FAMOUS SAYINGS AND THEIR AUTHORS

FAMOUS SAYINGS AND THEIR AUTHORS

A Collection of Historical Sayings in English, French, German, Greek, Italian, and Latin

BY

EDWARD LATHAM

AUTHOR OF "A DICTIONARY OF NAMES, NICKNAMES AND SURNAMES,"
"A DICTIONARY OF ABBREVIATIONS," "IDIOMATIC PHRASES
(FRENCH-ENGLISH)," ETC.

DETROIT
Gale Research Company · Book Tower
1970

This is a facsimile reprint of the
1904 edition published in London
by Swan Sonnenschein & Co., Lim.

Library of Congress Catalog Card Number 68-26582

PREFACE.

I know not what profit there may be in the study of history, what value in the sayings of wise men, or in the recorded experience of the past, if it be not to guide and instruct us in the present.—*Speech of Benjamin Disraeli*, July 2, 1849.

In some shape or other doubt has been thrown on the majority of the best known historical sayings. Indeed, after perusing E. Fournier's *L'Esprit dans l'Histoire*, we are tempted to come to the conclusion that there is very little truth in any of them; but it must, on the other hand, be borne in mind that M. Fournier deals almost exclusively with those sayings concerning which there *is* some question : the authentic sayings are scarcely mentioned at all. Still, it is not to be wondered at that so little reliance is to be placed upon such a large number of historical sayings—these landmarks of history, as they may be called—when we have Dr. Johnson's opinion that "We must consider how very little history there is ; I mean real authentic history. That certain kings reigned, and certain battles were fought, we can depend upon as true ; but all the colouring, all the philosophy of history is conjecture." (Boswell's *Life*, 1824 ed., vol. ii, pp. 340-1). Carlyle (*French Revolution*, pt. i, bk. 7., ch. 5) remarks : "Remarkable Maillard, if fame were not an accident, and History a dis-tillation of Rumour, how remarkable wast thou!" The doubtful points in historical sayings may be roughly classified as follows :

(1) inaccuracy of form, slight or considerable ;
(2) inauthenticity, invention after the events to which they relate ;
(3) attribution to another person than the real author.

(1) In considering the first point we have only to reflect how difficult it is, even with the best intentions, to faithfully report another person's words, and how treacherous the memory is as to exact words. (Historic sayings, occurring in speeches that have the advantage of being "taken down" in shorthand, stand the best chance, but even here discrepancies creep in.) Further, if the words uttered are not concise or pithy enough to suit the taste of posterity, it is only to be ex-

pected that a little alteration or improvement will be made to enable them to be handled more easily or render them more effective.

(2) With regard to invented sayings, or those for which no authority has been found (e.g., *L'état, c'est moi*). Sainte-Beuve puts their case very strongly when he writes (*Causeries du Lundi*, vol. xiii. pp. 107-8), referring to a *mot* of Villars which seems never to have been uttered by him . . "*le mot est si bien dans sa nature que, s'il ne l'a pas dit, il a dû le dire*"* In these cases the Italian saying, "*se non è vero è ben trovato*, is often very appropriate; and, on the other hand, as Boileau writes (*L'Art poétique*, iii, 48), "*Le vrai peut quelquefois n'être pas vraisemblable.*" So that there is something to be said in favour of these (from one point of view useful) inventions after all.

(3) There is often a very good reason for a saying being fathered on the wrong person. Molière's words (*Amphytrion*, act ii, sc. 2) seem very appropriate here:

> "*Tous les discours sont des sottises,*
> *Partant d'un homme sans éclat:*
> *Ce seroient paroles exquises*
> *Si c'étoit un grand qui parlât.*"

Pope, too, expresses a similar idea in his *Essay on Criticism*, pt. ii, ll. 220-1.

> "But let a Lord once own the happy lines,
> How the wit brightens! how the style refines!"

But, without either adopting M. Fournier's apparently pessimistic attitude towards historic sayings in general, or going to the other extreme and accepting them all without question, the compiler's object in the following pages has been to bring together, in their original language, what he hopes may be considered a fairly representative collection of historic sayings, real or apocryphal, improved or altered, rightly or wrongly attributed, as the case may be; answering the questions by whom said, and under what circumstances; giving authorities as far as he has been able to ascertain them, varying versions, and, by means of frequent cross-references, enabling interesting comparisons to be made between them. The task of selection has been by no means an easy one, for a similar-sized volume might have been easily filled with sayings in any one of the six languages chosen.

Bon mots, as such, have not been included, for as Voltaire

* Tacitus (*Annals*, I, 74) has it: " *Quia vera erant, dicta etiam credebantur.*"

writes (*Essai sur les mœurs et l'esprit des nations*, ch. cxlv).
"*La plupart des bons mots ne sont que des redites.*" This
criticism, as will be seen in these pages, applies also, although
perhaps in a less degree, to many historical sayings.

A number of "dying words" have been included, not so
much because of any particular intrinsic merit they may
possess, but rather on account of the interest they acquire
from their having been uttered (or said to have been uttered)
by famous persons. With regard to these M. Fournier writes
(p. 377, *idem*) "*Défiez-vous des mots prêtés aux mourants.
La mort n'est point bavarde : un soupir, un regard noyé dans
les ombres suprêmes, un geste de la main se portant vers le cœur,
quelques paroles confuses, mais surtout sans déclamation, voilà
seulement ce qu'elle permet à ceux qu'elle a frappés.*" Still, if
correctly reported, they are likely to proceed from the heart of
the speakers.

> *Gaunt* : "O, but they say, the tongues of dying men
> Enforce attention, like deep harmony ;
> Where words are scarce, they are seldom spent in vain ;
> For they breathe truth, that breathe their words in pain."—
> Shakespere, *Richard II*, II, i, ll. 5-8.

On the whole, it is perhaps better, while keeping an open
mind on the point of their accuracy, to value historical sayings—
like history—for what they teach. Rousseau (*Émile*, 1838
ed., vol. i, p. 307) writes : "*Les anciens historiens sont remplis
de vues dont on pourroit faire usage quand même les faits qui les
présentent seroient faux . . . Les hommes sensés doivent
regarder l'histoire comme un tissu de fables, dont la morale est
très appropriée au cœur humain.*" Here are the sayings—
fables or otherwise, partly true or wholly false—it is for my
readers to draw their own moral from any of them, or draw
none at all as they please. For my part, to conclude these
desultory remarks—as they began—with a quotation,

> I cannot tell how the truth may be ;
> I say the tale as 'twas said to me.
> Sir W. Scott, *Lay of the Last Minstrel*, ca. ii, st. 23.

It only remains for me to express my indebtedness and
thanks for the valuable assistance rendered me by Mr. Swan
Sonnenschein, Mr. W. A. Peplow, and Mr. F. Thorold
Dickson, of the Inner Temple, Barrister-at-Law.

Errors there must be in such a compilation, and particulars of
any such that may be noticed will be gratefully received if
forwarded through the publishers.

EDWARD LATHAM.

CONTENTS.

	PAGE
ENGLISH AND AMERICAN SAYINGS, - - - -	1
FRENCH SAYINGS, - - - - - -	82
GERMAN ,, - - - - - -	190
GREEK ,, - - - - - -	209
ITALIAN ,, - - - - - -	232
LATIN ,, - - - - - -	237
INDEX OF NAMES OF PERSONS, - - - -	253

ENGLISH AND AMERICAN SAYINGS

. . a battle of giants.

DUKE OF WELLINGTON (1769-1852) — in a conversation with Samuel Rogers, referring to the battle of Waterloo (June 18, 1815): in allusion to the Legendary *Gigantomachia* of classical (post-Homeric) antiquity : cf. Plato, *Republic* 378 C; Horace, *Odes* iii, 1, 5-8, iii, 4, 49-58, where the giants are mentioned by name.

A bishop ought to die on his legs.

JOHN WOOLTON, Bishop of Exeter (1535-94),—Last words. See Decet imperatorem, &c ; Un roi de France peut mourir, &c. It is related of Siward, Earl of Northumberland (d. 1055) that, when near his end, he put on his armour, saying that "it became not a man to die like a beast ;" and died standing. (*Percy Anecdotes*, vol ii, p. 102).

A bishop should die preaching.

BISHOP JEWELL (1522-71)—in reply to his friends, who were endeavouring to persuade him to desist from pulpit services owing to his state of health (*Percy Anecdotes*, vol. iii, p. 285).

. . a born gentleman.

DR SAMUEL JOHNSON (1709-84): "Adventitious accomplishments may be possessed by all ranks, but one may easily distinguish the born gentleman."

Above all things—Liberty.

JOHN SELDEN (1584-1654)—Motto placed by him upon his books.

. . a burglar of others' intellects.

BENJAMIN DISRAELI [Earl of Beaconsfield] (1804-81)—in a speech in the House of Commons, May 15, 1846, referring to Sir Robert Peel. Preceded by "His life has been one great Appropriation Clause"; and followed by "Search the index of Beatson from the days of the Conqueror to the termination of the last reign, there is no statesman who has committed political petty larceny on so great a scale."

. . a city of cities, an aggregation of humanity, that probably has never been equalled in any period of the history of the world, ancient or modern.

BENJAMIN DISRAELI [Earl of Beaconsfield] (1804-81)—in a speech

I

in the House of Commons, May 1, 1873, referring to London.

A Conservative Government is an organized hypocrisy.

BENJAMIN DISRAELI, [Earl of Beaconsfield] (1804-81)—in a debate in the House of Commons, March 17, 1845, on agricultural distress.

A Conservative is only a Tory who is ashamed of himself.

J. HOOKHAM FRERE (1769-1846) —when the terms Conservative and Liberal were beginning to take the place of Tory and Whig.

. . a crowning mercy.

OLIVER CROMWELL (1599-1658) —in a despatch, dated Sep. 4, 1651, announcing the preceding day's victory at Worcester : " The dimensions of this mercy are above my thoughts. It is, for aught I know, a crowning mercy."

Actors speak of things imaginary as if they were real, while you preachers too often speak of things real as if they were imaginary.

THOMAS BETTERTON (1635-1710) —in reply to the Archbishop of Canterbury, who asked why actors were more successful than preachers in impressing their auditors.

. . a delusion, a mockery, and a snare.

LORD DENMAN (1779-1854)— in giving judgment in the case of O'Connell and others *v.* the Queen, in the House of Lords, Sept. 4, 1844. (Clark and Finnelly's *Reports of Cases in the House of Lords*, vol. xi, p. 351.) " If it is possible that such a practice as that which has taken place in the present instance should be allowed to pass without a remedy (and no other remedy has been suggested), trial by jury itself, instead of being a security to persons

who are accused, will be a delusion, a mockery, and a snare."

A dinner lubricates business.

LORD STOWELL (1745-1836). (Boswell's *Johnson* VIII, 67 note).

A dying man can do nothing easy.

Last words of BENJAMIN FRANKLIN (1706-90)—to his daughter, who had advised him to change his position in bed, to breathe more easily. See J'avais cru plus difficile de mourir.

. . a free breakfast table.

JOHN BRIGHT (1811-89)—a phrase used in addressing the Edinburgh Chamber of Commerce, in 1868, in favour of the repeal of the duties on tea, sugar and coffee.

A friend may be often found and lost ; but an old friend can never be found, and nature has provided that he cannot easily be lost.

DR. SAMUEL JOHNSON (1709-84): See A man, sir, should keep &c.

After I am dead, you will find 'Calais' written upon my heart.

QUEEN MARY I (1517-58)—Last words, alluding to England's loss of that town. Another version is : " When I die, 'Calais' will be found written on my heart : " cf. " Were I to die at this moment, 'want of frigates' would be found stamped on my heart ! " : LORD NELSON (1758 1805), in his despatches to the Admiralty (1798). (Southey, *Life of Nelson*, ed. 1888, p. 186)

. . a 'gentleman of the press.'

BENJAMIN DISRAELI [Earl of Beaconsfield] (1804-81) thus styled himself in a speech in the House of Commons on England's relations with France, Feb. 18, 1853. " And

ENGLISH AND AMERICAN SAYINGS 3

as for the Press, I am myself a 'gentleman of the Press,' and I bear no other scutcheon. I know well the circumstances under which we have obtained in this country the blessing of a free Press."

. . a great master of gibes and flouts and jeers.

BENJAMIN DISRAELI [Earl of Beaconsfield] (1804-81)—referring to Lord Salisbury (b. 1830) in 1874. He also spoke of him as "not being a man who measures his phrases."

Ah, a German and a genius! a prodigy, admit him!

DEAN SWIFT (1667-1745)—Last words, when Händel (1685-1759) was announced. Another version: "It is folly; they had better leave it alone," alluding to preparations that were being made for honouring his birthday anniversary.

. . a hasty plate of soup.

GENERAL WINFIELD SCOTT (1786-1866)—in a letter to Governor Marcy (1786-1857) in 1846.

A horse! a horse! my kingdom for a horse.

Attributed to Richard III (1452-85) at the battle of Bosworth Field (Aug. 23, 1485), where he was slain. (Shakspere, *King Richard III*, act 5, sc. 4, l. 7): See All my possessions for one moment of time.

Ah! very well.

Last words of DR. THOMAS ARNOLD (1795-1842)—to his physician, Dr. Bucknill (*Stanley's Life of Arnold*)

A jealous love lights his torch from the firebrands of the furies.

EDMUND BURKE (1729-97)—in his speech on the plan for Economical Reform, Feb. 11, 1780.

A kiss from my mother made me a painter.

BENJAMIN WEST (1738-1820).

A little more grape, Captain Bragg!

GENERAL ZACHARY TAYLOR (1784-1850)—to Captain (afterwards General) Bragg (1815-76), at the battle of Buena Vista, Mexico, Feb. 23, 1847. Observing that a discharge of grape-shot caused the Mexicans to waver, General Taylor shouted these words.

All free governments are party governments.

PRESIDENT J. A. GARFIELD (1831-81)—in an address on the death of O. P. Morton. He also wrote "All free governments are managed by the combined wisdom and folly of the people"—in a private letter from him, dated Apr. 21, 1880.

All government, indeed every human benefit and enjoyment, every virtue, and every prudent act is founded on compromise and barter.

EDMUND BURKE, (1729-97)—in a speech on Conciliation with America, March 22, 1775.

All human knowledge here is but methodized ignorance.

DR. PARR (1747-1825).

All my possessions for one moment of time.

QUEEN ELIZABETH (1533-1603) —said to have been her dying words. Another version is that, in answer to the question who should succeed her, she said, "I will have no rogue's (rascal's) son in my seat," alluding to Lord Beauchamp, son of the attainted Earl of Suffolk. See A horse! a horse! my kingdom for a horse!

All right ; you can go out now.

DR. DAVID LIVINGSTONE (1813-73)—Last recorded words, to his servant Susi. He was found dead in the attitude of prayer.

All that is valuable in the United States Constitution is one thousand years old.

WENDELL PHILLIPS(1811-84)—in a speech at Boston, Mass., Feb. 17, 1861.

All wise men are of the same religion.

Sir Anthony Ashley Cooper, afterwards first EARL OF SHAFTESBURY, (1671-1713)—attributed to, by John Toland, *Clidophorus*, 1720, ch. 13. When asked by a lady what that was, he replied " Madam, wise men never tell." In a note by Speaker Onslow to Burnet's *History of his Own Times*, ed. 1823, vol. i, p. 164, it is given as " People differ in their discourse and profession about these matters, but men of sense are really but of one religion . ' Madam, men of sense never tell it." And, further, J. A. Froude in *Short Studies on Great Subjects*, vol. i : *A Plea for the Free Discussion of Theological Difficulties* (ed. 1888, p. 216) writes : ' Of what religion are you, Mr. Rogers?' said a lady once. ' What religion, madam ? I am of the religion of all sensible men.' ' And what is that?' she asked. ' All sensible men, madam, keep that to themselves.' Lord Beaconsfield has ' As for that,' said Waldershare, 'sensible men are all of the same religion.' ' And pray what is that?' inquired the prince. ' Sensible men never tell.' (*Endymion*).

A man may be a fool to choose a profession, but he must be an idiot to give it up.

LORD CHARLES BOWEN (1835-94) —to the Dean of Wells. Preceded by " I simply hate law."

A man may be allowed to change his opinions, never his principles.

GEORGE III (1738-1820)—on appointing Sir James Mackintosh (1765-1832) to the Recordership of Bombay, being assured of the change in Mackintosh's views. (W. Jerdan, *Men I have known*, 1866, p. 299)

A man's best gift to his country— his life's blood.

PRESIDENT WILLIAM MCKINLEY (1843-1901)—in a speech at San Francisco, May 23, 1901.

A man should pass a part of his time with the laughers.

DR. SAMUEL JOHNSON (1709-84).

A man, sir, should keep his friendship in constant repair.

DR. SAMUEL JOHNSON (1709-84) —to Sir Joshua Reynolds (1723-92). See A friend may be often found and lost &c. Preceded by " If a man does not make new acquaintance as he advances through life, he will soon find himself left alone."

A man who attempts to read all the new productions, must do as the fleas do— skip.

SAMUEL ROGERS (1763-1855).

A man who could make so vile a pun would not scruple to pick a pocket.

JOHN DENNIS (1657-1734)—to Rowe, referring to a pun made by Dr. Garth (1660-1719), the Doctor having sent his snuff-box to the last-named, with the two Greek letters Φ Ρ (Phi Ro) written inside the lid. (*Gentleman's Magazine*, vol. 51, p. 324 note). Another version is : " Sir, the man that will make such an execrable pun as that in my company, will pick my pocket." (Benjamin Victor, *An Epistle to Sir Richard Steele* (1722, p. 28) In this account the pun is stated to have been made by DANIEL PURCELL (c. 1660-1717.)

A man will turn over half a library to make one book.

DR. SAMUEL JOHNSON (1709-84) Preceded by " Yes, sir, when a man writes from his own mind, he writes very rapidly. The greatest part of a writer's time is spent in reading in order to write; a man" &c. (Boswell, *Life of Johnson*, 1775, ed. 1824, vol ii, p. 322.)

Amazing, amazing glory! I am having Paul's understanding.

CHARLES READE (1814-84)—last words, alluding to 2 *Corinthians*, xii, 1-4, which had been recently discussed.

Amen.

W. E. GLADSTONE (1809-98)— last words. Also of GEORGE BULL, Bishop of St. David's (1634-1710).

America must be conquered in France: France can never be conquered in America.

CHARLES JAMES FOX (1749-1806) —in the House of Commons, referring to the assistance given by France to the American colonies and the resulting hostilities between England and France.

. . amicably if they can, violently if they must.

JOSIAH QUINCY (1772-1864)— in a speech, Jan. 14, 1811, to Congress, referring to a Bill for the admission of the Orleans territory as a State (*Abridged Cong. Debates*, vol. iv, p. 327). HENRY CLAY (1774-1852) in a speech Jan. 8, 1813, said that " the gentleman [Mr. Quincy] cannot have forgotten his own sentiment, uttered even on the floor of this House, ' Peaceably if we can, forcibly if we must '."

Am I not a man and a brother?

JOSIAH WEDGWOOD (1730-95)— inscription on a medal (1768) representing a negro in chains, in a supplicating posture. Adopted as a seal by the Anti-Slavery Society of London.

An ambassador is an honest man sent abroad to lie (or to lie abroad) for the commonwealth.

See Legatus est vir bonus &c.

A national debt is a national blessing.

DANIEL WEBSTER (1782-1852)— in his speech Jan. 26, 1830, replying to Hayne, of South Carolina, said: " The gentleman has not seen how to reply to this otherwise than by supposing me to have advanced the doctrine that a national debt is a national blessing."

A nation is not governed which is perpetually to be conquered.

EDMUND BURKE (1729-97)— alluding to the character of the Americans.

. . and he adores his maker.

JOHN BRIGHT (1811-89)—when told that he ought to give Benjamin Disraeli (1804-81) credit for being a self-made man.

And, if this inauspicious union be not already consummated, in the name of my country I forbid the banns.

WILLIAM PITT (1759-1806)— Conclusion of one of his speeches.

And is it so, sweetheart? then are we perfect friends again.

HENRY VIII (1491-1547)—to his wife, Catherine Parr (1513-48), after a theological argument. The king, on the queen declining the conversation, had said, " You are now become a doctor, Kate ; and better fitted to give than receive instruction " ; but she replied that she had ventured sometimes to feign a contrariety of sentiments in order to give him the pleasure of refuting her. (Hume, *Hist. of England.*)

And let God be judge between you and me.

OLIVER CROMWELL (1599-1658) —when dissolving the second Parliament of the Protectorate, Feb. 4, 1658.

And they know the reason why.

SIR JAMES GRAHAM (1792-1861) —in a speech on the advantages derived from the recent measures of commercial legislation. Alluded to by BENJAMIN DISRAELI (1804-81) in his speech in the House of Commons, Dec. 16, 1852, on the Budget. "Well, I've given him now the 'reason why.'"

And you, *madam* I may not call you ; *mistress* I am ashamed to call you : so I know not what to call you, but yet I do thank you.

QUEEN ELIZABETH (1533-1603) —on taking leave of Archbishop Parker's wife, after being entertained at Lambeth Palace. The Queen greatly disapproved of marriage among the clergy.

. . an irrepressible conflict between opposing and enduring forces.

WILLIAM HENRY SEWARD (1801-72)—in a speech at Rochester, N.Y., Oct. 25, 1858, referring to the antagonism between freedom and slavery.

A noble life, crowned with heroic death, rises above and outlives the pride and pomp and glory of the mightiest empire of the earth.

PRESIDENT J. A. GARFIELD

(1831-81)—in the house of Representatives, Dec. 9, 1858.

A noble manhood, nobly consecrated to men, never dies.

PRESIDENT WILLIAM MCKINLEY (1843-1901)—in a speech at Albany, Feb. 12, 1895.

. . another place.

A formula used to refer to the House of Lords in the House of Commons or *vice versâ*. It occurs in the former sense several times in Benjamin Disraeli's (1804-81) speech of Apr. 11, 1845, on the Maynooth Bill. The same statesman applied the term to the House of Commons in his speech in the House of Lords, Mar. 28, 1879. Cf. "Sir, you have taught me to look for the sense of my subjects in another place than the House of Commons " (Walpole, *Memoirs of the Reign of George II*, vol. ii, p. 331). It was also used by GEORGE II (1683-1760) to WILLIAM PITT, Earl of Chatham (1708-78) when the latter pleaded unsuccessfully with him for Admiral Byng (Feb. 1757), urging that the House of Commons was inclined for mercy. (See also *Dict. Nat. Biog.*, vol. lix, p. 203). " . . . delusion that the majority of the House of Commons is the majority of the nation " (*Marchmont Papers*, vol. ii, p. 123). Also by SIR ROBERT WALPOLE (1676-1745) —see *Dict. Nat. Biog.*, vol. lix, p. 203.

. . an untoward event.

The DUKE OF WELLINGTON (1769-1852)—alluding to the battle of Navarino (Oct. 20, 1827), because it appeared likely to disturb the 'balance of power.' The phrase occurs in the speech of George IV. at the opening of Parliament in 1828. " His Majesty deeply regrets that this conflict should have occurred with the naval force of an ancient ally; but he still entertains a confident hope that this untoward event will not be followed by further hostilities" (S. Walpole, *Hist. of England*, vol. ii, pp. 556-7; see also *Dict. Nat. Biog.*, vol. lx, p. 195).

Any man can do what any other man has done.

DR. THOMAS YOUNG (1773-1829).

Any man may get a reputation for benevolence by judiciously laying out five pounds a year.

DEAN SWIFT (1667-1745).

Anything but history, for history must be false.

SIR ROBERT WALPOLE (1676-1745)—to his son, who offered to read history to him. (*Walpoliana*, 1799, vol. i. p. 60, No. 79) See Voilà ce que c'est l'histoire; cf. . . "History, a distillation of Rumour" (Carlyle, *French Revolution*, Pt. i, bk. 7, ch. v).

A painter is a companion for kings and emperors.

BENJAMIN WEST (1738-1820)—in the course of a conversation.

' Apologies only account for that which they do not alter.'

Quoted by BENJAMIN DISRAELI [Earl of Beaconsfield] (1804-81)—in a speech on the prosecution of war, May 24, 1855, and in another on the order of business, July 28, 1871.

A precedent embalms a principle.

BENJAMIN DISRAELI [Earl of Beaconsfield](1804-81)—in a speech in the House of Commons on the expenditure of the country, Feb. 22, 1848. Cf. The acts of to-day become the precedents of to-morrow.

A reform is a correction of abuses : a revolution is a transfer of power.

LORD LYTTON (1805-72)—in the House of Commons, alluding to the Reform Bill of 1866.

Are the doctors here ?

PRESIDENT BENJAMIN HARRISON (1833-1901)—Last words, to his wife, who enquired whether he wanted anything.

Are we not children, all of us ?

JANE TAYLOR (1783-1824)—Last words.

. . a safe and honourable peace.

BENJAMIN DISRAELI [Earl of Beaconsfield] (1804-81)—Concluding words of a resolution moved in the House of Commons, May 24, 1855. See also Peace with honour.

As a man advances in life, he gets what is better than admiration—judgment, to estimate things at their true value.

DR. SAMUEL JOHNSON (1709-84) (Boswell's *Life of Johnson*, ed. 1824, vol ii, p. 335).

. . as good as a play (a comedy).

CHARLES II (1630-85)—said to have been uttered by him when listening to a debate on Lord Ross's Divorce Bill (see Macaulay, *Review of the Life . . of Sir William Temple*).

A shocking bad hat.

FREDERICK AUGUSTUS, DUKE OF YORK (1763-1827), second son of George III—referring to Walpole, who was wearing a low-crowned, broad-brimmed hat at Newmarket. He said : "Then the little man wears a shocking bad hat." He had previously asked who the stranger [Walpole] was. (Capt. R. H. Gronow, *Recollections*, 4th Series, 1866, pp. 153-4).

. . Asian mystery.

BERESFORD HOPE (1820-87)—during the discussion in the House of Commons, Apr. 12, 1867, referring to Benjamin Disraeli (1804-81). The latter, in his speech, said : " All his [Beresford Hope's] exhibitions in this House are distinguished by a prudery which charms me, and when he talks of Asian mysteries I may, perhaps, by way of reply, remark that there is a Batavian * grace about his exhibition which takes the sting out of what he has said."

* [Alluding to Beresford Hope's descent from the family of Hope of Amsterdam, and his action while speaking].

. . a social animal.

DUKE OF WELLINGTON (1769-1852)—in a letter to Thomas Raikes, March 1, 1841.

Assassination has never changed the history of the world.

BENJAMIN DISRAELI [Earl of Beaconsfield] (1804-81)—in a speech in the House of Commons, May, 1865, on the death of President Lincoln (1809-65) who was assassinated on April 15th.

. . a star for every State, and a State for every star.

ROBERT C. WINTHROP (b. 1809) —in an address on Boston Common in 1862.

A strange sight, sir, an old man unwilling to die.

EBENEZER ELLIOTT (1781-1849) the Corn Law Poet—Last words.

. . a ' superior person '.

BENJAMIN DISRAELI [Earl of Beaconsfield] (1804-81)—in a speech on a vote of censure against the government, July 8, 1864, alluded to the Rt. Hon. Edward Horsman (1807-76) as the ' superior person ' of the House of Commons.

A treaty is the promise of a nation.

FISHER AMES (1758-1808)—in a speech on the British Treaty, April 28, 1796.

A university should be a place of light, of liberty, and of learning.

BENJAMIN DISRAELI [Earl of Beaconsfield] (1804-81)—in a speech in the House of Commons, March 11, 1873, on the University Education Bill (Ireland).

. . a watcher of the atmosphere.

BENJAMIN DISRAELI [Earl of Beaconsfield] (1804-81)—a euphemism employed in his speech on the Address, Jan. 22, 1846, alluding to Sir Robert Peel (1788-1850).

. . a whale stranded upon the sea-shore of Europe.

EDMUND BURKE (1729-97)—referring to modern Spain : See He will be left alone &c.

. . a wise and salutary neglect.

EDMUND BURKE (1729-97)—in a speech on Conciliation with America, March 22, 1775. Cf. the more modern phrase " masterly inactivity," which originated with Sir James Mackintosh, *Vindiciæ Gallicæ* : " The Commons, faithful to their system, remained in a wise and masterly inactivity " (ed. 1837. p. 14).

Be a whole man to one thing at a time.

THOMAS CARLYLE (1795-1881).

Before this time to-morrow, I shall have gained a peerage, or Westminster Abbey.

LORD NELSON (1758-1805)—just before the Battle of the Nile (Aug. 1, 1798) ; " when his officers rose from table and went to their respective stations." (Southey, *Life of Nelson*, ch. 5)

Be good, be virtuous, my lord ; you must come to this.

LORD GEORGE LYTTELTON (1709-73)—Last words, addressed to his son-in-law, Lord Valentia.

" Be just and fear not."

JOHN BRIGHT (1811-89)—his favourite maxim.

Be of good cheer, Master Ridley, and play the man. We shall this day light such a candle, by God's grace, in England, as I trust shall never be put out.

HUGH LATIMER (c. 1472-1555) —to BISHOP NICHOLAS RIDLEY (c. 1500-55). Both were burned at the stake, Oct. 16. Hume records : " Be of good cheer, brother ; we shall this day kindle such a torch in England, as, I trust in God, shall never be extinguished." See Be of good comfort &c.

Be of good comfort, brother, for we shall have a merry supper with the Lord this night : if there be any way to heaven on horseback or in fiery chariots, this is it.

JOHN BRADFORD (d. 1555)—Last words, addressed to a fellow martyr. See Be of good cheer &c.

Blessed be God, I have kept a conscience void of offence to this day, and have not deserted the righteous cause for which I suffer.

SIR HENRY VANE (1612-62), beheaded for treason, June 14—Last words.

. bloated armaments.

BENJAMIN DISRAELI [Earl of Beaconsfield] (1804-81)—in a speech (1862) during the American Civil War. He advocated " putting an end to these bloated armaments which naturally involve States in financial embarrassment."

Blücher or night.

DUKE OF WELLINGTON (1769-1852)—at the Battle of Waterloo (June 18, 1815), after looking at his watch. (Cf. Hugo, *Les Misérables* : *Cosette*, bk. 1, ch. 10).

Books, churches, governments, are what we make them.

WENDELL PHILLIPS (1811-84)— in a speech at Boston, Mass., Oct. 4, 1859.

Born and educated in this country, I glory in the name of Briton.

GEORGE III. (1738-1820)—added to his first speech to Parliament in 1760. See Thank God, I—I also —am an American.

Brother, I am too old to go again on my travels ; you may, if you choose it.

CHARLES II. (1630-85)—referring to the hasty counsels of his brother, James, Duke of York, afterwards James II. (1633-1701), which gave him great uneasiness.

But ere this be done Take up our sister's handkerchief.

WILLIAM SHAKSPERE (1564-1616—when playing the King in one of his own tragedies before Queen Elizabeth. The Queen dropped her handkerchief on the stage as if by accident, to see whether he would depart from his regal dignity. The poet is said to have promptly exclaimed the above words.

But may heaven avert her principles from our minds, and her daggers from our hearts!

EDMUND BURKE (1729-97)—in a speech on the Alien Bill (1792), at the same time producing a dagger, and throwing it on the floor. Preceded by : "These are the presents which France designs for you ! By these she would propagate her freedom and fraternity !" He had stated that there were 3,000 daggers then being manufactured at Birmingham, but whether for exportation or home consumption had not been ascertained. See Liberté, égalité, fraternité.

By my soul, maun, I have heard but rawly of thee.

JAMES I. (1566-1625)—to Sir Walter Raleigh (1552-1618), when meeting him for the first time.

By seizing the Isthmus of Darien you will wrest the keys of the world from Spain.

SIR WALTER RALEIGH (1552-1618)—Advice given to Queen Elizabeth (1533-1603).

By such means as these we shall make the name of Englishman as great as that of Rome's most palmy days.

OLIVER CROMWELL (1599-1658) —referring to his foreign policy, after reading one of Blake's despatches : See I would have the English republic &c.

Can this last long ?

WILLIAM III. (1650-1702)—Last words, addressed to his physician.

Carry my bones before you on your march, for the rebels will not be able to endure the sight of me, alive or dead.

EDWARD I, of England, surnamed "Longshanks," (1239-1307) —Last words, addressed to his son Edward. The king died whilst endeavouring to subdue a revolt in Scotland.

Children are excellent physiognomists, and soon discover their real friends.

REV. SYDNEY SMITH (1771-1845)

"Christ's rood !"

KING HAROLD (d. 1066)—his battle cry at the Battle of Hastings, Oct. 14, 1066. Cf. "I like that ancient Saxon phrase which calls The burial-ground God's acre !—" (Longfellow, *Goa's-Acre.*)

Civil equality prevails in Britain, social equality prevails in France.

BENJAMIN DISRAELI [Earl of Beaconsfield] (1804-81)—in a speech at Glasgow University, Nov. 19, 1873. Followed by, "The essence of civil equality is to abolish privilege ; the essence of social equality is to destroy class."

Close this eye, the other is closed already ; and now farewell !

REV. CHARLES WOLFE (1791-1823), author of *The Burial of Sir John Moore*—Dying words. He then uttered part of the Lord's prayer. (Rev. J. A. Russell, *Remains of Rev. Charles Wolfe.*)

Colonies do not cease to be colonies because they are independent.

BENJAMIN DISRAELI [Earl of Beaconsfield] (1804-81)—in a speech in House of Commons, Feb. 5, 1863.

Come, my son, and see how a Christian can die.

SIR HENRY HAVELOCK (1795-1857)— Last words. See I have sent for you &c., and Venez voir comment meurt &c.

Comfort the poor, protect and shelter the weak, and, with all thy might, right that which is wrong. Then shall

the Lord love thee, and God himself shall be thy great reward.

ALFRED THE GREAT (849-901)— Last words.

Commend your souls to God, for our bodies are the foes !

SIMON DE MONTFORT, Earl of Leicester (1206-65)— Last words ; at the battle of Evesham. Another version is : " Now let us commend our souls to God, for our bodies belong to our enemies." Also given as " It is God's grace."

Confidence is a plant of slow growth in an aged bosom :

WILLIAM PITT, first Earl of Chatham (1708-78)—in a speech, Jan. 14, 1766. (*Dict. Nat. Biog.*, vol. xlv., p. 360.) Followed by— " Youth is the season of credulity." Cf. Disraeli's words in a speech at the Mansion House, Nov. 9, 1867 : " I see before me the statue of a celebrated minister, who said that confidence was a plant of slow growth. But I believe, however gradual may be the growth of confidence, that of credit requires still more time to arrive at maturity." " Rashness is the error of youth, timid caution of age" (Colton, *Lacon*) and " True friendship is a plant of slow growth, and must undergo and withstand the shocks of adversity before it is entitled to the appellation." (G. Washington, *Social Maxims : Friendship*.)

Consummate master of language.

BENJAMIN DISRAELI [Earl of Beaconsfield] (1804-81) — referring to W. E. Gladstone, in a speech on the Black Sea Conference, Feb. 24, 1871.

Corporations have no souls.

SIR EDWARD COKE (1552-1633) —in the case of Sutton's Hospital (*10 Law Reports*, 39): "They [i.e., corporations] cannot commit trespass, nor be outlawed, nor excommunicated ; for they have no souls." Lord Thurlow is stated to have said later, "You never expected justice from a company, did you ? They have neither a soul to lose nor a body to kick."

Cramming is the tribute which idleness pays to the excellence of industry.

LORD CHARLES BOWEN (1835-94) —in a speech at a distribution of prizes at the City of London School, Dec. 1888.

Cranmer has got the right sow by the ear.

HENRY VIII (1491-1547) — of Cranmer's opinion as to the best method of procuring the divorce from Catherine of Aragon (Hume, *Hist. of England.*). Sir Robert Walpole (1676-1745), when asked how he had overcome Sir Spencer Compton, Earl of Wilmington, replied " He got the wrong sow by the ear, and I the right " (*Anecdotal Hist. of Parliament*).

Customs may not be as wise as laws, but they are always more popular.

BENJAMIN DISRAELI [Earl of Beaconsfield] (1804-81)—in a speech in the House of Commons on the Irish Land Bill, Mar. 11, 1870.

Damn your principles ! Stick to your party.

BENJAMIN DISRAELI [Earl of Beaconsfield] (1804-81)—to Bulwer Lytton, at Spa, Belgium, the latter having said that he could not vote for some Bill in Parliament it being " against his principles."

Dear gentlemen, let me die a natural death.

SIR SAMUEL GARTH (c. 1660-1718)

—Death-bed utterance, on seeing his doctors in consultation.

. . deep dream of peace.

JAMES HENRY LEIGH HUNT (1784-1859)—Last words.

Democracy is like the grave : it never gives back what it receives.

LORD LYTTON (1805-73)—of Lord Palmerston's Reform Bill, in 1860.

Depend upon it, of all vices, drinking is the most incompatible with greatness.

SIR WALTER SCOTT (1771-1832). See Sir, I can abstain &c.

Desperate diseases require desperate remedies.

GUIDO (GUY) FAWKES (1570-1606) —when taken before King James I. (see *Dict. Nat. Biog.*, vol. xviii, p. 268).

Dictionaries are like watches : the worst is better than none, and the best cannot be expected to go quite true.

DR. SAMUEL JOHNSON (1709-84).

Did you know Burke ?

RICHARD BRINSLEY SHERIDAN (1751-1816)—Last words ; alluding to Edmund Burke.

Die, my dear doctor ! that's the *last* **thing I shall do.**

LORD PALMERSTON (1784-1865) —Death-bed utterance.

Difference of religion breeds more quarrels than difference of politics.

WENDELL PHILLIPS (1811-84)— in a speech, Nov. 7, 1860, on Abraham Lincoln's election to the Presidency of the U.S.

. . distilled damnation.

DR. ROBERT HALL (1764-1831) —in replying to a request for a glass of brandy-and-water : "That is the current, but not the appropriate, name ; ask for a glass of liquid fire and distilled damnation." (Gregory, *Life of Hall*).

Do as I have done—persevere.

GEORGE STEPHENSON (1781-1848)—when addressing some young men.

Doctor Livingstone, I presume ?

Sir H. M. STANLEY (b. 1840)—to Dr. David Livingstone, when he found him at Ujiji in 1871.

Do not let poor Nelly starve !

CHARLES II (1630-85)—Dying words, referring to Nell Gwynn, the celebrated actress, his mistress. Another version is : "Let not poor Nelly starve !" (Burnet, *Hist. of is own Times*, vol. ii, 473).

Don't give up the ship !

CAPT. JAMES LAWRENCE, American naval officer (1781-1813)—when mortally wounded in the engagement between the *Chesapeake* and the *Shannon* he gave orders to "fire faster, and not give up the ship." This is according to the evidence of the surgeon's mate, Dr. John Dix, at the trial of Lieut. Cox, Apr. 14, 1814.

Don't quote Latin; say what you have to say, and then sit down.

DUKE OF WELLINGTON (1769-1852)—Advice to a new Member who asked him how to get on in the House of Commons.

Don't think, but try ; be patient, be accurate.

JOHN HUNTER (1728-93)—Advice to Edward Jenner, when consulted as to the latter's views on the prophylactic virtues of cow-pox.

Don't you know, as the French say, there are three sexes,— men, women, and clergymen?

Rev. SYDNEY SMITH (1771-1845) —Lady Mary Wortley Montagu (1689-1762) had said "The world is made up of men, women and Herveys."

Dost thou think, man, I can make thy son a painter? No! only God Almighty makes painters!

SIR GODFREY KNELLER (1648-1723)—when declining to take the son of his tailor as a pupil.

Do you call that nothing? But so much the worse for them.

JAMES II. (1633-1701)—after inquiring the cause of a great uproar in the camp, June 30, 1688, and being told by Lord Faversham: "it was nothing but the rejoicing of the soldiers for the acquittal of the bishops." (Hume, *Hist. of Engl.*)

Do you not know that I am above the law?

JAMES II. (1633-1701)—to the Duke of Somerset, who said that he could not obey him without breaking the law. See Ego sum rex Romanus et supra grammaticam.

. . driving a coach and six through an Act of Parliament.

SIR STEPHEN RICE (1637-1715), appointed Chief Baron of the Irish Exchequer 1686 and removed in 1690, before he was made judge, said that he would "drive a coach and six horses through the Act of Settlement (of Ireland)" (*Memoirs of Ireland*, pub. anon. in 1716, but attributed to Oldmixon; see also *Dict. Nat. Biog.*, vol. xlviii, p. 103). See also I can drive a coach and six &c.

Duty determines destiny.

PRESIDENT WILLIAM McKINLEY (1843-1901)—in his Jubilee speech at Chicago, Oct. 19, 1898.

Dying, dying.

THOMAS HOOD (1792-1845)— Last words.

Early and provident fear is the mother of safety.

EDMUND BURKE (1729-97)—in a speech on the Petition of the Unitarians. Cf.

La méfiance

Est mère de la sûreté
(Prudence is the mother of safety)
La Fontaine, *Le Chat et le vieux Rat*

England began this war with all Europe on her side; she will end it with all Europe against her.

LORD NELSON (1758-1805)—alluding to the war with Russia.

England can never be ruined except by a parliament.

SIR WILLIAM CECIL, LORD BURLEIGH (1520-98).

England does not love coalitions.

BENJAMIN DISRAELI [Earl of Beacon-field] (1804-81)—in the last sentence but one of a speech on the Budget, Dec. 16, 1852: "Yes! I know what I have to face. I have to face a coalition. The combination may be successful. But coalitions, although successful, have always found this, that their triumph has been short. This too I know, that England," &c. Attributed also to John Scott (1751-1838), 1st Earl of Eldon. Cf. "The noble Lord [Palmerston] cannot bear coalitions" (Speech by Disraeli in the House of Commons, Feb. 29, 1857)

England expects every man to do his duty.

LORD NELSON (1758-1805)— Words caused to be signalled to the fleet before the Battle of Trafalgar, Oct. 21, 1805. Nelson at first used the word 'confides' in place of 'expects.'; but Capt. Pasco, his flag-lieutenant, suggested that 'expects' should be substituted, as it was in the signalling vocabulary, whereas the former would have had to be spelt out.

" England for the English ! "
Rallying-cry of the people under Earl Godwin (c. 990-1053) and Harold (d. 1066) when driving out the Norman priests and nobles whom Edward the Confessor tried to bring into England.

England is a domestic country; there the home is revered, the hearth sacred.
BENJAMIN DISRAELI [Earl of Beaconsfield](1804-81)—in a speech at Manchester, Apr. 3, 1872.

England is the Mother of Parliaments.
JOHN BRIGHT (1811-89)—in a speech at Birmingham, Jan. 18, 1865.

England is the only country which, when it enters into a quarrel that it believes to be just, never ceases its efforts until it has accomplished its aim.
BENJAMIN DISRAELI [Earl of Beaconsfield](1804-81)—in a speech June 3, 1862, in the House of Commons on Mr. Walpole's resolution. Preceded by ". . the real cause of that influence of England—which influence is, perhaps, on an average, the most permanent throughout the Continent—has arisen from this circumstance, that England ", &c.

English soldiers of the steady old stamp—depend upon it, there is nothing like them in the world in the shape of infantry.
DUKE OF WELLINGTON (1769-1852).

Eternal vigilance is the price of liberty.
JOHN PHILPOT CURRAN (1750-1817)—in a speech at Dublin in 1790.

Ever speak the truth ; for, if you will do so, you shall never be believed, and 'twill put your adversaries (who will still hunt counter) to a loss in all their dispositions and undertakings.
SIR HENRY WOTTON (1568-1639) —Advice given to a person setting out on a foreign mission. See An Ambassador is &c.

Every Englishman has a Turk on his shoulders.
JOHN BRIGHT (1811-89)—in a speech in the House of Commons, March 31, 1854, said, "Gentlemen, I congratulate you, that every man of you has a Turk upon his shoulders."

Every man has his price.
This saying is said to have originated from the following remark by SIR ROBERT WALPOLE (1676-1745) to Mr. Leveson: "You see with what zeal and vehemence those gentlemen oppose, and yet I know the price of every man in this house except three, and your brother [Lord Gower] is one of them." "Flowery oratory he despised. He ascribed to the interested views of themselves or their relatives the declarations of pretended patriots, of whom he said, All those men have their price." (Coxe, *Memoirs of Walpole* (1800) vol. iv, p. 369.) "All those men, he said of 'the patriots,' have their price" (Coxe, vol. i, p. 757 ; *Walpoliana* vol. i, p. 88 ; see *Dict. Nat. Biog.* vol. lix, p. 203). "But

in case it be a septennial parliament, will he not then probably accept the £500 pension, if he be one of those men that has a price?" (*Speech of Sir Robert Walpole*, 1734, Feb. 26 ; see vol. ii, p. 261 of Coxe.) See Gentlemen, I am poor, very poor &c.

Every man meets his Waterloo at last.

WENDELL PHILLIPS (1811-84)— in a speech at Brooklyn, on John Brown, Nov. 1, 1859.

Every step of progress the world has made has been from scaffold to scaffold, and from stake to stake.

WENDELL PHILLIPS (1811-84)— in a speech in favour of Woman's Rights, at Worcester (Mass.), Oct. 15, 1851.

Excellence is never granted to man but as the reward of labour.

SIR JOSHUA REYNOLDS (1723-92)—See Nothing is denied &c.

Facing the music.

Saying said to be of military origin, one of the difficulties in training horses for the army being to get them to ' face ' the regimental band. According to Barrère (*Dict. of Slang, Jargon, and Cant*) it was " originally army slang (American) applied to men when drummed out to the tune of the ' Rogue's March.' " The expression ' Wake up, hoss, and face the music ' is said to be generally used in the United States as an exhortation to men as well as to horses. Walsh (*Literary Curiosities*) says : " Face the Music : a proverbial phrase probably derived from the stage, where it is used by actors in the green-room when preparing to go on the boards to literally face the music. Another explanation traces it to

militia-muster, where every man is expected to appear fully equipped and armed, when in rank and file, facing the music." The phrase is employed by R. L. Stevenson and Lloyd Osbourne in *The Ebb Tide*, ch. xv (1894, p. 211): "If I'd ast you to walk up and face the music I could understand." It was in constant use by English journalists in 1900-1 in connection with Cecil Rhodes and the Jameson Raid.

Fain would I climb, yet fear I to fall.

SIR WALTER RALEIGH (1552-1618)—said to have been scratched on a pane of glass in Queen Elizabeth's presence. Her answer written underneath was : " If thy heart fails thee, why then climb at all?" (see Fuller, *Worthies*). Another version is :

" Fain would I climb, but that I fear to fall," and " If thy mind fail thee, do not climb at all."

(Scott, *Kenilworth*, ch. xvii) Cf. " Fain would I, but I dare not ; I dare and yet I may not." (First line of a lyric by Sir Walter Raleigh) ; and Aut non tentaris, aut perfice (Either attempt not, or perform) (Ovid, *De Arte Amandi*, I, 389).

Fame is a revenue payable only to our ghosts.

SIR G. MACKENZIE (1626-1714).

Farewell, a long farewell to all my greatness !

CARDINAL WOLSEY (1471-1530) — put in his mouth by Shakspere (*King Henry VIII*, act 3, sc. 2, l. 351 ; but see Had I served my God &c.

Farewell, France, farewell ! I shall never see thee more.

See Adieu, chère France ! je ne vous verrai jamais plus !

Farewell, Oxford without a head !

DUKE OF ORMOND (1665-1745) —when taking leave of Robert Harley, Earl of Oxford (1661-1724) in the Tower. The latter replied : "Farewell, Duke without a duchy!" (P. H. Stanhope (Lord Mahon) *Hist. of Eng.* 1836, vol. i, p. 189). See Adieu, prince sans terre.

Father abbot, I am come to lay my weary bones among you.

CARDINAL WOLSEY (1471-1530) —to the abbot and monks of Leicester Abbey, Nov. 26, 1529.

Few die, and none resign.

THOMAS JEFFERSON (1743-1826) —in a letter to a committee of the merchants of New Haven in 1801 : "If a due participation of office is a matter of right, how are vacancies to be obtained ? Those by death are few : by resignation, none."

Finality is not the language of politics.

BENJAMIN DISRAELI [Earl of Beaconsfield] (1804-81)—in a speech in the House of Commons, Feb. 28, 1859.

Fish is almost the only rare thing by the sea-side.

JOHN WILKES (1727-97).

Fold up the map of Europe !

WILLIAM PITT (1759-1806)— after his return from Bath to his house at Putney (Jan. 1806)—just after the battle of Austerlitz (Dec. 2, 1805) — observing a map of Europe unrolled, turned to his niece and said : " Roll up that map : it will not be wanted these ten years." (*Dict. Nat. Biog.*, vol. xlv, p. 383).

Force is no remedy.

JOHN BRIGHT (1811-89) —referring to the land troubles in Ireland in 1880. ⌐ ʹified in 1882 by him

as applying " not to outrages but to grievances."

Forget not what I have said ; and when I am gone call it often to mind.

CARDINAL WOLSEY (1471-1530) —Last words, to Sir William Kingston.

For me it will be enough that a marble stone should declare that a queen having reigned such a time lived and died a virgin.

QUEEN ELIZABETH (1533-1603) —in reply to a petition from the House of Commons in 1559 on the subject of her marrying (Hume, *Hist. of Engl.*, ch. xxxviii).

For shame! are you afraid to die in my company ?

WILLIAM III. (1650-1702)—to some sailors in 1691, during a rough passage to Holland.

For the name of Jesus and the defence of the Church I am willing to die.

THOMAS À BECKET (1117-70) Archbishop of Canterbury, assassinated in Canterbury Cathedral—Last words. (Hume, *Hist. of Engl.*) Froude (*Short Studies on Great Subjects*, 1886, vol. iv, p. 175) gives them as follows : " I am prepared to die for Christ and for His Church."

For the queen ! for the queen ! a plot is laid for my life !

EARL of ESSEX (1567-1601)—on his way to the city, having previously detained several officers of state sent by Elizabeth to learn the cause of the unusual commotion.

Friendship may and often does grow into love, but love never subsides into friendship.

LORD BYRON (1788-1824).

Friend, you do not well to trample on a dying man.

HUGH PETERS (1599-1660)— Last words, in reply to a remark by the hangman. Peters was executed Oct. 16, 1660.—(*Percy Anecdotes*, vol. iii, p. 417).

Gentlemen, I am poor, very poor ; but your king is not rich enough to buy me.

GENERAL JOSEPH REED, President of Congress (1741-85)—when offered a bribe of 10,000 guineas to desert his country's cause during the American revolution. Another version is : " I am not worth purchasing, but such as I am, the King of England is not rich enough to buy me." (*Encycl. Americana*, vol. iv, p. 329). See Every man has his price.

Gentlemen of the jury, you will now consider of your verdict.

CHARLES ABBOTT, Lord Tenterden (1762-1832)—Last words. The *Dict. Nat. Biog.* (vol. i, p. 29), however, gives them as "Gentlemen, you are all dismissed."

Gentle shepherd, tell me where.

DR. SAMUEL HOWARD (d. 1782)—line of a song of his, repeated by WILLIAM PITT, first Earl of Chatham, when asked by George Grenville in a debate on the financial statement of 1762 where a tax should be levied : "Let them tell me where. I say, sir, let them tell me where. I repeat it, sir : I am entitled to say to them, tell me where." It was long before Grenville lost the nickname of 'Gentle shepherd,' which Pitt fixed upon him. (Macaulay. *Essay on Chatham*).

" Give Cæsar his due."

CHARLES I (1600-49)—Motto inscribed on his standard at Nottingham, 1642.

Give Dayrolles a chair.

LORD CHESTERFIELD (1694-1773) —Last words.

Give me back my youth.

JOHN WOLCOT, M.D. [" Peter Pindar "] (1738-1819)—Last words, in reply to Taylor, who asked if there was anything he could do for him. See Quinctili Vare, legiones redde.

. . give me liberty, or give me death.

PATRICK HENRY (1736-99)—in a speech in the Virginia Convention (March, 1775). " Is life so dear, or peace so sweet, as to be purchased at the price of chains and slavery? Forbid it, almighty God ! I know not what course others may take ; but, as for me, give," etc. Cf.

We must be free or die, who speak the tongue
That Shakespeare spake : the faith and morals hold
Which Milton held.

(Wordsworth, *Poems dedicated to National Independence*, pt. 1, Sonnet xvi.)

Give me time, and I will yet produce works that the Academy will be proud to recognise.

JOHN FLAXMAN (1755-1826)—to his father, on failing to win the gold medal at the Royal Academy.

Give them a corrupt House of Lords.

RICHARD BRINSLEY SHERIDAN (1751-1816)—in 1810, alluding to the liberty of the press : "Give them a corrupt House of Lords, give them a venal House of Commons, give them a tyrannical prince, give them a truckling court, and let me

2

have but an unfettered press, I will defy them to encroach a hair's breadth upon the liberties of England."

Give them the cold steel, boys.

LEWIS ADDISON ARMISTEAD (1817-63)—Last words.

Glory be to the Father, and to the Son, and to the Holy Ghost.

VEN. BEDE (673-735)—Last words.

God and liberty.

VOLTAIRE (1694-1778)—said in English when blessing Franklin's grandson (1778). He added " *C'est la seule bénédiction qui convienne au petit-fils de M. Franklin.*" (It is the only fitting benediction for M. Franklin's grandson). See Dieu et la liberté.

God bless you.

EDMUND BURKE (1729-97)—Last words.

God bless you all.

SIR WALTER SCOTT (1771-1832) —Last words. Other versions are : " I feel as if I were to be myself again ; " "My dear, be a good man ; be virtuous ; be religious— be a good man. Nothing else can give you any comfort when you come to lie here" (to Lockhart) ; "There is but one book ; bring me the Bible" (to Lockhart).

God bless you, my dear !

DR. SAMUEL JOHNSON (1709-84)—Last words, to Miss Morris, who asked his blessing.

God has put into every white man's hand a whip to flog the black.

THOMAS CARLYLE (1795-1881) —to Ralph Waldo Emerson (1803-82).

God help me, my very children have forsaken me.

JAMES II (1633-1701)—when told that his daughter Anne, as well as Mary, was on the side of William of Orange. Hume substitutes 'own' for ' very '.

God may forgive you, but I never can.

QUEEN ELIZABETH (1533-1603— is credited with having used these words to the dying Countess of Nottingham (in 1603), who confessed that she had kept a ring given her by the Earl of Essex to be returned to the Queen. Elizabeth is said to have even shaken the dying woman in her bed (Hume, *Hist. of Engl.* ch. 44).

God reigns, and the government at Washington still lives.

GENERAL GARFIELD (1831-81) —concluding words of a brief speech at New York, April 15, 1865, the day of President Lincoln's death. Garfield became President in 1881, but was assassinated Sep. 19 of the same year. Cf.
God's in his heaven—
All's right with the world.
(R. Browning, *Pippa Passes.*)

God's will be done.

BISHOP THOMAS KEN, author of the Doxology and *Praise God from whom all blessings flow* (1637-1711) —Last words.

God's wounds ! the villain hath killed me.

GEORGE VILLIERS, Duke of Buckingham (1592-1628), assassinated by John Felton—Last words. Hume's version is simply : "The villain has killed me."

God who placed me here, will do what he pleases with me hereafter, and he knows best what to do. May he bless you.

VISCOUNT HENRY ST. JOHN BOLINGBROKE (1678-1725)—just before his death, to Lord Chesterfield.

Good Americans, when they die, go to Paris.

THOMAS GOLD APPLETON (1812-84), American wit and author. (Cf. Holmes, *Autocrat of the Breakfast Table*, ch. 66).

Good-bye, General ; I'm done. I'm too old.

COL. HENRY CLAY EGBERT (1840-99)—Last words. He was killed near Manila in the war between the U. S. and the Phillipines (Cf. *N. Y. Daily Sun*, Mar. 27, 1899). Said to General Wheaton, who, bending over him, exclaimed, " Nobly done, Egbert ! "

Government is founded on property.

DANIEL WEBSTER (1782-1852)—in his Plymouth oration, Dec. 22, 1820, said : " It would seem, then, to be part of political wisdom to found government on property," &c. (*Works*, Boston, 1851, vol i, p. 39).

Government of the people, by the people, for the people.

ABRAHAM LINCOLN (1809-65)—in a speech at the dedication of the National Soldiers' Cemetery at Gettysberg, Nov. 19, 1863. " We here highly resolve that the dead shall not have died in vain, that this nation shall, under God, have a new birth of freedom, and that government of the people, by the people, for the people, shall not perish from the earth." The phrase was, perhaps unconsciously, adapted from Theodore Parker, in whose address to the Anti-Slavery Society on May 13, 1854 (*Additional Speeches*, vol. ii, p. 25) occur the words " a government of all the

people, by all the people, and for all the people." Daniel Webster, in a speech, Jan. 26, 1830, spoke of " The people's government, made for the people, made by the people, and answerable to the people."

Gratitude is a lively sense of favours to come.

SIR ROBERT WALPOLE (1676-1745)—his definition of the gratitude of place expectants ; quoted by Hazlitt in his lecture " On Wit and Humour " (*Lectures on Engl. Comic Writers*) as " a lively sense of future favours." Cf.

A grateful sense of favours past,
A lively hope of more to come
(authorship unknown).

See Toutes les fois que je donne une place etc. ; L'ingratitude est l'indépendance du cœur.

Great and burning questions.

BENJAMIN DISRAELI [Earl of Beaconsfield] (1804-81)—in a speech March 20, 1873, explaining his reasons for refusing to take office. The phrase " brennende Fragen " (burning questions), however, occurs in the preface of Hagenbach's *Grundlinien der Liturgik und Homiletik*, 1803.

Great God ! what a genius I had when I wrote that book !

DEAN JONATHAN SWIFT (1667-1745)—alluding to *The Tale of a Tub*.

Great objects can only be seen at a distance.

JAMES NORTHCOTE (1746-1831). See You must stand afar off, &c.

Great revolutions, whatever may be their causes, are not lightly made, and are not concluded with precipitation.

BENJAMIN DISRAELI [Earl of Beaconsfield] (1804-81)—in a speech in the House of Commons, Feb. 5, 1863.

Had I served (my) God as diligently as I have (served) the king, he would not have given me over in my gray hairs.

CARDINAL WOLSEY (1471-1530) —to Sir William Kingston, who arrested him. See Si j'avois fait pour Dieu, &c. ; Cf.
"O Cromwell, Cromwell, Had I but served my God with half the zeal I serv'd my king, he would not in mine age Have left me naked to mine enemies." (Shakspere, *King Henry VIII*, act 3. sc. 2, ll. 455-8.)

Hailing with horrid melody the moon.

BENJAMIN DISRAELI [Earl of Beaconsfield] (1804-81)—Phrase applied to the oratory of Robert Lowe [Lord Sherbrooke]. Cf.
"I had rather be a dog and bay the moon, Than such a Roman." (Shakspere, *Julius Cæsar*, act 4, sc. 3, ll. 27-8.)

Happiness is not the end of life : character is.

Rev. HENRY WARD BEECHER (1813-87).

Happy !

SIR JAMES MACKINTOSH (1765-1832)—Last word.

Happy is the king who has a magistrate possessed of courage to execute the laws; and still more happy in having a son who will submit to the punishment inflicted for offending them.

HENRY IV. (1366-1413)—to Sir William Gascoigne, who had imprisoned Prince Henry (afterwards Henry V). Cf.
" 'Happy am I, that have a man so bold, That dares do justice on my proper son; And not less happy, having such a son,

That would deliver up his greatness Into the hands of justice'" (Shakspere, *King Henry IV*, 2nd Part, act 5, sc. 2, ll. 108-12 : King Henry V, quoting his father's words).

Happy is the man who has been twice thanked by his country !

BENJAMIN DISRAELI [Earl of Beaconsfield] (1804-81)—in a speech in the House of Commons, July 2, 1868, referring to Sir Robert Napier and the Abyssinian expedition.

Hard pounding this, gentlemen ! let's see who will pound longest.

DUKE OF WELLINGTON (1769-1852)—at the Battle of Waterloo (June, 1815). See It is warm work &c.

. . hare-brained chatter of irresponsible frivolity.

BENJAMIN DISRAELI [Earl of Beaconsfield] (1804-81)—in a speech at the Mansion House, Nov. 9, 1878. " The government of the world is carried on by sovereigns and statesmen, and not by anonymous paragraph writers or by the," &c.

Heaven !

WILLIAM WILBERFORCE (1759-1833)—Last words. Another version is : " I now feel so weaned from earth, my affections so much in Heaven, that I can leave you all without regret ; yet I do not love you less, but God more."

He has more wit than to be here.

LADY FAIRFAX—Reply when Lord Fairfax's name was called by the crier in forming the Court in Westminster Hall, Jan. 20, 1649, to try Charles I for treason. When the charge against the king " In the name of the people of England " was read, she exclaimed " Not a tenth part of them."

He has set his heart on being a martyr, and I have set mine on disappointing him.

WILLIAM III (1650-1702)—of Professor Dodwell (of Oxford), a bitter Jacobite.

He serves his party best who serves the country best.

PRESIDENT ' RUTHERFORD B. HAYES (1822-81)—in his Inaugural Address, delivered March 5, 1877.

He smote the rock of the national resources, and abundant streams of revenue gushed forth.

DANIEL WEBSTER (1782-1852)—in a speech on Alexander Hamilton, March 10, 1831, in allusion to Moses smiting the rock (*Exodus* xvii, 6). Followed by: "He touched the dead corpse of public credit, and it sprang upon its feet." See Millions for defence, not a cent for tribute !

He was a bold man who first swallowed an oyster.

JAMES I (1566-1625). Cf. "He was a bold man that first ate an oyster (Swift, *Polite Conversation*, Dialogue II).

He who would make a pun, would pick a pocket.

DR. SAMUEL JOHNSON (1709-84). Also attributed to Dr. John Donne (1573-1631); but see A man who could make so vile a pun &c.

He will be left alone like a whale upon the strand.

EDMUND WALLER (1605-87)—of James II (1633-1701). See A whale stranded &c.

. . hog is not bacon, until it be well hanged.

SIR NICHOLAS BACON (1510-79) —to a criminal named Hog, who

asked for mercy, claiming kindred. Preceded by : "But you and I cannot be kindred except you be hanged, for " &c.

Hold the Fort ! I am coming.

GENERAL WILLIAM TECUMSEH SHARMAN (1820-91)—Signal to General Corse, Oct. 5, 1864.

How beautiful God is !

CHARLES KINGSLEY (1819-75). Death-bed utterance. His *last* words were from the Burial Service (*Letters and Memoirs*, by his wife).

How beautiful to be with God.

FRANCES ELIZABETH WILLARD (1839-98) —Last words.

How men undervalue the power of simplicity, but it is the real key to the heart.

WILLIAM WORDSWORTH (1770-1850).

How sweet it is to rest.

JOHN TAYLOR, "the Water Poet " (1580-1654)—Last words.

I always get the better when I argue alone.

OLIVER GOLDSMITH (1728-74)— See Il me bat dans la chambre &c.

I am almost dead ; lift me up a little higher.

HENRY DORNEY (1613-83)— Last words, to his wife.

I am already married to my country.

WILLIAM PITT (1759-1806)— Reply to Horace Walpole, who was trying to arrange a marriage between him and Necker's daughter, afterwards Mme. de Staël : Cf. Brougham, *Life of Pitt*, also *Quarterly Review*, no. 97, p. 568, and J. W. Croker, *Memoirs*, vol.

ii, 340 note. Camillo Benso, Conte di Cavour (1810-61), who died unmarried, is credited with a similar saying when joked by the king as to his celibacy. He said, "Italy is my wife: I will never have another."

I am a priest! Fie! Fie! All is gone.

DAVID BEATON, Cardinal and Archbishop(1494-1546),assassinated in May, 1546—Last words.

I am come among you 'unmuzzled.'

W. E. GLADSTONE (1809-98)— at Manchester, July 18, 1865 (Sir W. Reid, *Life*, 1899, p. 476).

I am dying.

GEORGE WHITEFIELD (1714-70), founder of the Calvinistic Methodist Church—Last words.

I am for equality. I think that men are entitled to equal rights, but to equal rights to unequal things.

CHARLES JAMES FOX (1749-1806).

I am glad I am not the eldest son. I want to speak in the House of Commons, like papa.

WILLIAM PITT (1759-1806)— then only seven years old, when told that his father had been made Earl of Chatham, Aug. 1776. See Oh, Pitt never was a boy!

I am going on my journey: they have greased my boots already.

SIR SAMUEL GARTH (1660-1719) —Death-bed utterance, after receiving the extreme unction. See Very well, then, I shall not take off my boots.

I am going where all tears will be wiped from my eyes.

REV. COTTON MATHER (1633-1728)—Last words, to his wife, who had wiped his eyes with her handkerchief.

I am ill—very ill, I shall not recover.

JOHN LOTHROP MOTLEY (1814-77)—Last words (Cf. Sir William W. Gull's account of his death).

I am not in the least afraid to die.

CHARLES DARWIN (1809-82)— Last words. See Remember! I do not fear death; My Lord, why do you not go on? &c.

I am on the side of the angels.

BENJAMIN DISRAELI [Earl of Beaconsfield] (1804-81)—at a meeting of the Oxford Diocesan Society, Nov. 25, 1864, referring to the subject of Darwinism. "The question is this: Is man an ape or an angel? My lord, I am on the side of the angels. I repudiate with indignation and abhorrence the contrary view, which is, I believe, foreign to the conscience of humanity." See I have no patience whatever with" &c.

I am perfectly resigned. I am surrounded by my family. I have served my country. I have reliance upon God, and am not afraid of the devil.

HENRY GRATTAN (1750-1820)— Last words.

I am ready.

CHARLES MATHEWS (1776-1836) —Last words.

I am ready at any time—do not keep me waiting.

JOHN BROWN (1800-59)—Last words before he was hanged for taking part in the Harper's Ferry insurrection.

I am satisfied with the Lord's will.

JOHN NEWTON (1725-1807), a friend of the poet Cowper—Last recorded words.

I am sweeping through the gates, washed in the blood of the Lamb.

REV. ALFRED COOKMAN (1828-71)—Last words.

I am weary of the times, and foresee much misery to my country ; but believe that I shall be out of it ere night.

LORD FALKLAND (1610-43), Secretary of State under Charles I. —on the morning of the battle of Newbury (Sep. 20, 1643), in which he was killed. (Hume, *Hist. of Engl.*)

I awoke one morning, and found myself famous.

LORD BYRON (1788-1824)—after the publication of the first two cantos of *Childe Harold.* (Moore, *Life of Byron.*)

I believe England will be conquered some day in New England or Bengal.

HORACE WALPOLE (1717-97)—In a letter to Sir Horace Mann in 1774.

I believe that, without party, Parliamentary government is impossible.

BENJAMIN DISRAELI [Earl of Beaconsfield] (1804-81)—in a speech at Manchester, April 3, 1872. Followed by " I look upon Parliamentary government as the noblest government in the world, and certainly the one most suited to England."

I believe this government cannot endure permanently half slave and half free.

PRESIDENT ABRAHAM LINCOLN (1809-65)—in a speech to the Illinois Whig State Convention at Springfield, June 16, 1858.

I called the New World into existence to redress the balance of the Old.

GEORGE CANNING (1770-1827)—in a speech on the relations between Great Britain and Portugal (Dec. 12, 1826). Alluded to by Daniel Webster, in his speech, Jan. 19, 1824. (H.C. Lodge, *Daniel Webster,* 1889, p. 134)

I can drive a coach and six through any act of Parliament.

DANIEL O'CONNELL (1775-1847). Anacharsis, laughing at Solon who was writing his laws, said that written laws were just like spiders' webs ; for, like them, they caught the weaker criminals, but were broken through by the stronger and more important. (Plutarch, *Life of Solon,* V.) Cf. "Où la guêpe a passé le moucheron demeure." (Where the wasp escapes the gnat is caught) (La Fontaine, *Le Corbeau voulant imiter l'aigle*) ; and see Driving a coach and six, &c.

I cannot bear it ; let me rest. I must die. Let God do his work.

FREDERICK WILLIAM ROBERTSON (1816-53)—Last words.

I committed my soul to God, and my cause to my country.

ROBERT JENKINS, master of a small sloop (fl. 1731-8)—when asked at the bar of the House of Commons (in 1738), what were his feelings when his ear was torn off (as was alleged) by the commander of a Spanish ship. The Spaniard bade him carry the ear to King George (the Second, 1683-1760) and tell him that he would serve him in the same manner if he caught him. (*Dict. Nat. Biog.* vol. xxix. p. 306.)

I could, if God please, lay my head back and die without terror this afternoon.

Dr. ISAAC WATTS (1674-1748) —Last words. Preceded by : " It is a great mercy to me that I have no manner of fear or dread of death."

I could wish this tragic scene were over, but I hope to go through it with becoming dignity.

JAMES QUIN (1693-1766)— Last words.

I die happy.

CHARLES JAMES FOX (1749-1806)—Last words. Another account gives : "Trotter will tell you," said to Mrs. Fox. See Now God be praised ! I die happy.

I die not only a Protestant, but with a heart-hatred of popery, prelacy, and all superstition whatever.

ARCHIBALD, 8th EARL OF ARGYLE (1598-1661)—on the scaffold.

I do forgive you.

WILLIAM HOWARD, VISCOUNT STAFFORD (1612-80)—to the executioner, who asked his forgiveness. (Bell's *Chapel and Tower.*) Another version is : " This block will be my pillow, and I shall repose there well, without pain, grief or fear "; and a further : " I thank God I am no more afraid of death, but as cheerfully put off my doublet at this time as ever I did when I went to bed." His only exclamation on hearing his sentence was " God's holy name be praised ! " (Hume, *Hist of Engl.*) George Wishart also forgave the executioner in a similar way : See I fear not this fire.

I do not believe that state can last in which Jesus and Judas have equal weight in public affairs.

THOMAS CARLYLE (1795-1881) —to an American clergyman who defended universal suffrage.

I do not fear death.

THOMAS BLOOD (1628-80)— Last words. See I am not in the least afraid to die ; My Lord, why do you not go on ?

I do not know a method of drawing up an indictment against a whole people.

EDMUND BURKE (1729-97)— in a speech on conciliation with America, Mar. 22, 1775.

I do not like giving advice, because it is an unnecessary responsibility under any circumstances.

BENJAMIN DISRAELI [Earl of Beaconsfield] (1804-81)—in a speech at Aylesbury, Sep. 21, 1865.

I don't think much of a man who is not wiser to-day than he was yesterday.

PRESIDENT ABRAHAM LINCOLN (1809-65)—when taxed with having changed his mind on some subject. Cf. " L'homme absurde est celui qui ne change jamais " (The stupid man is he who never alters.) (Barthélemy, *Ma Justification,* 1832)

I drink with pleasure the health of all unfortunate princes.

GEORGE II (1683-1760)—when challenged at a masked ball by a Jacobite lady to drink to the health of the Pretender.

If all our wishes were gratified, most of our pleasures would be destroyed.

ARCHBISHOP WHATELY (1787-1863).

If all the swords in England were brandishing over my head, your terrors would not move me.

THOMAS à BFCKET (1117-70), Archbishop of Canterbury—to his murderers.

If anyone attempts to haul down the American flag, shoot him on the spot.

JOHN A. DIX (1798-1879)—Telegraphic order dated from Washington, Jan. 29, 1861, regarding the arrest of Capt. Breshwood, commander of the revenue cutter, *McClennand*, at New Orleans.

I fear not this fire.

GEORGE WISHART (1502-46), burned at the stake—Last words. Preceded by : " For the sake of the true Gospel, given one by the grace of God, I suffer this day with a glad heart. Behold and consider my visage. Ye shall not see me change colour." The executioner had asked for and obtained his forgiveness.

I feel now that I am dying.

JEREMY BENTHAM (1748-1832)— Last words.

I feel the flowers growing over me.

JOHN KEATS (1796-1821)—Last words. Another version is : " I die of a broken heart."

If I am alive, I shall be glad to see him ; if I am dead, he'll be glad to see me.

LORD HOLLAND (1705-74)— when told by his physicians that he had scarcely half-an-hour to live. Preceded by " Should Mr. Selwyn call within the next half-hour, show him in at once."

If I die, I die unto the Lord. Amen.

REV. EDWARD IRVING (1792

1834)—Last words. Another version is : " In life and in death, I am the Lord's."

If I granted your demands, I should be no more than the mere phantom of a king.

CHARLES I (1600-49)—Reply to the demand of the Long Parliament for the control of military, civil, and religious appointments.

If I had a son, I should endeavour to make him familiar with French and German authors. Greek and Latin are only luxuries.

DR. RICHARD PORSON, the Greek scholar, (1759-1808).

If I had strength enough to hold a pen, I would write down how easy and pleasant a thing it is to die.

DR. WILLIAM HUNTER (1717-83—Last words.

If I have been deceived, doubtless it was the work of a spirit ; whether that spirit was good or bad I do not know.

JOANNA SOUTHCOTT (1750-1814) —Last recorded words.

If I have done the public any service, it is due to nothing but industry and patient thought.

SIR ISAAC NEWTON (1642-1727) —to Dr. Richard Bentley.

I firmly believe that if the whole materia medica could be sunk to the bottom of the sea, it would be all the better for mankind and all the worse for the sea.

OLIVER WENDELL HOLMES (1809-94)—in a lecture before the Harvard Medical School.

If I tremble with cold, my enemies will say it was from

fear : I will not expose myself to such reproaches.

By CHARLES I (1600-49)—Remark when asking for two shirts,
the morning of his execution, Jan.
30, 1649. (Lingard, *Hist. of Engl.*,
x, ch. 5.) See *Tu trembles, Bailly.*
Drake, when a midshipman, was
observed to tremble very much on
the eve of an engagement, and, on
being asked the cause, replied,
" My flesh trembles at the anticipa-
tion of the many and great dangers
into which my resolute and un-
daunted heart will lead me." (*Percy
Anecdotes*, vol. i., p. 203.)   Cf.
" Why dost thôu quiver man?" (*Dick*).
" The palsy, ànd not fear, provoketh me."
(*Lord Say.*)
(Shakspere, *King Henry VI*, 2nd
Part, act iv, sc. 7, ll. 95-6).

If I were an American, as I am
an Englishman, while a
foreign troop was landed in
my country, I never would
lay down my arms—never !
never ! never !

WILLIAM PITT, 1st Earl of
Chatham (1708-78) – in a speech
Nov. 18, 1777, referring to the
employment of German soldiers.

If learning could have kept a
man alive, our brother had
not died.

RICHARD JOHNSON Master of
the Temple, (d. 1674)—over the
grave of John Selden in the Temple
Church, London. Cf. " Lord, if
thou hadst been here, my brother
had not died." (*St. John* xi. 32)

If my head would win him a
castle in France, it should
not fail to go.

SIR THOMAS MORE (1480-1535)
—of Henry VIII.

I forgive him, and I hope I shall
as easily forget the wrongs
he has done me, as he will
forget my pardon.

RICHARD I (1157-99)—of his
brother, John, who had endeavoured
to prevent Richard's release by
Henry VI. Emperor of Germany.

I found there was nothing for it
but to take off my flesh and
sit in my bones.

REV. SYDNEY SMITH (1771-
1845)—alluding to the heat.

If this be treason, make the most
of it.

PATRICK HENRY (1736-99) —
in a speech in the Virginia House
of Burgesses against the Stamp Act,
May, 1765 (Wirt, *Life*).   Preceded
by " Cæsar had his Brutus—Charles
the First, his Cromwell—and George
the Third ('Treason !' cried the
Speaker)—may profit by their example.   If &c."

If you like the terms of the loan,
down with the dust !

DEAN JONATHAN SWIFT (1667-
1745)—in a short charity-sermon on
the text " He that hath pity upon
the poor lendeth unto the Lord "
(*Prov.* ch. xix., v. 17).

If you love my soul, away with
it !

JOHN HOOPER, Bishop of Glou-
cester and afterwards Bishop of
Worcester (c. 1495-1555) — Last
words.   Other versions are: "Lord
Jesus, receive my spirit," and
" Good people, give me more fire."
(The faggots were green, and had to
be rekindled three times.)

I give Thee thanks, O God, for
all Thy benefits, and with
all the pains of my soul I
humbly beseech Thy mercy
to give me remission of those
sins I have wickedly com-
mitted against Thee ; and
of all mortal men whom
willingly or ignorantly I
have offended, with all my
heart I desire forgiveness.

EDWARD, THE BLACK PRINCE (1330-76)—Last words.

Ignorance never settles a question.

BENJAMIN DISRAELI [Earl of Beaconsfield](1804-81)—in a speech in the House of Commons, May 14, 1866.

I go from a corruptible to an incorruptible crown.

CHARLES I (1600-49) — on the scaffold. He added "where no disturbance can have place" (Hume, *Hist. of Engl.*)

I hate all Boets and Bainters.

GEORGE I (1660-1727)—when refusing to allow a poem to be dedicated to him. (Campbell, *Life of Lord Mansfield*, ch. 30 note.)

I have always endeavoured, to the best of my ability, to serve God, my king and my country. I go to the place God has designed for those who love him.

ANTHONY COLLINS (1676-1729) —Last words.

I have been nearer you when you have missed me.

SIR GEORGE LISLE (Aug. 28, 1648)—Last words, to one of the soldiers appointed to shoot him. (*Percy Anecdotes*, vol. ii, p. 114.)

I have desired to have the obedience of my subjects by love, and not by compulsion.

QUEEN ELIZABETH (1533-1603) —to her parliament. See Nothing, no worldly thing.

I have done England little good, but I should be sorry to do it any harm.

KATHARINE OF ARAGON (1486-1536)—to the commissioners, after her divorce by Henry VIII (1491-1547).

I have ever cherished an honest pride; never have I stooped to friendship with Jonathan Wild, or with any of his detestable thief-takers; and, though an undutiful son, I never damned my mother's eyes.

JACK SHEPPARD (1701-24), noted highwayman and burglar, hanged at Tyburn—Last words.

I have given my life to law and politics; law is uncertain, and politics are utterly vain.

DANIEL WEBSTER (1782-1852) —to Professor Silliman (1772-1864).

I have had wealth, rank, and power, but, if these were all I had, how wretched I should be!

PRINCE ALBERT (1819-61)— Dying words.

I have heard, indeed, that two negatives make an affirmative; but I never heard before that two nothings ever made anything.

DUKE OF BUCKINGHAM (1627-88)—in a speech in the House of Lords.

I have known thee all the time.

JOHN GREENLEAF WHITTIER (1807-92)—Last words, to his niece, who asked whether he knew her. Another version is: "Give my love to the world."

I have learnt again what I have often learnt before, that you should never take anything for granted.

BENJAMIN DISRAELI [Earl of Beaconsfield] 1804-81)—in a speech at Salthill, Oct. 5, 1864.

I have long been of the opinion that a British army could

bear neither success nor
failure.

DUKE OF WÈLLINGTON (1769-
1852)—written from Coimbra, May
31, 1809, to the Rt. Hon. J. Villiers.
See The English nation is never so
great as in adversity.

I have long been of the opinion
that the foundations of the
future grandeur and stability
of the British Empire lie in
America.

BENJAMIN FRANKLIN (1706-90)
—written in 1761 to Lord Kames.

I have neither eyes to see, nor
ears to hear, save as the
Commons of England do
direct.

SPEAKER LENTHALL (1591-1662)
—reply, Jan. 4, 1642, to Charles I
(1600-49), who had entered the
House for the purpose of arresting
Pym, Hampden, Holles, Hazlerig
and Strode. Hume (*Hist. of Engl.*)
has it : "I have, sir, neither eyes
to see, nor tongue to speak, in this
place, but as the House is pleased
to direct me, whose servant I am ;
and I humbly ask pardon that I
cannot give any other answer to
what your majesty is pleased to
demand of me."

I have no patience whatever
with these gorilla damnifica-
tions of humanity.

THOMAS CARLYLE (1795-81)—
referring to the Darwinian theory
of development. See I am on the
side of the angels.

I have not yet begun to fight.

PAUL JONES, Naval Commander
(1747-92)—to the captain of the
Serapis, who asked if he had struck
his colours, during a lull in the
engagement.

I have no wish to believe on that
subject.

THOMAS PAINE, author of *The
Rights of Man*, &c. (1737-1809)—
Last words, in reply to his physician's
question, "Do you wish to believe
that Jesus is the Son of God?"

I have often read and thought
of that scripture, but never
till this moment did I feel its
full power, and now I die
happy.

BISHOP JOSEPH BUTLER (1692-
1752)—Last words, to his chaplain
who read to him chapter vi. of St.
John, calling his attention to the
37th verse : "All that the Father
giveth me shall come to me ; and
him that cometh to me I will in no
wise cast out."

I have Old England set against
me, and do you think I will
have New England also ?

SIR ROBERT WALPOLE (1676-
1745)—in 1739, when sounded by
Lord Chesterfield as to a project for
the taxation of America. The *Dict.
Nat. Biog.* (vol. lix, p. 202) gives
the last word as "likewise."

I have opened it.

ALFRED LORD TENNYSON (1809-
92)—Last recorded words, pre-
sumably referring to a volume of
Shakspere opened by him at
. . . Hang there like fruit my soul,
Till the tree die.
(*Cymbeline*, act 5. sc. 5 ll. 263-4)
or perhaps to one of his last poems:
"Fear not, thou, the hidden purpose of
that Power,
Which alone is great,
Nor the myriad world, his shadow, nor the
silent
Opener of the Gate."
(see *Memoir*, by his son).

I have pain—there is no arguing
against sense—but I have
peace, I have peace! (a
little later) I am almost well.

RICHARD BAXTER (1615-91)—
Last words.

I have peace, perfect peace. 'Thou wilt keep him in perfect peace whose mind is stayed on thee.'

BENJAMIN FRANKLIN BUTLER (1795-1858), Attorney General of the U.S. 1831-4—Last words

I have seen many a man turn his gold into smoke, but you are the first who has turned his smoke into gold.

QUEEN ELIZABETH (1533-1603) —to Sir Walter Raleigh. The latter made a wager with the Queen that he could weigh the smoke from his tobacco-pipe, and she used the above words on paying him the bet. He weighed the tobacco before smoking and the ashes afterwards.

I have sent for you that you may see how a Christian can die.

JOSEPH ADDISON (1672-1719) —shortly before his death, to his step son, Lord Warwick. Another account gives the words as " See in what peace a Christian can die." Cf. Venez voir comment meurt, &c.

I have sought Thee in the fields, and gardens, but I have found Thee O God, in thy Sanctuary—thy Temple.

FRANCIS BACON (1561-1626)— Last words. Preceded by : " Thy creatures, O Lord, have been my books, but Thy Holy Scriptures much more."

I have sought the Lord night and day that he would rather slay me than put me upon the doing of this work.

OLIVER CROMWELL (1599-1658)—referring to the dissolution of the Long Parliament, Apr. 20, 1653. Preceded by, addressing the House : " It is you that have forced me upon this." (Hume, *Hist. of Engl.*)

I hold that the characteristic of the present age is craving credulity.

BENJAMIN DISRAELI [Earl of Beaconsfield] (1804-81)—in a speech at Oxford, Nov. 25, 1864.

I know I have the body but of a weak and feeble woman ; but I have the heart and stomach of a king, and of a king of England too.

QUEEN ELIZABETH (1533-1603) —in her address to the troops assembled at Tilbury to oppose the Spanish Armada in 1588. See No. 6798 *Harleian MSS.*

I know no method to secure the repeal of bad or obnoxious laws so effective as their stringent execution.

ULYSSES S. GRANT (1822-85)— in his inaugural address as President of the U.S. Mar. 4, 1869.

I know not what profit there may be in the study of history, what value in the sayings of wise men, or in the recorded experience of the past, if it be not to guide and instruct us in the present.

BENJAMIN DISRAELI [Earl of Beaconsfield] (1804-81)—in a speech on the state of the nation, July 2, 1849. See Anything but history, &c.

I know that all things on earth must have an end, and now I am come to mine.

SIR JOSHUA REYNOLDS (1723-92) —Last words. Preceded by : " I have been fortunate in long good health, and constant success, and I ought not to complain."

" I know that my Redeemer liveth."

ANNE STEELE (1716-78)—Last words.

I know what you are thinking of, but I have nothing to communicate on the subject of religion.

MARY WOLLSTONECRAFT, afterwards Mrs. Godwin (1759 97)—Last words, to her husband.

I learn more from conversation than from all the books I ever read.

CHARLES JAMES FOX (1749-1806)—Cf. " A great thing is a great book, but a greater thing than all is the talk of a great man." (Disraeli, *Coningsby.*)

I leave this world without a regret.

HENRY DAVID THOREAU (1817-62)—Last words.

I like thee better because thou livest unmarried.

QUEEN ELIZABETH (1533-1603)—to Dr. Whitehead, who replied, "I like you the worse for the same cause." See, And you, *madam* I may not call you, &c.

I'll bell the cat.

ARCHIBALD DOUGLAS, 5th Earl of Angus (1449-1514)—to the Scotch nobles in 1482 at a midnight council in the church of Lauder (cf. La Fontaine, *Conseil tenu par les Rats*).
Princes and favourites long grew tame
And trembled at the homely name
          Archibald " Bell-the-Cat."
(Scott, *Marmion* v, 14 and note.)

I'll be shot if I don't believe I'm dying.

LORD THURLOW (1732-1806)—Last words.

I'll have a 'Gazette' of my own.

LORD NELSON (1758-1805)—in his journal referring to his services at the siege of Calvi, in Corsica (1794), not having been mentioned in the official report. " They have not done me justice. But, never

mind, I'll have a ' Gazette' of my own." (Southey, *Life of Nelson*, ed. 1888, p. 99). Later (1797), in a letter to his wife, he wrote "One day or other I will have a long ' Gazette' to myself," (ibid, p. 131).

Illustrious predecessor.

PRESIDENT MARTIN VAN BUREN (1782-1862)—in his inaugural address, March 4, 1837. "I shall tread in the footsteps of my illustrious predecessor [Genl. Jackson]." The expression occurs, however, in Burke's *Thoughts on the Present Discontents*, vol. 1, p. 456.

I look to the event with perfect resignation.

GEORGE WASHINGTON (1732-99)—a few hours before his death, Dec. 14, 1799.

I make this vow, that mine eyes desire you above all things.

CATHERINE OF ARAGON (1486-1536)—Concluding words of a tender letter written to Henry VIII shortly before her death. He had divorced her in 1533. (Hume, *Hist. of Engl.*)

I mak siccar ! (*Scotch for* sure).

KIRKPATRICK, of Closeburn, one of Robert Bruce's followers, the latter having in a rage stabbed John Comyn, a claimant for the Scottish Crown. Bruce cried, " I doubt I have slain the Red Comyn !" " You doubt !" said Kirkpatrick, " I mak siccar !" The words have been adopted as the motto of the Kirkpatricks.

I may say of our literature that it has one characteristic which distinguishes it from almost all the other literatures of modern Europe, and that is its exuberant reproductiveness.

BENJAMIN DISRAEL [Earl of

Beaconsfield] (1804-81) — in a speech at the Royal Literary Fund Dinner, May 6, 1868.

I mistrust the judgment of every man in a case in which his own wishes are concerned.

DUKE OF WELLINGTON (1769-1852).

I mix them with (my) brains, sir.

JOHN OPIE (1761-1807)—Reply, when asked how he mixed his colours. "With Brains, Sir" is the title of a paper (1st series, 2nd paper) in Dr. John Brown's *Spare Hours* (Boston 1883), and the paper begins with the anecdote of Opie. A similar saying is recorded of William Etty, R.A. (1787-1849). He replied, when questioned as to the 'medium,' saying, "Tell them the only medium I use is brains." (Gilchrist, *Life of Etty*, vol. ii, p. 191).

Impossible, sir! don't talk to me of impossibilities.

WILLIAM PITT, [Earl of Chatham] (1708-78)—to Mr. Cleveland, who brought a message from Lord Anson that it was impossible to fit out the ships for a naval expedition by a given time. See, Le mot impossible n'est pas français.

I must arrange my pillows for another weary night.

WASHINGTON IRVING (1783-1859)—Last (coherent) words.

I must sleep now.

LORD BYRON (1788-1824)—Last words.

In a progressive country change is constant.

BENJAMIN DISRAELI, [Earl of Beaconsfield] (1804-81)—in a speech

at Edinburgh, Oct. 29, 1867, on the Reform Bill.

Increased means and increased leisure are the two civilisers of man.

BENJAMIN DISRAEL [Earl of Beaconsfield] (1804-81)—in a speech at Manchester, April 3, 1872.

Indemnity for the past and security for the future.

WILLIAM PITT, [Earl of Chatham] (1708-78)—attributed to him by De Quincey, *Theol. Essays*, vol. ii, p. 170. (see also Russell, *Memoir of Fox*, vol. iii, p. 345.) Pitt, in a letter to the Earl of Shelburne, Sep. 29, 1770, speaks of "reparation for our rights at home and security against the like future violations."

Individuals may form communities, but it is institutions alone that can create a nation.

BENJAMIN DISRAELI, [Earl of Beaconsfield] (1804-81)—in a speech at Manchester (1866).

Inebriated with the exuberance of his own verbosity.

LORD BEACONSFIELD, (1804-81) —in a speech at Knightsbridge (July 28, 1878) on his return from Berlin, referring to Mr. Gladstone. The latter had shortly before described the Convention of Constantinople as an insane convention. "A sophistical rhetorician, inebriated with the exuberance of his own verbosity, and gifted with an egotistical imagination, that can at all times command an interminable and inconsistent series of arguments to malign his opponents, and to glorify himself."

I never heard of a king being drowned.

WILLIAM II, (1056-1100) in 1099, when about to embark at Southampton for Normandy, being entreated by the sailors not to put to sea in an old crazy ship, when the wind was contrary, and the waves high. " I never heard of a king being drowned," cried Rufus, "make haste, loose your cables ; you will see the elements join to obey me." (Freeman, *Life of William Rufus*, vol. ii, 284 and note.) Another version is " Weigh anchor, hoist sail and begone. Kings never drown ! " See Queens of England are never drowned.

I never knew a man of merit neglected ; it was generally by his own fault that he failed of success.

DR. SAMUEL JOHNSON (1709-84) —Preceded by : " All the complaints which are made of the world are unjust."

I never knew a man that was bad fit for service that was good.

EDMUND BURKE (1729-97)—of Warren Hastings.

I never read a book before reviewing it, it prejudices a man so.

REV. SYDNEY SMITH (1771-1845)

In honour I gained them, and in honour I will die with them.

LORD NELSON (1758-1805)—of his decorations *(not* at the battle of Trafalgar, Oct. 21, 1805, but on a previous occasion), when it was hinted that they rendered him a conspicuous mark for the enemy. (Southey, *Life of Nelson*, ed. 1888, p. 366.)

In me behold the end of the world with all its vanities.

SIR PHILIP SIDNEY (1554-1586) —Last words, when mortally wounded at Zutphen, Sep. 22, 1586. See, Take it, thy necessity is greater than mine.

Innocuous desuetude.

PRESIDENT GROVER CLEVELAND (b. 1837) — in a message to the Senate, Mar. 1, 1886 : " And so it happens that after an existence of nearly twenty years of an almost innocuous desuetude these laws are brought forth, apparently the repealed as well as the unrepealed, and put in the way of an executive who is willing, if permitted, to attempt an improvement in the methods of administration." He declined to furnish papers relative to suspensions from office during the recess of the Senate, as demanded by that body.

Instruction ladled out in a hurry is not education.

LORD JUSTICE BOWEN (1835-94) —in a lecture on Education. In the same lecture he said : " In ancient times when duty to the State was the keynote of civilisation, education was that culture of mind and body which tended to turn out the ideal citizen."

Insurrection of thought always precedes insurrection of arms.

WENDELL PHILLIPS (1811-84) —in a speech at Brooklyn, on John Brown, Nov. 1, 1859. See Revolutions never go backward.

In this country ministers are king.

GEORGE II (1683-1760).

In times of danger it is the custom of England to arm.

QUEEN ELIZABETH (1533-1603) —referring to a possible attack by the French.

Into thy hands, O Lord, I commend my spirit.

THOMAS A. BECKET, Archbishop óf Canterbury (1117-70), assassinated in Canterbury Cathedral—

Dying words (Hume, *Hist. of Engl.*) See In manus, Domine &c., and For the name of Jesus &c.

I once ate a pea.

" BEAU " BRUMMEL (1778-1840) —when asked if he never ate vegetables.

I only regret that I have but one life to give to my country.

NATHAN HALE (1755-76) American patriot, executed as a spy—Dying words.

I praise God, I am willing to leave it, and expect a better— that world wherein dwelleth righteousness, and I long for it.

SIR HENRY WOTTON (1568-1639) —Last words. Preceded by : " I now draw near to the harbour of death—that harbour that will rescue me from all the future storms and waves of this restless world."

I pray God to spare my friends from a similar clemency.

SIR THOMAS MORE (1480-1535)— when told that the sentence of death pronounced upon him had been changed to one of simple decapitation, by clemency of the king. Another version is : " God preserve all my friends from such favours."

I pray you all pray for me.

CARDINAL HENRY BEAUFORT (1370-1447) — Last words. Cf. Shakspere, *King Henry VI, pt.* ii, act 3, sc. 3.

I propose to get into fortune's way.

DUKE OF WELLINGTON (1769-1852)—a favourite phrase of his. (*Dict. Nat. Biog.*, vol. lx, p. 203.)

I really do not see the signal !

LORD NELSON (1758-1805)—at the Battle of Copenhagen, Apr. 2,

1801, on a signal being made to him to leave off action, putting his glass to his blind eye. Preceded by: "Leave off action ? Now, damn me if I do ! You know, Foley," turning to the Captain, " I have only one eye,—I have a right to be blind sometimes." (Southey, *Life of Nelson*, ed. 1888, p. 279).

I regret nothing, but am sorry that I am about to leave my friends.

ZACHARY TAYLOR (1784-1850) —Last words. Preceded by : " I am about to die. I expect the summons soon. I have endeavoured to discharge all my official duties faithfully."

Ireland is in a state of social decomposition.

BENJAMIN DISRAELI [Earl of Beaconsfield] (1804-81)—in a speech in the House of Commons, July 2, 1849. Cf. :
"Something is rotten in the state of Denmark." (Shakspere, *Hamlet*, act 1, sc. 4, l. 90.)

I resign my spirit to God, my daughter to my country.

THOMAS JEFFERSON (1743-1826) —Last words.

I sat by its cradle, I followed its hearse.

HENRY GRATTAN (1750-1820)— referring to the rise of Irish independence in 1782 and its fall 20 years later.

I say *ditto* to Mr. Burke—I say *ditto* to Mr. Burke.

MR. CRUGER, who was returned as member for Bristol conjointly with Edmund Burke (1729-97) in 1774 (Prior's *Life of Burke*, p. 152).

I see earth receding ; Heaven is opening ; God is calling me.

DWIGHT LYMAN MOODY (1837-

3

99)—Last words (*New York Times*, Dec. 23, 1899).

I see no reason why the existence of Harriet Martineau should be perpetuated.

HARRIET MARTINEAU (1802-76) —Last words. Preceded by: " I have had a noble share of life, and I do not ask for any other life."

I shall be satisfied with Thy likeness—satisfied !

CHARLES WESLEY (1708-88)— Last words.

I shall retire early ; I am very tired.

THOMAS BABINGTON, LORD MACAULAY (1800-59)—Last words ; to his butler.

I shall soon know the grand secret.

ARTHUR THISTLEWOOD (1770-1820,—Dying words, at his execution for high treason, May 1, 1820. (*Annual Register*). See Je vais quérir un grand peut-être.

I should like to record the thoughts of a dying man for the benefit of science, but it is impossible.

DR. GEORGE MILLER BEARD (1839-83)—Last words. See I wish I had the power of writing &c.

I should not be a better king, however splendidly I was dressed.

EDWARD I (1239-1307).

Is Lawrence come—is Lawrence come ?

JOHN HENRY FUSELI (c. 1742-1825)—Last words ; alluding to his friend. (*Life of Fuseli*)

Is that you, Dora ?

WILLIAM WORDSWORTH (1770-1850)—Last words. (*Memoirs of Wordsworth*, vol. ii, p. 506.)

" Is this a dagger which I see before me ? "

WILLIAM POWELL (1735-69)— when on his death-bed, suddenly quoted the above line from Shakspere, *Macbeth*, act ii, sc. 1, l. 33, with an appropriate attitude. A moment after he cried ' O God!' and expired.

Is this death ?

GEORGE LIPPARD (1822-54)— Last words, to his physician ; also attributed to JOHN QUICK (1748-1831).

Is thy servant a dog, that he should do this thing ?

REV. SYDNEY SMITH (1771-1845) —when advised to have his portrait painted by Landseer. Cf. " Is thy servant a dog, that he should do this great thing?" (*2nd Book of Kings*, ch. viii, v. 13).

I still live !

DANIEL WEBSTER (1782-1852) —Last words.

I strike my flag.

COMMODORE ISAAC HULL (1775-1843)—Last words.

I succeed him ; no one could replace him.

THOMAS JEFFERSON (1743-1826) —Reply, when asked by the Comte de Vergennes if he replaced Mr. Franklin.

It came with a lass, and it will go with a lass.

JAMES V. of Scotland (1512-42) —Last recorded words, referring to the Scottish crown. Hume's version is : " The crown came with a woman, and it will go with one." (*Hist. of Engl.*)

It grows dark, boys : you may go.

Dr. ALEXANDER ADAM, Head Master, High School, Edinburgh (1741-1809)—Last words.

I thank you for all your faithful services ; God bless you.

WILLIAM BROMLEY CADOGAN (1751-97)—Last words, to an old servant.

It has all the contortions of the sibyl, without the inspiration.

EDMUND BURKE (1729-97)—referring to Croft's *Life of Dr. Young,* which was spoken of as a good imitation of Dr. Johnson's style. " No, no," said he, " it is not a good imitation of Johnson ; it has all his pomp without his force ; it has all the nodosities of the oak, without its strength ; it &c. (Prior's *Life of Burke,* p. 468.)

It hath been said, that an unjust Peace is to be prefer'd before a just War.

SAMUEL BUTLER (1612-80) (*Two Speeches made in the Rump Parliament,* 1659—Butler's *Remains,* 1759, vol. I, p. 284). Followed by : " because the Safety of the People, the End of all Government, is more concerned in the one than the other. Cf. : There never was a good war or a bad peace (B. Franklin, *Letter to Quincy,* Sep. 11, 1773).

I think I shall die to-night.

DANTE GABRIEL ROSSETTI (1828-82)—Last words.

I think it would, madam—for a toad.

DR. SAMUEL JOHNSON (1709-84)—on a lady showing him a grotto she had made and asking him if it would not be a cool habitation in summer.

I think the author who speaks about his own books is almost as bad as a mother who talks about her own children.

BENJAMIN DISRAELI [Earl of Beaconsfield] (1804-81)—in a speech at Glasgow, Nov. 19, 1870.

I think you had better send for the doctor—I am so faint.

JOHN SHERMAN (1823-1900)—Last words.

It is a difficult task to lead the House of Commons, a more difficult one to manage a Cabinet Council ; but to lead an army in the field must be the most difficult of all.

W. E. GLADSTONE (1809-98)—in later life. Sir W. Reid's *Life,* 1899, pp. 479-80).

It is all the same in the end.

TITUS OATES (1620-1705)—Last words.

It is a very easy thing to devise good laws : the difficulty is to make them effective.

VISCOUNT BOLINGBROKE (1678-1751).

It is beautiful.

ELIZABETH BARRETT BROWNING (1805-61)—Last words.

It is better to wear out than to rust out.

BISHOP CUMBERLAND (1632-1718)—see Richard Sharp, *Letters and Essays.* p. 29. Cf. " Horrible as it is to us I imagine that the manner of his [General Gordon's] death was not unwelcome to himself. Better wear out than rust out, and better break than wear out." Huxley, Letter to Sir J. Donnelly, 16th Feb. 1885 (*Life and Letters,* 1900, vol. ii, p. 95).

It is done.

HORACE GREELEY (1811-72)—Last words.

It is likely you may never need to do it again.

JAMES HOGG, "the Ettrick Shepherd" (1772-1835)—Last words ; to his wife, whom he had asked to watch by his bedside during the night.

It is much easier to be critical than to be correct.

BENJAMIN DISRAELI [Earl of BEACONSFIELD] (1804-81)—in the debate on the Queen's Speech, Jan. 24, 1860) Cf. "La critique est aisée et l'art est difficile" ("Criticism is easy and art difficult.")—Néricault-Destouches, *Le Glorieux*, act. ii, sc. 5.

It is not best to swap horses when crossing a stream.

ABRAHAM LINCOLN (1809-65)—on being re-nominated to the Presidency of the United States, June 9, 1864. He said, "I have not permitted myself, gentlemen, to conclude that I am the best man in this country ; but I am reminded in this connection of the story of an old Dutch farmer, who remarked that it was not best to swap horses when crossing a stream."

It is not that women are not often very clever (cleverer than many men), but there is a point of excellence which they never reach.

JAMES NORTHCOTE, R.A. (1746-1831).

It is not the first time they have turned their backs upon me.

DUKE OF WELLINGTON (1769-1852)—to Louis XVIII, on the latter apologising to him for the French marshals turning their backs on him and leaving the king's levée. Preceded by : "Don't distress yourself, sire, it is not" &c.

It is small, very small indeed.

ANNE BOLEYN (1507-36) wife of Henry VIII—Last words, just before being beheaded, alluding to her neck, which she clasped with her hands when speaking.

It is still our duty to fight for our country, into what hands soever the government might fall.

ADMIRAL ROBERT BLAKE (1598-1657)—to his seamen. After the victory of Santa Cruz, April 20, 1657, being ill with dropsy and scurvy, he hastened home, but died in sight of land, off Plymouth, Aug. 17, 1657. (Hume, *Hist. of Engl.*)

It is the custom here for but one man to be allowed to stand covered.

CHARLES II, (1630-85)—at the same time removing his hat while William Penn, the Quaker, remained covered. Penn said, "Friend Charles, keep thy hat on." Another version is : "Friend Penn, it is the custom of this court for only one person to be covered at a time." (*Percy Anecdotes*, vol. vi, p. 331)

It is the day of *no* judgment that I am afraid of.

EDMUND BURKE (1729-97)—Reply to William Pitt, who had said in 1791, speaking of French affairs, that England and the British Constitution were safe until the day of judgment.

It is the duty of a minister to stand like a wall of adamant between the people and the sovereign.

RT. HON. W. E. GLADSTONE (1809-81)—in a speech at Garston, Nov. 14, 1868.

It is warm work, and this day may be the last to any of us at a moment.

LORD NELSON (1758-1805)—at

the Battle of Copenhagen (April 2, 1801). He added " But, mark you ! I would not be elsewhere for thousands." (Southey, *Life of Nelson*, ed. 1888, p. 278) See Hard pounding &c.

It is well.

GEORGE WASHINGTON, first President of the U.S. (1732-99)— Last words. Washington had said to his secretary, Mr. Lear, " I am just going ; have me decently buried, and do not let my body be put into the vault until three days after I am dead—do you understand me ? " On receiving Mr. Lear's reply that he did, Washington added. " It is well."

It is well known what a middle-man is : he is a man who bamboozles one party and plunders the other.

BENJAMIN DISRAELI [Earl of Beaconsfield] (1804 81)—on the proposed increased grant to May-nooth College, April 11, 1845. Preceded by : " Something has risen up in this country as fatal in the political world as it has been in the landed world of Ireland—we have a great Parliamentary middle-man ; " and followed by : " till having obtained a position to which he is not entitled, he cries out, ' Let us have no party questions, but a fixity of tenure.' "

It matters little to me ; for if I am but once dead they may bury me or not bury me as as they please. They may leave my corpse to rot where I die if they wish.

GEORGE BUCHANAN (1506-82)— Last words ; to his servant, who asked who would defray the expenses of his burial.

It matters not where I am going whether the weather be cold or hot.

LORD CHANCELLOR JOHN SCOTT ELDON (1750-1838)—Last words ; to someone who spoke to him about the weather.

It was a great day for England.

WILLIAM IV (1765-1837)—Last words, on hearing the cannons firing on the anniversary of the Battle of Waterloo.

It was not British blood which had been spilt, but it was British honour that bled at every vein.

RICHARD BRINSLEY SHERIDAN (1751-80)—in the House of Commons, Oct. 29, 1795, alluding to the conduct of Commodore Warren at Quiberon, Oct. 27, 1795. Preceded by : " . . it was true, the blood of French emigrants only had flowed—it was not British blood " etc. (*Speeches of Sheridan*, 1816, vol. iv, pp. 106-7)

It will be but a momentary pang.

MAJOR JOHN ANDRÉ (1751-80)— Last words before being shot as a spy, Oct. 2, 1780, during the American Revolution. Preceded by : " All I request of you, gentle-men, is that you will bear witness to the world that I die like a brave man." These are sometimes quoted as his last words. Another account says : " But I pray you to bear witness that I die like a soldier." (*Percy Anecdotes*, vol. 2, p. 161)

I want, oh, you know what I mean the stuff of life.

BAYARD TAYLOR (1825-78)— Last words.

I want to go away.

ALICE CARY (1820-71)—Last words.

I were miserable, if I might not die.

DR. JOHN DONNE (1573-1631)— Last words. Other versions: " Thy will be done"; and "I repent of my life except that part of it which I spent in communion with God, and in doing good."

I will be your captain. Come with me into the fields and you shall have all you ask.

RICHARD II (1367-1400)—to the rebels who were about to avenge Wat Tyler's death, 1381. (*Dict. Nat. Biog.*, vol. xlviii, p. 147)

I will die in the last ditch.

WILLIAM III (1650-1702)—to the Duke of Buckingham: There is one certain means by which I can be sure never to see my country's ruin: I will die in the last ditch." (Hume, *Hist of Engl.* ch. 65)

I will govern according to the common weal, but not according to the common will.

JAMES I (1566-1625)—Reply to a demand of the House of Commons in 1621.

I will lie down on the couch; I can sleep, and after that I shall be entirely recovered.

ELIZABETH CHUDLEIGH Duchess of Kingston (1720-88)—Last words.

I will lose all, or win all.

JAMES II (1633-1701)—to the Spanish Ambassador, who advised moderation after the trial of the Seven Bishops, June 1688.

I will maintain the liberties of England and the Protestant religion.

WILLIAM III (1650-1702)—words displayed upon his banner when landing in England, 1688.

I will not stand at the helm during the tempestuous night, if that helm is not allowed freely to traverse.

SIR ROBERT PEEL (1788-1850) —during the agitation for the repeal of the Corn Laws.

I will sit down now, but the time will come when you shall hear me.

BENJAMIN DISRAELI [Earl of Beaconsfield](1804-81)—Conclusion of his maiden speech in the House of Commons, Dec. 7, 1837. (Cf. Sir M. E. Grant Duff's *Notes from a Diary*, vol. I, p. 112.) Samuel Smiles (in *Self-help* ch. 1, p. 23) quotes the words thus: "I shall sit down now, but the time will come when you will hear me." See Give me time, and I will yet &c.

I wish I had the power of writing, for then I would describe to you how pleasant a thing it is to die.

WILLIAM CULLEN (1712-90)— Last words. See I should like to record &c.

I wish Vaughan to preach my funeral sermon, because he has known me longest.

ARTHUR PENRHYN STANLEY, Dean of Westminster (1815-81)— Last recorded words.

I wish you to understand the true principles of government; I wish them carried out. I ask nothing more.

WILLIAM HENRY HARRISON, President of the United States (1773-1841)—Last words.

I would have the English Republic as much respected as ever the Roman commonwealth was.

OLIVER CROMWELL (1599-1658) See By such means as these we shall make &c.

I would not give up the mists that spiritualize our mountains for all the blue skies of Italy.

WILLIAM WORDSWORTH (1770-1850).

I would rather be a poor beggar's wife and be sure of heaven than queen of all the world and stand in ˛doubt thereof by reason of my own consent.

KATHARINE OF ARAGON, wife of Henry VIII (1486-1536).

I would rather be the author of that poem [i.e. Gray's *Elegy*] than take Quebec.

GENERAL JAMES WOLFE (1726-59)—beforeQuebec, Sep. 12, 1759, the day before the battle in which he was killed. See Je donnerais une de mes pièces pour les avoir faits ; and Je donnerais pour l'avoir fait &c.

I would rather eat a dry crust at a king's table than feast on luxuries at that of an elector.

ELIZABETH OF BOHEMIA, daughter of James I of England (1596-1662)—to her husband, the Elector Palatine Frederick V, when urging him to accept the crown of Bohemia.

James, take good care of the horse.

WINFIELD SCOTT (1786-1866)—Last words ; to his servant. (Appleton's *Cyclo. of Amer. Biog.*)

Jesus! precious Saviour!

BISHOP GEORGE DAVID CUMMINGS (1822-76)—Last words.

Joy.

HANNAH MORE (1744-1833)—Last word.

Just two years younger than your majesty's happy reign.

FRANCIS BACON (1561-1626)—to Queen Elizabeth, in 1572, on her asking his age. He was then eleven.

Kings govern by means of popular assemblies only

when they cannot do without them.

CHARLES JAMES FOX (1749-1806)—in the House of Commons, Oct. 31, 1776.

Knowledge is wooed for her dowry, not for her diviner charms.

LORD CHARLES BOWEN (1835-94)—in a lecture on Education. Preceded by : " The system of competitive examinations is a sad necessity." (*Law Times*, Aug. 16, 1902)

Language is the picture and counterpart of thought.

MARK HOPKINS, D.D., (b. 1802) —in an address delivered at the dedication of Williston Seminary, Dec. 1, 1841. See La parole a été donnée à l'homme &c.

Lay me quietly in the earth and put a sun-dial over my grave, and let me be forgotten.

JOHN HOWARD (1726-90)—Last words. Preceded by : " Suffer no pomp at my funeral, nor monumental inscription where I am laid."

Learned men are the cisterns of knowledge, not the fountainheads.

JAMES NORTHCOTE, R.A. (1746-1831).

Let him be hanged by the neck.

Formula written in the margin of the calendar against the name of a person condemned to be executed ; formerly *sus. per coll.*, an abbreviation of *suspendatur per collum* This, with the signature of the judge, is the sheriff's authority. Wharton, (*Law Lexicon*, 1883, p. 804) says that, in the case of a capital felony, it is written opposite to the prisoner's name, ' Hanged by the neck.' *Sus. per coll.* is quoted by Sir W. Scott in *The Antiquary*, ch. 8.

Let no guilty man escape.

PRESIDENT GRANT (1822-85)—
Words endorsed on a letter of July
29, 1875, relating to the prosecution
of those violating the laws with regard to the tax on distilled spirits.
" Let no guilty man escape, if it
can be avoided. No personal
consideration should stand in the
way of performing a public duty."

**Let our object be : our country,
our whole country, and
nothing but our country.**

DANIEL WEBSTER (1782-1852)—
in a speech at the laying of the
corner-stone of the Bunker Hill
Monument, June 17, 1825.

Let posterity cheer for us.

GEORGE WASHINGTON (1732-
99)—attributed to him when some
of the American troops cheered as
Cornwallis's sword was given to
him by General O'Hara at York-
town, Oct. 19, 1781. Its authenticity is denied.

**Let the child win his spurs, and
let the day be his.**

EDWARD III (1312-77)—at the
Battle of Crecy, Aug. 26, 1346,
referring to his son Edward, the
Black Prince, and refusing to send
him help, although he was then hard
pressed by the French. The prince
had been knighted only a month
before. The king, on returning to
the camp, exclaimed, " My brave
son ! persevere in your honourable
course ; you are my son ; for
valiantly have you acquitted yourself to-day, and worthy are you of
a crown." (Hume, *Hist. of Engl.*)

**Let there be no fuss about me ;
let me be buried with the
men.**

SIR HENRY LAWRENCE (1806-
57)— Last words.

Let us go over the river, and sit

under the refreshing shadow
of the trees.

THOMAS JONATHAN [" STONE-
WALL "] JACKSON (1824-63)—Last
words, spoken in delirium.

Let us have peace !

ULYSSES S. GRANT (1822-85)—
concluding phrase of a letter accepting his nomination to the Presidency
of the United States, dated May
29, 1868.

**Liberalism is trust of the people,
tempered by prudence ; Con-
servatism, distrust of the
people, tempered by fear.**

RT. HON. W. E. GLADSTONE,
1809-98). See Le gouvernement de
France est une monarchie absolue
&c.

**Liberty *and* Union, one and in-
separable, now and for
ever !**

DANIEL WEBSTER (1782-1852)—
conclusion of a speech in the
United States Senate, Jan. 26,
1830. Otherwise given " Liberty
and Union, now and for ever, one
and inseparable."

**Liberty exists in proportion to
wholsome restraint.**

DANIEL WEBSTER (1782-1852)—
in a speech delivered May 10,
1847.

**Liberty is no negation. It is a
substantive, tangible reality.**

PRESIDENT J. A. GARFIELD
(1831-81)—in the House of Representatives, Jan. 13, 1865.

**Liberty must be limited in order
to be enjoyed.**

EDMUND BURKE (1729-97).

**Life would be tolerable were it
not for its amusements.**

SIR GEORGE CORNEWALL LEWIS
(1806-63)—attributed to him by

Mrs. C. M. Simpson, who writes: "It was to Mrs. Austin that I heard Sir George [Cornewall] Lewis one day in our house make his celebrated speech that ' Life would be very tolerable if it were not for its amusements.' (*Many Memories of Many People*, p. 118). Cf. " O what pleasure is it to lacke pleasures, and how honorable is it to fli from honors throws " (in a letter of Sir John Cheke included in Sir Henry Ellis's *Letters of Eminent Literary Men*, Camden Society, 1843, vol. xxiii, p. 8)

Like the measles, love is most dangerous when it comes late in life.

LORD BYRON (1788-1824).

Literature is a very good walking-stick, but very bad crutches.

GEORGE COLMAN, the younger (1762-1836)—alluding to the uncertain rewards of the profession of literature. Also attributed to Sir Walter Scott, but *his* saying was: "I determined that literature should be my staff, not my crutch, and that the profits of my literary labour, however convenient otherwise, should not, if I could help it, become necessary to my ordinary expenses," alluding to the principle of action that he laid down for himself, that he must earn his living by business, and not by literature.

Lord, forgive my sins ; especially my sins of omission.

JAMES USSHER (Usher) (1580-1656)—Last words. Another version is : " God be merciful to me a sinner."

Lord, help my soul !

EDGAR ALLAN POE (1811-49)—Last words.

Lord into thy (thine) hands I commend my spirit.

LADY JANE GREY (1537-54). Last words. See Lord, take my spirit.

Lord, Jesus, receive my soul.

JONATHAN WILD, the thief-taker (1682-1725)—Last words ; but authenticity very doubtful.

Lord John is a host in himself,

DUKE OF WELLINGTON (1769-1852)—attributed to him by Samuel Rogers, as said in allusion to Lord John Russell in 1838 or 1839. Cf. Pope's *Iliad*, bk. iii, l. 293 ; "the great, himself a host " (alluding to Ajax).

Lord, Lord, Lord, receive my spirit.

WILLIAM HUNTER (1536-55)—Last words. He was burned at the stake. (Foxe, *Book of Martyrs*) See Lord, take my spirit.

Lord, now let thy servant depart in peace.

DAVID BRAINERD (1718-47). Last words.

Lord, open the eyes of the King of England.

WILLIAM TYNDALE (c. 1477 or 1484—1536)—Last words. He was strangled and his body afterwards burned. Alternatively : " Lord, open the King of England's eyes."

Lord, receive my soul.

WILLIAM LAUD, Archbishop of Canterbury, (1573-1645) — Last words ; to the headsman as a signal to strike. See Lord, take my spirit Another version is : " Thou hast broken the jaws of death." See also No one can be more willing &c.

Lord, receive my spirit.

JOHN ROGERS, Canon of St.

Paul's (1509-55)—Last words. He was burned at the stake. Also attributed to REV. DR. ROWLAND TAYLOR, burned at the stake in 1555.

Lord, take my spirit.

EDWARD VI. (1537-53)—Last words. See Lord, receive my soul; Lord, into thy hands &c; Lord, Lord, receive my spirit.

Madam, I have but ninepence in ready money, but I can draw for a thousand pounds.

JOSEPH ADDISON (1672-1719)—to a lady who remarked upon his taking so small a part in conversation. (Boswell's *Life of Johnson*.)

Madam, I have heard men say that those who would make fools of princes are the fools themselves.

SIR WILLIAM CECIL, LORD BURLEIGH (1520-98)—to Queen Elizabeth.

Manners makyth man.

WILLIAM OF WYKEHAM, Bishop of Winchester and Lord High Chancellor of England (1324-1404) —motto inscribed on buildings founded by him at Oxford and Winchester.

. . measurable distance.

RT. HON. W. E. GLADSTONE (1809-98)—attributed to. Cf "..he's as far from jealousy as I am from giving him cause; and that, I hope, is an immeasurable distance." (Shakspere, *Merry Wives of Winsor*, act 2, sc. 1, l. 107-9—*Mrs. Page*)

Meddle and muddle.

LORD DERBY (1799-1869)—in a speech in the House of Lords, Feb. 1864, referring to the policy of Lord Russell, Minister for Foreign Affairs, as a policy of meddle and muddle. Disraeli, in a letter to Lord Grey de Wilton in 1865,

brought an accusation against Mr. Gladstone's government of "blundering and plundering"— perhaps an adaptation of Lord Derby's phrase.

Millions for defence, not a cent for tribute!

C. C. PINCKNEY (1746-1825)— Reply, in 1796, to the hint that money paid the United States might have a favourable effect : in allusion to the treaty made by John Jay with England and the refusal of the Directory to receive the American minister. Another version is : " Millions for defence, but not one cent for tribute." See He smote the rock of the national resources &c.

Mind is the great lever of all things.

DANIEL WEBSTER (1782-1852)— in an address at the laying of the corner-stone of the Bunker Hill Monument, June 17, 1825. Followed by "human thought is the process by which human ends are alternately answered." Cf. " Thought is the measure of life." (C. G. Leland, *The return of the Gods*.)

Ministers are the trustees of the nation and not the dispensers of its alms.

LORD SALISBURY (b. 1830). See Public office is a public trust.

Molly, I shall die.

THOMAS GRAY (1716-71)—Last words.

Monks! Monks! Monks!

HENRY VIII (1491-1547)—Last words ; probably referring to his suppression of the monasteries.

Most good lawyers live well, work hard, and die poor.

DANIEL WEBSTER (1782-1852). See There is always room at the top.

Mr. Speaker, I smell a rat; I see him floating in the air; but mark me, sir, I will nip him in the bud.

SIR BOYLE ROCHE (1743-1807) —a famous example of mixed metaphor.

Muscular Christianity.

CHARLES KINGSLEY (1819-75)— attributed erroneously to him (Cf. his *Life*, vol. ii, pp. 74-5) Lord Lytton uses the phrase : " The Rev. John Stalworth Chillingly was a decided adherent to the creed of what is called ' Muscular Christianity,' and a very fine specimen of it too." (*Kenelm Chillingly*, ch. 2.)

My anchor is well cast, and my ship, though weatherbeaten, will outride the storm.

REV. SAMUEL HOPKINS (1721-1803)—Last words.

My Christ.

JOHN BROWN (1720-87)—Last words.

My desire is to make what haste I may to be gone.

OLIVER CROMWELL (1599-1658) —Last words. Another version has it that his last words were " Then I am safe," on being assured by his chaplain that " once in grace is always in grace."

My God !

DR. EDWARD BOUVERIE PUSEY (1800-82)—Last words.

**" My God, my Father, and my Friend,
Do not forsake me at my end."**

WENTWORTH DILLON, Earl of Roscommon (1633-84)—Last words ; quoted from his own translation of the *Dies Irae*. (*Dict. Nat. Biog.*, vol. xv, p. 88)

My heart is fixed, O God ! my heart is fixed where true joy is to be found.

ROBERT SANDERSON, chaplain to Charles I (1587-1663)—Last words.

My heart is resting sweetly with Jesus, and my hand is in His.

HOWARD CROSBY (1826-91)— Last words.

My hope is in the mercy of God.

FISHER AMES (1758-1808)— Last words. Preceded by " I have peace of mind. It may arise from stupidity, but I think it is founded on a belief of the Gospel."

My Lord, why do you not go on ? I am not afraid to die.

MARY II, wife of William III, (1662-94)—Last words ; to Archbishop Tillotson, who, overcome with grief, paused in reading a prayer. See I do not fear death ; I am not in the least afraid to die.

My rigour relents. I pardon something to the spirit of liberty.

EDMUND BURKE (1729-97)—in a speech on Conciliation with America Mar. 22, 1775. (*Works*, 1897, vol I, p. 462)

My sayings are my own, my actions are my ministers.

CHARLES II (1630-85)—Reply to the following lines written by the Earl of Rochester and fastened to the king's bed-chamber door :
" Here lies our Sovereign Lord the king,
Whose word no man rely'd [relies] on,
Who never said a foolish thing,
Nor ever did a wise one."

My servant will give you more gold if you do your work well.

JAMES SCOTT, DUKE OF MONMOUTH (1649-85)—Last words. Preceded by : " There are six guineas for you, and do not hack me as you did my Lord Russell. I have heard that you struck him three or four times."

My trust is in God.

JEREMY TAYLOR (1613-67)—Last words.

My ways are as broad as the king's high-road, and my means lie in an inkstand.

ROBERT SOUTHEY (1774-1843).

My work is done; I have nothing to do but to go to my Father.

SELINA, COUNTESS OF HUNTINGDON (1707-91)—Last words.

Nationality is the miracle of political independence. Race is the principle of physical analogy.

BENJAMIN DISRAELI [Earl of Beaconsfield] (1804-81)—in a speech in the House of Commons, Aug. 9, 1848. Preceded by: "There is a great difference between nationality and race." Cf. "The difference of race is unfortunately one of the reasons why I fear war may always exist ; because race implies difference, difference implies superiority, and superiority leads to predominance"—in his speech in the House of Commons, Feb. 1, 1849.

Nature can do more than physicians.

OLIVER CROMWELL (1599-1658) —said during his last illness.

Nature is religious only as it manifests God.

MARK HOPKINS, D.D. (b. 1802) —in a sermon before the Pastoral Association of Massachusetts, May 30, 1843.

Never forget what a man says to you when he is angry.

HENRY WARD BEECHER (1813-87).

Necessity is the argument of tyrants ; it is the creed of slaves.

WILLIAM PITT (1759-1806)—In a speech on the Indian Bill, Nov. 18, 1783, in the House of Commons. "It was true, the bill was said to be founded on necessity ; but what was this ? Was it not necessity, which had always been the plea of every illegal exertion of power, or exercise of oppression ? Was not necessity the pretence of every usurpation ? Necessity was the plea for every infringement of human freedom. It was the argument of tyrants : it was the creed of slaves." (*Speeches of the Rt. Hon. Wm. Pitt in the House of Commons (1806), vol. i, pp. 90-1*) Cf. also *Parly. Register, vol. xii, p. 51*.
Cf. "So spake the Fiend, and with necessity,
The tyrant's plea, excused his devilish deeds."—Milton, *Paradise Lost*, bk. IV., ll. 393-4.

Never has my mind wandered from Him.

(Hume, *Hist. of Engl., ch. 44.*)
QUEEN ELIZABETH (1533-1603) —Reply, on her death-bed, to the Archbishop of Canterbury's exhortation to turn her thoughts to God.

Never heed ! the Lord's power is over all weakness and death.

GEORGE FOX (1624-90) founder of the Society of Friends—Last words.

Never mind ! I shall soon drink of the river of Eternal Life.

HENRY TIMROD (1829-67)—Last words, on not being able to swallow some water.

Never mind ! let them fire away ; the battle's won, and my life is of no consequence now.

DUKE OF WELLINGTON (1769-1852)—when remonstrated with by

one of his staff for exposing his life at Waterloo (June 18, 1815).

Never mind! we'll win this battle yet.

DUKE OF WELLINGTON (1769-1852)—during the Battle of Waterloo (June 18, 1815), when the issue seemed doubtful.

No!

EUGENE ARAM (1704-59)—Last word, when asked if he had anything to say on the scaffold.

Nobody, nobody but Jesus Christ ; Christ crucified is the stay of my poor soul.

ANDREW BURN (1742-1814), Major General in the Royal Marines —Last words, when asked if he wished to see anyone.

No furniture so charming as books, even if you never open them, or read a single word.

REV. SYDNEY SMITH (1771-1845).

No ; it is not !

OLIVER GOLDSMITH (1728-74)—Last words, to the physician who asked whether his mind was at ease.

No ! it was one Tom Campbell.

THOMAS CAMPBELL (1777-1844) —Last words, to his friends, who, in order to ascertain whether he was conscious or not, spoke of the poem *Hohenlinden* as being by someone else.

No man can be a good critic who is not well-versed in human nature.

DR. PARR (1747-1825).

No man can write my epitaph.

ROBERT EMMET (1780-1803)—in his speech on his trial and conviction for high treason, Sept., 1803. " Let there be no inscription upon my tomb ; let no man write my epitaph: no man can write my epitaph."

No man, I fear, can effect great benefits for his country without some sacrifice of the minor virtues.

REV. SYDNEY SMITH (1771-1845) Cf. " Le bien public requiert qu'on trahisse, et qu'on mente, et qu'on massacre." — Montaigne, *Essais*, bk. 3, ch. 1. (The public weal requires that a man should betray, and lie, and massacre.)

No man who ever held the office of President would congratulate a friend on obtaining it. He will make one man ungrateful, and a hundred men his enemies, for every office he can bestow.

JOHN ADAMS (1735-1826)—alluding to the election of his son as President of the U. S. (Quincy, *Figures of the Past*, 74.) See J'ai fait dix mécontents et un ingrat.

No mortal man can live after the glories which God has manifested to my soul.

REV. AUGUSTUS MONTAGUE TOPLADY (1740-78) author of the hymn *Rock of Ages*—Last words.

None but Christ ! none but Christ !

JOHN LAMBERT (d. 1538), burnt at the stake—Last words. His real name was Nicholson.

No, no !

EMILY BRONTË (1818-48) —Last words, to her sister, who entreated her to let them put her to bed. She died sitting upon the sofa.

No one can be more willing to send me out of life than I am desirous to go.

WILLIAM LAUD (1573-1645), Archbishop of Canterbury—Last words. Executed Jan. 10, 1645.

(Hume, *Hist. of Engl.*)   But see Lord receive my soul.

No one ever laid down the book of Robinson Crusoe without wishing it longer.

DR. SAMUEL JOHNSON (1709-84).

No popery!

Popular Cry, on the occasion of the Gordon Riots, Lord George Gordon (1750-93) having on 2nd June, 1780, assembled a vast mob, which broke into the lobby of the House of Commons. (Hume, *Hist. of Engl.*)   The cry was again raised in 1807, when a bill was brought forward to enable Roman Catholics to serve in the army and navy in England as well as in Ireland.

No popery!   No slavery!

Party Cry, on the occasion of the election of a new parliament which met at Oxford, 21st March, 1681. (Hume, *Hist. of Engl.*)

Nothing except a battle lost can be half so melancholy as a battle won.

DUKE OF WELLINGTON (1769-1852)—in a despatch of 1815. Emerson, in his essay on *Quotation and Originality*, quotes (on the authority of Samuel Rogers) the following reply by Wellington to a lady who " expressed in his presence a passionate wish to witness a great victory." " ' Madam, there is nothing so dreadful as a great victory—excepting a great defeat.' " Emerson continues ; " But this speech is also D'Argenson's, and is reported by Grimm."

Nothing has a better effect upon children than praise.

RICHARD BRINSLEY SHERIDAN (1751-1816).   See Praise is the best diet for us after all.

Nothing is denied to well-directed

labour ; nothing is to be obtained without it.

SIR JOSHUA REYNOLDS (1723-92).   See Excellence is never granted, &c.

Nothing is so contemptible as a despised prince.

CHARLES I (1600-49)—just before his execution.

Not till the general resurrection : strike on !

ALGERNON SYDNEY (1622-83)— Last words, when asked by the executioner if he would like to. rise again, after laying his head on the block (7th Dec., 1683).

Now am I about to take my last voyage—a great leap in the dark.

THOMAS HOBBES (1588-1679)— Last words.   Another version is : " I am going to take a great leap into obscurity."   " He was very much afraid of death, which he called ' taking a leap in the dark.' " (Watkins, *Anecdotes of Men of Learning and Genius*, 1808, p. 276.) Cf. Sir John Vanbrugh, *The Provoked Wife*, act 5, sc. vi, produced 1697.   " ' Tis enough ; I'll not fail. (Aside.) Só, now, I am in for Hobbes' Voyage ; a great leap in the dark. " (*Heartfree*). (The Mermaid Series, 1896, pp. 306-7).   [A note refers to the Voyage of Ulysses (Hobbes' translation), but it appears to be rather an allusion to his last words] See Je vais quérir &c.

Now comes the mystery.

HENRY WARD BEECHER (1813-87)—Last words.   See I shall soon know the grand secret.

Now God be praised !   I die happy.

GENERAL JAMES WOLFE (1726-59), killed in the battle of Quebec— Last words, on hearing the cry

" They run !" and being told that it was the enemy. Another version is : "Then God be praised ! I shall die happy." See I die happy. There is still another version : "Support me, let not my brave soldiers see me drop. The day is ours! Oh, keep it !"—uttered to those who were near him when he was wounded.

Now God be with you, my dear children ; I have breakfasted with you, and shall sup with my Lord Jesus Christ.

ROBERT BRUCE (c. 1554-1631)— Last words.

Now I die.

JOSEPH BLANCO WHITE (1775-1841), author of the sonnet *On Night*—Last words (Thom's *Life of White*).

Now I know that I must be very ill, since you have been sent for.

HENRY WADSWORTH LONG-FELLOW (1807-82)—Last words, to his sister, who had journeyed from Portland (Maine).

Now I shall go to sleep.

LORD BYRON (1788-1824)—Last words (Moore's *Life of Byron*, ch. lvi. Other versions are : "I must sleep now" ; and "I wish it to be known that my last thoughts were given to my wife, my child, and my sister."

Now it is come.

JOHN KNOX (1505-72) — Last words. Another version is : "Live in Christ, live in Christ ; and the flesh need not fear death."

Now or never.

DUKE OF WELLINGTON (1769-1852)—to General Alava at the battle of Waterloo (18th June, 1815), after the signal for the advance had

been given (*Notes and Queries*, 9th ser., vol. xxxii).

Now pass thee onward as thou wast wont, and Douglas will follow thee or die.

SIR JAMES DOUGLAS (c. 1286-1330)—referring to the heart of Robert Bruce in a casket, which he threw before him in a battle on the plains of Andalusia in Spain. Other versions are : "Onward as thou wert wont, Douglas will follow thee." (*Dict of Nat. Biog.*, vol. xv., p. 304.) "Pass first in fight, as thou wert wont to do, and Douglas will follow thee or die." Cf.

Heart ! that didst press forward still.
(Mrs. Hemans, *Heart of Bruce in Melrose Abbey*, l. 1)
and
Pass on, brave heart, as thou wert wont
    The embattled hosts before :
Douglas will die or follow thee
    To conquest as of yore.
(Lady Flora Hastings, *Legend of the Heart of Bruce*.)

O Diamond, Diamond ! little do you know the mischief you have done me !

SIR ISAAC NEWTON (1642-1727) —addressed to his little dog, Diamond. The animal is said to have overturned a lighted taper upon some valuable MS. Another version is : "Oh, Diamond, Diamond ! thou little knowest what mischief thou hast done." Sir David Brewster, however, denies the authenticity of the story. Dr Thomas Cooper (c. 1517-94) is said to have remarked to his wife, she having destroyed the materials for his edition of the *Bibliotheca Elyota*, "Dinah, thou hast given me a world of trouble," and sat down to another eight years' labour to replace the notes thus lost. Another account says that the work destroyed was his *Thesaurus*. "He patiently set to work and re-wrote it." (*Dict. of Nat. Biog.*, vol. xii. p. 149.)

O God—if there be a God—I desire Thee to have mercy on me.

MATTHEW TINDAL (1657-1733) —Last words.

Oh, better !

ROBERT GREEN INGERSOLL (1833-99)—Last words, in reply to his wife's inquiry as to how he felt.

Oh, don't let the awkward squad fire over me !

ROBERT BURNS (1759-96)— Last words, alluding to the Dumfries militia, to which he belonged.

Oh, for an hour of Dundee.

By ALEXANDER GORDON OF GLENBUCKET (? 1678-1728)—at the battle of Sheriffmuir (1715), when the Jacobites were hard pressed by the Royalists : referring to John Graham of Claverhouse, Viscount Dundee.
Oh, for a single hour of that Dundee,
Who on that day the word of onset gave.
(Wordsworth, *In the Pass of Killiecrankie.*—Sonnet, ll. 11-12).

Oh, he's a dear good fellow.

WALT WHITMAN (1819-92) : Last words, referring to his friend (and biographer) Thomas Donaldson.

Oh, my country ! how I love my country !

WILLIAM PITT (1759-1806)— Last words. The word "love" was afterwards stated by Stanhope to have been "leave" (Stanhope, *Life of Pitt*, ch. 43) Cf. Timbs' *Historic Ninepins*, p. 205, and Stanhope, vol. iv., app. p. 31 and *Dict. of Nat. Biog.* vol. xlv, p. 383.

O Hobbema, Hobbema, how I do love thee !

JOHN CROME (1766-1821)—Last words, alluding to the Dutch landsscape painter Meindert Hobbema (c. 1638-63).

Oh, Pitt never was a boy.

WILLIAM WINDHAM (1750-1810)—in a conversation on the bad policy of suppressing innocent amusements of the common people, Pitt's name being mentioned among those whose opinion might be valuable. See This is a man !

Oh Puss, chloroform—ether —or I am a dead man.

SIR RICHARD F. BURTON (1821-90)—Dying words, to his wife. He repeated the words, "I am a dead man,"—and expired.

Oh, that peace may come.

QUEEN VICTORIA (1819-1901)— Last words attributed to her, referring to the war in South Africa.

Oh, the depth of the riches of the goodness and knowledge of God !

JOHN LOCKE (1632-1704)— author of *Essay concerning Human Understanding*—Last words. Another version is : "Cease now," said to Lady Masham, who was reading a Psalm of David to him.

O Lord Almighty, as thou wilt.

JAMES BUCHANAN (1791-1868) —Last words.

O Lord, forgive the errata !

ANDREW BRADFORD (1686-1742) —Last words.

O Lord, save my country! O Lord, be merciful to . . .

JOHN HAMPDEN (1594-1643)— Last words.

One country, one constitution, one destiny.

DANIEL WEBSTER (1782-1852) —Toast given at a banquet in New York in 1837. See Une seule loi, etc.

One, on God's side, is a majority.

WENDELL PHILLIPS (1811-84)—

in a speech at Brooklyn, on John Brown, 1st Nov. 1859. See Dieu est toujours pour les gros bataillons.

One tongue is sufficient for a woman.

JOHN MILTON (1608-74)—when asked whether he would instruct his daughters in foreign languages.

Only three Crowns.

SIR ROBERT WALPOLE (1676-1745)— to Queen Caroline, who had asked what would be the cost of inclosing St. James's Park, and making of it a private garden to the Palace. Leslie Stephen (*Life of Henry Fawcett*, 2nd edit., p. 311) refers to the phrase as mythical. Horace Walpole (*Memoirs of George II*, vol. ii, p. 62) states that Sir Robert Walpole's reply to Queen Caroline was: "Only a crown madam." In the *Gentleman's Magazine*, Feb. 1781 (vol. li, p. 75) Sir Robert is said to have replied: "O, a trifle, madam," and, when asked to be more definite, added: "Why, madam, I believe the whole will cost you but three crowns."

On the first year of freedom, by God's blessing, restored, 1648.

Legend engraved on the new great Seal; on which the House of Commons was represented, ordered to be made by the Commons, after having voted the abolition of the House of Peers and the Monarchy. (HUME, *Hist. of Engl.*)

On the ground.

CHARLES DICKENS (1812-70)—Last words, fearing he would fall to the floor.

Open the gates! Open the gates!

SARAH WESLEY (1726-1822) wife of Charles Wesley—Last words.

Oppression is but another name for irresponsible power, if history is to be trusted.

WILLIAM PINKNEY (1764-1822) —in a speech on the Missouri Question Feb. 15, 1820.

Orthodoxy is my doxy, heterodoxy is another man's doxy.

BISHOP WARBURTON (1698-1779 —to Lord Sandwich, in a debate in the House of Lords on the Test laws, the latter saying that he did not know precisely what "orthodoxy" and "heterodoxy" meant. (Priestley, *Memoirs*, vol. i, p. 372).

O, that beautiful boy!

RALPH WALDO EMERSON (1803-82)—Last words.

Our country, right or wrong.

STEPHEN DECATUR (1779-1820), American naval officer—in a toast proposed by him at a dinner at Norfolk, Va., in April 1816 "Our country! In her intercourse with foreign nations may she always be in the right; but our country right or wrong." (Mackenzie *Life.*) Cf. the remark of J. J. Crittenden, of Kentucky, "I hope to find my country in the right: however, I will stand by her, right or wrong."

Our differences are policies, our agreements principles.

PRESIDENT WILLIAM MCKINLEY (1843-1901)—in a speech at Des Moines in 1901.

Our domestic affections are the most salutary basis of all good government.

BENJAMIN DISRAELI [Earl of Beaconsfield] (1804-81)—in a speech at Salthill, Oct. 5, 1864.

Our Federal Union: it must be preserved.

PRESIDENT ANDREW JACKSON (1767-1845)—Toast at a banquet at Washington, April 30, 1830, the Jefferson Birthday Celebration. (Benton's *Thirty Years' View*, vol i, p.148.)

Our past has gone into history.

PRESIDENT WILLIAM McKIN-
LEY, (1843-1901)—in a speech at
Memphis, Apr. 30, 1901. See The
past, at least, is secure.

**Our self-made men are the glory
of our institutions.**

WENDELL PHILLIPS (1811-84)—
in a speech at Boston (Mass.), Dec.
21, 1860.

O, what triumphant truth !

TIMOTHY DWIGHT (1752-1817)
—Last words.

O yes ! O yes ! O yes !

Words used by town-criers, even
at the present day, before making
their proclamations. A corruption
of the old Norman-French word
Oyez—Hear !, or listen !

**Parliamentary speaking, like
playing on the fiddle, requires
practice.**

BENJAMINE DISRAELI [Earl of
Beaconsfield](1804-81)—in a speech
in the House of Commons, July 13,
1871. Cf. "Speaking truth is like
writing fair, and comes only by
practice." (Ruskin, *Seven Lamps
of Architecture*: *Lamp of Truth*, I)

Party is organised opinion.

BENJAMIN DISRAELI [Earl of
Beaconsfield] (1804-81)—in a speech
at Oxford, 25th Nov. 1268.

Peace !

ALDEN BRADFORD (1765-1843)
Last words.

Peace, retrenchment and reform,

Watchword of the Liberal party.
According to Sir Charles Dilke
(*Morning Herald*, 2nd Aug. 1899) the
the above is an emendation, brought
about by Joseph Hume, of the old
Whig watchword of 'Peace and
Reform.' (*Dict. Nat. Biog.*, vol.
xxviii, p. 231). A variant : "Re-
orm, retrenchment, peace " was

used to refer to Earl Grey's ministry
on coming into office in 1830.

Peace with honour.

BENJAMIN DISRAELI [Lord
Beaconsfield] (1804-81)—on his
return from the Berlin Congress,
July 16, 1878, said : "Lord Salisbury and myself have brought you
back peace—but a peace, I hope,
with honour, which may satisfy our
Sovereign, and tend to the welfare
of the country." Cf. "The superior
power may offer peace with honour
and with safety."—*Burke's Speech
on Conciliation with America*,
March 22, 1775. (Works, vol i,
p. 455, Bohn's Libraries, ed. 1897).

The phrase is also to be found in
Sir Anthony Weldon's *Court and
Character of King James* (London,
1650, p. 185) Cf.
"That it shall hold companionship in peace
With honour, as in war, since that to both
It stands in like request?"
(Shakspere, *Coriolanus*, act iii, sc.
ii, ll. 49-51)

The words *pax cum honore* are in
a letter from Theobald, Count of
Champagne to Louis le Gros (reigned
1108-37) (Walter Mapes, *De Nugis
Curialium*, Camden Soc. edn. p.,
220.) See A safe and honourable
peace.

**Pity that should be cut, that has
not committed treason.**

SIR THOMAS MORE (1480-1535)
—Last words on the scaffold, put-
ting aside his beard. (Froude's *Hist.
of Eng.*, ch. 9). Another version is :
"For it never committed treason."
(Hume, *Hist. of Engl.*)

**Poetry is only the eloquence and
enthusiasm of religion.**

WILLIAM WORDSWORTH (1770
1850).

**Poetry should only occupy the
idle.**

LORD BYRON (1788-1824)—to

Count Gamba, father of the Countess Guiccioli.

Poets succeed better in fiction than in truth.

EDMUND WALLER (1605-87) (English poet)—Reply to Charles II, who complained that Waller's eulogy of Cromwell was better than his congratulations on the Restoration.

Politeness is benevolence in trifles

WILLIAM PITT (1708-78), first Earl of Chatham. Cf.:

"Few to good breeding make a just pretence ;
Good breeding is the blossom of good sense."

(Young, *Love of Fam* , Sat. V.)

Politeness is the art of choosing among one's real thoughts."

MME. DE STAËL—(Abel Stevens, *Life of Mme. de Staël*, ch. iv)

. . political Cave of Adullam.

JOHN BRIGHT (1811-89)—in a speech on the Reform Bill of 1866. He said that Mr. Horsman had "retired into what may be called his political Cave of Adullam." (Reid, *Life of W. E. Gladstone*, p. 486.) An allusion to the cave Adullam. (Cf. 1 Samuel xxii, 1, 2.) Bishop Wilberforce wrote at the time about "Gladstone's new Commandment," which was "Thou shalt not commit Adullamy. (*Life of W. E. Gladstone*, p. 486, note.)

Politics is business.

LORD SALISBURY (b. 1830)

Poor little boys !

HENRY THOMAS BUCKLE (1822-62)—Last words.

Poor souls ! for a little money they would do as much against their commanders.

CHARLES I (1600-49)—after his sentence, referring to the soldiers, who, instigated by their superiors, were brought to cry aloud for justice. One soldier, who had asked a blessing on oppressed and fallen majesty, was, in the King's presence, beaten to the ground by his officer. Charles said, "The punishment, methinks, exceeds the offence." (Hume, *Hist. of Engl.*)

Possible ! is anything impossible? Read the newspapers.

DUKE OF WELLINGTON (1769-1852). (*Words of Wellington*, 1881 ed., p. 196.)

Posterity is a pack-horse, always ready to be loaded.

BENJAMIN DISRAELI [Earl of Beaconsfield](1804-81)—in a debate, 3rd June, 1862, on fortifications and works, he accused Lord Palmerston (1784-1865) of seeming to "think that posterity &c." In a speech on the Address, 22nd Jan. 1846, Disraeli, alluding to Sir Robert Peel's appeal to posterity, said (addressing the Speaker) "Sir, very few people reach posterity. Who amongst us may arrive at that destination. I presume not to vaticinate. Posterity is a most limited assembly. Those gentlemen who reach posterity are not much more numerous than the planets."

Praise is the best diet for us, after all.

REV. SYDNEY SMITH (1771-1845). See (*Wit and Wisdom of the Rev. Sydney Smith*, 1858, p. 434). See Nothing has a better effect upon children than praise.

Precious salvation !

JAMES HERVEY (1714-58)—Last words.

Presbytery is no religion for a gentleman.

CHARLES II. (1630-85)—to the Earl of Lauderdale.

Privilege of parliament ! priviledge of parliament !

Cry with which Charles I. (1600-49) was greeted in passing through the streets the day after a scene in the House of Commons on 3rd Jan., 1642. Hume, *Hist. of England.* One of the people threw into the king's coach a paper on which were written the words, " To your tents, O Israel ! " (1 Kings xiii, v. 16).

Property is not a principle, but an expedient.

BENJAMIN DISRAELI [Earl of Beaconsfield] (1804-81)—in a speech 17th March, 1845, on the subject of agricultural distress.

Promise me you will never again marry an old man.

WILLIAM WYCHERLEY (1640-1715)—Last words, to his wife.

Protection has its duties as well as its rights.

MARQUIS OF NORMANBY (1797-1863)—in a letter, written when lord lieutenant of Ireland (Earl Mulgrave). Also attributed to Chief Baron Woulfe (1787-1840), and to Thomas Drummond (1797-1840); but cf. " A landlord is not a land merchant ; he has duties to perform as well as rents to receive." (*Sketch of the state of Ireland, Past and Present*, Dublin, 1808 [by Rt. Hon. John Wilson Croker]) Cf. "Entendue de la sorte, qu'est-ce que la propriété? C'est le vol. (Viewed in this light, what is property? It is robbery.) (L. Blanc, *L'Organisation du Travail.*)

Protection and patriotism are reciprocal.

J. C. CALHOUN (1782-1850)—in a speech, 12th Dec., 1811. Followed by " This is the road that all great nations have trod."

Public office is a public trust.

PRESIDENT GROVER CLEVELAND (b. 1837)—A saying derived from him. In accepting the nomination to the mayoralty of Buffalo (New York) in 1882 he said, " When we consider that public officials are the trustees of the people, and hold their places and exercise their powers for the benefit of the people, there should be no higher inducement to a faithful and honest discharge of public duty." See Ministers are the trustees of the nation &c.

Put not your trust in princes, nor in the sons of men, for in them there is no salvation. (*Psalm* 146, v. 3.)

THOMAS WENTWORTH, EARL OF STRAFFORD (1593-1641)—on being assured that Charles I. had signed the Bill of Attainder. (Hume, *Hist. of Engl. ; Dict. of Nat. Biogr.*, vol. lx. p. 283). See Nolite confidere in principibus &c.

Put your trust in God, my boys, and keep your powder dry.

OLIVER CROMWELL (1599-1658)—advice to his troops when crossing a river. (Col. Blacker, *Oliver's advice*, 1834) Another version is : " Put your trust in God ; but mind to keep your powder dry." (Hayes's *Ballads of Ireland*, vol. i, p. 191.)

Queens of England are never drowned.

HENRIETTA MARIA (1609-69), wife of Charles I.—in a storm in the North Sea, crossing from Holland to Yorkshire, Feb., 1642. See I never heard of a king being drowned.

Rather than submit to the hard terms proposed by Pitt, I would die in the room I now stand in.

GEORGE III. (1738-1820)—to Grenville, when accepting his resignation after the obnoxious legislation against America in 1763.

Reaction is the law of life ; and it is the characteristic of the House of Commons.

BENJAMIN DISRAELI [Earl of Beaconsfield] (1804-81) — in the debate on the Address in reply to the Queen's Speech, 6th Feb., 1867.

"... Reason thus with life, If I do lose thee I do lose a thing That none but fools would keep : a breath thou art." (Shakspere, *Measure for Measure*, act iii, sc. i, ll. 6-8).

PATERSON (d. 1758)—Last words. He was playing the Duke, and had no sooner uttered the above lines than he expired. They are engraved on his tomb at Bury St. Edmunds, where he was buried.

Rebellion to tyrants is obedience to God.

PRESIDENT JOHN BRADSHAW— from an inscription on the cannon near which his ashes were laid, on the top of a hill near Martha Bay in Jamaica. (Ezra Stiles, *Hist. of Three of the Judges of King Charles I*, p. 107.) "In a public print of 1775, it was said, ' " The following inscription was made out three years ago on the cannon near which the ashes of President Bradshaw were lodged, on the top of a high hill near Martha Bay in Jamaica, to avoid the rage against the regicides exhibited at the Restoration." '

[The inscription ends as follows :] " And never, never forget THAT REBELLION TO TYRANTS IS OBEDIENCE TO GOD," (*ibid.* pp. 106-7). Found among the papers of Thomas Jefferson (1743-1826) and in his handwriting. Supposed to be one of Dr. Franklin's inspirations. (Randall's *Life of Jefferson*, vol. iii, p. 585.) Cf. : Where justice reigns, 'tis freedom to obey. (J. Montgomery, *Greenland*, canto iv.), and see L'insurrection est le plus saint des devoirs.

Remember !

CHARLES I (1600-49)—Last words to Bishop Juxon (1582-1663) : said to be intended as a message to his son. Another account says that his last words were " I fear not death ; death is not terrible to me." See I am not in the least afraid to die.

Rescue and retire.

W. E. GLADSTONE (1809-98)— Phrase applied to the policy announced by him in Feb., 1885 ; to support the Khedive of Egypt in regaining his authority over the Soudan, but without a permanent English occupation of the country.

Responsible government.

Phrase first used in 1829 in a petition presented to Parliament from Upper Canada. (Cf. Egerton's *History of Colonial Policy*, p. 304.)

Revolutions are not made, they come.

WENDELL PHILLIPS (1811-84)— in a speech to the Anti-Slavery Society at Boston (Mass.), 28th Jan. 1852.

Revolutions never go backward.

WENDELL PHILLIPS (1811-84)— in a speech at Boston (Mass.), Feb. 17, 1861. See Insurrection of thought &c.

Rich beyond the dreams of avarice.

DR. SAMUEL JOHNSON (1709-84) — when asked what he thought was the value of his friend Thrale's brewery, which was being sold, replied, " We are not here to sell a parcel of boilers and vats, but the potentiality of growing rich," &c. (Boswell, *Life of Johnson*, Fitzgerald's edition, vol. ii., p. 462.)

Ridicule is the best test of truth.

LORD SHAFTESBURY (1671-1713). " It is commonly said, and more particularly by Lord Shaftesbury, that ridicule is the best test of truth ; for that it will not stick where it is not just. I deny it." (Lord Chesterfield's *Letters to his Son.* Feb. 6, 1752.) The following variants, however, occur in Lord Shaftesbury's *Characteristics.* "How comes it to pass, then, that we appear such cowards in reasoning, and are so afraid to stand the test of ridicule." (*Letter concerning Enthusiasm,* sec. 2). "Truth, 'tis supposed, may bear all lights ; and one of those principal lights or natural mediums by which things are to be viewed, in order to a thorough recognition, is ridicule itself." (*Sensus Communis* &c., sec. 1.)

Save me from my friends.

See Je vais combattre &c.   Cf.
But of all plagues, good Heaven, thy
        wrath can send,
Save, save, oh save me from the candid
        friend."—(Canning, *New Morality,* in
                        The Anti-Jacobin.)

. . sea of upturned faces.

DANIEL WEBSTER (1782-1852)—in a speech, 30th Sept., 1842, which is generally supposed to be the origin of the phrase, but it occurs in Sir Walter Scott's *Rob Roy* (ch. 20) : "I next strained my eyes, with equally bad success, to see if, among the sea of upturned faces which bent their eyes on the pulpit as a common centre, I could discover the sober and business-like physiognomy of Owen."

See me safe up, for my coming down I can shift for myself.

SIR THOMAS MORE (1480-1535) —to Kingston, on ascending the scaffold, July 6, 1535. (Froude, *Hist. of Engl.* ch. ix.) Hume (*Hist. of Engl.*) has : "Friend, help me up : when I come down again, I can shift for myself."

See, there is Jackson standing

like a stone wall ; rally on the Virginians.

GENERAL BERNARD E. BEE—during the battle of Bull Run near Washington (June 21, 1861). The origin of the sobriquet "Stonewall," applied to General T. Jonathan Jackson (1824-63.)

Sentiment clothes the title of Emperor with bad associations.

ROBERT LOWE (1811-92), afterwards Lord Sherbrooke : quoted by Lord Beaconsfield (1804-81) in his speech on the Royal Titles Bill. Mar. 9, 1876.

Shame, shame, on a conquered king !

HENRY II (1133-89) — Dying words.

Sir Boyle Roche's bird.

SIR BOYLE ROCHE (1743-1807) —a phrase alluding to a remark of his, when it was said that the sergeant-at-arms should have stopped someone in the rear of the House when he was trying to catch him in the front. Roche asked whether it was thought that the sergeant-at-arms could be "like a bird, in two places at once?" In a play, written at the end of the 17th century, *The Devil of a Wife,* by Jevon, occur the words :
"I cannot be in two places at once.
—Surely no—unless thou wert a bird."

Sir Earl, by God, you shall either go or hang.

EDWARD I (1239-1307) —to Humphrey de Bohun, Earl of Hereford and Constable of England (died—1298) when in a passion, the Earls of Hereford and Norfolk having refused to take command of the forces Edward proposed to send to Guienne. The Earl replied, "By God, Sir King, I will neither go nor hang." (Hume, *Hist. of*

England.) The *Dict. of Nat. Biog.*
(vol. v, p. 26) gives the words as :
" By God, earl, you shall either go
or hang, and " By God, O king, I
will neither go nor hang," and says
that the king addressed himself to
Roger Bigod, Earl of Norfolk and
marshal of England.

**Sir, I can abstain ; but I can't
be moderate.**

Dr. SAMUEL JOHNSON (1709-84)
—referring to his own habits. See
Depend upon it, of all vices &c.

**Sir, I have tasted your sherry,
and I prefer the gout.**

EARL OF DERBY (1799-1869)—
to a wine-merchant who recom-
mended his sherry as not having
gout in a hogshead of it.

**Sir, I shall be glad to have a new
sense given to me.**

DR. SAMUEL JOHNSON (1709-84)
—to Dr. Burney, who had said " I
believe, sir, we shall make a musi-
cian of you at last," observing the
Doctor listening attentively to Miss
Thrale's playing on the harpsichord.

**Sir, I would rather be right than
be president.**

HENRY CLAY (1777-1852)—to
Mr. Preston, of Kentucky, when
told that the measures which he
advocated would injure his chances
of becoming president.

**Sir Joshua is the ablest man I
know on a canvas.**

GEORGE SELWYN (1719-91)—a
silent English M.P.—when told
that Reynolds intended to stand
for Parliament.

Sister ! sister ! sister !

THOMAS DE QUINCEY (1785-
1859)—Last words.

**Six hours' sleep is enough for a
man, seven for a woman, and
eight for a fool.**

GEORGE III (1738-1820)—to a
tradesman who had twice been late
for an appointment made by the
king. The king had asked what
sleep he took, and had been told
" usually eight hours."

. . smash the Mahdi.

GENERAL GORDON (1833-85)—
26th Feb. 1884 : referring to his expedition to Khartoum, where he
was killed, 26th Jan. 1885. "You
must smash the Mahdi, or the
Mahdi will smash you."

Solier, second thought.

FISHER AMES (1758-1808)—in a
speech on Biennial Elections, Jan.
1788. " I consider biennial elections as a security that the sober,
second thought of the people shall be
law." Cf. Posteriores cogitationes,
ut aiunt, sapientiores solent esse
(Second thoughts, they say, are apt
to be the best) (Cicero, *First Phil-
ippic*).

**So, Flaxman, I am told you are
married ; if so, sir, I tell you
you are ruined for an artist.**

SIR JOSHUA REYNOLDS (1723-92)
—to John Flaxman (1755-1826),
shortly after the latter's marriage.
Sir Joshua was a bachelor. Events
falsified Sir Joshua's opinion. Cf.
" He that hath wife and children
hath given hostages to fortune ; for
they are impediments to great
enterprises either of virtue or of
mischief." (Bacon, *Essays, viii :
Of Marriage and Single Life.*)

Soldiers, fire !

SIR CHARLES LUCAS, shot August
28, 1648—Last words, to the
soldiers.

So little done, so much to do.

(*The Daily Telegraph*, March 28,
1902.)

CECIL JOHN RHODES (1853-1902)
—Dying words, to Mr. Michell.

The actual last word was "Elm-
hirst," the name of his brother
(Major Elmhirst Rhodes).   Cf.
So many worlds, so much to do,
  So little done, such things to be.
        (Tennyson, *In Memoriam*, lxxiii)

**Some men has plenty money and
no brains, and some men
has plenty brains and no
money. Surely men with
plenty money and no brains
were made for men with
plenty brains and no money.**

CLAIMANT TO THE TICHBORNE
ESTATES (d. 1898)—written in his
note-book (signed R. C. Tichborne,
Bart.) ; rendered famous during the
Tichborne case, which lasted from
June, 1871 till Feb. 28, 1874.

**Some men have only one book in
them ; others a library.**

REV. SYDNEY SMITH (1771-1845)

**Some things can be done as well
as others.**

SAMUEL PATCH (c. 1807-29) to
the Rev. Dr. Bushnell (1802-76).
The latter met Patch at Rochester
(New York) just before his fatal attempt to jump the Genesee Falls
and, asked why he wished to expose
his life, Patch replied :   "To shew
people that some things can be done
as well as others." (*Life and Letters
of Horac Bushnell*, p. 52.)

**Sooner than make our colonies
our allies, I should wish to
see them returned to their
primitive deserts.**

CHARLES TOWNSHEND (1725-
67)—in a speech in the House of
Commons, 17th Dec. 1865, in support of the Stamp Act.

**So perish all Queen Elizabeth's
enemies !**

DR. RICHARD FLETCHER, Dean
of Peterborough (d. 1596), at the
execution of Mary, Queen of Scots.
(Hume, *Hist. of Engl.*, ch. xlii)

The *Dict. of Nat. Biog.* (vol. xix, p.
318) gives the words as :   "So perish
all the queen's enemies," crediting
the Earl of Kent with them, and
Dr. Fletcher with saying "Amen" ;
whereas Hume's account is that
the Earl of Kent said "Amen."

**So the heart be right, it is no
matter which way the head
lies.**

SIR WALTER RALEIGH (1552-
1618)—at his execution, when
asked on which side he preferred
to lay his head on the block.

Speak, good mouth !

QUEEN ELIZABETH (1533-1603)
—to the Mayor of Bristol, who, on
welcoming her, stopped short after
saying, "I am the mouth of the
town."—"Speak, good mouth !"

. . stagger humanity.

PRESIDENT KRUGER (born c.
1825)—referring to the war in
South Africa.

**Stop, and you shall have some-
thing more to take down !**

LORD PLUNKET (1764-1854)—
in the Irish House of Commons,
when someone called out that his
words should be taken down.

Stopped !

JOSEPH HENRY GREEN (1791-
1863)—Last words, referring to his
pulse.   See The artery ceases to
beat.

Struck with sterility.

LORD JUSTICE BOWEN (1835-
94)—in reference to certain premises
which he held to be not rateable
owing to their unproductiveness.

**Take care of the pence, and the
pounds will take care of
themselves.**

LORD CHESTERFIELD—quoted in
Letters to his Son (Oct. 9, 1746) as

being a saying of WILLIAM LOWN-
DES (1652-1724). Chesterfield's
advice took the shape of, "I re-
commend you to take care of the
minutes, for the hours will take care
of themselves."

**Take it, thy necessity is greater
than mine.**

SIR PHILIP SYDNEY (1554-86)
—to a wounded soldier at the Battle
of Zutphen (Sept. 22, 1586) who
looked wistfully at some water
which had been obtained with
difficulty for Sir Philip, who was
himself mortally wounded. Other
versions are: "This man's necessity is still greater than mine."
(Hume, *Hist. of Engl.*) "Thy
necessity is yet greater than mine."
(*Percy Anecdotes*) Cf. *Sydney at
Zutphen*, F. T. Palgrave.

**Take notes on the spot: a note
is worth a cart-load of recollections.**

RALPH WALDO EMERSON (1803-
82).

**Take not this for a threatening,
for I scorn to threaten any
but my equals.**

CHARLES I. (1600-49)—in his first
speech to his third parliament,
having referred to using 'those
other means which God had placed
in his hands,' if the members did
not do their duty 'in contributing
to the necessities of the state.' He
added, "but as an admonition from
him who, by nature and duty, has
most care of your preservation and
prosperity." (Hume, *Hist. of Engl.*)

**Take short views, hope for the
best, and trust in God.**

REV. SYDNEY SMITH (1771-1845)
—Favourite maxim.

Tell Hill he must come up.

ROBERT EDMUND LEE (1806-70)
—Last words (his mind wandering).

Texas! Texas! (followed, after a
pause, by his wife's name)
Margaret!

SAMUEL HOUSTON (1793-1862),
President of Texas and afterwards
United States Senator—Last words.

**Thank God, I have done my
duty!**

LORD NELSON (1758-1805)—Last
words. (Southey, *Life*, 1888, p.
377) (*Dict. Nat. Biog.*, vol. xl., p.
206) See also They've done for
me at last, Hardy.

**Thank God, I—I also—am an
American!**

DANIEL WEBSTER (1782-1852)
—in a speech at the completion of
the Bunker Hill Monument, June
17, 1843. In a speech at the
laying of the corner-stone, June
17, 1825, he said, "I was born
an American; I live an American;
I shall die an American!" See Born
and educated in this country &c.

Thank God! Thank Heaven!

SIR MOSES MONTEFIORE (1784-
1885)—Last words.

**Thank God, to-morrow I shall
join the glorious company
above.**

SAMUEL DREW (1765-1833)—
Last recorded words.

**That is enough to last till I get
to Heaven.**

WILLIAM WARHAM Archbishop
of Canterbury, (1450-1532)—Last
words, to his servant, who had informed him that he had thirty
pounds still left.

**That's a pretty sum to begin
the next world with.**

THOMAS ERSKINE (1750-1823)
—when told that one of his ac-
quaintances had died worth two
hundred thousand pounds.

That's right, Brother Taylor; parry them off as well as you can.

JOSEPH SMITH (1805-44), founder and first prophet of the Mormon Church—Last words, to John Taylor, who was endeavouring to drive back the mob.

That we shall succeed, is certain: who may live to tell the story, is a very different question.

LORD NELSON (1758-1805)—to Captain Berry before the Battle of the Nile (1 Aug., 1798). Captain Berry had said "If we succeed, what will the world say?" Nelson answered, "There is no *if* in the case; that," &c. (Southey, *Life*, ed. 1888, p. 172)

That which I said then I said, but that which I say now is true.

SIR THOMAS WYATT, the Younger (1521-54)—Last words, on the scaffold, referring to the accusation of the complicity of Princess Elizabeth and Lord Courtenay in the rebellion against Queen Mary.

That which is called firmness in a king is called obstinacy in a donkey.

THOMAS ERSKINE (1750-1823).

The accident of an accident.

LORD THURLOW (1732-1806)—in replying to the Duke of Grafton, who (during a debate on Lord Sandwich's administration of Greenwich Hospital) had reproached him his with his humble origin, expressed astonishment at his grace's speech, and said that the noble duke "could not look before him, behind him, and on either side of him without seeing some noble peer who owes his seat in this House to his successful exertions in the profession to which I belong. Does he not feel

that it is as honourable to owe it to these as to being the accident of an accident?" (Butler, *Reminiscences*, vol. i, p. 142)

The acts of to-day become the precedents of to-morrow.

LORD HERSCHELL (1837-99)—in a speech May 23, 1878. See A precedent embalms a principle; and cf. "One precedent creates another. They soon accumulate, and constitute law. What yesterday was fact, to-day is doctrine." Junius (Dedication of his *Letters to the English Nation*)

The air of England has long been too pure for a slave, and every man is free who breathes it.

LORD MANSFIELD (1704-93)—in the case of a negro slave who claimed his freedom on being brought to England. Cf.
"Slaves cannot breathe in England; if their lungs.
Receive our air, that moment they are free;
They touch our country, and their shackles fall."
         (Cowper, *The Task*, ii., 40).

The American people never ran away from a difficult question or from a well-defined duty.

PRESIDENT WILLIAM MCKINLEY (1843-1901)—in a speech at Redlands (Cal.), May 8, 1901.

The Angel of Death has been abroad throughout the land; you may almost hear the beating of his wings.

JOHN BRIGHT (1811-89)—in the House of Commons, Feb. 23, 1855, referring to the Russian War.

The atrocious crime of being a young man.

(John Almon, *Anecdotes and Speeches of the Earl of Chatham*, 1793.)
WILLIAM PITT, EARL OF CHATHAM (1708-78)—in a speech on

Mar. 10, 1740, beginning, " The atrocious crime of being a young man, which the hon. gentleman [Horace Walpole] has with such spirit and decency charged upon me, I shall neither attempt to palliate nor deny, but content myself with wishing that I may be one of those whose follies may cease with their youth, and not of that number who are ignorant in spite of experience." Brougham (*Statesmen of the Time of George III.*, vol. i., p. 19) says "many of his [Chatham's] earlier speeches as now preserved were avowedly the composition of Dr. Johnson," &c. Cf. Disraeli's allusion to Sir Robert Peel, in a speech on the Address, Jan. 22, 1846, " I want to know how it is that the right honourable gentleman, who certainly enjoys the full maturity of manhood," &c.; also, " I beseech you let his lack of years be no impediment to let him lack a reverend estimation ; for I never knew so young a body with so old a head." (Shakspere, *Merchant of Venice*, act iv., sc. 1 : Bellario's letter)

The balance of power in Europe.

BENJAMIN DISRAELI [Earl of Beaconsfield] (1804 - 81) — Phrase used in the House of Commons in a speech on the Black Sea Conference, Feb. 24, 1871. See An untoward event. "William [of Orange] now laid before Parliament his views upon the European situation, showing how the ' balance of power '— an old expression which now came into common use—had been affected by the accession of a Bourbon prince to the throne of Spain. (Wolseley, *Life of Duke of Marlborough*, 1894, vol. ii., p. 379)

The bane of England and the opprobrium of Europe.

BENJAMIN DISRAELI [Earl of Beaconsfield] (1804-81)—conclud-

ing words of a speech in the House of Commons, Aug. 9, 1843, on the Arms Bill (Ireland) referring to the then state of things in Ireland.

The battle of Waterloo was won on the playing fields of Eton.

DUKE OF WELLINGTON (1769-1852)—words attributed to him, but their authenticity denied. Another version is : " It was there that the battle of Waterloo was won." It is said that the Duke made the remark when looking at the boys engaged in their sports in the playground at Eton.

The belief in the immortality of the soul is the only true panacea for the ills of life.

LORD BYRON (1788-1824).

The best legacy I can leave my children is free speech, and the example of using it.

ALGERNON SYDNEY (1622-83).

The best of all is God is with us.

JOHN WESLEY (1703-91)—Last words.

The best of life is just tolerable : 'tis the most we can make of it.

DEAN SWIFT (1667-1745). See There is little or nothing in this life &c.

The best of prophets of the future is the past.

LORD BYRON (1788-1824).

The best part of every man's education is that which he gives to himself.

SIR WALTER SCOTT (1771-1832). Cf. " Every person has two educations, one which he receives from others, and one, more important, which he gives to himself." (Gibbon, *Decline and Fall.*)

The best physicians are Dr. Diet,

Dr. Quiet, and Dr. Merryman.

REV. SYDNEY SMITH (1771-1845.) Cf.

The best of all the pill-box crew,
  Since ever time began,
Are the doctors who have most to do
  With the health of a hearty man.
And so I count them up again
  And praise them as I can :
    There's Dr. Diet
    And Dr. Quiet
And Dr. Merryman !
(S. W. Duffield, *Praise of Good Doctors*.)
also "Si tibi deficiant medici, tibi fiant
    Haec tria ; mens læta, requies,
    moderata diæta."

The bitterness of death is now past.

LORD WILLIAM RUSSELL (1639-83)—executed for complicity in the Rye House Plot, July 21, 1683, on taking leave of his wife on the same day. (Hume, *Hist. of Engl.*)

The blue ribbon of the turf.

BENJAMIN DISRAELI, [Earl of Beaconsfield] (1804-81)—to Lord George Bentinck, referring to the Derby Race. (Disraeli, *Biog. of Lord George Bentinck*.)

The broad direct line is the best.

DUKE OF WELLINGTON (1769-1852) Preceded by : "It is difficult to say what will be successful, and what otherwise, in these governments of intrigue ; but, in my opinion, the," &c.

The Church of England hath a Popish liturgy, a Calvinistic creed, and an Arminian clergy.

WILLIAM PITT, Earl of Chatham (1708-78)—Quoted by Burke, in a speech, Mar. 2, 1790, on the Repeal of the Corporation and Test Acts, as, "We have a Calvinistic creed, a Popish liturgy, and an Arminian clergy."

The Classes and the Masses.

W. E. GLADSTONE (1809-98), but cf.
Too true it is she's bitten sadly
With this new rage for rhyming badly
Which late hath seized all ranks and classes
Down to that new estate, "the Masses."
(MOORE, *The Fudges in England*, Letter 4.)

The Continent will not suffer England to be the workshop of the world.

BENJAMIN DISRAELI [Earl of Beaconsfield] (1804-81)—in a speech in the House of Commons, March 15, 1838.

The de'il i' my saul, sirrah, an you be not quiet I'll send you to the five hundred kings in the House of Commons : they'll quickly tame ye.

JAMES I (1566-1625)—to his unruly horse.

The elegant simplicity of the three per cents.

LORD STOWELL (1745-1836) (Campbell's *Chancellors*, vol. x, ch. 212). See The sweet simplicity &c.

The English nation is never so great as in adversity.

BENJAMIN DISRAELI, [Earl of Beaconsfield] (1804-81)—in a speech in the House of Commons, Aug. 11, 1857. See I have long been of the opinion &c.

The Exe cannot be made to flow back to its source.

LORD PALMERSTON (1784-1865)—when asked whether he would be in favour of a return to Protection.

The field is won. Order the whole line to advance.

DUKE OF WELLINGTON (1769-1852)—at the battle of Waterloo, June 18, 1815. Sometimes quoted as "Let the whole line advance."

The glorious uncertainty of the law.

MR. WILBRAHAM—According to the *Gentleman's Magazine* (Aug., 1830) this phrase originated at a dinner of the judges and counsel at Serjeants' Hall not long after Wm. Murray, Earl of Mansfield's (1704-93) elevation to the Lord Chief Justiceship in 1756. A Mr. Wilbraham gave the words as a toast (alluding to Lord Mansfield's frequent reversals of former decisions) after that of "the glorious memory of King William" had been drunk.

The grand old man.

A term applied to the Rt. Hon. W. E. Gladstone (1809-98) and attributed by Sir W. V. Harcourt (in a speech at Derby, April 25, 1882) to Sir Stafford Northcote (now Lord Iddesleigh). Whoever first applied it to Mr. Gladstone did not, however, originate it. It occurs in Hook's *Lives of the Archbishops of Canterbury* (1860, vol. 1, ch. 4), applied to Theodorus, an early archbishop, a native of Tarsus in Cilicia. It is said that the vogue of the title arises from a speech by Charles Bradlaugh, M. P. (1833-91) at Northampton in which he repeatedly used it to designate Mr. Gladstone. He derived it from Henry Labouchere, M.P. The term was applied to Lord Brougham (1778-1868) in a leading article in the *Illustrated London News* (May 16, 1868) beginning "The grand old man has passed away from us." Charlotte Brontë so styled the Duke of Wellington. To Mr. Gladstone, however, belongs the distinction of the words being written and printed with capital letters. Cf.

And thus he bore without abuse
　The grand old name of gentleman,
　Defamed by every charlatan,
And soil'd with all ignoble use.
Tennyson's *In Memoriam* (1850) can.cxi.

The great business of life is, to be, to do, to do without, and to depart.

JOHN MORLEY, M. P. (b. 1838) —in an address on Aphorisms before the Edinburgh Philosoph. Institute, (Nov. 1887).

The greater the truth the greater the libel.

LORD MANSFIELD (1704-93)— circa 1789 ; also attributed to Lord Ellenborough (1750-1818). The latter is said to have used the words at a trial, adding, "If the language used was true, the person would suffer more than if it was false." Cf.

Dost not know that old Mansfield, who
　writes like the Bible,
Says the more 'tis a truth, sir, the more
　'tis a libel." (Burns.)

The greater the truth, the worse the libel, is quoted at the head, and also forms the last line of the poem *A Case of Libel*, by Thomas Moore. "For the same reason it is immaterial with respect to the offence of a libel, whether the matter of it be true or false," &c. (Blackstone's *Commentaries*, 1795,vol. iv, p. 150, note by Mr. Christian) In *State Trials* (1770) vol. xx, p. 902 it is stated that Lord Mansfield said ". . . . my brother Glynn has admitted that the truth or falsehood of a libel, whether public or private, however prosecuted, is out of the question." At this assertion of Lord Mansfield every man in court was shocked. Serjeant Glynn was astonished, and, ... asked them, 'Good God ! Did I admit anything like what Lord Mansfield says?' . . . . Lord Mansfield begged Mr. Glynn's pardon, and turned it off with great dexterity, just saying slightly, 'Oh ! I find I was mistaken ; well then, my brother Glynn is of a different opinion.'"

The greatest happiness of the greatest number.

Benjamin Disraeli [Earl of Beaconsfield] (1804-81)—concluding words of a speech on the Budget, Dec. 3, 1852. "Priestley was the first (unless it was Beccaria) who taught my lips to pronounce this sacred truth,—that the greatest happiness of the greatest number is the foundation of morals and legislation." (Jeremy Bentham's *Works*, vol. x, p. 142.) The phrase was used by Dr. Joseph Priestley (1733-1804) in his Essay on Government, published in 1768. The Marquis Beccaria's rendering (in Italian) is "La massima felicità divisa nel maggior numero." (Cesare Beccaria Bonesana, *Dei delitti e delle pene*, Monaco, 1764, p. 4) The origin of the phrase may, however, be said to be in Hutcheson's *Inquiry into the Original of our Ideas of Beauty and Virtue* (London, 1725, p. 164): "That Action is best, which accomplishes the greatest Happiness for the greatest Numbers."

The greatest history-painters have always been the ablest portrait-painters.

James Northcote (1746-1831).

The great unknown.

James Ballantyne (1772-1833) —a term applied to Sir Walter Scott (1771-1832), alluding to the extraordinary success made by *The Waverley Novels* on their first (anonymous) appearance.

The great unwashed.

Lord Brougham (1779-1868).

The Greek historians generally told nothing but truth, while the Latin historians told nothing but lies.

Charles James Fox (1749-1806).

The hero of a hundred fights.

Applied to the Duke of Wellington. (1769-1852). Cf. :
For this is England's greatest son,
He that gain'd a hundred fights,
Nor ever lost an English gun.
(Tennyson, *Ode on the Death of the Duke of Wellington*)

The history of superannuation in this country is the history of spoliation.

Benjamin Disraeli [Earl of Beaconsfield] (1804-81)—in a speech on the Civil Service Superannuation Bill, Feb. 15, 1856. Followed by :
"It is a very short history, for it may be condensed in one sentence, 'You promised a fund and you exacted a tax.'"

The human face is my landscape.

Sir Joshua Reynolds (1723-92)— alluding to his non-enjoyment of the scenery of Richmond.

The ignorant impatience of taxation.

Lord Castlereagh (1769-1822) —when the Income-Tax Bill was thrown out in 1816. Referred to by W. E. Gladstone when introducing his Budget in 1860, saying that if the author of that phrase could again take his place in the House he would be more likely to complain of "an ignorant patience of taxation."

The Iron Duke.

Surname applied to the Duke of Wellington (1769-1852) "said to have been borrowed from a steamboat (Gleig iv. p. 305), but "it attached itself to him by its fitness." (*Dict. Nat. Biog.*, lx., 203) "The term Iron Duke was first applied to an iron steamboat called by its owners the Duke of Wellington and afterwards, rather in jest than earnest, to the Duke himself." (*The Words of Wellington*, 1869, p. 179) A correspondent of *Notes & Queries*

(Aug. 30, 1902, p. 172) says that a locomotive called the Iron Duke was built at the Great Western Railway works in 1847.

The term was applied to the Duke of Wellington in 1850, according to the *Engl. Histor. Dict.*

The key of India is not Herat or Candahar. The key of India is London.

BENJAMIN DISRAELI [Earl of Beaconsfield] (1804-81)—in the House of Lords, Mar. 4, 1881, in a speech on the evacuation of Candahar.

The local sentiment in man is the strongest passion in his nature.

LORD BEACONSFIELD [Earl of Beaconsfield] (1804-81)—in a speech at Salthill, Nov. 5, 1864. Followed by:
"This local sentiment is the parent of most of our virtues."

The march of the human mind is slow.

EDMUND BURKE (1729-97)—in a speech on conciliation with America, Mar. 22, 1775.

The miseries of Italy have been the dangers of Europe.

W. E. GLADSTONE (1809-98)—in a speech on Italy, Mar. 7, 1861. He added: "The consolidation of Italy, her restoration to national life—if it be the will of God to grant her that boon—will be, I believe, a blessing as great to Europe as it is to all the people of the Peninsula." (Sir W. Reid's *Life*, 1899, p. 428).

The more happy I am, the more I pity kings.

VOLTAIRE (1694-1778)—written (in English) in a letter to Lord Keith, Oct. 4, 1759.

The murder of the Queen had been represented to me as a deed, lawful and meritorious. I die a firm Catholic.

ANTHONY BABINGTON (1561-86)— executed for conspiring against the life of Queen Elizabeth—Last words.

Then it was a bad speech.

CHARLES JAMES FOX (1749-1806) —when told that a speech read well. (Moore, *Life of Sheridan*, vol. ii, p. 12, note.)

Then let this Earl govern all Ireland.

HENRY VII (1456-1509)—Reply to someone who, speaking of Thomas Fitzgerald, eighth Earl of Kildare, said "All Ireland cannot govern this Earl." (Froude's *Hist. of Engl.* vol. ii, ch. 8).

The noble lord is the Prince Rupert of parliamentary discussion.

BENJAMIN DISRAELI, [Earl of Beaconsfield] (1804-81)—of Lord Derby, then Lord Stanley, in the House of Commons, April 1844. Cf.
The brilliant chief, irregularly great,
Frank, haughty, rash—the Rupert of debate.
    Bulwer Lytton, *The New Timon*,
        1846, pt. i, st. 6.

The officer who forgets that he is a gentleman does more harm to the moral influence of this country than ten men of blameless life can do good.

EARL OF DERBY (1799-1869)—to the Addiscombe students.

The only objection against the Bible is a bad life.

EARL OF ROCHESTER (1647-80)— Last words.

The oppression of a majority is detestable and odious: the oppression of a minority is only by one degree less detestable and odious.

W. E. GLADSTONE (1809-98)—
in the House of Commons, on the
second reading of the Irish Land
Bill in 1870.

**The Orangeman raises his war-
whoop ; Exeter Hall sets up
its bray.**

LORD MACAULAY (1800-59)—in
a speech in the House of Commons
in April, 1845, on the second reading
of the Maynooth College Bill.

The past, at least, is secure.

DANIEL WEBSTER (1782-1852)—
alluding to the history of Massachusetts in the Union. See Our
past has gone into history.

The people my trust.

PRESIDENT JAMES A. GARFIELD
(1831-81)—Last words.

**The people never give up their
liberties except under some
delusion.**

EDMUND BURKE (1729-97)—in a
speech at a county meeting of
Buckinghamshire, 1784.

**The people of England, in my
opinion, committed a worse
offence by the unconstitu-
tional restoration of Charles
II than even by the death of
Charles I.**

CHARLES JAMES FOX (1749-1806)
—in the House of Commons, Dec.
10, 1795. See The worst of revolutions is a restoration.

**The people's liberties strengthen
the king's prerogative, and
the king's prerogative is to
defend the people's liberties.**

CHARLES I (1600-49).

**The poorest man may in his
cottage bid defiance to all
the force of the crown.**

WILLIAM PITT, Earl of Chatham
(1708-78)—in a speech on the
Excise Bill.   He continued, "It

may be frail ; its roof may shake ;
the wind may blow through it ; the
storms may enter, the rain may
enter,—but the King of England cannot enter ! all his forces dare not
cross the threshold of the ruined
tenement." (Brougham's *Statesman
of George III*, 1st series, p. 41) Cf.

For a man's house is his castle,
et domus sua cuique tutissimum
refugium ; for where shall a man be
safe, if it be not in his house. (Sir
E. Coke, *Third Institute*, 1648 edit.
p. 162)

**The press is like the air, a
chartered libertine.**

WILLIAM PITT, Earl of Chatham
(1708-78)—about 1757, when his
attention was called to some of the
press comments against him.   The
allusion is to the following lines in
Shakspere's *King Henry V* (act 1,
sc. 1)

. . . . "that, when he speaks,
The air, a charter'd libertine, is still."
Cf. " That Man, the lawless libertine,
        may rove,
    Free and unquestion'd through the
        wilds of love ;
    (Rowe, *Jane Shore*, act 1, sc. 2).

**The programme of the Con-
servative party is to maintain the Constitution of the
country.**

BENJAMIN DISRAELI, [Earl of
Beaconsfield] (1804-81)—in a speech
at Manchester, April 3, 1872.

**The progress of the times, Mr.
Speaker, is such, that little
children who can neither
walk nor talk may be seen
running about the streets,
cursing their Maker !**

SIR BOYLE ROCHE (1743-1807)—
alluding to the manners of " Young
Ireland."

The public is poor.

EDMUND BURKE (1729-97)—in a
speech on the plan for economical
reform, Feb. 11, 1780.

The pursuit of knowledge under difficulties.

LORD BROUGHAM (1778-1868)—Title given to a book published in 1830 under the auspices of the Society for the Diffusion of Useful Knowledge. According to Charles Knight's *Passages of a Working Life* (vol. ii, p. 135) Lord Brougham suggested the phrase as an improvement upon Professor Craik's own title for the book: *The Love of Knowledge overcoming Difficulties in its Pursuit.*

The Queen of Scots is the mother of a fair son, and I but a barren stock.

QUEEN ELIZABETH (1533-1603)—Remark on hearing of the birth of James VI, in June, 1566.

There are three things that every man fancies he can do : farm a small property, drive a gig, and write an article for a review.

REV. SIDNEY SMITH (1771-1845).

There is a higher law than the Constitution.

WILLIAM HENRY SEWARD(1801-72)—in a speech, March 11, 1850. See There is something behind the Throne &c. "The Constitution devotes the national domain to union, to justice, to defence, to welfare, and to liberty. But there is a higher law than the Constitution, which regulates our authority over the domain, and devotes it to the same noble purposes."

There is always room at the top.

DANIEL WEBSTER (1782-1852)—when advised not to become a lawyer as the profession was overcrowded. See Most good lawyers live well, work hard, and die poor.

There is another and a better world.

JOHN PALMER (1742-98)—Last words. He died on the stage of the Liverpool Theatre, while acting in *The Stranger*, a play by Kotzebue, and the above words are a line in the play, act i, sc. i, translated by A. Schink, London, 1799.

There is little or nothing in this life worth living for, but we can all of us go straight forward and do our duty.

DUKE OF WELLINGTON (1769-1852). See The best of life is just tolerable.&c.

There is no sovereignty of any first-rate State which costs so little to the people, as the sovereignty of England.

BENJAMIN DISRAELI [Earl of Beaconsfield](1804-81)—in a speech at Manchester, April 3, 1872.

There is nothing that is meritorious but virtue and friendship ; and, indeed, friendship is only a part of virtue.

ALEXANDER POPE (1688-1744)—Last words (Johnson, *Life of Pope*). Another version : " I am dying, sir, of a hun!red good symptoms," said to a friend who called to inquire concerning his health.

There is no time to be lost.

ERASMUS DARWIN (1731-1802)—Last words, having asked to be bled.

There is something behind the Throne greater than the King himself.

WILLIAM PITT [Earl of Chatham] (1708-78)—in a speech, March 2, 1770. Preceded by " A long train of these practices has at length unwillingly convinced me that," etc. (*Chatham Correspondence*). Quoted by Lord Mahon, "greater than the Throne itself." (*Hist. of England*),

5

vol. v, p. 258) See There is a higher law than the Constitution.

The religion of all sensible men.

See All wise men are of the same religion.

The resources of civilisation are not yet exhausted.

W. E. GLADSTONE (1809-98)—in a speech at a banquet in his honour at Leeds, Oct. 7, 1881.

The right honourable gentleman [Sir Robert Peel] caught the Whigs bathing, and walked away with their clothes.

BENJAMIN DISRAELI [Earl of Beaconsfield] (1804-81)—in a speech on the opening of letters by government, Feb. 28, 1845.

The right honourable gentleman is indebted to his memory for his jests, and to his imagination for his facts.

RICHARD BRINSLEY SHERIDAN (1751-1816)—in the House of Commons, alluding to Mr. Dundas. (*Sheridaniana;* see also Moore's *Life of Sheridan*). Cf. ". . et on peut dire que son esprit brille aûx dépens de sa memoire." (It may be said that his wit shines at the expense of his memory) (Le Sage, *Gil Blas*, bk. iii, ch. 11).

The right man in the right place.

SIR AUSTEN H. LAYARD(1817-94) —in a speech in the House of Commons, Jan. 15, 1855. "I have always believed that success would be the inevitable result if the two services, the army and the navy, had fair play, and if we sent the right man to fill the right place." (Hansard, *Parl. Debates*, 3rd Series, vol. 138, p. 2077)

The Schoolmaster is abroad.

LORD BROUGHAM (1779-1868)— in a speech in the House of Commons, Jan. 29, 1828. Followed by: "and I trust more to him, armed with his primer, than I do to the soldier in full military array, for upholding and extending the liberties of his country."

The secret of success is constancy to purpose.

BENJAMIN DISRAELI [Earl of Beaconsfield] (1804-81)—in a speech at the Crystal Palace, June 24, 1872.

The sick man of Europe [or of the East].

See L'homme malade.

The South! The South! God knows what will become of her!

JOHN CALDWELL CALHOUN (1782-1850)—Last words.

The splendid bridge from the Old World to the New.

THOMAS CARLYLE (1795-81)—to Ralph Waldo Emerson, of Edward Gibbon, the historian.

The standard of St. George was hoisted on the mountains of Rasselas.

BENJAMIN DISRAELI [Earl of Beaconsfield] (1804-81)—in moving a vote of thanks, July 2, 1868, in the House of Commons, to Sir R. Napier's army after the Abyssinian campaign. "He led the elephants of Asia, bearing the artillery of Europe, over African passes which might have startled the trapper, and appalled the hunter of the Alps." The above precedes, but not immediately, the phrase "The standard of St. George," &c.

The sweet simplicity of the three per cents.

BENJAMIN DISRAELI [Earl of Beaconsfield (1804-81)—in a speech on agricultural distress, Feb. 19, 1850. "The sweet simplicity of the three per cents." (Idem, *Endy-*

mion 1880) See The elegant simplicity &c.

The Tower is to me the worst argument in the world.

WILLIAM PENN, founder of Pennsylvania, (1644-1718)—when threatened with imprisonment for joining the Quakers.

The true poet ascends to receive knowledge ; he descends to impart it.

WILLIAM WORDSWORTH (1770-1850).

The uncrowned king of Ireland.

W. E. FORSTER (1818-86)—in a speech in the House of Commons Feb. 22, 1883, on Ireland, spoke of Charles Stuart Parnell as " ' the uncrowned king' as the honourable member for Dungarvan called him." Mr. O'Donnell, however, denied having ever said anything of the kind.

The unspeakable Turk.

THOMAS CARLYLE (1795-1881)—in a letter written to a meeting at St. James's Hall, London, in 1876, convened to discuss the Eastern question. "The unspeakable Turk should be immediately struck out of the question, and the country be left to honest European guidance." A correspondant of *Notes and Queries* (1899, 1st half, p. 177) quotes as follows : "The unspeakable Turk should be immediately struck out of the question, and the country left to European guidance."—letter from Thomas Carlyle to George Howard, M.P., dated Nov. 24, 1876. He also used the phrase in 1831, in an article on the *Nibelungen Lied* in the *Westminster Review* (no. 29) "that unspeakable Turk, King Machabol."

The volunteer force is the garrison of our hearths and homes.

BENJAMIN DISRAELI [Lord Beaconsfield] (1804-81)—in a speech at Aylesbury, Feb. 18, 1879. Preceded by : "The British Army is the garrison of our Empire, but . . . ," and followed by : "Patriotism never had a better inspiration than when it established that effective and powerful institution."

The weapon of the advocate is the sword of the soldier, not the dagger of the assassin.

SIR ALEXANDER COCKBURN (1805-80)—combating Brougham's opinion that an advocate in discharging his duty regards only the interests of his client, even if he involves his country in confusion.

The wisdom of many, and the wit of one.

LORD JOHN RUSSELL (1792-1878—Impromptu definition of a proverb, one morning at breakfast— "One man's wit and all men's wisdom." (*Memoirs of Mackintosh*, vol. ii, p. 473.)

The wisdom of our ancestors.

EDMUND BURKE (1729-97)—in a speech on conciliation with America, Mar. 22, 1775, but SIR WILLIAM GRANT (1754-1832) is credited with having first used the phrase.

The world is a comedy to those who think, a tragedy to those who feel.

HORACE WALPOLE (1717-97)—in a letter, 1770, to Sir Horace Mann.

The world itself is but a large prison, out of which some are daily led to execution.

SIR WALTER RALEIGH (1552-1618)—when returning to prison from his trial.

The worst of revolutions is a restoration.

CHARLES JAMES FOX (1749-1806) —referring to that of Charles II. See The people of England &c.

The Youth of a nation are the Masters of Posterity,

BENJAMIN DISRAELI [Earl of Beaconsfield] (1804-81)—in a speech at the Manchester Athenæum, Oct. 23, 1844.

There's nothing to beat that, Hugh. It is a paraphrase of the words of Paul : ' I know whom I have believed, and am persuaded that he is able to keep that which I have committed unto Him, against that day.'

HENRY DRUMMOND (1851-97)— Last intelligible or connected words; referring to the following lines which Dr. Barbour had just joined with him in singing :—

> I'm not ashamed to own my Lord,
> Or to defend His cause,
> Maintain the glory of His cross,
> And honour all His laws.

There's plenty of time to win this game and to thrash the Spaniards too.

(*Dict. Nat. Biog.*, xv, p. 437.)

SIR FRANCIS DRAKE (1540-96)— who was playing at bowls with Lord Howard of Effingham and others on a cliff overlooking the sea, when news was brought to him that the Armada had been seen off Lizard Point, July 19, 1588. (Cf. C. Kingsley's *Westward Ho !* ch. 30)

They may ring their bells now ; before long they will be wringing their hands.

SIR ROBERT WALPOLE (1676-1745)—when the bells were rung in London on war being declared against Spain in 1739. (Coxe, *Life*, i, 579.)

They planted by your care ! No,

your oppression planted them in America.

ISAAC BARRÉ (1726-1802)—in reply to Charles Townshend in Feb. 1765. The latter asked if Colonies planted by British care would grudge taxation.

They've done for me at last, Hardy !

LORD NELSON (1758-1805)— Dying. words. "I hope not !" cried Hardy. "Yes," he replied. "my back-bone is shot through." He afterwards asked Hardy to kiss him (*Dict. Nat. Biog.*, vol. xl., p. 206 ; Southey, *Life*, ch. 9, ed. 1888, pp. 373-7.) See Thank God, I have done my duty.

They will never agree : they are arguing from different premises.

REV SYDNEY SMITH (1771-1845) —on seeing two women abusing each other from opposite houses.

They will not let my play run ; and yet they steal my thunder.

JOHN DENNIS (1657-1734)— finding that the manager of Drury Lane Theatre was using some artificial thunder that Dennis had invented for a play of his own that had been acted but a short time. (*Biog. Britannica*, vol. v. p. 103.) *The Dict. Nat. Biog.*, (vol. xiv. p. 370) says that Dennis was at a performance of ' Macbeth ' (shortly after " Appius and Virginia " was withdrawn) and, on hearing the thunder, exclaimed, " that's my thunder, by God ! the villains will play my thunder, but not my plays." (Cibber, *Lives*, iv. 234) In the *Life of Mr. John Dennis* (anon., London, 1734, p. 31) his exclamation is given as ' 'Sdeath ! that's my Thunder.'

They will receive a terrible blow

this parliament, and yet they shall not see who hurts them.

Concluding words of a letter sent to Lord Monteagle (1575-1622), a Catholic and brother-in-law of Francis Tresham, one of the conspirators, warning him not to attend parliament. The letter was communicated to the king and led to the discovery and frustration of the famous Gunpowder Plot, (Nov. 5, 1605.)

Thirty millions, mostly fools.

THOMAS CARLYLE (1795-1881)— when asked the population of England. Cf.

Les sots depuis Adam sont en majorité.
(Since Adam's days fools are in the majority).
Delavigne, *Epître à Messieurs de l'Académie française.*
" En toutes compaignies il y a plus de folz que de saiges."
(In every company there are more fools than wise men)
Rabelais, *Pantagruel*, ii, 10
See Combien faut-il de sots pour faire un public.

This day let me see the Lord Jesus.

JOHN JEWELL Bishop of Salisbury, (1522-71)—Last words.

This hand hath offended—this uuworthy hand.

THOMAS CRANMER, [Archbishop of Canterbury] (1489-1556)—Last words, at the stake.
" . . . and he called aloud several times, ' This hand hath offended.'"
(Hume, *Hist. of Engl.*)

This is a man !

EARL OF CHATHAM (1708-78)— in a letter to his son William Pitt, then aged 14. " How happy, my loved boy, is it that your mama and I can tell ourselves that there is at Cambridge *one* without a beard, and all the elements so mixed up in him, that Nature might stand up and say, ' this is a man ! '" Cf.

" His life was gentle ; and the elements
So mix'd up in him, that Nature might stand up
And say to all the world, This was a man !"
Shakspere, *Julius Caesar*, act v. sc. 5, ll. 73-5 (Mark Antony).
See Oh, Pitt never was a boy !

This is the head of a traitor.

Formula used by the headsman at executions for treason, holding up the decapitated head in view of the people.

**This is the Jew
That Shakespeare drew.**

By a gentleman in the pit (Feb. 14, 1741,) of the theatre witnessing Macklin's performance of Shylock, in the *Merchant of Venice*. The gentleman is said to have been Alexander Pope, (*Biog, Dram.*, vol I, pt. 2, p. 469 ; also *Dict. Nat. Biog.*, vol. xxxv. p. 180: " Pope's often quoted but apocryphal distich.")

This is the last of earth ! I am content !

JOHN QUINCY ADAMS, 6th president of the U. S. (1767-1848),— Last words.

This I will now truly say, that as long as I have lived, I have striven to live worthily, and after my life to leave to the men that come after me a remembering of me in good works.

ALFRED THE GREAT (849-901).

This republic can never fail, so long as the citizen is vigilant.

PRESIDENT WILLIAM McKINLEY (1843-1901)—in a speech at Redlands (Cal.) May 8, 1901.

Thomas Jefferson still survives.

JOHN ADAMS, 2nd President of the U. S. (1735-1826)—Last words. Jefferson, however, was already dead. In his *Life* by J. Q. Adams his last words are given as "Independence for ever." He died on Independence Day (4th. July)

Those things which are not practicable are not desirable.

EDMUND BURKE (1729-97)—in a speech on the plan for economical reform, Feb. 11, 1780.

Those who would give up essential liberty for the sake of a little temporary safety deserve neither liberty nor safety.

BENJAMIN FRANKLIN (1706-90) —during the French war, in 1755.

Those who have loved longest love best.

DR. SAMUEL JOHNSON (1709-84).

Three acres and a cow.

Phrase referring to the Small Holdings and Allotments Bill introduced by Mr. Jesse Collings in 1882. Quoted derisively by Sir Michael Hicks Beach, and promptly disavowed by him in that sense, the phrase has become a saying useful alike to advocates and opponents of the general idea of allotments and small holdings. The phrase is, however, traced to John Stuart Mill's *Principles of Political Economy* (bk. ii, ch. 6, sect. 5), who quotes it from a treatise on Flemish husbandry : "When the land is cultivated entirely by the spade, and no horses are kept, a cow is kept for every three acres of land, &c." Bentham, in his criticism of a Bill introduced by Pitt in 1797, points out that each cow would require for her sustenance three acres of land, and asked how this was to be provided. [The Bill provided, *inter alia*, for purchasing cows for poor people] (Cf. Bentham's *Works*, vol. viii. p. 448).

Throughout every part of my career I have felt pinched

and hampered by my own ignorance.

SIR WALTER SCOTT (1771-1832).

Thus far shalt thou go and no farther.

KING CANUTE (995-1035)—with reproving his courtiers for their flattery, telling them that there was one Being alone who could say to the ocean, Thus far, &c. (Hume, *Hist. of Engl.*) It is said that he ordered his chair to be set on the sea-shore while the tide was rising and bade the waters retire and obey the voice of Him who was lord of the ocean. Quoted by Edmund Burke in his speech on Conciliation with America, Mar. 22, 1775 (*Works*, 1897 edition, vol i, p. 468). Cf. "And said, Hitherto shalt thou come, but no further and here shall thy proud waves be stayed ?" (*Job*, ch. 38, v. xi) Cf. *King Canute*, a poem by W. M. Thackeray. (*Ballads and Songs*.) also Henry of Huntingdon, *Historia Anglorum*, Vitâ Canuti.

"Thy kingdom come, thy will be done."

SIR EDWARD COKE, Lord Chief Justice of England (1552-1633) —Last words.

Time is on our side.

W. E. GLADSTONE (1809-98)— in the debate on the Reform Bill under Earl Russell's administration in 1866. See Le temps et moi.

Time is precious, but truth is more precious than time.

BENJAMIN DISRAELI [Earl of Beaconsfield] (1804-81)—at Aylesbury, Sep. 21, 1865. Followed by " and, therefore it is for you calmly to consider what I have said today." (*The Times*, Sept. 22, 1865, p. 4, col. 5) Cf.
For truth is precious and divine,
Too rich a pearl for carnal swine
(S. Butler, *Hudibras*, pt. ii, canto 2, l. 257)

See Truth takes no account of centuries.

'Tis a sharp remedy, but a sure one for all ills.

SIR WALTER RALEIGH (1552-1618)—on the scaffold, feeling the edge of the axe. (Hume, *Hist. of Engl.*) Another version : " This gives me no fear. It is a sharp and fair medecine to cure me of all my troubles."

'Tis gone!

RICHARD SAVAGE (1696-1743)— Last recorded words, to a prison official, after saying " I have something to say to you, sir," but being unable to recollect what it was.

To anyone who has reached a very advanced age, a walk through the streets of London is like a walk in a cemetery.

RICHARD BINSLEY SHERIDAN (1751-1816).

To be like Christ is to be a Christian.

WILLIAM PENN (1644-1718), founder of Pennsylvania — Last words.

To be prepared for war is one of the most effectual means of preserving peace.

GEORGE WASHINGTON (1732-99) —in a speech to Congress, Jan. 8, 1790. Cf. ". . . the surest way, therefore, said he, [Edward Fox, Bishop of Hereford (1496-1538)], to Peace, is a constant preparedness for War " (*Statesmen of England*, 1665, p. 55). Cf.

Paritur pax bello (Peace is begotten of war).

Cornelius Nepos, *Epaminondas*, v) ; and Qui desiderat pacem praeparet bellum (Let him who desires peace prepare for war).

(Vegetius, *De Re Militari*, iii.) ; and Nissuno stato pubblico può godersi la quieta, nè ribattere l'injurie, nè diffendere le leggi, la religione e la liberta senza arme.

(No State can enjoy tranquillity, nor repel hostile attacks, nor defend its laws, its religion and its liberty, unless it be armed). (Montecuceoli, *Memorie*, bk. 1, xliv. ed. 1704, p. 55)

To recover my father's kingdom. (*Dict. Nat. Biog.* vol. xvii, p. 104.)

PRINCE EDWARD (1453-71), son of Henry VI. (1421-71)—to Edward IV. (1441-83) when asked what had brought him to England.

To that quarter of an hour I owe everything in life.

LORD NELSON (1758-1805)—to an upholsterer who had promised to see some goods off at six o'clock. Nelson said " A quarter before six," and added the above words. Another version is : " I owe all my success in life to having been always a quarter of an hour before my time." Cf. Lord `Chesterfield's remark, alluding to the Duke of Newcastle, " His Grace loses an hour in the morning, and is looking for it all the rest of the day." See L'exactitude est la politesse des rois. Sir Spencer Compton, Earl of Wilmington, (1673-1743) said of the Duke of Newcastle that he always loses half an hour in the morning which he is running after the rest of the day without being able to overtake it. (*Dict. Nat. Biog.* vol. xi., p. 451)

To the memory of the Man, first in war, first in peace, and first in the hearts of his countrymen.

GENERAL HENRY LEE (1756-1816)—in his eulogy on Washington, delivered Dec. 26, 1799. (*Memoirs of Lee*) In Marshall's *Life of Washington* the Resolutions presented to the House of Representatives, on the Death of General Washington, Dec. 1799, contain the above words, except that the last is " fellow-citizens " (instead of " countrymen ").

Trust in God and you need not fear.

JONATHAN EDWARDS (1703-58) —Last words, to some one who lamented his approaching death as a heavy blow to the church.

Truth takes no account of centuries.

WILLIAM WORDSWORTH (1770-1850). See Time is precious, but truth is more precious than time.

Up guards—make ready !

DUKE OF WELLINGTON (1769-1852)—to the Foot Guards at the battle of Waterloo, June 18, 1815. Generally quoted "Up guards and at them !" (Alison; Charles Lever) but the saying in either form is discredited. In answer to a letter from J. Wilson Croker (author of *Memoirs*) to Mr. Greville (the Duke's secretary) Mar. 14, 1852, the Duke himself wrote "What I must have said, and possibly did say, was, 'Stand up, guards !' and then gave the commanding officer the order to attack." See also Maxwell's *Life* (vol. ii, p. 82), *Dict. Nat. Biog.*, vol. lx., p. 191, Sir Wm. Fraser, *Words on Wellington*, (p. 88). W. Jerdan's *Autobiography* mentions the Duke's denial of having said "Up, boys, and at 'em !" Although the Duke himself denied or said he did not remember using the words, yet in a letter from Capt. Batty, of the Grenadier Guards, dated June 22, 1815, published in Booth's *Battle of Waterloo*, it is stated that the Duke said, "Up, guards, and at them again !"

Verify your references.

Dr. MARTIN JOSEPH ROUTH, president of Magdalen College Oxford (1755-1854)—advice given to the Rev. J. W. Burgon in 1847.

"Presently he brightened up and said, 'I think, sir, since you care for the advice of an old man, sir, you will find it a very good practice' (here he looked me archly in the face),—'always to *verify your references*, sir !'" (J. W. Burgon, *Lives of Twelve Good Men*, 1891, p. 38)

Very well, then I shall not take off my boots.

DUKE OF WELLINGTON (1769-1852)—during a storm at sea, when told that it would soon be all over with them. See I am going on my journey &c.

Victory of common sense.

GENERAL J. MEREDITH READ—in a speech in 1896 on William McKinley's election to the Presidency of the U. S.

Victory ! or Westminster Abbey !

See Westminster Abbey, or Victory !

Village tyrants

W. E. FORSTER (1818-86)—a term used in introducing the first Coercion Bill, Jan 24, 1881, referring to persons committing agrarian outrages in Ireland. "It is not that the police do not know who these village tyrants are." (T. P. O'Connor, *The Parnell Movement*, p. 218). "It is not (said Mr. Forster) that the police do not know who these village tyrants are. The police know perfectly well who plan and perpetrate these outrages, and the perpetrators are perfectly aware of the fact that they are known. (Hansard, vol. cclvii, p. 1226)

Volunteers are not, I believe, liable to go abroad except in case of invasion.

LORD JUSTICE BOWEN (1835-94).

Vy, sir, your Highness plays like a prince.

GEORGE FREDERICK HANDEL (1684-1759)—to a member of the royal family, who asked how he liked his playing on the violoncello.

Wally, what is this? It is death, my boy : they have deceived me.

GEORGE IV (1762-1830)—Last words, to his page, Sir Walthen Waller.

Water !

GENERAL ULYSSES SIMPSON GRANT (1822-85), President of the U. S.—Last words, to an attendant who enquired if he wished for anything. Also of SAMUEL JONES TILDEN (1814-86), who suffered from thirst during his last hours.

We are all Federalists, we are all Republicans.

THOMAS JEFFERSON, President of the U. S. (1743-1826).

We are all going to Heaven, and Van Dyck is of the party (or company).

THOMAS GAINSBOROUGH (1727-88)—Last words. Quoted by Ruskin (*Art of England* iii).

We are all Socialists, now-a-days.

EDWARD VII (when Prince of Wales)—in a speech at the Mansion House, London, in 1895.

We can only reason from what is : we can reason on actualities, but not on possibilities.

VISCOUNT BOLINGBROKE (1678-1751). Cf. "What can we reason but from what we know?" (Pope, *Essay on Man*, 1, 18)

We cultivate literature upon a little oatmeal.

REV. SYDNEY SMITH (1771-1845) —Motto suggested for *The Edinburgh Review*. Cf.

. . tenui musam meditamur avenâ. (Vergil, *Eclogues* 1, 2).

We have dished the Whigs.

EDWARD STANLEY, fourteenth Earl of Derby (1799-1869)—referring to the Reform Bill of 1867.

We have his Majesty's coronation oath to maintain the laws of England ; what need we, then, take his word?

JOHN PYM (1584-1643)—in 1628, when the House of Commons was asked if they would rely on the king's word.

Welcome the cross of Christ, welcome everlasting life.

LAWRENCE SAUNDERS (1516-58) —Last words, when burned at the stake in the reign of Queen Mary. (Foxe, *Book of Martyrs*)

Well, ladies, if I were one hour in Heaven, I would not be again with you, as much as I love you.

MARY, COUNTESS OF WARWICK (1625-78)—Last words.

We must all hang together, else we shall all hang separately.

BENJAMIN FRANKLIN (1706-90) —in reply to a remark of John Hancock, while the Declaration of Independence was being signed (July 4, 1776) that they must all hang together.

We must beat the red-coats, or Molly Stark's a widow.

JOHN STARK, American general (1728-1822), is credited with the following brief address to his troops before the battle of Bennington (Aug. 16, 1777). "There, my boys, are your enemies, the red-coats and Tories : you must beat them, or my wife sleeps a widow to-night."

We must consider how very

little history there is ; I mean real authentic history. That certain kings reigned, and certain battles were fought, we can depend upon as true ; but all the colouring, all the philosophy of history is conjecture.

DR. SAMUEL JOHNSON (1709–84) (Boswell's *Life*, 1824 ed., vol. 2, pp. 340-1) See Anything but history, for history must be false.

We must consult Brother Jonathan.

GEORGE WASHINGTON (1732-99)—a remark frequently made by him, referring to his secretary and aide-de-camp, Col. Jonathan Trumbull, of Connecticut. The origin of the term 'Brother Jonathan' as applied to America.

We must now at least educate our masters.

RT. HON. ROBERT LOWE, Lord Sherbrooke (1811-92)—alluding to the passing of the Reform Bill under Lord Derby's administration. Cf. Lord Beaconsfield's remark at a Conservative banquet at Edinburgh, Oct. 29, 1867, "I had to prepare the mind of the country, and to educate,—if it be not arrogant to use such a phrase,—to educate our party."

We part to meet again, I hope, in endless joys.

JOHN HOUGH (1651-1743)—Bishop of Oxford and afterwards Bishop of Worcester—Last words.

Were the church of Christ what she should be, twenty years would not pass away without the story of the cross being uttered in the ear of every living person.

SIMEON HOWARD CALLOUN (1804-76)—Last words.

We shall never war except for peace.

PRESIDENT WILLIAM McKINLEY (1843-1901)—in a speech at El Paso, May 6, 1901.

We shall there desire nothing that we have not, except more tongues to sing more praise to Him.

ROBERT BOYLE (1626-91)—Last words.

Westminster Abbey, or victory !

LORD NELSON (1758-1805)—Exclamation when boarding the *San Josef* from the *San Nicolas*, Feb. 14, 1797 (Southey, *Life of Nelson*, ch. 4, ed. 1888, p. 136.)

What an idle piece of ceremony this buttoning and unbuttoning is to me, now.

RICHARD BROCKLESBY (1722-97) —Last words.

What can it signify ?

WILLIAM COWPER (1731-1800)—Last words to Miss Perowne, who offered him refreshment.

What dost thou fear ? Strike, man ! strike !

SIR WALTER RALEIGH (1552-1618)—Last words to the executioner, who hesitated at the last moment.

What grave contains such a father and such a son ? What sepulchre embosoms the remains of so much human excellence and glory ?

DUKE OF WELLINGTON (1769-1852)—at the funeral of William Pitt, who was interred in his father's grave in Westminster Abbey.

What has become of the king and his cavaliers? And whither are they fled ?

Said by the populace on passing Whitehall, Charles I (1600-49) having retired to Hampton Court shortly after the scene in the House of Commons, 1642. (Hume, *Hist. of Engl.*)

What I am I have made myself: I say this without vanity, and in pure simplicity of heart.

SIR HUMPHRY DAVY (1778-1829).
Cf. Je ne dois qu'à moi seule toute ma renommée.
(I owe my fame to myself alone.)
Corneille, *Excuse à Ariste*, l. 50

What I cannot utter with my mouth, accept, Lord, from my heart and soul.

FRANCIS QUARLES (1592-1614)—Last words.

What is childhood but a series of happy illusions!

REV. SYDNEY SMITH (1771-1845).

What is that?

ROBERT LOUIS STEVENSON (1850-94)—Last words, clasping his forehead with both hands, in pain.

What is valuable is not new, and what is new is not valuable.

DANIEL WEBSTER (1782-1852)—at Marshfield, Sep. 1, 1848. Cf. "Our best thoughts came from others." (R. W. Emerson.—*Quotation and Originality*)

What, madam, have you not forgiven God Almighty yet?

JOHN WESLEY (1703-91) or GEORGE WHITEFIELD (1714-70)—Rebuke to a lady who was wearing the deepest mourning a considerable time after her husband's death.

What masks are these uniforms to hide cowards!

DUKE OF WELLINGTON (1769-1852)—speaking of military men. (R. W. Emerson, *Old Age*.)

What shadows we are, and what shadows we pursue.

EDMUND BURKE (1729-97)—in a speech at Bristol, on declining the Poll, Sep. 1780, alluding to the sudden death of one of the candidates (Mr. Coombe). "The worthy gentleman who has been snatched from us at the moment of the election, and in the middle of the contest, whilst his desires were as warm and his hopes as eager as ours, has feelingly told us what shadows we are, and what shadows we pursue." Cf. Quid umbras, fumos, fungos, sequimur.
(Sir H. Grimston, *Strena Christiana*, 1644.)

What shall we do with this bauble? Here, take it away.
(Hume *Hist. of Engl.*)

OLIVER CROMWELL (1599-1658)—referring to the mace of the House of Commons, Apr. 20, 1653. Another version is: "Take away that shining bauble and lock up the doors." See I have sought the Lord night and day &c.

What the Puritans gave the world was not thought but action.

WENDELL PHILLIPS (1811-84)—in a speech at a dinner of the Pilgrim Society at Plymouth (Mass.), Dec. 21, 1855.

What we call wisdom is the result, not the residuum, of all the wisdom of past ages.

HENRY WARD BEECHER (1813-87).

**When Adam delved and Eve span,
Where was then the gentleman?**

Lines used by JOHN BALL an itinerant preacher (d. 1381)—in an address to the populace on Blackheath, June 12, 1381, under the

leadership of Wat Tyler and Jack
Straw (Hume, *Hist. of Engl.*)
  " But when Adam delved and Eve span,
  Who was then a gentleman?"
  Jack Straw, act i, *Parson Ball* (c. 1604;
  but author unknown—see *Dodsley's Col-
  lection*).
  " When Adam dalf, and Eve span,
  Wo was thenne a gentilman?"
  (*Dict. of Nat. Biog.* vol. iii, p. 74.)
  The lines are quoted by Burke, in
*an Appeal from the New to the Old
Whigs* (Bohn's Lib., ed. 1896, vol.
iii, p. 88). He says " Of this sapi-
ent maxim, however, I do not give
him as the inventor." &c.

**When Dido found Æneas would
  not come,
She mourned in silence, and was
  di-do-dum.**

DR. PORSON (1759-1808)—when
asked to make a rime on the Latin
gerund, in reply to his offer to make
a rime on any subject. (Porson,
Facetiæ Cantabrigiensis) Another
version is found, however, in the
*Choice Humourous Works of Theo-
dore Hook* (1889, p. 522):
  On the Latin gerunds.
  When Dido's spouse to Dido would not
  come,
  She mourn'd in silence, and was Di, Do,
  Dumb!

**When I can't talk sense, I talk
  metaphor.**
(Moore, *Life of Sheridan*, vol. ii,
p. 29 note.
    J. P. CURRAN (1750-1817.)

**When I forsake my king in the
  hour of his distress, may my
  God Forsake me!**

EDWARD LORD THURLOW
(1732-1806)—in a speech on the
Regency question, in 1788. Sometimes quoted " When I forget my
king (sovereign) may my God forget
me!" (27 *Parl. Hist.* 680; *Ann.
Reg.* 1789) John Wilkes is reported
to have remarked " God forget you!
He'll see you d— first," and Burke
to have added: " The best thing
that could happen to you."

**When I was young, I used to
  say good-natured things,
  and nobody listened to me.
  Now that I am old, I say ill-
  natured things, and everybody listens to me.**
  SAMUEL ROGERS (1763-1855).

**When literature is the sole busi-
  ness of life it becomes a
  drudgery.**
  RICHARD BRINSLEY SHERIDAN
(1751-1816).

**When one begins to turn in bed
  it is time to turn out.**
  DUKE OF WELLINGTON (1769-
1852).

**When the sun shines on you, you
  see your friends. It requires
  sunshine to be seen by them
  to advantage.**
  LADY BLESSINGTON (1789-1849).

**When you strike at a king you
  must kill him.**
  RALPH WALDO EMERSON (1803-
82)—to a young man who wrote an
essay on Plato and mentioned the
subject to Emerson.

When law ends, tyranny begins.
  EARL OF CHATHAM (1708-78)—
in a speech on Wilkes' case Jan. 9,
1770.. " Unlimited power corrupts
the possessor; and this I know,
that, where law ends, there tyranny
begins."

While there is life there is hope.
  REV. PATRICK BRONTË (1774-
1861) father of Charlotte, Emily,
and Anne Brontë—Last words. He
died standing. Cf. " While there
is life there's hope." (Gay. *Fables*,
pt. i, XXVII)

**Who drives fat oxen should him-
  self be fat.**
  DR. SAMUEL JOHNSON (1709-84)
—Boswell, *Life of Dr. Johnson*,

1784 (1824 edit. vol. iv, p. 304). A tragedy by Henry Brooke, containing the line " To rule o'er freemen should themselves be free," was read in Dr. Johnson's presence, and the company admired it much. " I cannot agree with you," said Johnson, it might as well be said, " Who drives, &c."

> " . . . for righteous monarchs,
> Justly to judge, with their own eyes should see ;
> To rule o'er freemen, should themselves be free."
> H. Brooke, *The Earl of Essex* (1761) end of act i.

Boswell, in the above edition, misquotes the line in Brooke's play as " Who rules o'er freemen should himself be free." See Les bons rois &c.

Whoever is right, the persecutor must be wrong.

WILLIAM PENN (1644-1718)— Maxim, with regard to religious toleration in Pennsylvania.

Who goes home?

Question asked of the members of the House of Commons by the door-keeper. " A relic of ancient times when all members going in the direction of the Speaker's residence went in a body to see him safe." " . . . a parliamentary man as great as Pitt having answered to the old lobby cry, ' Who goes home?'" (Reid, *Life of W. E. Gladstone*, 1899, pp. 516-7).

Whose house is this? What street are we in? Why did you bring me here?

WILLIAM CULLEN BRYANT (1794-1878)—Last words. He fell upon some stone steps, receiving a blow on the head which caused his death. Taken into the house before which he fell, he asked the above questions.

Why are we so fond of that life which begins with a cry, and ends with a groan?

MARY, COUNTESS OF WARWICK (1625-78).

Why, certainly, certainly !

EDWARD T. TAYLOR (" Father Taylor "(1793-1871). Last words to a friend who asked him if Jesus was precious.

Why should the Devil have all the good tunes?

REV. RÓLAND HILL (1744-1833).

Why should we legislate for posterity?
What has posterity ever done for us?

SIR BOYLE ROCHE (1743-1807) —in the Irish Parliament. Cf. " The man was laughed at as a blunderer, who said in a public business, ' We do much for posterity, I would fain see them do something for us.'" (Mrs. Elizabeth Montagu, *Letters*, letter dated Jan. 1, 1742, ed. 1809, vol ii, p. 91.) Cf. also

> "What has poster'ty done for us,
> That we, lest they their rights should lose,
> Should trust our necks to grip of noose?"

(John Trumbull, *McFingal*, canto ii, l. 124. edit. 1776. p. 24).

See Pourtant j'avais quelque chose là !

Why, then, be as wise as Solomon; write proverbs, not histories.

CHARLES II (1630-85)—to Gregorio Leti (1630-1701) the Italian historian. The king told him to take care that his work on the History of the Court of England (*Teatro Britannico*) gave no offence. Leti replied that " if a man were as wise as Solomon, he would scarcely be able to avoid giving offence."

Will my people ever forgive me?

EDWARD VII. (b. 1841)—First words, on recovering consciousness after the operation for perityphlitis, performed June 24, 1902, referring to the postponement of his coronation, which had been fixed for June 26, 1902. It took place, Aug. 9, 1902. (*Daily Telegraph*, June 28, 1902).

Will you tell the Archdeacon?— will you move a vote of thanks for his kindness in performing the ceremony?

DEAN ALFORD (1810-71)—Last words, referring to his funeral service.

Win hearts, and you will have all men's hearts and purses.

LORD BURLEIGH (1520-98)—to Queen Elizabeth (1533-1603).

Without courage there cannot be truth, and without truth there can be no other virtue.

SIR WALTER SCOTT (1771-1832).

Wit is in general the finest sense in the world. I had lived long before I discovered that wit was truth.

DR. PORSON (1759-1808).

Woe is me!

THOMAS FITZ-STEPHEN, Captain of the *White Ship*, which struck on a rock off the Normandy coast. All on board perished, including Prince William, son of Henry I., with the exception of a butcher of Rouen named Berold. The captain, swimming above the wreck, asked one of the survivors where the prince was and, on being told that he had not appeared, uttered the above words and sank : (see Mrs. Hemans' poem "He never smiled again.") Another version is : " Woe ! woe to me !" (Dickens, *Child's History of Engl.*, ch x.)

Woman is ilke the reed, which bends to every breeze, but breaks not in the tempest.

ARCHBISHOP WHATELY (1787-

1863). Cf. La Fontaine's fable, *Le Chêne et le Roseau.*

Woman have the understanding of the heart, which is better than that of the head.

SAMUEL ROGERS (1763-1855). Cf. Montaigne's " Les femmes ont l'esprit primesautier." (Women have ready wits)

Wonderful, wondreful, this death!

WILLIAM ETTY (1787-1849)— Last words.

World without end. Amen!

JOHN BUNYAN, author of *Pilgrim's Progress* (1628-88)—Last words. Preceded by : " Weep not for me, but for yourselves. I go to the Father of our Lord Jesus Christ, who no doubt will receive me, though a sinner, through the mediation of our Lord Jesus Christ ; where I hope we shall ere long meet to sing the new song and remain happy for ever—for ever."

Would you be surprised to hear?

SIR JOHN COLERIDGE (1821-94) —a phrase frequently used by him in the course of the famous Tichborne trial.

The civil and criminal proceedings lasted from June, 1871, till Feb 28, 1874.

It is said that it was Charles Bowen (1835-94) who, in consultation, invented the phrase. " The object with which it was devised," says Sir Herbert Stephen, " was to abstain from giving in the form of the question the least hint as to whether it would be correctly answered in the affirmative or in the negative."

Ye be burly, my Lord of Burghley, but ye shall make less stir in our realm than my Lord of Leicester.

QUEEN ELIZABETH (1533-1603).

Yes, it would be rash to say that they have no reasons.

THOMAS CARLYLE (1795-1881)— Last words, to Froude. Preceded by: "I am very ill. Is it not strange that these people should have chosen the very oldest man in all Britain to make suffer in this way?" Froude said "We do not know exactly why those people act as they do. They may have reasons we cannot guess at." Carlyle replied as above. His mind was wandering.

Yes, yes, sing that for me. I am poor and needy.

CORNELIUS ("COMMODORE") VANDERBILT (1794-1877) — Last words, to some one who was singing to him the hymn "Come, ye sinners, poor and needy."

You are fighting for an earthly crown; I am going to receive a heavenly one.

COLONEL JAMES GARDINER (1688-1745)—Last words attributed to him, but see Doddridge's *Life*, 1747, p. 187, and note to Scott's *Waverley*, ch. xlvii.

You are going to leave us, but I will never leave you while your head is upon your shoulders.

JOHN PYM (1584-1643) — when Sir Thomas Wentworth was raised to the peerage as Earl of Strafford.

You are no longer a parliament : I tell you, you are no longer a parliament.

OLIVER CROMWELL (1599-1658) —when dissolving the Long Parliament, Apr. 20, 1653. Preceded by: "For shame, get you gone ; give place to honester men ; to those who will more faithfully discharge their trust," and followed by: "The Lord has done with you : he has

chosen other instruments for carrying on his work." (Hume, *Hist. of Engl.*) See also What shall we do with this bauble?

You can always get the truth from an American statesman after he has turned seventy, or given up all hope of the Presidency

WENDELL PHILLIPS (1811-84)— in a speech (Nov. 7, 1860,) on the election of Abraham Lincoln to the Presidency of the U.S.

You have not to do with Holbein, but with me ; I tell you of seven peasants I can make as many lords ; but of seven lords I could not make one Holbein.

HENRY VIII. (1491-1547)—to a nobleman who complained of some rude treatment by the painter. See Avec quatre aunes de drap &c. Je puis faire des nobles quand je veux &c.
JAMES I. (1566-1625) is credited with saying, "I can make a lord, but only God Almighty can make a gentleman."

You have risen by your gravity : I have sunk by my levity.

JOHN HORNE TOOKE (1736-1812) —remarking to his more prosperous brother that *they* had reversed the natural order of things.

You have swept away our constitution, you have destroyed our parliament, but we will have our revenge. We will send into the ranks of *your* parliament a hundred of the greatest scoundrels of the kingdom.

HENRY GRATTAN (1750-1820)— referring to the Irish representatives in the British parliament after the Union.

You make me drink. Pray leave

me quiet.   I find it affects
my head.

PRINCESS AUGUSTA CHARLOTTE,
daughter of George IV. and Queen
Caroline (1796-1817)—Last words,
dying in childbed.

**You may call it the accidental
and fortuitous concourse of
atoms.**

LORD PALMERSTON (1784-1865)
—of the combination of parties, led
by Disraeli and Gladstone, which
defeated the government on the
Chinese War, Mar. 5, 1857. (See
Quarterly Review, 1835, vol. liii,
p. 270)

**You may go on, sir : so far, the
court is quite with you.**

LORD ELLENBOROUGH (1750-
1818)--to a young barrister who
began his speech, "The unfortunate
client who appears by me"—and
stopped short after repeating the
words several times. (Campbell
Life.)

**You may polish the pewter till it
shines without its becoming
silver.**

LORD JUSTICE BOWEN (1835-94)
—in a lecture on Education.

**You must not contrast too
strongly the hours of court-
ship with the years of possession.**

BENJAMIN DISRAELI [Earl of
Beaconsfield](1804-81)—in a speech,
Mar. 17, 1845, on agricultural dis-
tress. Preceded by : "There is no
doubt a difference in the right
honourable gentleman's [Sir Robert
Peel] demeanour as leader of the
Opposition and as minister of the
Crown.   But that's the old story ;
you must not, &c.

**You must stand afar off to judge
St. Peter's.**

WENDELL PHILLIPS (1811-84)—

in a speech at Boston (Mass.) Feb.
17, 1861.   See Great objects can
only be seen, &c.

**You need not be anxious con-
cerning to-night.   It will be
very peaceful and quiet with
me.**

WILLIAM ELLERY CHANNING
(1780-1842)—Last words.

**Young man, you have heard, no
doubt, how great are the
terrors of death : this night
will probably afford you
some experience ; but you
may lea~n, and may you profit by the example, that a
conscientious endeavour to
perform his duties through
life, will ever close a
Christian's eyes with comfort
and tranquillity.**

WILLIAM BATTIE (1704-76)—
Last words. '

**Your highness has made me too
great for my house.**

SIR NICHOLAS BACON, father of
Lord Bacon (1510-79)—to Queen
Elizabeth when on a visit to him in
1572.   Elizabeth had remarked that
his house was too small.

Your Majesty is not a gentleman.

DUKE OF WELLINGTON (1769-
1852)—reply to George IV in 1822,
on the latter protesting that he
could not "on his honour as a gentleman" appoint Canning secretary for
foreign affairs.   "Your Majesty, I
say, is not a gentleman, but the
sovereign of England, with duties to
your people far above any to yourself", &c.

**Your warrant is written in fair
characters, legible without
spelling.**

CHARLES I (1600-49)—to one
Joyce, who came with some troopers
to conduct him to the army (June 5,

1647) and, in answer to the king's enquiries for his authority, pointed to the soldiers. See Vous avez fait, monsieur, trois fautes d'orthographe.

You sit upon a form, but you stand upon a ceremony.

ARCHBISHOP WHATELY (1787-1863)—replying to his own question, what is the difference between form and ceremony?

Youth, I forgive thee!

RICHARD I (1157-99)—to an archer, named Gourdon, who had wounded him while besieging the castle of Chaluz. He added "Loose his chains, and give him a hundred shillings." The king died next day, but his order was disobeyed and the archer flayed alive and hanged.

You will be hanged if you do.

THOMAS (afterwards) LORD ERSKINE (1750-1823)—reply on a slip of paper to a message from Thelwall, charged with high treason, whom he was defending. Thelwall wrote "I'll be hanged if I don't plead my own cause." After Erskine's reply, Thelwall wrote "Then I'll be hanged if I do."

You will never get credit by beheading me, my neck is so short.

SIR THOMAS MORE (1480-1535)—to the executioner, who had previously asked his forgiveness, which was granted (Hume, *Hist. of Engl.*) Anne Boleyn (c. 1507-36), wife of Henry VIII, remarked to the Lieutenant of the Tower "The executioner is, I hear, very expert; and my neck is very slender."

6

FRENCH SAYINGS

A cœurs vaillants rien d'impossible. (Nothing is impossible to valiant hearts.)

Motto of JACQUES CŒUR (1400-56)—son of a merchant furrier of Bourges : appointed master of the mint there by Charles VII. Lent the king (1449) 200,000 gold crowns enabling him to undertake the conquest of Normandy. Cf. " It is a strong castle, and strongly guarded ; but there is no impossibility to brave men." (Sir Walter Scott, *Quentin Durward*, ch. iii.)

Adieu, chère France ! je ne vous verrai jamais plus ! (Adieu, dear France ! I shall never see you more !)

Farewell of MARY STUART (1542-87) to France.

The lines

" Adieu, plaisant pays de France.
" O ma patrie
" La plus chérie ! " etc.

at one time attributed to her, were written by a journalist, G. Meusnier de Querlon (1702-80) who published them as hers in 1765 (*Dict. of Nat. Biog.*, vol. xxxvi, p. 389). Another version :

(*Adieu, France ! Adieu, France ! je pense ne vous voir plus.*" (Adieu, France ! Adieu, France ! I think that I shall never see you more.) Brantôme, vol. v, pp. 92-4.

Cf. " Adieu, charmant pays de France
" Que je dois tant chérir !
" Berceau de mon heureuse enfance
" Adieu ! te quitter c'est mourir."
Béranger, *Adieu de Marie Stuart.*
(Farewell, farewell, sweet land of France,
Enshrined in my heart !
Home of my childhood's happy hours,
Farewell ! 'tis death from thee to part).
also " Mary, Queen of Scots," Poem by Henry Glassford Bell. See Farewell, France, farewell, &c.

Adieu, mon cher Morand, je me meurs. (Adieu, my dear Morand, I am dying.)

VOLTAIRE (1694-1778)—Last words. Wagnière, *Relation du Voyage de M. de Voltaire à Paris en 1778, et de sa mort* (*Mémoires sur Voltaire*, etc. Longchamp and Wagnière, Paris, 1826, p. 163.)

Adieu, prince sans terre. (Adieu, landless prince.)

LAMORAL, COMTE D'EGMONT (1522-68)—when taking leave of WILLIAM OF ORANGE (1533-84) " the Silent," who had escaped from what he considered the murderous intentions of Philip II of Spain. Orange replied : " *Adieu, comte sans tête.*" (Adieu, headless count.) The Count is one of the principal characters in Goethe's tragedy of *Egmont.* See Farewell, Oxford without a head !

Ah ! c'est que vous ne savez pas combien il peut rester de bonheur dans trois arpents

de terre. (Ah ! you do not know how much happiness can remain in three arpents [3 to 4½ acres] of land.)

Saying of HELVETIUS'S widow (1719-1800) at Auteuil, to NAPOLEON (1769-1821), who was astonished at her cheerfulness in her reduced circumstances.

Ah ! c'est une spoliation véritable ; c'est une indignité. (Ah ! it's a downright spoliation ; it's an insult.)

LOUIS ADOLPHE THIERS (1797-1877)—alluding to the large amount (£200,000,000) of the war indemnity exacted by the Germans after the Franco-German War, 1870-1.

Ah ! le bon billet qu' a La Châtre ! (Ah ! what a fine promise La Châtre has !)

Remark by NINON DE LENCLOS (1620-1705) on remembering her written promise to remain faithful to the Marquis de La Châtre during his absence. Voltaire quotes the phrase as " . . . *le beau billet qu' a La Châtre ;*" in a letter to the Comtesse de Lutzelbourg, Sep. 14, 1753 ; also as " On sait l'aventure du *beau billet qu'a La Châtre*" in a letter *Sur Mlle. de Lenclos* à *M.* . . . (1751) (Cf. *Nouveaux mélanges philosophiques*, etc.) The anecdote is told by Saint Simon in ch. 151 of his *Mémoires*.

Ah ! pour Dieu, monsieur, n'ayez pitié de moi, mais plutôt de vous-même, qui combattez contre votre foi et votre roi. (Ah ! for God's sake, sir, don't pity me, but rather pity yourself, who are fighting against your religion and your king.)

Reply made by BAYARD (1475-1524) when mortally wounded (Apr. 30, 1524) in Italy, to the traitorous constable Charles de Bourbon. Said to be Bayard's last words. Another version is : " *Ce n'est pas moi qu'il* "*faut plaindre, mais vous, qui* "*combattez contre votre roi et votre* "*patrie.*" (It is not I who should be pitied, but you, who are fighting against your king and country.)

Ah ! sainte Vierge, ayez pitié de moi et recevez mon âme. (Ah ! holy Virgin, have pity on me and receive my soul.)

Dying words of CARDINAL MAZARIN, (1602-61), March 8-9, 1661.

Ah ! si je n'étais pas roi, je me mettrais en colère. (Ah ! if I were not a king, I should lose my temper.)

LOUIS XIV (1638-1715). (Dreux du Radier, *Tablettes hist. et anecdotes des rois de France*, vol.3, p. 199, 2nd edit.)

Ah ! si le roi le savait ! (Ah ! if the king knew it !)

Saying of the people, dating from, at least, feudal times, when oppressed by the nobles.

Ah ! s'il se fallait méfier de celui-là, en qui pourrait-on mettre sa confiance ? (Ah ! if *he* must be mistrusted, in whom could confidence be placed.)

Said by CARDINAL MAZARIN (1602-61) of Fabert (1599-1662) when doubts were cast upon the latter's fidelity.

Ah ! sire, la pluie de Marly ne mouille pas. (Ah ! sire, the rain at Marly does not wet anyone.)

Said by the CARDINAL DE POLIGNAC (1661-1741) to LOUIS XIV (1638-1715)

Ah, sire, qu'est-ce qui n'a pas soixante ans ? (Ah, sire, who isn't sixty ?)

Reply made by the MARÉCHAL DE GRAMONT (1604-78) to LOUIS XIV (1638-1715), on the latter complaining of being 60 years of age.

Ai-je donc sur les épaules la robe de Nessus? (Have I then on my shoulders the shirt of Nessus?)

Said by LAZARE HOCHE (1768-97)—referring to the spitting of blood at the beginning of his last illness.

A l'aide de deux axiomes : Tout est possible et tout le monde a raison. (By the help of two axioms: Everything is possible and everybody is right.)

Attributed to FONTENELLE (1657-1757) when asked how he had contrived to have so many friends and no enemies. Cf. "Whatever is, is right." Pope, *Essay on Man*, Epistle 4, l. 394, also Epistle 1, l. 294.

A la lanterne ! (To the street lamp !)

Cry of the populace during the Revolution in the ears of the 'aristocrats,' alluding to the '*lanterne de la Grève*,' a street-lamp hung against a gibbet, at the corner of the *rue de la Vannerie*, and the *place de la Grève*, where several summary executions took place. The expression owes its notoriety to the ABBÉ MAURY'S (1746-1817) reply to the mob who used it to him. He said : "*Eh bien ! quand vous m'aurez mis à la lanterne, y verrez-vous plus clair ?*" (Well, and when you have hanged me to the lamp, will you see any better there ?)

A l'immortalité. (To immortality.)

Motto of the FRENCH ACADEMY, established under Richelieu in 1635. Hence the surname of

"Immortels" applied to the members (40 in number).

Allez-vous-en, vous avez chacun gagné votre teston. (Go away, you have, each of you earned your teston. *)

(Claude Le Peletier, *Mémoire, etc., de Mr. Molé.*)

Said by President MATTHIEU MOLÉ (1584-1656) to the rioters who came to his house, after asking them what they wanted with him and getting no reply.

Allons, Danton, point de faiblesse ! (Come, Danton, no weakness !)

DANTON'S (1759-94) remark at the foot of the scaffold, after shedding a few tears at the thought of his wife. Preceded by : "*Oh, ma bien-aimée ! faut-il que je te quitte ?*" (Oh, my beloved ! must I leave thee ?) See Tu montreras ma tête &c.

Allons donc ! j'ai refusé mieux ! (How absurd ! I have refused better !)

Reply of BEAUMARCHAIS (1732-99) to the COMTE DE LA BLACHE'S challenge to fight. He was referring to the Duc de Chaulnes (? 1741-93)

Allons, petite créole, venez vous mettre dans le lit de vos maîtres. (Come, little creole, put yourself in the bed of your masters.)

Said, laughingly, by NAPOLEON (1769-1821) to JOSEPHINE (1763-1814) the day he took possession of the Tuileries (Feb. 19, 1800.) Cf. the remark of NÉPOMUCÈNE LEMERCIER (1771-1840) to NAPOLEON 4 years later, at the inauguration of the Empire : "*Vous vous amusez à refaire le lit des Bourbons ; vous n'y coucherez pas*"

*Small piece of money received each day by the rioters.

(You are amusing yourself by re-making the bed of the Bourbons; you will not sleep in it.)

Amis jusqu' aux autels (Friends as far as the altar.)

By FRANCIS I (1494-1547) to HENRY VIII (1491-1547) who pressed him to renounce the pope's authority.

Amis, souvenez-vous de Rocroy, de Fribourg et de Nordlingen! (Friends, remember Rocroy, Fribourg and Nordlingen!)

The GREAT CONDÉ (1621-86) is credited with having thus addressed his soldiers before the battle of Lens (Aug. 20, 1648), but the authenticity of the words is doubtful. In Mme. de Motteville's account of Condé's harangue (cf. her *Mémoires*, No. 38 of the *Collection Petitot*, 2nd series) there are no such words.

A moi Auvergne, voilà les ennemis. (Help, Auvergne, there's the enemy.)

Attributed to the CHEVALIER D'ASSAS (1738-60) by Voltaire (*Siècle de Louis XV*, ch. 33) but said by Grimm (*Mémoires inédits*, vol. 1, p. 188) to have been uttered by sergeant DUBOIS, belonging to his company, in the night of Oct. 15-16, 1760, at Clostercamp, when both perished. Grimm's version is: "A nous, Auvergne, c'est l'ennemi." (Help, Auvergne, it is the enemy) Cf. also Lombard de Langres, *Mémoires*, bk. 2, ch. 10 (vol 1, pp. 330-4) and Mrs. Hemans' poem *The Fall of d'Assas*.

A moi, mes amis, à moi! (Help, friends, help!)

Last words of JEAN PAUL MARAT (1744-93). *Hist. populaire de la France*, 1863, vol. 4, p. 136. Other versions are: "A moi, ma chère amie (mon amie), à moi!" Carlyle's version is as follows: "*A moi, chère amie*, help dear!" *The French Revolution*. bk iv, ch. I. (Charlotte Corday.)

Appuyez-moi contre cet arbre, et placez-moi de telle sorte que j'aie le visage tourné vers les ennemis. Jamais je ne leur ai tourné le dos ; je ne veux pas commencer en mourant, car c'est fait de moi. (Prop me up against this tree, and place me so that my face is turned towards the enemy. I have never turned my back to them ; I don't want to begin when I am dying, for all is over with me.)

Words used by the CHEVALIER BAYARD (1475-1524) when mortally wounded between Romagnano and Gattinara, Italy (Apr. 30, 1524.)

Après nous le déluge! (After us the deluge !)

MME. DE POMPADOUR (1721-64) to LOUIS XV after the battle of Rosbach (1757), to console the king. (p. xix of *Essai sur la Marquise de Pompadour*, by Desprez, prefacing *Mémoires de Mme. du Hausset*.)

"*A quoi bon vous tourmenter et vous rendre malade? après nous le déluge!*" (What is the use of worrying and making yourself ill? after us the deluge !) He had said, alluding to the resistance made by Parliament: "*Les choses, comme elles sont, dureront bien autant que moi.*" (Things as they are will last as long as I shall.)

Cf. "Il m'a raconté aussi que "peignant Mme. de Pompadour, le "roy, après l'affaire de Rosbach, "arriva fort triste, elle luy dit: qu' il "ne falloit point qu' il s'affligeât, "qu' il tomberoit malade, qu'au "reste, après eux le déluge." (He told me also that, when painting Mme. de Pompadour, the king, after the battle of Rosbach arrived very downcast, she said to him that he ought not to upset himself, that he would be ill, that for the rest, after them the deluge.) Ch. Desmaze, *Le Reliquaire de M. Q. de La Tour*: *Note de Mlle Fel sur de La Tour* (1874, p. 62)

Cf. "'Εμοῦ θανόντος γαῖα μιχθήτω πυρί." ("When I am dead let earth with fire be mingled.") ANON. (*Quoted by Suetonius, Nero*, 38.)

A quelle sauce voulez-vous être mangés? (With what sauce do you wish to be eaten?)

Concluding words of lines under a caricature directed against CALONNE (1734-1802) circulated in the reign of Louis XVI (1754-93).

Cf. Grimm's *Correspondance*, April, 17 /.

A qui donc parle-t-il? (To whom does he speak, then?)

FREDERICK THE GREAT of Prussia (1712-86) to D'ALEMBERT. The king asked whether d'Alembert had seen the king of France (Louis XV) "Yes, when presenting to him my reception speech at the French Academy."—"Well, what did he say to you?"—"He did not speak to me, Sire." Frederick then made the above remark. Chamfort, *Œuvres choisies*, p. 69. (A. Houssaye.)

Arrière-pensée. (Ulterior motive). Lit. Back-thought. *Magasin pittoresque*, vol. 8, p. 87.

Phrase attributed to the ABBÉ SIEYÈS (1748-1836), but also to be found in Destouches, *Le Dissipateur* (1736) act 5, sc. 9.

"Les femmes ont toujours quelque arrière-pensée." (Women have always some hidden thought) and, still earlier, in the *Discours politiques et militaires de* François de La Noue, *Discours* xxvi (Bâle, 1587.)

Au centre les ânes. (Donkeys to the centre).

Phrase used by the French soldiers in Egypt when forming their batal-lions into squares, into the centre of which the savants who accompanied the expedition, mounted on donkeys, were invited for protection. A friendly action on the part of the soldiers.

Aucun fiel n'a jamais empoisonné ma plume. (No gall has ever poisoned my pen.) *Œuvres de Crébillon*, 1818, vol 1, p. 13 of introduction and vol 2, p. 339.

In the speech (in rime) by CRÉBILLON (1674-1762) at his reception by the French Academy, Sep. 27, 1731.

Au nom de Dieu, Sire, faites la paix pour la France, moi je meurs. (In the name of God, Sire, make peace for France, *I* am dying.) *Revue des Deux Mondes*, April 15, 1857, p. 904.

Dying words of MARSHAL LANNES, duc de Montebello (1769-1809) to NAPOLEON. Mortally wounded at Essling, May 22, 1809; died nine days after. The words, as reported in the *Moniteur*, were "Sire, je meurs avec la conviction et la gloire d'avoir été votre meilleur ami. (Sire, I die with the conviction and the glory of having been your best friend).

Aux grands hommes la patrie reconnaissante. (Lit. To great men, the grateful country.—Erected in honour of great men by their grateful country.) (Decree of the Constitutional Assembly, Apr. 4, 1791.)

Inscription over the front of the *Pantheon français*, composed by the MARQUIS DE PASTOR ET(1756-1840).

Aux yeux d'un sage, les amis qui se refroidissent sont comme des meubles, qu' on change quand ils s'usent. (In a wise man's eyes, friends who grow old are like furniture that is renewed when worn out.)
FONTENELE (1657-1757).

Avec quatre aunes de drap, le roi peut faire en deux minutes un homme comme vous ; et il faut un effort de la nature et vingt ans de travail pour faire un homme comme moi. (With four ells of cloth the king can make a man like you in two minutes ; and it requires an effort of nature and 20 years' work to make a man like me.)
LEKAIN (1728-78)—to an officer who sought to humiliate him. See You have not to do with Holbein &c.

Avez-vous lu Baruch ? (Have you read Baruch ?) L. Racine, *Œuvres*, vol. 5, p. 156.
LA FONTAINE (1621-95), to whom Racine had lent a copy of the Bible which included the lesser prophets, said to him : *C'était un beau génie que ce Baruch ; qui était il ?* (That Baruch was a great genius ; who was he ?) The question has become proverbial, to express astonishment at anything which has greatly struck anyone.

A votre âge Napoléon était mort et vous ne serez que le Sieyès, d'une constitution mort-née. (At your age Napoleon was dead, and you will only be the Sieyès of a still-born constitution.) *Journal Officiel*, Débats parlementaires, p. 1636.
Words addressed by M. FLOQUET, president of the Council, to GENERAL BOULANGER (1837-91), June 4, 1888, alluding to a resolution, presented by the latter, for revision of the laws of the constitution.

Baiser Lamourette. (Lamourette kiss.)
Saying used to express a short-lived reconciliation, derived from the impression made by a speech of the ABBÉ ADRIEN LAMOURETTE (1742-94), July 7, 1792, causing political opponents to embrace each other. Three days after, however, the opposing parties were as great enemies as ever.

Béni serait le jour qui . . . (Blessed would be the day that . . .)
In a letter from GENERAL (then Colonel) BOULANGER (1837-91), dated May 8, 1880, to the ï JC D'AUMALE on the latter relinquishing command of the 7th corps. "Je serai toujours fier d'avoir servi un chef tel que vous, et *béni serait le jour qui* me rappellerait sous vos ordres." (I shall always be proud of having served under such a chief as yourself, and blessed would be the day that would again place me under your orders.)

Bien, nous n'aurons pas besoin de sable. (Good, we shan't want any sand [to blot with].)
JUNOT (1771-1813)—at the siege of Toulon (1793), Napoleon had just finished dictating a letter to Junot, (then only a sergeant) when a bullet covered it with earth, causing the above remark.

Bois ton sang, Beaumanoir, la soif te passera. (Drink thy blood, Beaumanoir, the thirst will pass off.)
Reply made by GEOFFREY DE BOVES to JEAN DE BEAUMANOIR, who, wounded, and tormented by

thirst, asked for drink. Combat
between thirty English and thirty
Bretons (March 27, 1351). *La
Bataille de trente Anglais et de
trente Bretons.*

**Bon roi, roi avare. J'aime mieux
être ridicule aux courtisans
que lourd au peuple.** (An
avaricious king is a good king.
I prefer being ridiculous to the
courtiers than oppressive to the
people.)
Saying of LOUIS XII (1462-1515).
He added : *Le menu du peuple est
la proye du gentilhomme et du soldat,
et ceux-ci sont la proye du diable.*
(The lower classes are the prey of
the gentleman and the soldier, and
these are the prey of the devil)

Brûler n'est pas répondre. (Burning is not replying.)—*Moniteur*, Jan. 10, 1794, p. 446.
Words quoted by CAMILLE DES-
MOULINS (1762-94) to ROBESPIERRE,
Jan. 7, 1794.—"*C'est fort bien dit,
Robespierre ; mais je te répondrai
comme Rousseau : 'Brûler n'est pas
répondre.'*" (It is very well said,
Robespierre; but I shall answer with
Rousseau that Burning, etc.). Grimm
(under date Sep. 15, 1762) says that
a brochure entitled *Mes doutes sur
la mort des jésuites* has been burnt
by order of Parliament, but that the
author [said to be the Abbé de
Caveirac] says, "*Brûler n'est pas
répondre.*"

**Ça fait tant de plaisir et ça
coûte si peu.** (That gives so
much pleasure, and costs so
little.)
Saying derived from a remark by
Mlle. GAUSSIN (d. 1767, aged 56),
a celebrated actress of the *Comédie-
Française.* "Que voulez-vous? cela
leur fait tant de plaisir, et il m'en
coûte si peu." (Under date Jan. 30,
1762)—Bachaumont, *Mémoires*, vol.
I, p. 34 note *a* (1777).

Also mentioned in Grimm's *Correspondance*, June 15, 1767, and Jan. 1778.

Ça ira. (That will succeed). See
(*La Révolution française*, pp.
513-29, June 4, 1899).
Title of a Revolutionary song
(1790), in France, the authorship of
which is uncertain. By some it is
attributed to DUPUIS (1742-1809),
by others to LADRÉ, a street singer.
The tune was taken from the *Caril-
lon National* (air de contredanse),
composed by BÉCOURT. It is said
that the expression is derived from
a saying of FRANKLIN (1706-90),
who, when asked what would become of the American Republic,
answered, "Ça ira, ça ira."—
Chronique de Paris, May 4, 1792,
p. 499. Franklin's words are given
as "Ça ira, ça tiendra" (That will
succeed, that will last), in G. de
Cassagnac's *Histoire des Girondins,
etc.* (É. Dentu) vol. I, p. 373.

**Camille, tu ne m'en veux pas ;
nous avons dès le commen-
cement défendu la même
cause ; je fais des vœux
pour que tu n'en sois pas
la victime ainsi que moi.**
(Camille, thou art not angry
with me ; we have defended
the same cause from the beginning ; I pray that thou
mayest not be the victim of it
as well as I.)
BARNAVE (1761-93) to CAMILLE
DESMOULINS, after being condemned to death by the revolutionary tribunal (1793).

Car tel est notre plaisir. (For
such is our pleasure.)
Formula appended to edicts, proclamations, orders, etc., of French
monarchs, and first used in the
reign (1461-83) of LOUIS XI. Sup-
pressed in the reign (1830-48) of
Louis-Philippe. The phrase under-
went various modifications in suc-

cessive reigns. Another form, often quoted, is " Car tel est notre bon plaisir," and there are instances of its use in the reign of Louis XVI. in 1787-8.

Catilina est aux portes de Rome et l'on délibère ! (Catilina is at the gates of Rome and you are deliberating !)

Honoré Gabriel Riquetti, COMTE DE MIRABEAU (1749-91)—in a speech to the Constituent Assembly. See Hannibal ad portas.

Ce fanfaron de crimes. (This boaster of crimes.)—St. Simon, *Mémoires*, vol. vi., p. 268. (Hachette).

LOUIS XIV (1638-1715)—of his nephew, the duc d'Orléans, afterwards Regent of France.

Ce gros garçon gâtera tout. (This fat fellow will spoil all.)

LOUIS XII. (1462-1515)—of his son-in-law, the comte d' Angoulème (afterwards Francis I.), who borrowed large sums on the strength of his royal relationship. See François Ier., apres tout &c.

Cela fera un bel effet. (That will have a fine effect.)—*Derniers momens*, p. 258.

GENERAL C.-F. DE MALET (1754-1812)—qn the road to the scaffold, when passing the place des Invalides, Paris, referring to the dome of the Hôtel des Invalides, then being gilded.

Cela ne va pas ; cela s'en va. (It doesn't go ; it's going away.)

FONTENELLE (1657-1757), when dying, was asked "Comment cela va-t-il ? " (How goes it ?) and replied as above—a *jeu de mots*.

Cela ne va pas si vite, Père Joseph. (Not so fast as that, Father Joseph.)

CARDINAL RICHELIEU (1585-1642) to PÈRE JOSEPH *à propos* of a military expedition, the latter making troops move on a map without taking obstacles into account. "Cela ne va pas si vite, Père Joseph ; où passeront les troupes ? " (Not so fast as that, Father Joseph ; where will the troops pass ?)

Ce livre est un ramas de chefs-d'œuvres. (This book is a heap of master-pieces.)

VOLTAIRE (1694-1778), when Frederick II (1712-86) was praising them, had said that not one of La Fontaine's fables would escape criticism if judged calmly. On reading them, however, he impatiently threw down the book saying the above words.

Ce mâtin-là remue tout Paris quand il prêche. (That rascal stirs all Paris when he preaches).

Said of BOURDALOUE (1632-1704) by a woman of the people, on seeing the crowd flocking to hear him preach.

Ce n'est pas moi qu'il faut pleurer, c'est la mort de ce grand homme. (It isn't for me that you should weep, but for the death of this great man.) *Mémoires de Saint Hilaire*, 1766, vol. i, p. 205.

SAINT HILAIRE, lieutenant-general of artillery—to his son. A bullet took off Saint Hilaire's arm and mortally wounded TURENNE, who fell dead (1675).

Ce n'est pas parler en roi. (That is not speaking like a king.)

BERNARD PALISSY, (1510-90) had embraced the Protestant faith and King Henry III, wishing to save him from the Leaguers, visited him in his prison to persuade him to be converted. "*Sire*," replied Palissy, "*vous m'avez dit plusieurs fois que vous aviez pitié de moi, mais, moi, j'ai pitié de vous qui avez prononcé ces mots : J'y suis contraint! Ce n'est pas parler en roi."* (Sire, you have several times told me you pitied me ; but I pity you who have uttered these words: I am compelled to do it ! That is not speaking like a king). Palissy died in prison at the age of 80 (1590).

Cependant, sire, la postérité distinguera toujours Louis le Grand de Louis le Gros. (Still, sire, posterity will always distinguish between Louis le Grand [Great] and Louis le Gros [Fat].)

Remark made by BOILEAU (1636-1711) to Louis XIV concerning the preference of the latter for the word *Gros* in place of *Grand*.

Ce sera la meilleure des républiques. (It will be the best of the republics.)—*Mémoires posthumes d'Odilon Barrot.*

Attributed to GENERAL LA FAYETTE (1757-1834) at his interview with the Duke of Orleans (afterwards Louis-Philippe), Aug. 1, 1830. The words ". . . c'est la meilleure des républiques" (it is &c.) are given in the *Moniteur universel* of Aug. 8, 1830, as having been said by Lafayette the day before, and M. Louis Blanc (*Histoire de dix ans*, vol. i, p. 347, 1841 edition) attributes to ODILON BARROT the phrase " *Le duc d'Orleans est la meilleure des républiques*" (The Duke of Orleans, &c) and as said on July 30, 1830, in reply to the republicans sent to the Hôtel de Ville by the Lointier meeting.

Ces gens tremblent, ils sont à nous. (These people tremble, they are ours.)

Attributed to the Duc ANNE DE JOYEUSE (1561-87), on seeing the king of Navarre's soldiers kneel down to pray before the battle of Coutras (1587). The duke thought they were on their knees for pardon.

CHARLES THE BOLD (1433-77) is said to have made a similar remark at the battle of Granson (1476) on seeing the Swiss kneel.

C'est à pareille époque que j'ai fait instituer le Tribunal révolutionnaire ; j'en demande pardon à Dieu et aux hommes. (It is at such a time that I have caused the revolutionary tribunal to be instituted ; I ask forgiveness for it of God and men.) H. Riouffe, *Mémoires d'un détenu* (Didot) p. 420.

DANTON (1759-94)—when awaiting the decision of the tribunal as to his own fate.

C'est assez de gémir sur la perte d'un fils dont je n'ai pas assez pleuré la naissance. (It is enough grieving over the loss of a son over whose birth I have not wept enough.)

MME. DE LA VALLIÈRE (c. 1642-1710) on learning the death of her son Louis de Bourbon, comte de Vermandois.

C'est bien, mais il y a des longueurs. (It is well, but there are lengthy portions.) *Esprit de Rivarol*, 1808, p. 161.

Reply by RIVAROL (1753-1801) when asked his opinion of a distich. Also attributed to TURGOT (1727-81).

C'est de la boue dans un bas de soie. (It is mud in a silk stocking.) Chateaubriand, *Mémoires d'outre tombe*, 1849, vol. 5, p. 402.

Attributed to LORD GRANVILLE, (1815-91) by Chateaubriand, alluding to TALLEYRAND.—In a footnote on the above-named page

Chateaubriand says, "J'affaiblis l'expression" (I soften the expression). Fournier (p. 424 note) says that the phrase is also attributed to Fox. C.-A. Ste-Beuve, in *M. de Talleyrand*, (Lévy, 1870, p. 37 note) gives it as "C'est un bas de soie rempli de boue" (It is a silk stocking filled with mud) and as having been said by LORD GRANVILLE, but that General Bertrand, in an account of a scene that he had witnessed between Napoleon and Talleyrand, added that the last words were: "Tenez, monsieur, vous n'êtes que de la m . . . . dans un bas de soie." (Look here, sir, you are only . . . in a silk stocking). The EARL OF LAUDERDALE (1759-1839), minister to France in 1806 is also credited with the phrase. All agree, however, that Talleyrand is alluded to.

C'est dommage de s'en aller ; ça commence à devenir amusant. (It is a pity to go away : it is beginning to be amusing.)

Death-bed utterance of JOSEPH-LOUIS GAY LUSSAC (1778-1850) —alluding to the various new scientific discoveries and inventions then being made.

C'est fini, messieurs, je pars pour le grand voyage. (It is ended, gentlemen ; I start for the great journey.)

GONTAUT-BIRON (1562-1602)— when condemned to death (beheaded, July 31, 1602). He is also said to have offered a glass of wine to the executioner, saying, "*Prenez, vous devez avoir besoin du courage au métier que vous faites.*" (Take some, you must need courage for the work you do)

C'est grand' pitie quand le valet chasse le maître. (It is a great pity when the valet turns out the master.)—L'Estoile.

ACHILLE DE HARLAY (1536-1616) chief president of the Paris Parliament, used these words to the DUC DE GUISE after the day of the Barricades when the victorious duke came to him in the hope of obtaining his adhesion.

C'est l'acteur qui m'empêche de vous entendre. (It is the actor who prevents my hearing you.) Goizet, *Hist. anecdotique, &c.* 1867, p. 56.

Attributed to ALEXIS PIRON (1689-1773). The poet was annoyed by some one next him humming all the tunes of Rousseau's *Devin du village* beforehand, and made an uncomplimentary remark. On the person in question asking whether this was addressed to him, Piron replied, "Oh, non ! monsieur, c'est à l'acteur, &c. (Oh, no sir, it is to the actor, &c.) A similar anecdote, however, is found in *Mélange amusant, &c.* vol 12, p. 452 (1829).

C'est le commencement de la fin ! (It is the beginning of the end !)

Attributed to TALLEYRAND (1754-1838) by Sainte-Beuve (see his work on *M. de Talleyrand*, ch. 3) alluding to the disasters of the Russian campaign, in 1812. Lockhart (in his Life of Napoleon, vol. 2, p. 205) also credits Talleyrand with the phrase, but Fournier (*L'Esprit dans l'Histoire*) says that it was suggested to him by M. de Vitrolles. Also quoted, *Voilà le commencement de la fin.* (There's the beginning of the end)

C'est le lapin qui a commencé. (The rabbit began it.)

The story goes that a dog passing through a market killed a rabbit and although its master offered to pay ten times the value of the rabbit, the rabbit's owner insisted on going before the police commissary. A boy, hearing the dispute, undertook for a consideration, to depose that the rabbit began it. The phrase attained equal popularity in Germany.

C'est magnifique, mais ce n'est pas la guerre (It is magnificent, but it is not war.)

GENERAL BOSQUET (1810-61), afterwards marshal of France, referring to the charge of the Light Brigade at Balaclava, Oct. 28, 1854.

C'est ma guerre à moi. (It is *my* war.)

Attributed to the EMPRESS EUGÉNIE (b. 1826) wife of Napoleon III, referring to the declaration of war between France and Germany in 1870. It is said, however, that it originates from a remark made by a politician at the time : *C'est la guerre à l'impératrice.* (It is the Empress's war)

C'est nous qui sommes des ancêtres. (It is we who are ancestors.) *Le Clairon*, March 11, 1882.

Attributed to MARSHAL SOULT (1769-1851), the Duc de Montmorency having said to him, " Vous êtes duc, mais vous n'avez pas d'ancêtres." (You are a duke, but you have no ancestors) " C'est vrai," replied Soult, " c'est nous," &c. (That is true, it is we, &c.,) Another version (A. Combes, *Hist. &c.*, *de Soult*, 1869, p. 102) gives the phrase as " Est-ce que je ne suis pas un ancêtre, moi ?" (Am *I* not an ancestor ?)

C'est par la gloire que les peuples libres sont menés à l'esclavage. (It is through glory that free nations are brought to slavery.)

CHATEAUBRIAND (1761-1848)— in the French Chamber, March 2, 1818. Cf. Fabre d' Eglantine, *Le*

Triomphe de Grétry : " *Le cri d'un peuple libre est celui de la gloire.*" (A free people's cry is that of glory).

C'est par le travail qu' on règne. (It is by work that one reigns.)

Saying of LOUIS XIV (1638-1715).

C'est plus qu'un crime, c'est une faute. (It is more than a crime, it is a blunder.)

Attributed both to JOSEPH FOUCHÉ (1763-1820) and TALLEYRAND* (1754-1838), referring to the death of the duc d'Enghien, who was tried by court-martial at 11 p.m., one day, found guilty and condemned to death at 2 a.m., and shot between 4 and 5 a.m., the next morning (Mar. 21, 1804). Fouché, in his *Mémoires*, says : " Je ne fus " pas celui qui osa s'exprimer avec " le moins de ménagement sur cet " attentat contre le droit des nations "et de l'humanité. 'C'est plus qu'un " crime, dis-je, c'est une faute ! ' " paroles que je rapporte parce " qu'elles ont été répétées et attri- " buées à d'autres." (I was not he who dared to express himself with the least moderation regarding this violation of the rights of nations and of humanity. " It is more than a crime, I say it is a blunder !" words that I record because they have been repeated and attributed to others) Napoleon, in his *Mémorial*, refers to ' Fouché as being the Talleyrand " of the clubs, and Talleyrand, the " Fouché of the Salons.' Ste. Beuve, *M. de Talleyrand* (1870) ch. 2. p. 79, quotes the phrase as " C'est *pire* qu'un crime, c'est une faute " and (pp. 79-80) says that he has been assured that it was in reality uttered by BOULAY (de la Meurthe). Boulay de la Meurthe, in *les Dernières anneés du duc d'Enghien*, says (referring to his execution) " Dans ce milieu où depuis long-

*But see *Histoire des deux Restaurations*, vol, I, p. 92, 1858.

"temps on se mêlait tout bas de
"juger Bonaparte, l'impression qui
"prévalut aussitôt fut celle d'une
"faute commise." (In this circle
where for a long time they had
taken upon themselves to judge
Bonaparte in whispers, the impression which at once prevailed was
that of a mistake committed) Cf.
"Il y a de mauvais exemples qui
"sont pires que les crimes : et plus
"d'états ont péri parce qu' on a violé
"les mœurs que parce qu' on a violé
"les lois." (There are bad examples
which are worse than crimes : and
more states have perished because
morality has been sinned against
than because laws have been broken).
Montesquieu, *Grandeur et Décadence
des Romains*, ch. viii. Also "Si
"comme vous le dites, Bonaparte
"s'est rendu coupable d'un crime,
"ce n'est pas une raison que je me
"rende coupable d'une faute."—
(If, as you say, Bonaparte has been
guilty of a crime, that is no reason
why I should become guilty of a
mistake) Lady C. J. Blennerhassett,
Talleyrand, Eine Studie, ch. 14
(Berlin, 1894, p. 324).

**C'est que vous n'avez pas été
sous la baguette du magicien.**
(You have never been under the
influence of the magician's wand.)
WILLIAM PITT (1759-1806)—in
reply to a Frenchman who expressed
his astonishment that a moral nation
like England should submit to be
governed by a man so wanting in
private virtue as Charles James Fox.

**C'est toujours avec un nouveau
plaisir. . .** (It is always with
renewed pleasure. . .)
Favourite expression of LOUIS
PHILIPPE (1773-1850)—much ridi-
culed in the newspapers, notably *La
Caricature*, May 16, 1833.

**C'est une croix de bois qui a
sauvé le monde.** (It is a
cross of wood that has saved
the world.) Chateaubriand,
Mémoires d'outre-tombe, vol. 3,
p. 235.
In a speech by MONTLOSIER
(1755-1838) to the Constituent Assembly (Nov. 2, 1789).

**C'est une médisance, sire, il n'y
a pas de jour que je ne fasse
au moins trois fois le tour de
mon cousin d'Aumont.** (It is
a slander, sire, not a day passes
but what I walk at least three
times round my cousin d'Aumont.)
Joking reply by the DUC DE
VIVONNE (1636-88) to Louis XIV,
who reproached him, in the presence of the DUC D'AUMONT (who
was very fat, like Vivonne) with
not taking enough exercise.

**C'est un grand diable d'Anglais
sec, qui va toujours droit devant lui.** (He is a tall thin
devil of an Englishman, who
always goes straight forwards.)
A Bourbon queen of Spain's * sar-
casm against JAMES FITZJAMES,
Duke of Berwick (1670-1734) her
untractable marshal. Cf. George
Darley's preface to the works of
Beaumont & Fletcher (1840).

**C'est un sale coup pour la fan-
fare ! †** (It is a great blow for
the band.)
Reported to have been said by a
captain of tirailleurs at Weissenburg,
Aug. 4, 1870, on seeing the musi-
cians decimated by the fire of the
Bavarians.

**C'est vous qui êtes le nègre ? Eh
bien, continuez !** (It is you
who are the "nègre" Well,
go on !)

---

* Probably Marie Louise Gabrielle de
Savoie (1688-1714) married to Philip
V. of Spain in 1701.

† i.e., military brass band.

Remark made by MARSHAL MACMAHON (1808-93) to a pupil at Saint Cyr at a review (see the Abbé L. C. Berry's biography of Mac-Mahon (1895, p. 64). The word "nègre" (= negro) is applied at Saint Cyr to the first pupil of his year. Unfortunately, it appears that the pupil addressed was a mulatto, and the term pursued him to such an extent that he at last sent in his resignation (cf. *Le Gaulois*, March 4, 1898).

Cet homme sera pendu, mais la corde cassera. (That man will be hanged, but the rope will break.)

SOPHIE ARNOULD (1744-1803)— of BEAUMARCHAIS.

Cette femme apprend à penser à ceux qui ne s'en aviseraient point ou qui l'avaient oublié. (That woman teaches to think those who would not dream of doing so or who had forgotten it.)

NAPOLEON (1769 - 1821) — of MME. DE STAËL.

Cette poutre durera plus que vous et moi. (This beam will last longer than you and I.)

Answer made by the DUC DE SULLY (1560-1641) to Henri IV, who sent for his three ministers, Villeroi, President Jeannin and Sully, in turn and pointed out to each a beam that seemed in danger of falling, to shew a Spanish ambassador their respective characters from their remarks. Villeroi said : "*Sans doute ; il faut la raccommoder, je vais donner des ordres.*"—(Of course, it must be repaired, I'll go and give instructions). Jeannin said : "*Il faudra s'en assurer.*" (It must be attended to). Sully said : "*Eh ! Sire, y pensez vous ? cette poutre durera plus que vous et moi.*" (Do you think so, sire ? this

beam will last longer than you or I). *Chamfort.*

Chacun chez soi, chacun pour soi. (Everyone in his own home, everyone for himself.)

Attributed, as a political maxim, to M. DUPIN (1783-1865) (Dec. 6, 1830), but he in his Memoirs (vol. 2, pp 267-9) claims to have said instead : "Chacun chez soi, chacun son droit." (Everyone in his own home, everyone his rights).—*Moniteur universel*, Dec. 8, 1830, p. 1648. The question before the Chamber of Deputies was whether France should assist Poland.

Chauvinisme. (Chauvinism, i.e., Jingoism.)

Term applied to an exaggerated patriotism, derived from the name (Chauvin) of one of the principal characters in a vaudeville *la Cocarde tricolore*, by Théodore and Hippolyte Cogniard (acted in 1831). The definition given in the 1878 edition of the dictionary of the French Academy is as follows : " *Terme très familier, qu'on a employé pour chercher à tourner en ridicule un sentiment exalté de la gloire des armes françaises.*" (Very familiar term, which has been used to turn into ridicule an exalted sentiment of the glory of the French arms)

Cherchez la femme. (or Où est la femme ?) (Find the woman. [or where is the woman ?])

Attributed to GABRIEL DE SARTINE (1729-1801) lieut.-general of police in 1759. Cf.

M. Jackal.—Que dis-je toujours, monsieur Salvator ? "Cherchez la femme !" Cette fois, la femme est trouvée.

Mme. Desmarest.—Comment, la femme est trouvée ? vous croyez qu'il y a une femme dans cette affaire ?

M. Jackal.—Il y a une femme

dans toutes les affaires; aussitôt qu'on me fait un rapport, je dis: "Cherchez la femme!" On cherche la femme et quand la femme est trouvée . . .

Mme. Desmarest.—Eh bien?

M. Jackal.—On ne tarde pas à trouver l'homme.

(*M. Jackal.*—What do I always say, monsieur Salvator? "Look for the woman!" This time the woman is found.

Mme. Desmarest.—What, the woman is found? you think there is a woman in this case?

M. Jackal.—There is a woman in every case; as soon as a report is made to me, I say: "Look for the woman!" The woman is sought for, and when she is found . . .

Mme Desmarest.—Well?

M. Jackal.—The man is soon found.)—Dumas, *Les Mohicans de Paris*, act 3, sc. 7. (5th tableau).

"Nulla fere causa est in qua non femina litem
Moverit: accusat Manilia, si rea non est." (Juvenal, sat. 6, ll. 242-3.) (There is hardly any matter about which a woman will not stir up a law-suit: if she is not defendant, Manilia is plaintiff).

"Such a plot must have a woman in it."
RICHARDSON, *Sir Charles Grandison*, letter 24 (1753).

Also A. Dumas, *Les Mohicans de Paris*, vol. 3, ch. x and xi.

Clameur (or cri) de Haro.

Phrase referring to a formula formerly in use in Normandy and used in Jersey to this day. "*Ha Ro à l'aide, mon prince.*"

(*Aa* or *Ha* is the exclamation of a person suffering, *Ro* is the Duke Rollo's name abbreviated) The phrase being said three times by the party aggrieved, the aggressor attempted anything further at his peril. Used at the funeral of William the Conqueror. (For an account of the scene see the Harleian MS. Some say that *Haro* is derived from the Celtic verb *haren* (to cry for assistance); *harau*—help. Only as recently as March 4, 1890, the formula was used in Guernsey (cf. The Morning Post, March 5, 1890) "Haro! Haro! Haro! A l'aide mon Prince! On me fait tort!" (Haro! Haro! Haro! Help, my Prince! I am being wronged.) Cf. "Haro and help, and hue and cry, every true man!"—Sir Walter Scott, *Kenilworth*, ch. xxiv. also P. Bourget, *Etudes et Portraits*, vol ii, p. 92.

Clemént, juge inique, je t'ajourne a comparaître dans quarante jours devant le tribunal du souverain juge. (Clement, iniquitous judge, I summon you to appear in forty days before the tribunal of the sovereign judge.)

Last words attributed to JACQUES DE MOLAY (c. 1244-1313 or 1314) last Grand Master of the Order of Templars. It is said that he summoned both the pope (CLEMENT V— c. 1264-1314) and the king (PHILIPPE LE BEL— 1268-1314).

Combien faut-il de sots pour faire un public? (How many fools are necessary to make a public?)

In Chamfort's *Caractères et Anecdotes* (vol 4, pp. 217-8) there is an anecdote of someone not named, who used these words, when the public was spoken of as having a different opinion to his own concerning a certain work. See Thirty millions, mostly fools.

Comme ami, je vous offre mon bras, comme maître, je vous promets justice. (As a friend,

I offer you my arm; as a master, I promise you justice.)

In a letter written Nov. 8, 1597, by HENRI IV (1553-1610) to DUPLESSIS-MORNAY. The above, although not the exact words used, are a *résumé* of the letter. A similar remark is also attributed to LOUIS XIV (1638-1715) in *Ménagiana*, vol. 3, p. 134 (1715 edition) *à propos* of a courtier who had received an offence.

Comment peut-on être Persan! (How can one be a Persian!)

A saying expressing astonishment at the appearance of anyone, not even being a European. Allusion to *Les Lettres persanes* written by Montesquieu (1689-1755) published in 1721.

Comme un seul homme. (As one man.)

Oft-quoted saying, the original of which is uncertain or unknown.

Courage, Père Joseph, Brisach est à nous. (Courage, Father Joseph, Brisach is ours.)

Said by CARDINAL RICHELIEU (1585-1642) to PÈRE JOSEPH, who was dying, at the Château de Ruel, when Brisach was capitulating.

Dans les révolutions, le pouvoir reste toujours dans les mains des petits; mais il vaut mieux être né pauvre pêcheur que de gouverner les hommes. (In revolutions the power always remains in the hands of nobodies; but it is better to be born a poor fisherman than to govern men.)

DANTON'S (1759-94) reflection when taken back to prison, after being sentenced to death. He added: "Les insensés! ils crieront: Vive la république! en me voyant marcher à l'échafaud." (The fools! they will cry: Long live the re-

public! when seeing me walk to the scaffold). *Derniers momens*, p. 201.

Débarrassons nous de ce qui nous gêne. (Let us rid ourselves of what troubles us. *Journal Officiel, Débats parlementaires*, p. 1057.

In a speech by M. MADIER DE MONTJAU in the chamber of Deputies, June 10, 1886, on the subject of members of families having reigned in France.

Défiez-vous des premiers mouvements; ils sont presque toujours bons. (Mistrust first impulses; they are nearly always good.)

Cynical saying sometimes attributed to TALLEYRAND (1754-1838), but really belonging to Count Montrond. (Capt. Gronow's *Recollections and Anecdotes*—Count Montrond)

Déjà, monseigneur? (Already, my lord?)—Louis Blanc, *Histoire de dix ans*, vol 5, p. 290.

It is said that LOUIS PHILIPPE (1773-1850) when visiting TALLEYRAND (1754-1838) shortly before his death (May 1838) used the above words. The king asked if he suffered and Talleyrand replied "Oui, comme un damné." (Yes, like the damned.) The anecdote, however, appears to be an invention, so far as concerns Talleyrand and the king; and *L'improvisateur*, Salentin (1804) relates the same story of BOUVARD, a learned doctor (1717-87) who remarked "*Déjà!*" of a patient, the archbishop of Reims (Monseigneur de la Roche-Aymond) when told that he was suffering "*comme un damné.*" —De Levis, *Souvenirs et portraits*, p. 241.

De l'audace, encore de l'audace,

toujours de l'audace. (Audacity, still audacity, audacity always.) *Moniteur*, Sep. 4, 1792.

In a speech by DANTON (1759-94), Sep. 2, 1792. He added, "*et la France est sauvée*" (and France is saved.) When reproached with his audacity, Danton said: "L'audace individuelle est, sans "doute, repréhensible; mais "l'audace nationale, dont j'ai tant "de fois donné l'exemple, est "permise, et je m'honore de la posséder." (Individual audacity is, of course, reprehensible; but national audacity, of which I have so many times given the example, is permissible, and I honour myself for possessing it.) *Derniers momens*, p. 200. GAMBETTA (1838-82) used the expression "*Du travail, encore du travail, et toujours du travail!*" (Work, still work, and work always!) in a speech at Versailles, June 24, 1872.

De plus fort en plus fort, comme chez Nicolet. (Stronger and stronger, as at Nicolet's).

A popular saying, alluding to the way in which NICOLET (1710-96) arranged his entertainments (Boulevard du Temple, Paris.)

Des choses et non des mots. (Things and not words.) Motto of LAZARE HOCHE (1768-97).

Devant un homme comme vous, je ne suis plus une femme comme moi. (In presence of a man like you, I am no longer a woman like myself.)

Reply of SOPHIE ARNOULD (1744-1803) to the lieutenant of police's enquiry who were the people who had supped at her house. Sophie did not remember. —'A woman like you ought to remember such things,' said he. To this she replied, 'Yes, but,' etc. Another account credits CORBINELLI (who lived to be more than 100) with having made a similar reply to the lieutenant of police d'Argenson (? 1652-1721) when questioned as to a supper, 1697, where he was present and at which songs were sung about Mme. de Maintenon. ". . . *devant un homme comme vous, je ne suis pas un homme comme moi.*"

Dieu ait votre âme; vous nous avez fait maints maux et douleurs (May God receive your soul; you have caused us many ills and griefs.)

Words uttered by RENE II, DUC DE LORRAINE (1451-1508) on visiting the body of CHARLES LE TÉMÉRAIRE which was found at a little distance from Nancy on Jan. 7, 1477. *Chronique de Jean de Troyes.*

Dieu a-t-il donc oublié ce que j'ai fait pour lui. (Has God then forgotten what I have done for him.)

LOUIS XIV (1638-1715)—after the battle of Malplaquet (Sep. 11, 1709).

Dieu est toujours pour les gros bataillons (God is always on side of the big battalions.)

Attributed to TURENNE (1611-75) by Joseph de Maistre. Cf. "Dieu est d'ordinaire pour les gros escadrons contre les petits."—Bussy Rabutin *Lettres*, iv, 91, Oct. 18, 1677. (God is usually for the big battalions against the little ones.) "Le nombre des "sages sera toujours petit. Il est "vrai qu'il est augmenté; mais ce "n'est rien en comparaison des "sots, et par malheur on dit que "Dieu est toujours pour les gros "bataillons." (The number of wise men will always be small. It is true that it has increased; but that is nothing compared with the fools,

7

and unfortunately it is said that God is always on the side of the big batallions.)—Voltaire, *Letter to M. Le Riche*, Feb. 6, 1770. Cf. " Wise men and Gods are on the strongest side."—Sir C. Sedley, *Antony and Cleopatra*, act 4, sc. 3 (1677, p. 38.) ; also " Deos fortioribus adesse (dixit)" (" The gods fight on the side of the stronger.") Tacitus, *History* IV, 42. See One, on God's side, is a majority.

Dieu et la liberté (*or* **Dieu et liberté**) (God and Liberty.)

VOLTAIRE (1694-1778)—to B. Franklin's grandson, in 1778, when asked to give him his blessing. Some say that he spoke in English. T. J. Duvernet, Vie de Voltaire, 1787, p. 300. See God and liberty.

Dieu, je te prie que tu fasses aujourd' hui pour la Hire autant que tu voudrois que La Hire fît pour toi s'il était Dieu et que tu fusses La Hire. (Oh, God, I pray thee do to-day for La Hire as much as you would like him to do for thee, if he were God and thou wert La Hire.)

Prayer attributed to LA HIRE (Etienne de Vignolles) (1390-1442) before a combat after receiving absolution from the chaplain. —*Chronique dela Pucelle.* CARLYLE (in his *Life of Frederick the Great*, bk. xv, ch. 14), credits LEOPOLD, PRINCE OF ANHALT-DESSAU (1676-1747) with a similar prayer before a battle : " Oh God, assist our side : at least, avoid assisting the enemy, and leave the result to me."

Dieu m'a confié l'honneur des Polonais, je ne le remettrai qu' à Dieu. (God has confided Poland's honour to me, I will only deliver it up to God !) Ch. Deulin, *l'Esprit public*, June 24, 1862.

A grenadier named Antoine Deleau, at the Prefecture du Nord, June 30, 1862, claimed to have heard these words uttered by PRINCE JOZEF ANTON PONIATOWSKI (1762-1813) at Leipsic, as he plunged into the Elster. The same person also affirmed that he heard CAMBRONNE repeat—" La garde," &c. (q. v.) twice.—*Journal des Débats*, July 7, 1862.

Dieu seul est grand, mes frères ! (God alone is great, my brethren !).

First words of the funeral sermon on LOUIS XIV, preached by J. B. MASSILLON (1663-1742).

Diviser pour regner. (Divide, to reign).

Machiavelian maxim put in practice by CATHERINE DE MÉDICIS (1519-89) and by LOUIS XI (1423-83) (See also Qui nescit dissimulare &c), but existing as a Latin one, " *Divide et impera.*" Voltaire has written " Dissimuler, vertu de roi et de femme de chambre." (To dissimulate, virtue of kings and chambermaids). —Cf. " Diviser pour régner : voilà sa politique." (Divide to reign : that is his policy). Voltaire, *Don Pèdre*, act 4, sc. 2.

Donnez-moi quelques lignes de l'écriture d'un homme, cela me suffira pour le faire pendre. (Give me a few lines of a man's hand-writing, that will be sufficient for me to get him hanged).

Saying attributed to CARDINAL RICHELIEU (1585-1642) (see Mme. de Motteville's Memoirs, (1723, vol i, p. 58) *à propos* of the chevalier de Jars'* case) although M. Fournier, in his *Esprit dans l'histoire*, credits either LAFFÊMAS or LAUBARDEMONT (Richelieu's instruments) with it. Mme. de. Motteville's version is ". . . *selon les manières même du cardinal, qui, à ce que j'ai oui conter à ses amis. avait accoutumé de dire qu' avec deux lignes de l'écritnre d'un homme on paurrait faire le procès au plus innocent.*" (. . . according to the methods of the cardinal himself, who, as I have heard his friends tell, was in the habit of saying that with two lines of a man's handwriting, an accusation could be made against the most innocent.) Another version is "Qu'on me donne six lignes écrites de la main du plus honnête homme, j'y trouverai de quoi le faire pendre." (Give me six lines written by the hand of the most honest man, I will find enough in them to hang him).

Donnez-moi un remède pour la fatigue, mais que ce remède ne soit pas le repos. Give me a remedy for fatigue, but let not that remedy be rest).
LAZARE HOCHE (1768-97)—to his doctor (1797). He died Sep. 18, 1797.

Du sublime au ridicule il n'ya qu'un pas. (There is only one step from the sublime to the ridiculous.) Abbé de Pradt, *Histoire de l'ambassade dans le Grande-duché de Varsovie en 1812* (1815 ed., p. 215), also, Mme. de Rémusat, *Mémoires* (1880, vol. 3, p. 56).
Favourite saying of NAPOLEON (1769-1821) ; also attributed to TALLEYRAND (1754-1838). Cf. "En général, le ridicule touche au

sublime."—Marmontel, *Éléménts de littérature.*—(1787, vol 5. p. 188).
"Le magnifique et le ridicule sont si voisins qu'ils se touchent."—(The magnificent and the ridiculous are so near each other that they touch).—Fontenelle, *Dialogues des Morts Anciens et Modernes, I* (*Scarron*). "One step above the sublime makes the ridiculous, and one step above the ridiculous makes the sublime again."—Thos. Paine, *Age of Reason*, pt. 2. ad fin. (note) "Du fanatisme à la barbarie il n'y a qu'un pas. (There is only one step from fanaticism to barbarity). Diderot, *Essai sur le Mérite et la Vertu. Dédicace.*

Du temps que j'étais roi ! (At the time when I was king !)
LOUIS XIV (1638-1715)—on his death-bed. Died Sep. 1, 1715.

Ecrasez l'infâme ! (Crush the infamous thing !)
Phrase often used by VOLTAIRE, (1694-1778) at the end of his letters, especially in the year 1762 and after. Sometimes he abbreviated it to "Ecr. l'inf." In a letter to D'ALEMBERT (1717-83) dated Nov. 28, 1762, he explains that by "infâme" he refers to superstition. "Vous pensez bien que je ne parle "que de la superstition : car pour "la religion chrétienne, je la respecte "et l'aime comme vous" . . . (You know that I only speak of superstition : as for the Christian religion, I respect it and love it as you do.)

Eh bien ! je n'avais pas oublié de vous obliger, mais j'avais oublié que je l'eusse fait. (Well ! I had not forgotten to oblige you, but I had forgotten that I had done so.)
Attributed to FONTENELLE (1657-1757) when spoken to on the subject of a service which he at first thought he had forgotten to render.

---

* François de Rochechouart, chevalier de Jars, was condemned to death in 1633 and was already on the scaffold when his pardon arrived (died 1670).

Eh bien, mes enfants, qu'est-ce que c'est? du canon? Eh bien! ça tue ça tue, voilà tout! (Well, boys, what is it? cannon? Well! that kills, that kills, that's all!)

M. DE SAINT-PERN—at the battle of Minden (1757), to the corps of the grenadiers of France (exposed to a severe fire from a battery), to induce them to be patient.

Eh! ne le tourmentez donc pas tant! Il est plus bête que méchant. (Don't torment him so! He is more stupid than wicked.)

Said by LA FONTAINE's (1621-95) nurse—during his last illness, to the priest who was urging him to repent.

Eh! qui nous fera grâce à nous? (Who will pardon us, eh?)

Attributed (but contradicted) to E. CLAVIER (1762-1817), magistrate and Hellenist, *à propos* of the trial of GENERAL MOREAU, in reply to Napoleon, who wished him to be condemned, promising to pardon him afterwards. Cf. *la Revue rétrospective* (2nd series), vol. 9, p. 458.

Elle me gêne. (It [the crown] is uncomfortable.)

LOUIS XVI, (1754-93), at his coronation at Reims (1774). On learning that he was king (May 10, 1774) he cried: "O mon Dieu, quel malheur pour moi." (O my God, what a misfortune for me.)

Elles s'embrassent, elles se baisent, elles se disent adieu pour ne se revoir jamais. (They embrace, they kiss, they say good-bye, never to see each other again.)

GUILLAUME BAUTRU, comte de Serrant (1588-1665)—of a group of two figures, Justice and Peace embracing each other.

Elles sont trop fortes, elles grossissent les objets. (They are too powerful, they magnify objects.)

Remark by LOUIS XV (1710-74) —on a visit to the printing-works of the Minister for War, after reading a paper in praise of himself with some spectacles lying near.

Embrassons-nous, si nous pouvons. (Let us embrace each other if we can.)

Said, on returning from a journey, by the DUC DE VIVONNE (1636-88) —to his sister MME. DE THIANGES. Both were very stout.

Empoignez-moi cet homme-là. (Seize me that man.)

COLONEL DE FOUCAULT, instructed to expel M. MANUEL from the Chamber of Deputies, Mar. 4., 1823, used the expression "Empoignez-moi M. Manuel." (Seize me M. Manuel). *Hist. des deux Restaurations*, vol. 6, p. 320. (1858). The same evening an actor used the words "Empoignez-moi cet homme-là" with great effect in a piece then being played, but was arrested and passed the night at the prefecture of police for his temerity. — Bouffé, *Mes souvenirs* (1880), p. 60 and following.

Enfans, je suis votre roi, vous êtes François, voilà l'ennemi; donnons! (Children, I am your king, you are Frenchmen, there are the enemy; let us charge!)

HENRI IV (1553-1610)—to his troops before the battle of Ivry (Mar. 14, 1590). See Ralliez-vous à mon panache blanc.

Enfin je vais me mesurer avec ce Vilainton. (At last I am going to cross swords with this Vilainton [Wellington].)

Attributed to NAPOLEON (1769-1821)—on the morning of the battle of Waterloo (June 18, 1815).

Enrichissez-vous ! (Enrich yourselves !)

In a speech by FRANÇOIS GUIZOT, (1787-1874) minister for foreign affairs, March 1st, 1843. "A "présent, usez de ces droits, fondez "votre gouvernement, affermissez "vos institutions, éclairez-vous, en-"richissez-vous, améliorez la con-"dition morale et matérielle de notre "France," etc. (Now, use those rights, establish your government, make firm your institutions, enlighten yourselves, enrich yourselves, improve the mental and physical condition of our France, etc.) *Le Moniteur*, March 2, 1843, p. 345. Guizot, *Histoire parlementaire de France*, vol. 4, p. 68. *Guizot* is also credited with having used the phrase "Enrichissez-vous "par le travail et par l'économie" (Enrich yourself by work and economy), to the electors in Normandy.

En voulez vous des z'homards ? (Do you want any lobsters ?)

A stupid line of a song 'created' by DUFOR at the Moulin Rouge (Paris) in 1895. It was for a long time in everybody's mouth.

Epée dont la poignée est à Rome et la pointe partout. (Sword of which the hilt is at Rome and the point everywhere).

Phrase used by ANDRÉ M. J. DUPIN (1783-1865) in the *Procès de tendance*, Nov. 26, 1825, but Rousseau quotes it (in a letter written to Brossette Mar. 25, 1716) as occurring in a book *Anti-Coton, ou Réfutation, &c., du Père Coton*, 1610, p. 73. The *mot* is there attributed to a "Polonois" (Pole). Rousseau writes "J'ay vu dans un "petit livre, *l'Anti-Coton*, que la

"Societé de Jésus est une épée dont "la lame est en France et la poignée "à Rome." (I have seen in a little book, the Anti-Coton, that the Society of Jesus is a sword of which the blade is in France and the hilt in Rome). Cf. also Diderot, *Œuvres choisies*, 1856, p. 298. Cf. also "C'est une sphère "infinie dont le centre est partout, "la circonférence nulle part." (It [Nature] is an infinite sphere, whose centre is everywhere, the circumference nowhere.) Pascal, *Pensées*, De la grandeur. . . la miserè des hommes, article 6, § iv.

Est-ce qu'on emporte sa patrie à la semelle de ses souliers ! (Is one's country to be carried away on one's shoe soles !)

DANTON'S (1759-94) reply, when he was advised to flee from France.

Est-il heureux.[1] (Is he lucky).

Saying of CARDINAL MAZARIN (1602-61). It was his first question when it was proposed that anyone should enter his service. Cf. *Mémoires, fragments historiques, &c.* published in 1832 by Busoni, p. 332.

Est-il permis de se faire remplacer ? (Is anyone allowed to take my place ?)

Question put by the CHEVALIER DE CHAMPESNETZ (1759-94) on being sentenced to death.

Et qu'êtes-vous allé faire là-bas, Monsieur ?—apprendre à penser,[2] Sire.—Les chevaux. (And what did you go to

---

[1] (Cé qui veut dire habile, adroit, industrieux, which means clever, adroit, industrious.) [Note by Ch. Barthélemy, *Erreurs et Mensonges historiques*, 10th series, p. 265].
[2] Penser = to think; and Panser = to dress wounds, &c. The King's reply was as if the latter word had been used.

do there, Monsieur? To learn
to think, Sire.—Horses.)

Louis XV (1710-74) is said to
have asked the above question of, and
received the above reply from
M. de Lauraguais, who had
returned from a journey to London
Authenticity denied by the prince de
Ligne (see *Œuvres choisies*, vol 2,
p. 342), but confirmed by Beaumarchais in a letter to M. de
Lauraguais. (de Loménie, *Beaumarchais et son temps*, 1856, vol 2,
p. 272.)

**Etre malheureux pendant quatre-
vingt-dix ans! car je suis
sûr que je vivrai jusque là.**
(To be unfortunate during 90
years! for I am sure that I
shall live as long.)

Louis XV (1710-74)—at the death
of Mme. de Châteauroux (1717-
44).

**Et vous, qui en êtes l'auteur, je
vous le pardonne.** (And you,
who are the cause of it, I
forgive you.)

Dying words of the Duc de
Guise (1519-63)—addressed to Admiral Coligny. Brantôme, vol 1, p.
435 (Pantheon edition). Montaigne
(Essays, bk. 1, ch. 23) relates an anecdote of the duc de Guise at the siege
of Rouen in 1562, in which a similar
sentiment is uttered by him to an
conspirator, "gentilhomme angevin,
ou manceau" (a gentleman of Angers
or Anjou or of Le Mans).

Excusez du peu! used ironically.
(Excuse the small quantity.)

Written by Rossini (1792-1868)
on the manuscript of a hymn to the
Emperor, composed specially for
the occasion and performed July
1st, 1867. The words referred to
the noise of bells and cannon
with which the piece concluded.
E. Rimmel, *Souvenirs de l'Exposi-
tion* (1868), p. 16.

**Faites comme eux, vous étiez
dessous, mettez-vous dessus.
Voilà la révolution.** (Act
like them, you were under-
most, put yourselves uppermost.
There's revolution.)

Reply by Danton (1759-94)
—when consulted as to what to do
with the aristocrats.

Faites des perruques. (Make
perukes.)

Saying used in the sense of Ne
sutor supra crepidam (Shoemaker,
stick to your last)—alluding to a
phrase repeated several times in a
letter from Voltaire (1694-1778)
to Charles André, a hairdresser,
who asked the former's opinion of a
tragedy he had written: "Monsieur
"André faites des perruques" was
the refrain of the letter.

**Faites-moi de bonne politique,
je vous ferai de bonnes fin-
ances.** (Only govern well and
you shall have sound finance.)

Form in which a *mot* of Baron
Louis (1755-1807) has become
popular. M. Guizot in his *Mémoires
pour servir à l'hist. de mon temps*,
vol. i, p. 44 (1858) says, quoting the
baron, "Gouvernez bien, vous ne
dépenserez jamais autant d'argent
que je pourrai vous en donner."
(Govern well, and you'll never be
able to spend as much money as I
shall be able to supply you with.)
In "*An account of a conversation
concerning a Right Regulation of
Governments for the common good of
Mankind.*" In a Letter to the
Marquis of Montrose, the Earls of
Rothes, Roxburg, and Haddington,
from London, the 1st of December,
1703, by Andrew Fletcher of Sal-
toun (1655-1716)—the dialogue described in the text as between
Fletcher himself, the Earl of
Cr[o]m[a]rty, Sir Ed[ward] S[ey]-
m[ou]r, and Sir Chr[istopher]

M[u]sgr[a]ve—occurs the following :
" I said, I knew a very wise man so
much of Sir Chr[istopher]'s sentiment, that he believed if a man were
permitted to make all the ballads,
he need not care who should make
the laws of a nation." (cf. The
Political Works of Andrew Fletcher,
London, 1737 ; also *Dict. Nat.
Biog.*, vol. xix, p. 295).

**Faites, sire, ce sacrifice ; c'est
un dernier trait de ressemblance avec votre divin
modèle.** (Make this sacrifice,
sire ; it is a last trait of resemblance to your divine model
[Jésus Christ].)

Advice given by the ABBÉ EDGE-
WORTH DE FIRMONT (1745-1807),
an Irish ecclesiastic, to LOUIS XVI,
when about to have his hands tied
before his execution (1793). He is
credited with having said to Louis
XVI at the foot of the scaffold :
Fils de saint Louis, montez au ciel ;
(Son of St. Louis, ascend to Heaven.)
but denied having any recollection
of these words (appearing in the
Républicain français the day following the execution). Another version
(*Mémoires de la duchesse d'Angou-
lême*) gives : *Allez, fils de saint
Louis, les portes de l'éternité vous
sont ouvertes ;* (Go, son of St. Louis,
the gates of eternity are open to
you) but this is no more likely than
the first. A third (in No. 192 of
the *Révolutions de Paris* (March 9-
16, 1793) is " *Allez, fils aîné de
Saint Louis, le ciel vous attend.*"
(Go, eldest son of St. Louis, heaven
awaits you.) E. Fournier (*L'Esprit
dans l'histoire*) affirms that the expression was invented by CHARLES
LACRETELLE (1766-1855),who in his
work *Dix années d'épreuves* (1842,
p. 134), says that he (Lacretelle) was
the first to quote it. A letter from
Miss Edgeworth, the abbé's sister,
o one of her friends, written Feb.

10,1793(published in the*Dutensiana*
pp. 213-8) thus quotes the abbé's
words: " *Sire, c'est encore un sacrifice
que vous avez à faire pour avoir un
nouveau trait de ressemblance avec
votre divin modèle.*" (Sire, it :
another sacrifice that you have to
make to have a new trait of resem
blance to your divine model.) The
following is from the *Dernières
heures de Louis XVI*, by the Abbé
Edgeworth de Firmont, Son Con
fesseur, pp. 124-5, vol. 9, of the
Bibliothèque des Mémoires (Barri
ére) : "Sire, lui dis-je avec larmes,
dans ce nouvel outrage je ne vois
qu'un dernier trait de ressemblance
entre votre majesté et le Dieu qui va
être as récompense." (Sire, said I in
tears, in this new outrage I only see
a last trait of resemblance between
your majesty and the God who is
going to be your reward.) For the
king's last words as there given,
see Je meurs innocent etc.

**Fi de la vie ! qu'on ne m'en parle
plus.** (Out upon life ! don't
talk of it to me any more.)

Last words of MARGARET OF
SCOTLAND (1425-45) wife of Louis
XI of France. Another version :
" Fi de la vie de ce monde ! ne
m'en parlez plus " (Beaucourt, *Hist.
de Charles VII*, iv, pp. 104-10).
Dict. Nat. Biog. vol. xxxvi, p. 138.

**Fils de saint Louis, montez au
ciel.**

See Faites, sire, ce sacrifice, etc.

Fin de siècle. (End of the century.)

Phrase often used towards and until the end of the nineteenth century.
Title of a play by MM. Micard and
de Jouvenot, produced at the
Château-d'Eau (Paris) Apr. 17,
1888.

**Fourbe il a vécu, fourbe il a voulu
mourir.** (Knave he has lived,

and knave he has chosen to
die.)
Said, by the courtiers, of CARD-
INAL MAZARIN (1602-61), when
dying.

**François Ier, après tout, n'était
qu'un héros de tournois, un
beau de salon, un de ces
grands hommes pygmées.**
(Francis I, after all, was only a
tournament hero, a drawing-
room beau, one of those pigmy
great men.)

NAPOLEON (1769-1821)—of Francis I. See Ce gros garçon gâtera
tout.

Frappe, mais va-t-en. (Strike,
but go away.)

Reply made by CHAPELLE (1626-
86)—to a lord at dinner, when the
latter threatened to cane the poets
who had satirised persons of quality.
A parody of the *mot* of Themistocles
Πάταξον μὲν, ἄκουσον δέ (which
see).

Frères, il faut mourir! (Brothers
we must die!)

Saying of the monks of La
Trappe when at the point of death
—*not* whenever they meet each
other, as alleged by Chateaubriand.

Fusillez-moi tous ces gens-là!
(Shoot me all those people!)

Attributed to PAUL ARMAND
CHALLEMEL-LACOUR (1827-1896),
but denied. He is said to have
written these words on a report
sent by him to General Bressolles
concerning the conduct of a
battalion of mobiles, near Lyons,
in Sept. 1870.

**Général, pourquoi versez-vous
des larmes? Je suis heureux
de mourir pour mon pays.**
(General, why do you shed
tears? I am happy to die for my
country.)

Dying words of F.-S. Desgraviers,
GENERAL MARCEAU (1769-96),

mortally wounded near Altenkirchen,
to GENERAL JOURDAN (1762-1833),
whose retreat he protected.

**Général, vous êtes grand comme
le monde!** (General, you are as
great as the world!)

GENERAL KLEBER (1753-1800)—
to NAPOLEON, seizing him round
the waist, at the battle of Aboukir
when the Turkish army was
destroyed (July 1799).

**Gonzalve menace de m'ôter un
reste de vie si vous ne, vous
rendez promptement. Mon
ami, regardez-moi comme
un homme déjà mort, et
faites votre devoir.** (Gonzalvo
threatens to take what remains
of my life if you do not surrender at once. My friend,
consider me as already dead;
and do your duty.)

Instructions given by JACQUES DE
LA PALICE (appointed Marshal in
1515, died 1525) to his lieutenant
Cornon. La Palice being wounded
in the head, was made prisoner by
the Spaniards (1503) when the town
of Ruvo fell into their hands, and
as the citadel still held out, Gonzalvo
threatened him with death if he did
not give his lieutenant orders to
surrender. Being led to the foot
of the ramparts he spoke to Cornon
as above. J. d'Authon, *Annales de
Louis XII.*

**Grâce aux prisonniers, Bon-
champ l'ordonne!** Pardon for
the prisoners, Bonchamp commands it!)

Dying words of the MARQUIS DE
BONCHAMP (1759-93) wounded
before Clolet, Oct. 17, 1793—referring to the republican prisoners
(numbering about 5,000) who were
going to be killed.

**Grands cœurs, cessez d'aimer,
ou je cesse d'écrire.** (Noble

hearts, cease to love, or I cease to write.)

In a speech by A. DUMAS FILS at the French Academy (Aug. 2, 1877) on the subject of prizes for virtue. A parody of the first line of Boileau's 8th epistle (1677) alluding to Louis XIV (1638-1715.) " *Grand roi, cesse de vaincre, ou je cesse d'écrire.*" (Great king, cease to conquer or I cease to write.)

Grattez le Russe, vous trouverez le Cosaque. (Scratch the Russian, you'll find the Cossack [Tartar].)

Attributed to NAPOLEON (1769-1821) Cf. " Plusieurs de ces " parvenus de la civilisation ont " conservé la peau de l'ours, ils " n'ont fait que la retourner, mais " pour peu qu'on gratte, le poil se " retrouve et se redresse." Quoted as said by the ARCHBISHOP OF TARENTE, CAPÈCE-LATRO (1744-1836) (Several of these *parvenus* of civilisation have retained the skin of the bear, they have only turned it, but however little it is scratched, the hair is there all the same and stands up again.) de Custine, *La Russie en* 1839 vol, 2 p. 308. Also : Zieht man einem solchen Gallier die weisse haut ab, so hat man einen Turco vor sich. (Strip off the white skin from such a Gaul, and you will find a Turco.) By PRINCE BISMARCK (1813-98.)

Guerre aux châteaux et paix aux chaumines. (War against castles and peace towards cottages.)

Motto proposed by CHAMFORT (1741-94) to the soldiers of the Republic. See Mort aux tyrans, paix aux chaumines. Quoted by J. Berchoux in his *Epître politique et galante à Ephrosine de N* . . .

" Guerre aux châteaux, paix aux chau- mières,
" Attendu que dans ces dernières,
" Le pillage serait sans prix."
(War against castles and peace towards cottages, Seeing that in these last, Pillage would be worthless.)

In the *Edinburgh Review,* Apr. 1800 (p. 240 note) the phrase " Guerre aux châteaux, paix à la chaumière " is ascribed to Cordorcet (1743-94). Thiers (*Hist. de la Rév. Française,* 1846, vol, 2, p. 283) credits Joseph Cambon (1754-1820 with it. In Lamartine's *Hist. des Girondins,* 1847, Merlin (1754-1838) is represented as exclaiming in the Assembly : " Déclarez la " guerre aux rois et la paix aux " nations." (Declare war against kings and peace to nations.)

Hé! Hé! sire, c'est le treizième (Eh! Eh! sire, it's the thir- teenth.)

Attributed by V. Hugo to TALLEY-RAND (1754-1838)—when taking the oath of allegiance to LOUIS-PHILIPPE.

Hélas! je n'en suis pas digne (Alas! I am not worthy of it.)

Dying words of CARDINAL RICHELIEU (1585-1642) in reply to a request to give those round him his blessing.
Cf. *Journal de ce qui s'est fait, etc à la mort de feu Mgr. de Richelieu,* etc. Biblio. nat. L b 36, No. 3315, pp. 2-3.

Henri IV fut un grand roi, Louis XIV fut le roi d'un beau regne. (Henry IV was a great king, Louis XIV was the king of a fine reign.)

ABBÉ VOISENON (1708-75). Cf. *Œuvres,* vol 4, p. 121). Cf. Vol- taire's letter to Mme. du Deffand, Sep. 23, 1752, in which he says (à propos of Louis XIV): " C'était, avec ses défauts, un grand roi ; son siècle est un grand siècle." (He was, with his faults, a great king ; his century is a great century.)

Honny soit qui mal y pense.
(Evil be to him who evil thinks [of it].)

Attributed to EDWARD III (1312-77), and is the motto of the Order of the Garter established by him in 1349 (April 23). Sir W. Scott, *Essay on Chivalry*. The popular tradition ascribes the origin of this Order to the picking up by the king of the Countess of Salisbury's garter at a ball, he remarking : " Those who laugh will be proud to wear a similar one," but the incident is of doubtful authenticity. Cf. Shakspere's *Merry Wives of Windsor*, act 5, sc. 5.

Il a été tué ! j'avais toujours dit que cet homme-là était plus heureux que moi. (He has been killed ! I always said that that man was more fortunate than I.)

Attributed (but discredited) to the DUC DE VILLARS (1653-1734) the priest having said that God had given him (Villars) time to prepare himself, while the Maréchal · de Berwick (1670-1734) had been killed before Phalsbourg by a cannon ball.

Il aurait un meilleur usage à en faire. (He could put it to a better use.)

Dying words of TALLEYRAND (1754-1838)—May 1838, after being informed that the Archbishop of Paris had said that he would give his life for M. de Talleyrand.

Il avait été a la peine, c'était bien raison qu' il fut a l'honneur (It had borne the brunt, it was only right that it should have the honour.)

Reply made by JOAN OF ARC (1412-31), when asked by her captors

why her standard was carried at the coronation of Charles VII at Reims, (July 17, 1429), rather than those of the other captains.

Il est bon que de chez lui un souverain puisse voir la maison du pauvre. (It is well that from his palace a sovereign should be able to see the house of the poor.)

DE ROUGEMONT (   )—alluding to the Louvre, Charles X (1757-1836) and the Hôtel Dieu respectively. Rougemont is also credited by Fournier (*L'Esprit dans l'Histoire*) with having invented the phrase La garde meurt, etc. (q.v.)

Il est mort aujourd'hui un homme qui faisait honneur à l'homme. (There has died to-day a man who did honour to mankind.)

GENERAL MONTECUCULLI (1608-81)—of MARSHAL TURENNE. The former was killed by a cannon-ball at Salsbach (July 27, 1675).

Il est mort guéri. (He died cured.)

DELON, a medical mesmerist, with regard to one of his patients who had died, when reminded of the promise he had made to cure him. *Œuvres de Chamfort*, p. 129 (1852).

Il est permis en littérature de voler un auteur pourvu qu' on le tue. (In literature it is permissible to rob an author provided he is killed.)

Attributed to MOLIÈRE (1622-73).
Cf. " Most writers steal a good thing when they can,
" And when 'tis safely got 'tis worth the winning.
" The worst of 't is we now and then detect 'em,
" Before they ever dream that we suspect 'em."

Barry Cornwall, *Diego de Montillo,*

iv. See On reprend son bien ou on le trouve.

Il est peu de distance (*or* il n'y à qu' un pas) du Capitole à la Roche Tarpéienne. (There is but a little distance from the Capitol to the Tarpeian Rock).

Words used by MIRABEAU (1749-91) in a speech to the Constituent Assembly (May 22, 1790).

" Et moi aussi, on voulait, il y a "peu de jours, me porter en "triomphe ; et l'on crie maintenant "dans les rues : *La grande trahison* "*du Comte de Mirabeau !* . . . Je "n'avais pas besoin de cette leçon "pour savoir qu' *il n'y a qu'* "*un pasdu Capitole à la roche* "*Tarpéienne !*" (And they wanted a few days ago to carry me too in triumph ; and now they cry *Great treason of Count Mirabeau,* in the streets ! . . . I did not need this lesson to know that, etc.) *Le Moniteur Universel,* May 24, 1790.

Note.—The Tarpeian rock is the rock from which criminals guilty of treason were precipitated and is near the Capitol where victors were crowned. The comparison is used to indicate that triumph is often followed by a fall.

Cf. " La roche Tarpéienne est près du Capitole." (The Tarpeian Rock is near the Capitol.) Jouy, *La Vestale,* act 3, sc. 3 (written 1807.)

Il est plus difficile d'entrer ici que d'y etre reçu. (It is more difficult to enter here than to be received here [i.e. to be elected a member].)

Joking remark by PIRON (1689-1773) —in a crowd, trying to obtain admission to a *séance* of the French Academy.

Il est temps que je fasse ce que j'ai tant de fois prêché aux autres. (It is time for me to do what I have so many times preached to others.)

Said by BOURDALOUE (1632-1704)—feeling death approaching.

Il est trop tard ! (It is too late !)

Reply by ODILON BARROT (1791-1873), to MM. de SÉMONVILLE (1759-1839) and D'ARGOUT, Charles X's envoys (expressing the opinion of the provisional government and La Fayette). *Mémoires posthumes d'Odilon Barrot.* Sometimes attributed to LA FAYETTE (1757-1834).

Il faut avouer que nous avons un grand roi. (It must be admitted that we have a great king.)

Phrase probably derived from the following remark by MME. DE SEVIGNÉ (1626-96). *Il faut avouer que le roi a de grandes qualités.* (It must be admitted that the king has some great qualities.) Bussy-Rabutin, *Hist. amoureuse des Gaules* vol. 1, pp. 309-10 (1856).

Il faut bin qu' Arnoul daîne. Il faut bien qu' Arnoul dîne. (Arnoul must have his dinner.)

By the wife of ARNOUL COCAULT, a well-known notary, to the PRINCE DE CONDÉ (1588-1646) in the year 1611.—The latter was made to wait until the former had dined. Neither husband nor wife knew who thei distinguished visitor was until afterwards.

Il faut quitter tout cela ! (I must leave all this !)

Words used by CARDINAL MAZARIN (1602-61) shortly before his death, which took place March 8-9, 1661. He added : " *Et encore cela ! Que j'ai eu de peine à acquérir toutes ces choses ! puis-je les abandonner sans regret ? . . . Je ne les verrai plus où je vais !* (And that also ! What trouble I have had to collect all these things ! can I leave them without regret ? . . . I shall see them no more where I am going !) Afterwards he said to the Comte de Brienne (1635-98) "*Ah! mon pauvre ami, il faut quitter tout cela! Adieu! chers tableaux que j'ai tant aimés, et qui m'ont tant coûté!*" (Ah! my poor friend, I must leave all this! Adieu, dear pictures that I have loved so dearly, and which have cost me so much!)—Comte de Brienne, *Mémoires*, etc.

Il faut tout prendre au sérieux, mais rien au tragique. (Everything should be taken seriously, but nothing tragically.)

LOUIS ADOLPHE THIERS (1797-1887) May 24, 1873, the day of his political defeat. *Journal Officiel*, May 25, 1873.

Il faut user des amis comme des meubles, que l'on change quand ils sont usés. (Friends should be used like furniture, changed when worn out.)

Saying attributed to FONTENELLE (1657-1757), but of doubtful authenticity. Cf. Dr. Johnson's saying: "If a man does not make new acquaintance as he advances through life, he will soon find himself left alone. A man, sir, should keep his friendship in constant repair."

Il faut vouloir vivre et savoir mourir. (We should wish to live and know how to die.)

Maxim of NAPOLEON (1769-1821) and repeated by him in May, 1805, after seeing Raynouard's (1761-1836) tragedy, *Les Templiers*.

Il m'arrive un grand malheur : hier Marat a dit du bien de moi. (A great misfortune has happened to me : yesterday Marat spoke well of me).

Reply of PIERRE VERGNIAUD (1759-93) to A. GENSONNÉ, a Girondist leader, who asked why he seemed depressed.

Il me bat dans la chambre, mais il n'est pas plutôt au bas de l'escalier que je l'ai confondu. (He beats me in the room, but he is no sooner at the bottom of the stairs than I have confounded him.)

PIERRE NICOLE (1625-95) of M. DE TRÉVILLE. The latter was a good talker, but the former was not. See I always get the better when I argue alone.

Il ne faut plus de bavards, il faut une tête et une épée. (We want no more talkers, we must have a head and a sword.)

ABBÉ SIEYÈS (1748-1836)—when he felt that it was time to prepare the *coup d'état* of le 18 brumaire, an VIII (Nov 9, 1799). The head was himself, the sword, Bonaparte.

Il neige ; nous n'aurons pas la révolution. (It snows ; we shall not have the revolution.)

M. ANISSON (1776-1852)—on the night of the 22nd Feb. 1848, putting his head out of the carriage-window. Authority of Mrs. Austin who was riding with him, in Paris. Sir M. E. Grant Duff, *Notes from a diary*, vol 1, p. 194.

Il ne s'agit pas de vivre, mais de partir. (It is not a question of living, but of departing.)

Reply made by MARSHAL SAXE (1696-1750), April 1745, when about starting to take command of the French Army in the Netherlands, to VOLTAIRE (1694-1778) who reminded him of his bad state of health.

Il n'est pas juste que j'expose un homme d'esprit comme moi contre un sot comme lui. (It is not just that a man of sense like myself should risk death at the hands of a fool like him.)

A saying of MIRABEAU (1749-91) when challenged to a duel.

Il n'est pas nécessaire de connaître quelqu'un pour lui ôter son chapeau. (It is not necessary to know anyone to take off your hat to him.)

MARSHAL CATINAT (1637-1712) —to a young man who came to ask his pardon for having treated him unceremoniously, not knowing who he was.

Il n'oserait! (He would not dare!) Sometimes quoted Ils n'oseraient. (they would not dare!)

Written by the DUC DE GUISE (1550-88) at the foot of a note found by him under his serviette at table (Dec. 22, 1588). The note, which he threw under the table, contained these words:—
"Donnez-vous de garde, on est "sur le point de vous jouer un "mauvais tour." (Take care, they are on the point of doing you a bad turn.) During the evening, his cousin the duc d'Elbeuf, told him that an attempt would be made next day on the life of the Catholic princes; he laughingly advised him to go to bed as he himself intended doing, adding:—
"Je vois bien, mon cousin, que "vous avez regardé votre almanach, "car tous les almanachs de cette "année sont farcis de telles "manaces." (I see clearly, cousin, that you have looked at your almanac, for all this year's almanacs are full of such threats.) The next day the duc de Guise was assassinated.

When Henri III. (1551-89) was assured that his great enemy was indeed no more, he came out from his cabinet, sword in hand, and exclaimed, spurning the corpse with his foot: "Nous ne sommes plus "deux! Je suis roi maintenant!" (There are no longer two of us! Now I am king!) After looking at the body a little time Henri said .

"Mon Dieu, qu'il est grand! Il "paraît encore plus grand mort que "vivant." (My God, how tall he is! He seems taller dead than alive.)—Journal de L'Estoile. See Morte la bête, mort le venin.

Il n'y a de nouveau que ce qui est oublié. (Nothing is new but what is forgotten.)

MLLE. BERTIN, a celebrated modiste, to MARIE ANTOINETTE (1755-93). The queen asked whether the model of a costume was quite new, for she thought she had seen a drawing of it in some old engravings. Cf.
"... Nothing is thought rare
"Which is not new, and followed; yet we know
"That what was worn some twenty years ago
"Comes into grace again." ...
J. Fletcher,
The Noble Gentleman. Prologue, ll. 4-7.
Also Il n'y a de nouveau que ce qui a vieilli. (Nothing is new but what has grown old). Motto of the *Revue rétrospective* 1st series, published in 1833. Also
"There n'is no newe guise, that it n'as old."
Chaucer, *The Knight's Tale*, Tyrwhitt's edition, vol. I, p. 66, l. 2127.
"... and there is no new thing under the sun." Ecclesiastes i, 9.

Il n'y a pas de question sociale. (There is no social question).

Favourite saying of LÉON GAMBETTA (1838-82). In his speech at Belleville, May 26, 1870, occur the words:—"car cette unité que l'on appelle la question sociale n'existe pas." (for the unity that is called the social question does not exist.) *Le Rappel*, May 28, 1870.
And in another at Havre, April 18, 1872:—"Croyez qu'il n'y a pas de remède social parce qu'il n'y a pas une question sociale." (Be sure

that there is no social remedy because there is no social question). *Le Rappel*, April 22, 1872.

Il n'y a plus de Pyrénées. (There are no more Pyrenees.)

Attributed by Voltaire (*Siècle de Louis XIV*, ch. 28) to LOUIS XIV (1638-1715) (but authenticity doubtful)—on the occasion of declaring Philip, duke of Anjou, king of Spain (Nov. 16, 1700), under the title of Philip V.

The *Journal du marquis de Dangeau* (vol. vii, p. 419) credits the Spanish ambassador with the words which probably gave rise to the above saying, namely :—

"L'ambassadeur d'Espagne dit fort "à propos que ce voyage * devenoit "aisé, et que présentement les "Pyrénées étoient fondues." (The Spanish ambassador said very *à propos* that this journey became easy and that now the Pyrenees had melted away.)

The poet Malherbe (1555-1628), however, previously used the words "aplanir les Pyrénées". (to remove, or smooth away, the Pyrenees.) Cf.

". . . Mountains interposed
"Make enemies of nations, who had else,
"Like kindred drops, been mingled into
one."
Cowper, *The Task*, bk. ii (The Timepiece).

Il n'y a plus une seule faute à commettre. (There is now not a single mistake left to make.)

LOUIS ADOLPHE THIERS (1797-1877), in a speech to the *Corps législatif*, Mar. 14, 1867, alluding to foreign affairs.—*Le Moniteur universel*, Mar. 15, 1867, p. 295.

Il n'y a point de héros pour un valet de chambre. (No one man is a hero to a valet.)

MME. CORNUEL (1605-94). Cf.

---

* Alluding to the permission given Nov. 16, 1700, by the new king of Spain to the young courtiers to follow him there.

Lettres de Mlle. Aïssé (Aug. 13, 1728), 5th édition p. 161. Cf.

"Il faut être bien héros pour l'être aux yeux de son valet de chambre." (It is necessary to be indeed a hero to be one to one's valet.) Said by the MARÉCHAL DE CATINAT (1637-1712).

The following occurs in Montaigne's *Essais*, bk. iii, ch. xi :—

"Tel a esté miraculeux au monde, "auquel sa femme et son valet n'ont "rien veu seulement de remarquable, "peu d'hommes ont esté admirez "par leurs domestiques," etc. (A man may astonish the world, an dhis wife and his valet see nothing even remarkable in him; few men are admired by their servants, etc.)

Cf. also A prophet is not without honour, *save in his own country, and in his own house.* St. Matthew, xiii, 57.

Heinrich Heine (1800-56) is reported to have remarked, when the above saying was quoted to him, That is not because the hero is not a hero, but because the valet is a valet.

Cf. Οὐ τοιαῦτά μοι ὁ λασανοφόρος σύνοιδεν.

(The carrier of my night-stool has not so good an opinion of me.)

ANTIGONUS THE ELDER (382-301 B.C.), King of Sparta—reply to verses by Hermodotus comparing him to the Sun and styling him a god.

Il n'y a point de place faible là où il y a des gens de cœur. (No place is weak where there are brave hearts.)

CHEVALIER BAYARD (1475-1524) —when it was proposed to destroy Mézières and ravage the neighbourhood to starve the enemy, Mézières being considered unable to sustain a siege. Bayard who had a horror of devastation replied "*il n'y avait "point de place faible là où il y avait* "*des gens de cœur pour la défendre.* (no place was weak where there were brave hearts to defend it.) He assembled soldiers and citizens, made them swear to fight to the death and gaily ended his harangue by saying: "*Si les vivres nous* "*manquent, nous commencerons* "*par manger nos chevaux, puis* "*nous salerons et mangerons . . . .* "*nos valets.*" (If our provisions do not hold out, we will begin by eating our horses, then we will salt and eat . . . . our servants.) The siege was raised at the end of five weeks (Sep. 17, 1521), and the question was asked of the Duke of Nassau on his return to the Netherlands, "*Eh quoi! vous aviez* "*quarante mille hommes et cent* "*pièces d'artillerie, et vous n'avez* "*pu prendre Mézières, un pigeon-* "*nier?*" (What! you had 40,000 men and a 100 pieces of cannon, and you could not take Mézières, a pigeon-house?) The Duke replied: "Le pigeonnier était gardé par un "aigle et par des aiglons autrement "becqués et membrés que toutes "les aigles de l'Empire." (The pigeon-house was guarded by an eagle and eaglets with beaks and limbs differing from all the eagles of the Empire.)—History of the Chevalier sans peur et sans reproche (Bayard) by the Loyal Serviteur (1527).

Il n'y a que les morts qui ne reviennent* pas. (It is only the dead who do not come back.)

In a speech by BERTRAND BARÈRE DE VIEUZAC (1755-1841) in the Convention, May 26, 1794, alluding to the English. *Le Moniteur*, May 29, 1794; also *Mémoires de Barère*, 1842, vol. 2, p. 120.

---

* (A *revenant* is a ghost.)

Il n'y a rien à dire; la strophe est belle. (There is nothing to be said; the stanza is fine.)

VOLTAIRE (1694-1778)—on hearing some lines by LEFRANC DE POMPIGNAN (in his *Ode sur J. B. Rousseau*.) Lefranc and Voltaire were literary enemies.

This is the stanza:

"Le dieu, poursuivant sa carrière, "Versait des torrents de lumière "Sur ses obscurs blasphémateurs.

(The god, pursuing his onward career, Poured floods of light On his obscure blasphemers.)

Il n'y a rien de changé en France, il n'y a qu'un Français de plus. (Nothing is altered in France, there is only one more Frenchman.)

Phrase put by TALLEYRAND in the mouth of the COMTE D'ARTOIS afterwards Charles X (1757-1836) (although never uttered by him) on the occasion of his entry into Paris (Apr. 12, 1814) and forming the concluding words of a speech composed for the newspapers [1] (as being made by the comte d'Artois) by the COMTE BEUGNOT (1761-1835), minister of the interior at the time. "Plus de divisions: la paix et la "France; je la revois, et rien n'y "est changé, si ce n'est qu'il s'y "trouve un Français de plus." (No more divisions: peace and France; I see it once more, and nothing is changed, unless it is that there is one more Frenchman.) On reading in the *Moniteur* the account of his entry into Paris, the comte d'Artois exclaimed "Mais je n'ai pas dit cela." (But I never said that.) It was pointed out to him that it was necessary that he should say it and the phrase remains historical.[2] *Revue rétrospective* (2nd series) vol.

---

[1] Le Moniteur universel, April 13, 1814.
[2] Memoirs du comte Beugnot. 1866, vol. 2, pp. 112-4.

9, p. 459. Also quoted "Rien "n'est changé en France, si ce n'est "qu'il s'y trouve un Français de plus." (Nothing is altered in France, unless it is that there is one more Frenchman.)

Il reviendra ! (He will return !)

Popular cry, dating from end of May, 1887, when General Boulanger (1837-91) left the ministry of War—*Le Soleil*, July 10, 1887. In 1814, Napoleon being at Elba, the soldiers used to console themselves by repeating "*Il reviendra.*"

Ils chantent, ils payeront. (They sing, they will pay.)

CARDINAL MAZARIN (1602-61) —when new taxes provoked new satirical songs. (*L'Encyclopédie Méthodique du XVIIIe siècle*, p. 63.) " . . . . tant mieux, reprenait "le cardinal, s'ils cantent la canson-nette, ils pagaront." . . . . (. . . . so much the better, resumed the cardinal, if they sing songs, they will pay.)

Note—The spelling indicates the cardinal's Italian accent.

Voltaire's version is—" Laissons "les dire et qu'ils nous laissent "faire." (Let them talk and let them let us do.)—*Letter to M. Hénin*, Sep. 13, 1772. See Je laisse tout dire, etc. The cardinal also said : "La nation française est la plus "folle du monde : ils crient et "chantent contre moi, et me laissent "faire ; moi, je les laisse crier et chanter, et je fais ce que je veux." (The French people are the maddest in the world : they cry out and sing against me and let me act ; I let them cry out and sing and I do what I like.) *Nouvelles lettres de la duchesse d'Orléans* (née princesse Palatine), 1853, p. 249.

Il se mettra en chemin un peu tard, mais il ira plus loin qu'un autre. (He will begin

his career rather late, but he will go further than another.)

CARDINAL MAZARIN (1602-61)— of LOUIS XIV. Followed by : Il y a en lui de l'étoffe pour faire quatre rois et un honnête homme. (There is in him the making of four kings and an honest man).—*Lettres de Guy Patin*, vol 2, pp. 192-223, also St. Simon, *Mémoires*, vol. 24, p. 84 (1840 edition).

Il serait honteux au duc de venger les injures faites au comte. (It would be disgraceful of the duke to avenge insults offered to the count.)

Saying of PHILIP, COMTE DE BRESSE, afterwards duc de Savoie (died 1497).—Suard, *Notes sur l'esprit d'imitation*. Earlier than *Le roi de France ne venge pas les querelles du duc d'Orléans* (q.v.). See also Evasisti.

Ils m'applaudirent ! (They applauded me !)

LOUIS PHILIPPE JOSEPH, duc d'Orléans, surnamed " Egalité " (1747-93)—on the way to the scaffold, referring to his loss of popularity with the people.

Ils m'ont laissé arriver, comme ils les ont laissés partir. (They let me arrive, as they let them leave.)

NAPOLEON (1769-1821)—to the COMTE MOLLIER (1758-1850) after his return to Paris from Elba (Mar. 20, 1815) alluding to the attitude of the people towards himself and Louis XVIII.

Ils n'ont rien appris, ni rien oublié. (They have neither learnt nor forgotten anything.)

Attributed to TALLEYRAND(1754-1838), but authenticity doubtful. A letter dated Jan. 1796, from the Chevalier de Panat (whom Talleyrand knew in London) to Mallet du

Pan, a celebrated journalist, contained the words : " . . . personne n'est corrigé, personne n'a su ni rien oublier, ni rien apprendre. (. . . no one has reformed, no one has known how to either forget or learn anything.)—*Mémoires et correspondance de Mallet du Pan*, 1851, vol. ii, p. 196. Twenty years later, at the time of the return of the Bourbons to France, the emperor ALEXANDER OF RUSSIA (1777-1825) exclaimed (a hope being expressed that misfortune had partly corrected their faults), " *Corrigés! ils sont incorrigés et incorrigibles.*" (Reformed ! they are unreformed and unreformable.)

Ils sont là quarante qui ont de l'esprit comme quatre. (There are forty there who have the wit of four.)

PIRON (1689-1773) — of the French Academy (composed of forty members).—*Œuvres complètes d' Alexis Piron*, 1777, vol. i, p. 122. Cf. " Elle a de l'esprit comme quatre." (She has the wit of four.) Molière, *George Dandin*, act 2, sc. 6.

Ils sont trop ! (They [i.e. the Germans] are too many.)

Words uttered by a wounded soldier at the battle of Paris, Mar. 30, 1814.—A. T. de Vaulabelle, *Hist. des deux Restaurations*, 1858, vol. i, p. 331.

Ils veulent être libres, et ils ne savent pas être justes. (They want to be free, and they do not know how to be just.)

ABBÉ SIEYÈS (1748-1836)—when the Constituent Assembly declared the *dîme* (tithes) abolished (Aug. 10, 1789).—*Le Moniteur*, Aug. 11-14, 1789, p. 165.

Il vaut mieux écouter ceux qui vous crient de loin : Soulagez notre misère, que ceux qui vous disent à l'oreille : Augmentez votre fortune. (It is better to listen to those who cry out to you from a distance : Alleviate our misery, than those who say in your ear : Increase your fortune.)

Saying of MARIE LECZINSKA (1703-68), wife of Louis XV.

Il y a des juges à Berlin. (There are judges in Berlin.)

Reply (See Ja, wenn das Berliner &c.) made by a miller to FREDERICK THE GREAT (1712-86). Popularised by Andrieux (1759-1833) in his tale in verse, *le Meunier de Sans-Souci*. (*Œuvres* [1818 edition] vol. 3, p. 208) " Oui, si nous n'avions pas de juges à Berlin." (Yes, if we had no judges in Berlin.) Cf. *The Court of Berlin* (Anon). (The 1000 Best Books in the world, 2nd series [Hutchinson & Co.]. Selected and arranged by Ernest Hope, p. 132.)

Il y a de l'écho en France quand on prononce ici les mots d'honneur et de patrie. (There is an echo in France when the words of honour and mother-country are pronounced here.)

GENERAL (Maximilien Sebastien, comte) FOY (1775-1825)—in the French Chamber, Dec. 30, 1820.

Il y a plus loin de rien à un que d'un à mille. (It is farther from nothing to one than from one to a thousand.)

MME. PILOU (1578-1668), wife of Jean Pilou, proctor at the Châtelet, to a woman who asked her advice in a love intrigue.

8

Il y a quelqu'un qui a plus d'esprit que Voltaire, c'ést tout le monde. (There is someone who has more wit than Voltaire, and that is everybody.)

Words used by TALLEYRAND (1754-1838) in defending the liberty of the Press against *la censure* (censorship), July 24, 1821. " Il y "a quelqu'un qui a plus d'esprit que "Voltaire, plus d'esprit que Bona-"parte, plus d'esprit que chacun "des directeurs, que chacun des "ministres passés, présents et à "venir, c'est tout le monde." (There is someone who has more wit than Voltaire, more wit than Bonaparte, more wit than each of the directors, each of the ministers past, present, and future, and that is everybody.) Quoted as follows in the *Journal anecdotique* de madame Campan (1824, p. 81): "Je connais quelqu'un qui a plus "d'esprit que Napoléon, que Vol-"taire, que tous les ministres "présents et futurs : c'est l'opinion." (I know someone who has more wit than Napoleon, than Voltaire, than all the ministers present and future : and that is public opinion.) Cf. " Ce Tout-le-Monde qui a plus "d'esprit que Voltaire et plus de "poésie que Virgil." (This Everybody who has more wit than Voltaire and more poetry than Virgil.) Jules Claretie, *Pierrille*, pt. i., ch. 14.

Il y a trop longtemps qu'elle est morte pour moi pour que je la pleure aujourd'hui. (She has been dead too long for me to weep for her now.)

LOUIS XIV (1638-1715) of MME. DE MONTESPAN (1641-1707) and MLLE. DE LA VALLIÈRE (abt. 1642-[4]-1710).

Impossible ! ne me dites jamais ce bête de mot ! See Le mot impossible n'est pas français.

J'ai cessé d'être heureux. (I have ceased to be fortunate.)

Saying of BAILLY (1736-93)— when harassed by administrative dissensions.

J'ai entendu plusieurs grands orateurs, j'en ai été content ; pour vous, toutes les fois que je vous entends, je suis très mécontent de moi-même. (I have heard several great orators, I have been pleased with them ; as for you every time I hear you, I am much displeased with myself.)

LOUIS XIV (1638-1715) — to MASSILLON, who preached at Versailles (1699), after hearing a certain number of his sermons.

J'ai été infidèle à Dieu, à mon Ordre, à mon Roi ; je meurs plein de foi et de repentir. (I have been unfaithful to God, to my Order, to my King ; I die full of faith and repentance.)

Attributed to GENERAL ARMAND LOUIS DE GONTAUT, DUC DE BIRON (1747-93)—when arriving near the guillotine. He was executed 31st Dec., 1793, or according to one authority, Jan. 1st, 1794.

J'ai été tailleur, j'ai taillé du drap. (I have been a tailor, I have cut out cloth.)

Attributed to the MARÉCHAL DE LUXEMBOURG (1628-95), surnamed the "*tapissier de Notre Dame.*" He is said to have added, drawing his sword, " *Voici l'instrument avec* "*lequel je coupe les oreilles à ceux* "*qui parlent mal de moi.*" (Here's the instrument with which I cut the ears of those who speak ill of me.)

J'ai failli attendre ! (I very nearly had to wait !)

Attributed to LOUIS XIV (1638-1715), but authenticity doubtful. See Pourquoi le grondez-vous ? Cf., however, *Mémoires*, &c., (1832, p. 38) of the Duchess of Orleans (Elisabeth-Charlotte). Referring to Louis XIV, she writes : " Il ne pouvait souffrir que l'on se fit attendre." (He could not bear to be kept waiting for anyone.)

J'ai fait dix mécontents et un ingrat. (I have made ten discontented and one ungrateful.) Saying of LOUIS XIV (1638-1715), when he appointed anyone to office. See No man who ever held &c.

J'ai froid. (I am cold.) Dying words of L.-M. LE PELLETIER, (1760-93) assassinated by a *garde du corps* named Pâris, Jan. 20, 1793. See Tu trembles &c.

J'ai interrompu mon agonie pour venir vous embrasser. (I have interrupted my death-agony to come and embrace you.) VOLTAIRE (1694-1778) to his old friend D'ARGENTAL (1700-88) on arriving at Paris (Feb., 1778). Voltaire died May 30, 1778.

J'aimais à faire des heureux. (I liked making people happy.) Reply of LOUIS XVI (1754-93) at his trial, when asked what he had done with a sum of money which he had given away in charity.

J'aime bien à prendre ma part d'un sermon ; mais je n'aime pas qu'on me la fasse. (I like to take my share of a sermon ; but I don't like one made to me.) Attributed to LOUIS XIV (1638-1715) after hearing a sermon in which the preacher, Bourdaloue, alluded to the king in these words : " Tu es ille vir ! " (Thou art that man !) The king was then living with the Marquise de Montespan. Cf. " And Nathan said to David, Thou art the man." 2 Samuel xii, 7.

J'aime mieux être guillotiné que guillotineur. (I prefer being guillotined to being guillotineur.) DANTON (1759-94)—reply to those who advised him to strike Robespierre to avoid a like fate himself.

J'aime mieux ma famille que moi-même ; j'aime mieux ma patrie que ma famille : mais j'aime encore mieux le genre humain que ma patrie. (I love my family better than myself ; I love my country better than my family : but I love humankind still better than my country.) Saying of FÉNELON (1651-1715). Cf. φιλῶ τέκν', ἀλλὰ πατρίδ' ἐμὴν μᾶλλον φιλῶ. (I love my children, but I love my country more)— Plutarch, *Praecepta gerendae reipublicae*, xiv. 809, D.

J'aime qui m'aime, j'estime qui le mérite, et je fais plaisir à qui je puis. (I love him who loves me, I esteem him who deserves it, and I please whom I can.) GILLES MÉNAGE (1613-92).

J'ai saisi cette terre de mes mains : tant qu'il y en a elle est à nous. (I have seized this land with my hands : as much as there is of it is ours.) WILLIAM THE CONQUEROR (1025-87) on landing in England (Sept. 28, 1066), stumbled and fell. A. Thierry, *Hist. de la Conquête de l'Angleterre*, etc., I, p. 334. This was considered a bad omen by his followers, but he, like Cæsar (See Teneo te Africa) averted the superstitious feeling by the above remark. " Qu'avez-vous ? quelle chose vous étonne ? J'ai saisi cette terre de mes mains, et, par la splendeur de Dieu, aussi loin qu'elle puisse s'étendre, elle est à moi, elle est à vous." (What is the matter? what is it that astonishes you? I have seized this land with my hands, and, by God's splendour, as far as it can extend, it is mine, it is yours.) *Ibid*, vol. 1, bk. 3, p. 290.

Edward III (1312-77) on landing at la Hogue-Saint-Vast, July 12, 1346, also fell, and his knights, considering this unlucky, urged him to return. He replied: *Pourquoi? Mais est un très bon signe pour moi, car la terre me désire.* (Why? But it is a very good sign for me, for the land wants me.)—Froissart, bk. 1, pt. 1, ch. 266.

J'ai souvent loué Dieu de ne m'avoir fait ni femme, ni prêtre, ni Turc, ni juif. (I have often praised God for not having made me either a woman, priest, Turk or Jew.) Saying of GUI-PATIN (1602-72).

J'ai toujours été le maître chez moi, quelquefois chez les autres : me m'en faites pas souvenir. (I have always been the master at home, sometimes abroad ; don't recall it to my mind.)

Words attributed to LOUIS XIV (1638-1715) (but questioned by Voltaire, *Siècle de Louis XIV*, ch. 23) with regard to LORD STAIR (1673-1747), the English ambassador, owing to his persistent representations as to the works at Mardyck being contrary to the treaty of Utrecht. Hénault, *Abrégé etc. de l'Histoire de France.* These were discontinued in April 1715.

J'ai trouvé la couronne par terre et je l'ai ramassée. (I found the crown in the dirt and I have picked it up.)

NAPOLEON (1769-1821), alluding to his resolve to make what he liked

of it (the crown). (Cf. *Mémorial de Sainte-Hélène.*)

J'ai vécu. (I lived.)

Reply of the ABBÉ SIEYÈS (1748-1836) when asked what he had done during the Terror. He died at Paris, June 20, 1836, aged 88 years. "Ce que j'ai fait, j'ai vécu." (What did I do, I lived.) *Notices historiques*, vol 1, p. 81.

Jamais homme d'honneur ne demandait argent la veille d'une bataille. (Never did a man of honour ask for money on the eve of a battle.)—Pierre Mathieu.

Answer made by HENRI IV (1553-1610) to the German COLONEL TICH DE SCHOMBERG before the battle of Ivry, on being asked for the troops' pay. Just before the engagement the king, remembering and regretting his harsh words, approached the Colonel and said "Monsieur de Schomberg, je vous ai offensé ; cette journée peut être la dernière de ma vie ; je ne veux point emporter l'honneur d'un gentilhomme ; je sais votre valeur et votre mérite : pardonnez-moi et embrassez-moi. (Monsieur de Schomberg, I have offended you ; this day may be my last ; I do not wish to take away the honour of a gentleman ; I know your valour and merit : forgive and embrace me) Schomberg replied : "Il est vrai, sire, Votre Majesté me blesse l'autre jour, et aujourd'hui elle me tue ; car l'honneur qu'elle me fait m'oblige de mourir pour son service. (It is true, sire, Your Majesty wounded me the other day, and to-day you kill me ; for the honour you do me compels me to die for you.) Schomberg kept his word ; he fought valiantly and was killed on the battle-field. H. de Péréfixe, *Histoire du roi Henri le Grand* (vol 1, pp. 153-6), says : "Est-ce le fait d'un homme d'honneur de demander de l'argent, quand il faut prendre les ordres pour combattre ? (Is it the act of a man of honour to ask for money, when it is necessary to receive orders to fight ?)

The rest differs but slightly from the version quoted above.

Jamais l'Italie ne s'emparera de Rome. (Never shall Italy take possession of Rome.)

EUGÈNE ROUHER (1814-84), at the time that Garibaldi threatened Rome, said (Dec. 5, 1867): ". . . l'Italie ne s'emparera pas de Rome ! Jamais." (Italy shall not take possession of Rome ! Never.) Often alluded to as the "jamais de Rouher". (Rouher's 'never.')

J'aurais voulu l'en guerir ; mais elle craignait trop Dieu. (I should have liked to cure her of it [her virtue], but she feared God too much.)

NINON DE LENCLOS (1620-1705) of MME. SCARRON, afterwards Mme. de Maintenon (1635-1719).

J'avais cru plus difficile de mourir. (I thought dying more difficult.)

Deathbed utterance of LOUIS XIV (1638-1715) to MME. DE MAINTENON (1635-1719). H. Martin, *Hist. de France*, xiv, bk. 91. See A dying man can do nothing easy.

Another version is : " J'avais " toujours ouï dire qu'il était " difficile de mourir ; je touche à " ce dernier moment, et je ne trouve " pas que ce soit si pénible." (I had always heard say that it was difficult to die ; I have come to that moment, and I do not find it so painful.)

J'avais résolu de renouveler à Cherbourg les merveilles de l'Egypte. (I had resolved to renew at Cherbourg the marvels of Egypt.)

Words graven on the pedestal of NAPOLEON's statue at Cherbourg, alluding to the works projected by him.

" Jean s'en alla comme il était venu." (John went away as he had come.)

LOUIS PHILIPPE (1773-1850) in bidding adieu to France. The words are the first line of La Fontaine's epitaph on himself.

Je donnerais pour l'avoir fait les succès de toute ma vie. (I would give the successes of my whole life to have made that.)

Marshal (Sebastien Le Prestre de) VAUBAN (1633-1707)—of the canal du Midi (opened 1681) connecting the Atlantic with the Mediterranean, and undertaken by COLBERT at the instigation of PAUL DE RIQUET. See Je donnerais une de mes pièces, etc.; and I would rather be the author, etc.

Je donnerais une de mes pièces pour les avoir faits. (I would give one of my pieces to have composed them.)

PIERRE CORNEILLE (1606-84) of the following lines by G. DE BRÉBEUF (1618-61), alluding to writing : " C'est de lui que nous vient cet " art ingénieux " De peindre la parole et de parler " aux yeux ; " Et par les traits divers de figures " tracées, " Donner de la couleur et du corps " aux pensées." (It is from it that we derive that ingenious art Of painting the word, and speaking to the eyes ; And by the varied traits of traced figures, Of giving colour and body to thoughts.) See I would rather be the author of etc. Cf. Lucan, *Pharsalia*, iii, 220-1 :— Phœnices primi, famæ si creditur, ausi Mansaram rudibus vocem signare figuris. (The Phoenicians were the first, if tradition may be trusted, to picture language by rude figures with the object of their remaining permanent.)

Je l'ai soigné, il a guéri.   (I attended him, he has recovered.)
Saying of CORVISART-DES-MARESTS (1755-1821), Napoleon's physician. Cf. the saying of AMBROISE PARÉ (1517-90). "Je le pansay, Dieu le guarist." (I attended him, God cured him.) Cf. *Œuvres complètes*, 1840, p. 296, Introduction. Cf. also. "Le roi te touche, Dieu te guérisse !" (The king touches thee, God cures thee !) Phrase used by the kings of France when touching for scrofula or King's evil, after being anointed.   According to Père Daniel's *Histoire de France*, Robert II (970-1031) surnamed le Pieux (the Pious), son of Hugues Capet, was the first to exercise this privilege, and the custom is said to have been maintained until the reign (1715-74) of Louis XV. Henry IV (1553-1610) at the battle of Ivry (Mar. 14, 1590) is said to have laid about him right and left with his sword, saying, "Je te touche, Dieu te guérisse !"   (I touch thee, may God cure thee !) Edward the Confessor is supposed to have had the power of curing scrofula conferred upon him.

Je l'ai vaincu, il faut me vaincre moi-même.   (I have conquered him, I must conquer myself.)
Phrase used by LOUIS XII (1462-1515) referring to GENERAL ALVIANO, commander of the Venetian army, who was taken prisoner and brought before the king.   The captive received the king's advances with brusqueness. Said he :   "Il vaut mieux le laisser, "je m'emporterais et j'en serais "fâché. Je l'ai vaincu," etc. (It is better to leave him, I might lose my temper and I should be sorry for it. I have conquered him, etc.)

Je louerois davantage vostre œuvre si elle ne me louoit tant
(*or* si elle me louoit moins.) (I should praise your work more if it did not praise me so much.)
Written at the beginning of her Memoirs by MARGUERITE DE VALOIS (1552-1615) (daughter of Henri II and Catherine de Médicis), addressing Brantôme, who had sent her his book, *Les Dames illustres*. She was a prisoner in the château d'Usson at the time. Said to have been repeated by LOUIS XIV (1638-1715) when Boileau read to him the last 40 lines of his first epistle. Said the king to the poet : "Voilà qui est très beau ; "cela est admirable.   Je vous "louerois davantage si vous ne "m'aviez pas tant loué (*or* si vous "m'aviez loué moins)." (That is very fine, admirable. I should praise you more if you had not praised me so much, *or* if you had praised me less.)

Je me nomme Elisabeth de France sœur du roi.   (My name is Elisabeth of France, sister of the king.)
Last words of MME. ELISABETH (Philippine-Marie-Hélène) DE FRANCE (1764-94), sister of Louis XVI—on the scaffold.—F. de Barghon Fort-Rion, *Mémoires de Mme. Elisabeth de France*, (1860, p. 78.)

Je m'en vais avec l'Europe.   (I am going away and Europe with me.)
Dying words attributed to the count JOSEPH DE MAISTRE (1753-1821), but contradicted by his son in the *Life* written by him (see *Revue de Genève*, Aug. 1851, p. 56).

Je m'en vais ou je m'en vas. L'un et l'autre se dit ou se disent.   (I am going away [Je m'en vais ou je m'en vas]. One and the other is said or are said.)

Last words of U. DOMERGUE (1745-1810), a celebrated French grammarian, when asked how he was. Père D. BOUHOURS (1628-1702) is also credited with a similar saying on his death-bed. "Je vais ou je vas bientôt mourir : l'un et l'autre se disent (I am going [je vais or je vas] to die soon : one and the other are said).

Je me sens fort bien. (I feel very well.)

Dying words of C.-J. DORAT (1734-80) to his servant. Preceded by : " Ils sont plaisants, ces médecins ! ils voient tout de mauvais œil. Le mien me trouve très-affaibli, et moi, je," etc.

(These doctors are very funny ! they see everything in an unfavourable light. Mine thinks me very weak and *I*, etc.) He then repeated two lines that he had just composed to begin a satire against doctors, and expired.

Je me souviens qu'il a été mon ami, et ses malheurs m'ont fait oublier le reste. (I remember that he has been my friend, and his misfortunes have made me forget the rest.)

Remark made by GUILLAUME DE LAMOIGNON (1617-77) chief president of the Paris parliament with regard to FOUQUET. The former presided over the judges by whom Fouquet was tried. He also said to Colbert (1619-83) who tried to prejudice him against Fouquet (1615-80) : *Un juge ne donne qu'une fois son avis et sur les fleurs de lis.* (A judge gives his opinion once only and on the fleurs-de-lis.)

Je meurs ; cela m'est égal, c'est pour la liberté ! (I am dying ; never mind, it is for liberty !)

Dying words attributed by Robespierre (in his report made May 7, 1794, to the Convention) to AGRICOLE VIALI (1780-93). A similar phrase : " Je meurs content, je meurs pour la liberté de mon pays." (I die content, I die for the liberty of my country) is attributed to LEPELLETIER DE ST.-FARGEAN (born 1760 ; assassinated in 1793), but those who were present deny that he said anything.

Je meurs en adorant Dieu, en aimant mes amis et en détestant la superstition. (I die worshipping God, loving my friends and hating superstition.)

Declaration made by VOLTAIRE (1694-1778), thinking his last hour had come (Feb. 28, 1778).

Je meurs innocent de tous les crimes qu'on m'impute. Je pardonne aux auteurs de ma mort, et je prie Dieu que le sang que vous allez répandre ne retombe jamais sur la France. (I die innocent of all the crimes laid to my charge. I forgive the authors of my death, and I pray God that the blood which you are about to shed may never fall on France.) *Dernières heures de Louis XVI.**

Last words of LOUIS XVI (1754-93) on the scaffold.

Je meurs satisfait, je désirais terminer ainsi ma vie. (I die content, I wished to end my life thus.)

Dying words of T. CORRET DE LA TOUR D'AUVERGNE surnamed " le premier Grenadier de la République" (1743-1800), killed June 27, 1800 at Oberhausen, Bavaria.

Another version : " Je meurs content ; c'est ainsi que j'avais toujours rêvé de finir ma carrière." (I die content ; it is thus that I had always dreamed of ending my

*(For exact reference see under **Faites**, sire, ce sacrifice, etc).

career). See Mort au champ d'honneur.

J'emporte avec moi le deuil de la monarchie ; après ma mort, les factieux s'en disputeront les lambeaux. (I carry away with me the mourning of monarchy ; after my death, the factionists will quarrel over the fragments.)
Dying words of MIRABEAU (1749-91), to FROCHOT. A. Mézières, *Vie de Mirabeau*, p. 323.

Je m'y ferai porter, et nous sauterons ensemble. (I'll have myself carried there, and we will be blown up together.)
Attributed to LOUIS XVIII (1755-1824), alluding to the bridge of Jena that Blucher wanted to blow up, but invented by count J.-C. BEUGNOT (1761-1835) who admits it in his *Mémoires* (1866, vol. 2, pp. 312-3).

Je n'ai jamais eu si froid que le jour où je fus brûlé. (I was never so cold as the day when I was burned.)
HENRI ESTIENNE (1528-98), the celebrated printer, on learning the date when his effigy was burned as a punishment for his violent attacks against the Romish Church in his *apologie d'Hérodote*. At the time he was wandering about in the depth of winter.

Je n'ai pas besoin de conseil, mais d'assistance. (I need no advice, but assistance.)
HENRY IV (1553-1610). June 3 [or 5], 1595—to those who begged him not to risk his life at Fontaine-Française (Côte d'Or). When, in the most critical position, he was advised to flee, he resolutely went to the assistance of Biron, saying : " *Il y a plus de peril à la fuite qu'à la chasse.*" (There is more danger in being chased than in chasing.)

Je n'ai trouvé que bons citoyens et braves soldats, mais pas un bourreau. (I found only good citizens and brave soldiers, but no executioners.)
Said to have been written in a letter from d'Aspremont, VISCOUNT ORTHE, the tyrannical and very unpopular governor of Bayonne, to the King, Charles IX, refusing to obey the orders of the Court after the massacre of Saint Bartholomew, but the letter is regarded as apocryphal.—d'Aubigné, *Histoire universelle.*
Viscount Orthe was one of the three provincial governors who refused to obey these orders ; the others were : le comte de Tende, governor of Provence, and Saint Hérem, governor of Auvergne.
Another version is : " Sire, je " n'ai trouvé, parmi les habitants " et les gens de guerre, que de bons " citoyens, de braves soldats et pas " un bourreau. Ainsi, eux et moi, " nous supplions Votre Majesté " d'employer nos bras et nos jours " à des services plus honorables."
(Sire, I have found, among the inhabitants and soldiers, only good citizens and brave soldiers and not one executioner. Therefore, they and I, we beg your Majesty to use our arms and our days for more honourable services.)

Je n'aurais pas cru qu'il fût mort horizontalement. (I should not have thought that he would have died horizontally).
Saying attributed to BOUVART (1717-87) on learning the death (1776) of his *confrère* and enemy Bordeu.

Je ne connais en Europe aucun ministre ni plénipotentiaire capable de faire la barbe à ce capucin, quoiqu'il y ait belle prise. (I do not know any minister or plenipotentiary in Europe capable of shaving this capuchin, although there is plenty to take hold of.) A *jeu de mots* on "faire la barbe" in its literal and figurative, senses of 'to shave' and 'to surpass.'

Said of his confidential agent, LE PÈRE JOSEPH (1577-1638), by RICHELIEU (1585-1642).

Je ne croirai pas à la Révolution, tant que je verrai ces carrosses et ces cabriolets écraser les passants. (I shall not believe in the Revolution as long as I see these coaches and cabriolets running over the pedestrians.)

CHAMFORT (1741-94).

Je ne croyais pas qu'on pût faire mourir un gentilhomme pour si peu de chose! (I didn't think that they could kill a gentleman for such a trifle!)

Dying words of J.-F.-J. LEFEBVRE, chevalier de Labarre (1747-66)—condemned to death for not having saluted a procession and having mutilated a crucifix.

Je ne fais pas assez de cas de la vie pour en faire part à quelqu'un. (I do not attach enough importance to life to share it with anyone.)

Reply made by the MARÉCHAL DE GASSION (1609-47), when spoken to on the subject of marriage.

Je ne lis plus, monsieur, je relis. (I no longer read, sir; I re-read.)

Remark made by P.-P. ROYER-COLLARD (1763-1846) to A. DE VIGNY (1797-1863), a candidate for the French Academy.—Ste-Beuve, *Notes et Pensées* (par. 204).

Je ne m'amuse pas à penser aux morts. (I don't amuse myself by thinking of the dead.)

NAPOLEON'S (1769-1821) reply at Berlin (1807), when it was hinted that he should appear sad on receiving news of the death of his nephew Napoleon (son of his brother Louis, king of Holland).

Je n'en vois pas la nécessité. (I don't see the necessity of it.)

Reply by MARC PIERRE DE VOYER, COMTE D'ARGENSON (1696-1764) to the ABBÉ DESFONTAINES (1685-1745) according to a letter from Voltaire, dated December 23, 1760 (to the Marquis Albergati Capacelli).

The abbé had been apologising for his frequent publication of libels and added, "Il faut que tout le monde vive." (Everybody must live.)

Attributed also to TALLEYRAND (1754-1838) and to the COMTE d'ARGENTAL (1700-88).

Referred to in a foot-note by Lord Mahon (1845-53 ed., vol. 2, p. 209) to a letter of Lord Chesterfield to his son, Jan. 23, 1752.

Cf. "Vivere ergo habes?" (What necessity is there that you should live?) Tertullian, Liber de idolatria, ch. V.

See πλεῖν ἀνάγκη ξῆν οὐκ, &c.

Cf. "Navigare necesse est, vivere non est necesse." (It is necessary to sail; it is not necessary to live.)—Inscription on a house, founded in 1525 in Bremen for invalided sailors and for the support of their widows and orphans.

Je ne souffre pas, mes amis, mais je sens une certaine difficulté d'être. (I do not suffer, my friends, but I feel a certain difficulty in existing.)

Last words of FONTENELLE (1657-1757).

Je ne suis pas grande, je suis seulement élevée. (I am not great, I am only elevated.)

MME. DE MAINTENON (1635-1719)--speaking of her position.

Je ne vois pas assez Dieu pour l'aimer au-dessus de toutes choses, et je vois beaucoup trop mon prochain pour l'aimer comme moi-même. (I do not see enough of God to love him above all things, and I see too much of my neighbour to love him as myself.)

Saying of the MARQUISE DE CRÉQUI (1714-1803). President Harlay (1639-1712) is said to have made the following confession : "Je me confesse de n'avoir pu aimer Dieu au-dessus de toutes choses, ni mon prochain comme moi-même." (I confess to not having loved God above all things, nor my neighbour as myself.)

J'entends, vous avez juroté. (I understand, you only partly swore.)

Reply of LOUIS XVIII (1755-1824) to BARENTIN (1738-1819) at Ghent, where the latter came to explain as well as he could his visit to Napoleon after the return to Paris from Elba (Mar. 20, 1815). " Je n'ai pas précisément juré," said Barentin (I did not exactly swear [fidelity to Napoleon]). "J'entends," replied the king, "vous avez juroté. A votre âge, on ne fait plus les choses qu'à demi." (I understand, you only partly swore. At your age, one no longer does things except by halves.)

Je perds en lui une moitié de mon âme. (In him I lose half of my soul.)

CARDINAL RICHELIEU (1585-1642)—at the death of PÈRE JOSEPH (1577-1638) surnamed " son Eminence grise " (His grey Eminence). — His real name was François le Clerc du Tremblay. Another version is :—" J'ai perdu ma consolation et mon appui." (I have lost my comforter and support) Cf. Bazin, *Hist. de France sous Louis XIII*, vol. 4, pp. 115-9.

Je perds sur ce que je vends, mais je me rattrape sur la quantité. (I lose on what I sell, but I make it up on the quantity.)

Popular saying, probably derived from the following anecdote : " Josserand, le maître du café de Foy ; c'est celui qui disait l'année dernière : ' Je perds sur chaque glace que je ' vends, plus de deux sous, mais je ' me sauve sur la quantité. '"—Note by Meister to Grimm's *Correspondence*, under date Aug. 1781, vol. 13, p. 12.

(Josserand, the master of the *café de Foy* ; he who used last year to say : ' I lose by every ice I sell, more than two sous, but I make it up on the quantity.') Cf. " Je perds sur tout ce que je vends . . . Mais il faut bien gagner sa vie ! "— (I lose on all I sell. . . But I must win my bread.) Cormon et Grangé, *Don Pèdre*, act 2, sc. 5 (1857).

Je prendrai le plus long. (I'll go the longest way.)

Reply of LA FONTAINE (1621-95) when told—on leaving the dinner-table before the others, saying that he was going to the Academy—that there was plenty of time and that he would arrive too early.

Je prie Dieu qu' il me condamne si j'ai eu autre intention que le bien de la religion et ˆde l'Etat. (I pray God to condemn me if I have had any other thought than the welfare of the Church and the State.)

Le père Griffet, vol. 3 p. 576, also *Récit de ce qui s'est passé un peu avant la mort, etc.*

Biblio. nat. MS. Fonds Dupuy, vol. DXC, fol. 298 recto.

Words uttered by CARDINAL RICHELIEU (1585-1642) shortly before he died. He is also credited with having said in reply to the question whether he forgave his enemies, that he had none except those of the State: "*qu'il n'en avait point que ceux de l'Etat*"— (cf. *Mémoires de Montglat*, collection Michaud, 3rd series, vol. 5, p. 133; also *Mémoires de Montchal*, 1718, p. 268). "Je n'ai jamais eu d'autres ennemis que ceux de l'Etat." (I have never had any other enemies than those of the State)—d'Avenel, *Richelieu et la monarchie absolue*, vol. 1, p. 89.

Je puis faire des nobles quand je veux, et même de très grands seigneurs; Dieu seul peut faire un homme comme celui que nous allons perdre. (I can make nobles when I will, and even great lords; God alone can create a man like the one we are about to lose.)

Attributed to FRANCIS I (1494-1547) on noticing the disdainful looks of the courtiers who had accompanied him on his visit to LEONARDO DA VINCI, who was dying. See You have not to do with Holbein, but with me &c. I can make a lord &c. Avec quatre aunes de drap, &c. Cf. "Le roi Louis XI [1423-83] disoit qu'il annobliroit assez, mais n'être en sa puissance faire un gentilhomme: cela venant de trop loin et de rare vertu." N.Du Fail, *Contes et Discours d'Eutrapel*, ch. vi. (1856 edition, *Propos rustiques*, etc., p. 176).

Je reprends mon bien partout ou je le trouve.

See On reprend son bien ou on le trouve.

Je saurai vous trouver jusqu'au fond de vos repaires. (I shall know how to find you even in the depths of your holes.)

In a speech at Cheronne, Aug. 16, 1881, by LÉON GAMBETTA (1838-82) when candidate for the elections of 21st Aug.—*La République française*, Aug. 1881.

Je serai toujours de l'avis de M. le Prince, surtout quand il aura tort. (I shall always be of M. the prince's opinion, especially when he is wrong.)

BOILEAU (1636-1711) to the great CONDÉ (1621-86) on the occasion of a dispute between them, when the latter was losing his temper.

Je serois bien marri d'avoir battu les buissons et qu'un autre eust les oisillons. (I should be sorry to have beaten the bushes and that another should have the young birds).

Words used by the DUKE OF BEDFORD (1389-1435) at the siege of Orleans, referring to PHILIP III, surnamed le Bon, Duke of Burgundy (died 1467). The phrase, "Battre les buissons sans prendre les oiseaux" (To beat the bushes without taking the birds) has become a proverb, and is quoted by Rabelais and Mme. de Sévigné.

Je suis la moins folle femme du monde, car de femme sage, il n'y en a pas. (I am the least stupid woman in the world, for there are no wise ones.)

Saying of ANNE DE BEAUJEU (1462-1522), daughter of Louis XI.

Je suis l'homme qui vous a donné plus de royaumes que vos ancêtres ne vous ont laissé de villes. (I am the man who has given you more kingdoms than your ancestors have left you towns.)—Voltaire, *Essai sur les Mœurs*, ch. 147.

FERNAND CORTEZ (1485-1547) to CHARLES-QUINT (1500-58). Being unable to obtain an audience of that monarch, Cortez mounted the carriage-step and made the above reply when Charles asked who he was. Prescott, however, doubts the authenticity of the phrase (Cf. *Conquest of Mexico* VII, 5 note).

Je suis né sans savoir pourquoi, j'ai vécu sans savoir comment, et je meurs sans savoir ni pourquoi, ni comment. (I was born without knowing why, I have lived without knowing how, and I am dying without either knowing why or how.) Dying words of P. GASSENDI (1592-1655), a French philosopher.

Je suis venu ici pour recevoir des hommages et non des leçons. (I have come here to receive homage and not lessons.) Reply of Charles X. (1757-1836) to the National Guards, when reviewing them at the Champ de Mars (Apr. 29, 1827). He was asked— " Is the Charter an outrage then?" —and replied as above.

Jésus! (Jesus!) Last words of JOAN OF ARC (1410-31) the " Maid of Orleans," burned at the stake, May. 31, 1431. —O'Reilly, *Les deux Procès de Jeanne Darc.*

Jeune homme, apprenez qu'il y a toujours bien loin de la poitrine d'un homme de bien au poignard d'un séditieux. (Young man, know that there is always a great distance between the breast of a good citizen and the dagger of a rebel)—Claude Le Peletier, *Mémoire, etc., de Mr. Molé.* Said by President MATHIEU MOLÉ (1584-1656) to the abbé de Chanvallon (afterwards archbishop

of Paris) on the Day of the Barricades, Aug. 26, 1648. Another version : " Il y a loin du poignard d'un assassin à la poitrine d'un honnête homme ! " (It is a great distance from the dagger of an assassin to the breast of an honest man !)

Je vais combattre les ennemis de Votre Majesté, et je vous laisse au milieu des miens. (I am going to fight your Majesty's enemies, and I leave you in the midst of my own). Said by the MARÉCHAL DE VILLARS (1653-1734) to LOUIS XIV (1638-1715) before starting for the Rhine army.

Je vais quérir un grand peut-être. (I am going to seek a great "perhaps.")—Sketch of Rabelais by P. Dupont, prefacing 1858 edition. See Tirez le rideau, la farce est jouée ; Now am I about to take etc. ; I shall soon know the grand secret ; Now comes the mystery. Another version, but contradicted : " Je m'en vais chercher un grand peut-être ; tirez le rideau, la farce est jouée."

Je veux bien que la langue espagnole demeure à l'Espagnol, l'allemande à l'Allemand ; maise toute la françoise doit être à moy. (I am willing that the Spanish language should belong to the Spaniards ; the German to the Germans ; but all the French should belong to me).—Mathieu, *Hist. de Henry le Grand*, vol. 2, p. 444. Saying of HENRY IV (1553-1610). Cf. Béranger, *Le bon Français :*

" J'aime qu' un Russe soit Russe,
Et qu 'un Anglais soit Anglais,
Si l'on est Prussien en Prusse,
En France soyons Français."

(I'd have a Russian be a Russian,
A Briton British I would see,
And if in Prussia one is Prussian,
Why then in France let's Frenchmen be.)

Je veux honorer dans ma vieillesse une charge qui m'a fait honneur quand j'étais jeune. (I wish to honour in my old age an office which honoured me when I was young.) Given by the COMTE DE RICHEMONT (1398-1458) as a reason for not delivering up his sword as Constable of France on acceding to the dignity of Duke of Brittany (1457) under the title of Arthur III.

Je veux que chaque laboureur de mon royaume puisse mettre la poule au pot le dimanche. (I desire that every labourer in my realm should be able to put a fowl in the pot on Sundays.) A wish attributed to HENRI IV (1553-1610), said to the DUC DE SAVOIE early in 1600. "Si Dieu me donne encore de la vie, je ferai qu'il n'y aura pas de laboureur en mon royaume qui n'ait moyen d'avoir une poule dans son pot." (If God spares my life, I will see that there is no labourer in my realm without means to have a fowl in his pot.) Mathieu, *Hist. des Années de Paix*. H.de Péréfixe,*Hist. de Henri le Grand*, 1749, p. 559. Cf. the following paraphrase in Legouvé's LA MORT DE HENRI IV (act IV, sc 1):

"Je veux enfin qu' au jour marqué pour le repos,
L'hôte laborieux des modestes hameaux,
Sur sa table moins humble, ait par ma bienfaisance,
Quelques-uns de ces mets réservés à l'aisance."
(I wish, in short, that on the day set aside for repose,
The hard-working host of the modest hamlets,
On his less humble table, should have by my beneficence,
A few of those dishes reserved for the well-to-do.)

Je vis par curiosité. (I live out of curiosity).—Mme. de Bawr, *Mes souvenirs*, p. 137.

Remark made by a singular personage named MARTIN (about whom very little is known) to his friend DUCIS during the Terror. Also ascribed to MERCIER (1740-1814) author of *Le Tableau de Paris* (cf. V. Hugo's *Marion Delorme*, act iv, sc. 8.)

Je vois bien qu' à la cour on fait argent de tout. (I see clearly that at the court money is made out of everything.) LOUIS XIV (1638-1715) referring to the princess de Montauban's offer to the princess d'Harcourt of 1000 crowns to take her place at Marly.

Je voudrois bien voir la grimace qu'il fait à cette heure sur cet échafaud. (I should like to see the grimace he is making now on that scaffold). Attributed (but denied) to LOUIS XIII (1601-43)—alluding to CINQ-MARS (1620-42) surnamed *M. le Grand.* — Tallement des Reaux, *Historiettes*, vol. 3, p. 58. According to M. Paulin Paris, the phrase originates from a saying of the DUC D'ALENÇON, (afterwards duc d'Anjou, 1554-84) when news was brought to him that the COMTE DE SAINT-AIGNAN had been killed at Antwerp, Jan. 19, 1583. "Je croy que quy eust pu prendre le loisir de contempler à cette heure-là Saint-Aignan, qu'on luy eust veu faire alors une plaisante grimace." (I think that whoever had the opportunity of looking at Saint Aignan then would have seen him make a lovely grimace.)—P. de l'Estoile, *Journal*, vol. 1, p. 156 (edition 1719). Another version (with regard to Cinq-Mars) is "Je crois qu' à cette heure 'cher ami' fait une vilaine mine." (I think "dear friend" is making an ugly grimace just now). Another:

"Je crois que 'cher ami' fait à présent une vilaine mine." (I think "cher ami" is making an ugly grimace now.) Louis XIII used to call Cinq-Mars "cher ami." "As the hour appointed for the execution was drawing nigh, the king, looking at his watch, remarked with much satisfaction that Monsieur le Grand 'passait alors un mauvais quart-d'heure.'—This is said to have been the origin of the phrase."—Lady Jackson, *Old Paris*, i, 227. See Le quart d'heure de Rabelais.

Je voudrais te la laisser en héritage. (I should like to leave it to you as an inheritance) Dying words of MIRABEAU (1749-91), to one of his friends who was supporting his head. Followed by: "J'emporte avec moi" etc. (q.v.)— A. Mézières,*vie de Mirabeau*, p. 322.

Je vous ai assemblés pour me mettre en tutelle entre vos mains, envie qui ne prend guère aux rois, aux barbes grises et aux victorieux. (I have called you together in order to place myself in your hands, a course which is not usually taken by kings, grey-beards or victors.) Words occurring in the speech made by HENRI IV (1553-1610) to the Assembly of Notables at Rouen (Nov. 4, 1596).

J'ignorais que j'eusse mérité ni la mort ni le pardon. (I did not know that I had deserved either death or pardon.) MICHEL DE L'HOSPITAL (1506-73) in 1572. The news of the massacre of St. Bartholomew reached him at Vignay, near Etampes, where he had retired. "Je ne pensois pas avoir jamais mérité ni pardon, ni mort advancée." (I did not think that I had deserved either pardon or premature death.)

J'y suis, j'y reste. (Here I am, here I stay.) MARSHAL MACMAHON (1808-93)—at Sebastopol, Sep. 8, 1855, on being asked whether he could retain the Malakoff which he had taken. "Dites à votre général, que j'y suis et que j'y reste". (Tell your general that I am there and that I remain there.) Cf. *Le Figaro*, Oct. 28, 1893. See Ci siamo e ci resteremo.

L'abîme de Pascal. (Pascal's abyss.) Saying, meaning an imaginary gulf, derived from an accident that happened to BLAISE PASCAL (1623-62) near the Seine, from which he narrowly escaped with his life. After the accident Pascal was haunted by the idea that there was always an abyss by his side ready to swallow him up, and, although he placed a chair near him, he was unable to dismiss the hallucination from his mind.

La carrière ouverte aux talents, voilà mon principe. (Professions [Lit. The career] open to talent, that is my principle). NAPOLEON (1769-1821) to O'MEARA (1786-1836). Quoted by Carlyle in his essay "Sir Walter Scott" (Critical and Miscellaneous Essays, vol. vi. p. 35). See Tout soldat français porte dans sa giberne &c.

La Charte sera désormais une vérité. (The Charter shall be henceforth a reality.) Concluding words of the DUKE OF ORLEANS' proclamation on being appointed (July 31, 1830) lieutenant-general of the realm—afterwards LOUIS-PHILIPPE (1773-1850). — Guizot, *Mémoires pour servir à l'histoire de mon temps*, vol. ii, p. 22. The proclamation in question was drawn up by M. Dupin aîné (cf. his Memoirs, vol. ii,p. 151).

La confiance doit venir d'en bas, le pouvoir doit venir d'en haut. (Confidence must come from below, power must come from above.)
The ABBÉ SIEYÈS (1748-1836).— Thiers, *Hist. du Consulat et de l'Empire*, vol. i, p. 98.

La cour rend des arrêts et non pas des services. (The court renders judgments and not services.)
Reply made by M. SÉGUIER (1768-1848), chief president of the court of Paris, to an influential person who asked a service in a case pending.—*Le Courrier de Vaugelas*, Nov. 15, 1886. Although the authenticity of the *mot* is confirmed by the president's grandson in the *Courrier de Vaugelas* as above, yet M. Séguier is said—in a letter that he wrote to M. DE PEYRONNET, (1775-1853), keeper of the seals (Nov. 28, 1828)—to have denied it (Cf. Crétineau-Joly, *Hist. de Louis-Philippe*).

La démocratie coule à pleins bords. (Democracy is flowing full-tide.)
The COMTE DE SERRE (1776-1824) brought before the Chamber of Deputies, on Dec. 3, 1821, a bill for increasing the penalties for illegalities by the Press, and in his speech used the words " . . si le torrent [of democracy] coule à pleins bords dans de faibles digues qui le contiennent à peine," &c. (. . . . if the torrent flows full-tide between feeble dykes which scarcely keep it within bounds, &c.) *Moniteur*, Dec. 4, 1821.

La force prime le droit.
See Macht geht vor Recht. Cf. " Il y a bien un droit du plus sage, mais non pas un droit du plus fort." (There is indeed a right of the wisest, but not a right of the strongest.) Joubert, *Pensées* xv., 4.

La France est assez riche pour payer sa gloire. (France is rich enough to pay for her glory.)
Phrase used in the *Journal des Débats*, Sep. 14, 1844, after the war in Morocco.

Le garde meurt et ne se rend pas. (The guard dies, and does not surrender).
Phrase attributed to CAMBRONNE (1770-1842) at the battle of Waterloo (June 18, 1815), but he denied having uttered it.—*L'Indépendant*, June 20, 1815 ; Thiers, *Histoire du Consulat et de l'Empire*. See Dieu m'a confié &c. Really said by GENERAL COUNT MICHEL (1772-1815). Cambronne is said to have uttered a single word, not fit for ears polite, but which V. Hugo has written at the end of Bk. i, ch. 14, of *Les Misérables* (Cosette). The inscription at the foot of Cambronne's statue at Nantes, however, remains.

La grande nation. (The great nation.)
NAPOLEON (1769-1821)—in his proclamation to the Italian people, Nov. 17, 1797.—Lanfrey, *Hist. de Napoléon*, vol. I., ch. x ; Joseph de Maistre, *Letter to M. Vignet des Etoles*, 1794.

L'aigle volera de clocher en clocher jusqu'aux tours de Notre-Dame. (The eagle will fly from steeple to steeple until it reaches the towers of Notre-Dame).
In a proclamation read by NAPOLEON (1769-1821) to his soldiers on landing at Cannes (Mar. 1, 1815). "L'aigle, avec les couleurs nationales, volera", etc. (The eagle, with the national colours, will fly, etc). —*Le Moniteur universel*, March 21, 1815. The phrase is used by V. Hugo at end of ch. 18, bk. 1 of *Cosette: Les Misérables*.

Laissez faire et laissez passer.
(Liberty of action and liberty
of movement.)

Maxim of the school of QUESNAY
(1694-1774), generally attributed to
GOURNAY (1712-59). Cf. Adam
Smith's *Wealth of Nations*, bk. iv,
ch. 9.

Laissez la verdure. (Leave the
green [i.e. do not cover my
tomb with anything, but let the
grass grow there].)

Last words of GEORGE SAND
[Pseudonym of Aurore Dupin, dame
Dudevant] (1804-76).

**Laissez-moi mourir au son de la
musique.** (Let me die to the
sound of music.)

Often given as the last words of
MIRABEAU (1749-91), but probably
a *résumé* of what he did say just
before his death. See Mon ami, je
mourrai aujourd'hui.

Laissez passer la justice du roi.
(Make way for the king's
justice.)

Inscription said to have been
placed, in the reign (1380-1422) of
CHARLES VI (1368-1422), on the
sacks in which the bodies of rebels
were sewn up and thrown into the
Seine during the night. (Cf. C.
Dareste, *Histoire de France*, vol. 2,
p. 552). Chamfort, *Tableaux
historiques de la Révolution* (Tableau
21) refers to July 22, 1789, when
(J.-J.) Foulon's (1715-89) head was
carried through the streets on a
pike preceded by a man who cried
out "Laissez passer la justice du
peuple!" (Make way for the
people's justice.) Cf. "We will
over with him into the Somme, and
put a paper on his breast, with the
legend, 'Let the justice of the
King pass toll-free.'" — Scott,
Quentin Durward, ch. xxviii.

**Laissez passer le tapissier de
Notre-Dame.** (Make way for
the tapestry-maker of Notre-
Dame.)

Remark made by the PRINCE DE
CONTI (1664-1709) when accompanying the MARÉCHAL DE LUXEM-
BOURG (1628-95) to Notre-Dame
(abt. 1694). — *Lettres de J.-B.
Rousseau*, vol. 3, p. 112 (1st
edition). The custom then was to
place in the cathedral the flags
taken from the enemy.

**La 'justice immanente des
choses.'** (The inherent justice
of things.)

LÉON GAMBETTA (1838-82) in
a speech at Cherbourg, Aug. 9,
1880, said, ". . et savoir s'il y a dans
les choses d'ici-bas une justice
immanente qui vient à son jour et
à son heure". (. . and know whether
there is in the things of this world
an inherent justice which comes at
its day and hour.) *La République
française*, Aug. 12, 1880, p. 2
(Résumé de l'agence Havas.)

**La lecture fait à l'esprit ce que
vos perdrix font à mes joues.**
(Reading does for the mind
what your partridges do for
my cheeks.)

Reply made by the DUC DE
VIVONNE (1636-88) when asked by
LOUIS XIV (1638-1715) what was
the use of reading. Vivonne was
stout and of ruddy complexion.
Another version : "Mais à quoi
sert la lecture?—"Sire, la lecture
fait à l'esprit ce que les perdrix de
votre table font à mes joues." (But
what is the use of reading?—Sire,
reading does to the mind what the
partridges of your table do to my
cheeks.)

La légalité nous tue. (Legality
is killing us.) *Œuvres* de
Carrel, vol. 3, p. 383.

J.-G. Viennet (1777-1868)
March 29, 1833. See Sorti de la
légalité etc.

**La littérature mène à tout . . à
condition d'en sortir.** (Litera-
ture leads to everything . . on
condition of leaving it.) A.
Cuvillier-Fleury, *Recueil des
Discours, etc.*, p. 92.
Attributed to A. F. Villemain
(1790-1870) when receiving X.
Marmier (1809-92) at the French
Academy, Dec. 7, 1871.

L' alphabet est à tout le monde.
(The alphabet belongs to everybody.) P. Bourget, *Études et
Portraits—Rivarol.*
Jacques Casanova (1725-1803)
when his title of De Seingalt was
questioned. See Milord, ils sont du
même alphabet.

**La marquise n'aura pas beau
temps pour son voyage.**
(The marchioness will not have
fine weather for her journey.)
Ste.-Beuve, *Causeries du lundi*,
vol. 2, p. 471.
Remark made by Louis XV
(1710-74) on seeing from a window
the coffin of Mme. de Pompadour
(1721-64) on its way from Versailles
to Paris.

La monnaie de Turenne. (Change
for Turenne). *Nouvelle Biographie Universelle.*
Mot of Mme. Cornuel (d.
1694) referring to the creation of
new marshals of France at the death
of Turenne in order to make way
for a *protégé* of Louvois. Often
erroneously ascribed to Mme. de
Sévigné.

**La montagne est passée, nous
irons mieux.** (The mountain
is passed, we shall get along
better now.)
Last words of Frederick the
Great (1712-86)—said to have
been uttered in delirium.

**La mort m'aura tout entier ou
n'aura rien.** (Death shall
have me entirely or shall
have nothing.)
Fabert (1599-1662)—after being
wounded in the thigh at the siege of
Turin (1640), amputation having
been declared necessary. The exact
words, however, were :—"Qui aura
le gigot aura le reste du corps"
(who has the leg of mutton shall have
the rest of the body.) "Il ne faut
pas mourir par pièces; la mort, etc.
(There is no need to die bit by bit,
death, etc.)

La mort sans phrase. (Death
without words.)
The Abbé Sieyès (1748-1836)
is credited with having used these
words in voting for the death of
Louis XVI (Jan. 16, 1793), but the
evidence is that he only voted for
la mort (death), the words *sans
phrase* being a note by the shorthand writer that Sieyès added no
remarks like some of the others did.
(Cf. the *Moniteur*, Jan. 20, 1793,
p. 102; also Lamartine, *Histoire des
Girondins.*)

**L'amour est le roi des jeunes
gens et le tyran des vieillards.**
(Love is the king of young
people and the tyrant of old
men.)
Saying of Louis XII (1462-
1515).

**L'amour est plus fort que toutes
les entraves qu'on lui oppose.**
(Love is stronger than all the
obstacles that may be put in its
way.) A. Mézières, *Vie de
Mirabeau*, p. 63.
Mirabeau (1749-91). Cf: Love
laughs at locksmiths (Proverb).

Were beauty under twenty locks kept
fast,
Yet love breaks through, and picks them
all at last.

Shakspere, *Venus and Adonis*,
v. 96.

9

L'âne de Buridan.   (Buridan's donkey.)

Saying derived from a hypothetical case invented by JEAN BURIDAN (c. 1295-1360) of a donkey equally pressed by hunger and thirst and placed between a bucket of water and a measure of oats at equal distances from it. — Cf. Montaigne's Essays, bk. 2, ch. xiv.

L'Angleterre, ah! la perfide Angleterre.   (England, ah! perfidious England.)

JACQUES BOSSUET (1627-1704)—in his first sermon on the Circumcision.   " L'Angleterre, ah ! la perfide Angleterre, que le rempart de ses mers rendoit inaccessible aux Romains, la foi du Sauveur y est abordée : *Britannorum inaccessa Romanis loca, Christo vero subdita.* (Tert. adv. Jud. v. 7, p 212) (England, ah ! perfidious England, which the ramparts of its seas rendered inaccessible to the Romans, the faith of the Saviour landed there : etc.) Bossuet (1836 vol. 3, p. 687.) Cf. "Je crois, en vérité, comme vous, que le roi et la reine d'Angleterre [James II. and his queen Mary of Este] sont bien mieux à Saint Germain que dans leur *perfide* royaume. (I really think, like yourself, that the king and the queen of England are much better at Saint Germain than in their perfidious realm.)—Mme. de Sévigné. Also Boileau's Ode on a rumour, in 1656, that Cromwell was going to war with France :—

" Jadis on vit ces parricides,
Aidés de nos soldats perfides," etc.

(Formerly we saw these parricides [alluding to the execution of Charles I], aided by our perfidious soldiers, etc.)   Here the word *perfide* is applied to the French soldiers.   In a speech by Barère de Vieuzac (1755-1841) 7 prairial (26th May) 1794 occur the words : " Ne croyez " pas à leur astucieux langage, c'est " un crime de plus de leur caractère " perfide et de leur gouvernement " machiavélique," etc. (Do not believe their [the English] crafty language, it is one more crime in their perfidious character and their Machiavelian government etc.) The speech concludes as follows :—" Que les esclaves anglais périssent, et l'Europe sera libre." (Let the English slaves perish, and Europe will be free.) The *Annual Register* (1794, p. 144) states that in Barère's speech of 30th May, 1794, he said " Do not trust to their artful language, which is an additional crime, truly worthy of their *perfidious character*, and their Machiavelian government." Cf. Les histoires qu'on relit à cause de cet évènement, ne sont pleines que de la perfidie des peuples.— (The stories that are re-read on account of this event, are full of nothing else than the perfidy of nations.) Mme. de Sévigné, *Lettres* (1836, vol. 2, p. 425.) (Letter dated 31/1/1689.) Also " France, by the perfidy of her leaders, has utterly disgraced the tone of lenient council [sic] in the cabinets of princes, and disarmed it of its most potent topics."—E. Burke, *Reflections on the Revolution in France* 1790 (Bohn's Library ed., vol. 2, p. 311.) See La perfide Albion.

La paix à tout prix.   (Peace at any price.)

Phrase used by M. DE MANTALEMBERT (1810-70), Nov. 18, 1840, and which came to be applied to the new ministry. Cf. " We love peace as we abhor pusillanimity ; but not *peace at any price.*—Douglas Jerrold —*Specimens of Jerrold's Wit. Peace.* Also " It would be a curious thing " to find that the party in this " country which on every public " question affecting England is in

"favour of war at any cost, when
"they come to speak of the duty
"of the Government of the United
"States, is in favour of 'peace at
"any price'".—Speech by John
Bright, Dec. 4, 1861, at Rochdale.
"Paris, May 14, 1848 . . . . The
bourgeoisie are eager for war . . . .
Lamartine having proclaimed, 'Paix
à tout prix,' is therefore thought an
obstacle." A. H. Clough's *Letters
and Remains* (London, 1865, p.
105). "Mihi enim omnis pax cum
"civibus, bello civili utilior vide-
"batur". ("I consider that any
peace with our fellow citizens is pre-
ferable to civil war.")—Cicero,
Philippica, 11, 15, 37.

**La parole à été donnée a l'homme
pour déguiser sa pensée.**
(Speech was given to man to
disguise his thoughts.)

Attributed to TALLEYRAND(1754-
1838), in Barère's *Mémoires*, but
claimed by HAREL (d. 1846). Cf.
Le Siècle, Aug. 24, 1846.

Cf. Voltaire, *Dialogue du Chapon
et de la Poularde* (1763) "Ils
"ne se servent de la pensée que
"pour autoriser leurs injustices et
"n'emploient les paroles que pour
"déguiser leurs pensées [written
1763]. (They only use thought to
warrant their injustices and words
only to disguise their thoughts.)
"The true use of speech is not so
"much to express our wants as to
"conceal them."—Goldsmith, *The
Bee*, Oct. 20, 1759.

"Where Nature's end of language is
declin'd,
"And men talk only to conceal the mind."

Young, *Love of Fame*, Satire 2,
l. 207 (1725-6). Imago animi
sermo est. (Speech is the mirror
of the mind.) Seneca, *De Moribus*, 72. Molière (*Le Mariage
forcé*, sc. vi) makes Panurge

say: "La parole a été donnée
"à l'homme pour expliquer sa
"pensée," etc. (Speech was given
to man to *explain* his thoughts
etc). That "speech is the shadow of
deeds" was a saying of DEMOCRITUS
(c. 460—c. 357 B.C)—Diog. L.,
Life. The comte J. d'Estournel in
his *Derniers souvenirs*, p. 319
(1860) attributes the French saying
to MONTROND, Talleyrand's *âme
damnée* (familiar evil spirit).
This is confirmed by Captain
Gronow in his *Recollections and
Anecdotes* (second series, 1863), but
he quotes the phrase as: "La
"parole a été donnée à l'homme
"pour l'aider à cacher sa pensée."
(Speech was given to man to help
him to conceal his thoughts.) Cf.
"Words were given to us to
communicate our ideas by, . . ."—
Lord Chesterfield, *Letters*, June 21,
1748. Also,

"Perspicito tecum tacitus, quid quisque
loquatur,
Sermo hominum mores et ceiat et indicat
idem."

(Note carefully what each man says
for speech Is cloak and index both
of character). — Dionysius Cato,
Disticha de Moribus, iv. 20. See
Language is the picture and counterpart of thought.

La perfide Albion. (Perfidious
Albion).

The following is the nearest
approach that we have as yet been
able to make to the source of this
expression. "L'Angleterre ainsi
"baptisé par nous sous le premier
"Empire et qui devint notre alliée
"sous le second. Logique des
"gouvernements impériaux. E.
"Parny n'appelle jamais l'Angle-
"terre 'qu'Albion'." (England thus
baptized by us during the first
Empire and who became our ally
during the second. Logic of imperial
governments. E. Parny never calls
England otherwise than "Albion.")

L. Rigaud, *Dict. des lieux communs,*
1887. See L'Angleterre, ah! la
perfide Angleterre.

La petite morale tue la grande.
(The little moral [of our daily
life] kills the great.)

Saying of MIRABEAU (1749-91)
Cf. Les petites considérations sont
le tombeau des grandes choses.
(Small considerations are the tomb
of great things). Voltaire.

La plus grande pensée du règne.
(The greatest thought of the
reign).

Attributed to E. ROUHER (1814-
84). MARSHAL E.-F. FOREY
(1804-72), in the course of the
debate on the address, spoke as
follows: "J'ai entendu
"une parole, je ne sais pas si elle
"est exacte ; l'Empereur aurait dit,
"en parlant de l'expédition du
"Mexique, que ce serait une des
"plus belles pages de son règne."
(I have heard one word, I do not
know whether it is correct ; the
Emperor is reported to have said,
speaking of the Mexican expedition,
that it would be one of the finest
pages of his reign.) *Moniteur,*
Mar. 19, 1865. Possibly M.
Rouher in repeating the Emperor's
words gave them the first-named
form.

**La politesse est de toutes les
nations ; les manières de
l'expliquer sont différentes,
mais indifférentes de leur
nature.** (Politeness is of all
nations ; the ways of expressing
it are different, but indifferent
in their nature).

Saying of FÉNELON (1651-1715).

L'appétit vient en mangeant.
(Appetite comes by eating).

Attributed to JACQUES AMYOT
(1513-93) who, having already the
abbey of Bellozane, wanted the

bishopric of Auxerre. On CHARLES
IX (1550-74) expressing astonishment at his greediness, Amyot
used the above phrase. It occurs
in Rabelais (*Gargantua,* bk. 1, ch.
5) as follows: "'L'appétit vient
en mangeant,' disoit Angeston ;
mais la soif s'en va en buvant."
(Appetite comes by eating, said
Angeston ; but thirst goes away by
drinking). Cf.
   " . . . cibus omnis in illo
      Causa cibi est."
(. . . food raises a desire for food
in him). (Ovid's *Metamorphoses,*
bk. 8, ll. 841-2).

**La première des femmes est celle
qui a fait le plus d'enfants.**
(The first among women is she
who has borne the most
children.)

NAPOLEON'S (1769-1821) reply to
MME. DE STAËL (1766-1817), who,
fishing for a compliment, asked him
who was the first among women.

**La première qualité du soldat est
la constance à supporter la
fatigue et la privation ; la
valeur n'est que la seconde.**
(The first quality of a soldier is
constancy in enduring fatigue
and privation ; valour is only
the second). Thiers, *Hist. du
Consulat et de l'Empire,* vol. 1,
p. 47.

NAPOLEON (1769-1821).

**L'arbre de la liberté ne croît
qu'arrosé par le sang des
tyrans.** (The tree of liberty
grows only when watered by the
blood of tyrants).

BERTRAND BARÈRE (1755-1841)
—in a speech to the Convention
Nationale (1792).

**La reconnaissance est la mémoire
du cœur.** (Gratitude is the
memory of the heart).

Written on a black-board by a

deaf-mute MASSIEU who was asked, in writing, at a *séance* of the abbé Sicard (1742-1822) for a definition of gratitude. Cf. "Animus memor" (Cicero) referring to gratitude. See *L'ingratitude est l'indépendance du cœur.*

La réflexion doit préparer et la foudre exécuter. (Reflection should prepare and lightning execute).

Saying of LAZARE HOCHE (1768-97). Cf. Deliberate slowly, execute promptly.

La république, elle est perdue ; les brigands triomphent. (The Republic is doomed ; the brigands triumph).

Reply made by ROBESPIERRE (1758-94), on his arrest being decreed by an immense majority of the National Convention (July 27, 1794) amid cries of *Vive la liberté ! Vive la République !* (Long live liberty ! Long live the Republic !)

La République est le gouvernement qui nous divise le moins. (The Republic is the government which divides us least).

L.-A. THIERS (1797-1877)—in a speech on public instruction, Feb. 13, 1850, said : " . . . elle [the Republic] est, de tous les gouvernements, celui qui nous divise le moins" (. . . . it is of all governments the one that divides us least). —*Discours parlementaires* vol. 8, pp. 608-9.

La République sera conservatrice, ou elle ne sera pas. (The Republic will be conservative, or it will not exist). *Journal Officiel*, Nov. 14, 1872.

In an address read by L.-A. THIERS (1797-1877) to the National Assembly, Nov. 13, 1872.

La révolution française est un bloc . . . . (The French revolution is a block. . . .)

E. CLÉMENCEAU (b-1841)—in a speech in the French Chamber *à propos* of Sardou's play *Thermidor* (represented at the Comédie-Française, Jan. 24 & 26, 1891). "Messieurs, que nous le voulions ou non, que cela nous plaise ou que cela nous choque, la Révolution française est un bloc . . M. MONTAUT.—Indivisible ! M. CLÉMENCEAU . . . un bloc dont on ne peut rien distraire parce que la vérité historique ne le permet pas." (Gentlemen, whether we like it or not, whether it pleases or shocks us, the French revolution is a block . . M. MONTAUT—Indivisible ! M. CLÉMENCEAU . . a block in which nothing can be changed, because historic truth does not permit it.) *Le Journal officiel*, Jan. 30, 1891, pp. 155-6.

La seule différence entre eux et moi, c'est qu'ils sont des descendants et que je suis un ancêtre. (The only difference between them and me is that they are descendants and I am an ancestor.)

GENERAL A. JUNOT'S (1771-1813) reply to those who spoke to him of the prejudices of the old French nobility. Cf. "Mon nom commence en moi : de votre honneur jaloux, "Tremblez que votre nom ne finisse dans vous." (My name begins in me : you jealous of your fame, Beware lest in yourself should end your name).—Voltaire, *Rome Sauvée*, act 1, sc. 5 (Cicéron). See Τὸ μὲν ἐμον ἀπ' ἐμοῦ γένος, etc.

La tragédie court les rues. (Tragedy runs in the streets.)

Reply made by the poet LEMIERRE (1723-93) to those who expressed their astonishment at his refusal to allow his tragedy, *Virginie*, to be acted. "Que voulez-vous, maintenant la tragédie court les rues?" (What would you have, now tragedy runs in the streets?) Nearly the same words were used by DUCIS* (1733-1816) and CHAMFORT (1741-94).

L'avenir appartient à tout le monde. (The future belongs to everyone.)—Lord Malmesbury, *Memoirs of an ex-Minister*, vol. 1, p. 323, 1884.

LORD MALMESBURY (1807-89)—in a letter to Lord Cowley, dated Foreign Office, Mar. 26, 1852.

L'avenir des enfants est l'ouvrage des mères. (The future of children is the work of mothers.)

NAPOLEON (1769-1821).

Laver son linge sale en famille. (To wash one's dirty linen in private).

Derived from a speech (Jan. 1, 1814) by NAPOLEON (1769-1821) to the *Corps législatif* in which he said: "*c'est en famille, ce n'est pas en public, qu'on lave son linge sale.*" (. . . . it is in private, not in public, that dirty linen is washed.)

La victoire sera au plus sage. (Victory will belong to the wisest).

L.-A. THIERS (1797-1877), addressing the National Assembly, Mar. 27, 1877, said:—"Messieurs, je m'adresse à tous les partis indistinctement. Savez-vous à qui appartiendra la victoire? Au plus sage. . . ." (Gentlemen, I am addressing myself to all parties without distinction. Do you know to whom victory will belong? To the

*See Campenon, *Essais de Mémoires* etc., Ducis (1824) p. 79.

wisest).—*Discours parlementaires*, vol. 13, p. 143.

La vieillesse est l'enfer des femmes. (Old age is woman's hell.)

Saying of NINON DE LENCLOS (1616-1705).

La vie n'est qu'un songe : le mien a été beau, mais il est court. (Life is but a dream ; mine has been beautiful, but it is short.)

Dying words of MARSHAL SAXE (1696-1750) to his physician SÉNAC (1693-1770).

La vile multitude. (The vile crowd).

Phrase used by L.-A. THIERS (1797-1877) in a speech in the National Assembly, May 24, 1850, to designate a class of vagabond citizens proposed to be eliminated from the list of voters.

Cf. "Learning will be cast into the mire, and trodden down under the hoofs of a *swinish multitude.*" E. Burke, *On the French Revolution*, (Bohn's Library ed., vol. 2, p. 351.)

Le boulet qui doit me tuer n'est pas encore fondu. (The bullet that is to kill me is not yet moulded).

NAPOLEON (1769-1821) at Montereau, in 1814. Charles V of Spain (1500-58) is said to have asked whether an emperor had ever been hit by a cannon ball.

Le chevalier sans peur et sans reproche. (The knight without fear and without reproach).

Surname applied to the Chevalier Pierre du Terrail, SEIGNEUR DE BAYARD (1476-1524). Francis I after the battle of Marignan (1515) was, at his own request, knighted by Bayard.

Le citoyen Jésus Christ est le premier sans-culotte du monde! (The citizen, Jesus Christ, is the first sans-culotte * in the world!)

F. CHABOT (1759-94)—Sep. 7, 1793.

CAMILLE DESMOULINS (1762-94) April 3, 1794, when stating his age to the revolutionary tribunal said: *J'ai l'âge du sans-culotte Jésus, trente-trois ans quand il mourut.* (I am the age of the *sans-culotte*, Jesus, thirty-three years when he died.) The abbé Maury (1746-1817) at the Constituent Assembly asked the president to 'silence the *sans-culottes*.' (Th. Barrau, Histoire de la Révolution francaise, 1862, p. 134.) Robespierre (1758-94) jokingly applied the term to a women's club, founded by the actress Lacombe, when he proposed to have it closed. Another version of Desmoulin's reply is: " J'ai l'âge de Jésus quand il mourut, 33 ans." (I am the age of Jesus when he died, 33 years).— *Derniers momens*, p. 200.

Le Cléricalisme, voilà l'ennemi! (Clericalism, there's the enemy!) *Journal Officiel*, May 5, 1877, p. 3284.

Concluding words of L. GAMBETTA'S (1838-81) speech in the French Chamber, May 4, 1877, quoting the phrase as being that of his friend Peyrat — ALPHONSE PEYRAT, a journalist, who died 1891.

Le Congrès ne marche pas, mais il danse. The Congress does not progress [walk], but it

* Term applied to the Republicans, because they wore trousers instead of knee-breeches.
Others say it was because the new legislators, mostly poor, had not a culotte to wear.

dances). *Journal des Débats*, Feb. 5, 1861).

The PRINCE DE LIGNE (1735-1814)—alluding to the lively slowness of the Vienna Congress, which began Nov. 1814. Quoted by Jacob Grimm in a letter dated Nov. 23, 1814 (*Briefwechs. d. Grimm*, 1881) to his brother William as: " Le Congrès danse beaucoup, mais il ne marche pas." (The Congress dances much, but it doesn't progress;) and (in German) by Varnhagen of Ense (*Galerie v. Bildnessen aus Rahels Umgang und Briefwechs*, 1836, 1, 171) as: " Der Kongress tanzt wohl, aber geht nicht." (The Congress dances much, but it doesn't progress) after saying that festivities were more thought of at the Congress than the business on hand.

Le contentement voyage rarement avec la fortune, mais il suit la vertu jusque dans le malheur. (Contentment rarely accompanies fortune, but it follows virtue even in misfortune.)

Saying of MARIE LECZINSKA (1703-68) wife of Louis XV.

Le couronnement de l'édifice. (The crowning of the edifice).

NAPOLEON III (1808-73) in a speech delivered Feb. 14, 1853, opening the parliamentary session at the Tuileries, said: " La liberté n'a jamais aidé à fonder d'édifice politique durable; elle le couronne quand le temps l'a consolidé." (Liberty has never helped to found any durable political edifice; it crowns it when time has consolidated it.) A letter (Jan. 1867) addressed to E. Rouher (1814-84) by the Emperor ends: " en achevant enfin le couronnement de l'édifice par la volonté nationale." (. . . completing at last the crowning of the edifice by the national will). The words also occur in a letter from the Emperor to M. Émile Ollivier, dated Jan. 13, 1867. The phrase appears, however, to have originated with CAMILLE JORDAN (1771-1821). Cf. *Vrai sens du Vote National sur le Consulat à vie*, p. 46.

" Le crime fait la honte, et non pas l'échafaud." (Crime makes the shame, and not the scaffold.) —Thomas Corneille, *Le comte d'Essex*, act iv, sc. 3.

Line quoted by MARIE-CHAR-LOTTE DE CORDAY D'ARMONT (1768-93) at the end of a letter of farewell to her father, after murdering J.-P. Marat (1744-93). Charlotte Corday was a descendant of Corneille.

Le diable m'emporte! laissez-les dire, mais qu'ils gardent l'honneur des dames. (The devil fly away with me! let them talk, only let them take care of the ladies' honour.)

Attributed to LOUIS XII (1462-1515) when complaint was made to him of the free language made use of by the Basochiens against his method of governing.

Le drapeau rouge n'a jamais fait que le tour du Champ-de-Mars, et le drapeau tricolore a fait le tour du monde. (The red flag has never made more than the circuit of the Champ-de-Mars and the tricolour has made the tour of the world.)

In a speech by LAMARTINE (1790-1869) to the crowd surrounding the Hotel de Ville, Paris, who were clamouring for the red flag to be officially adopted. ". . . car le drapeau rouge que vous nous rapportez n'a jamais fait que le tour du Champ-de-Mars, traîné dans le sang du peuple en '91 et en '93, et le drapeau tricolore a fait le tour

du monde avec le nom, la gloire et la liberté de la patrie !" (. . . for the red flag that you bring us has, etc., dragged through the blood of the people in '91 and '93, and the tricolour etc., with the name, the glory, and the liberty of the country). —Lamartine, *Hist. de la Révolution de* 1848, bk. 7, ch. 27.

Le droit d'être vêtu simplement n'appartient pas à tout le monde. (The right to dress simply does not belong to everyone.)

Saying of NAPOLEON (1769-1821). Cf. the remark of HENRI DE NAVARRE after the battle of Coutras (1587) on seeing the brilliant costume of the *duc de Joyeuse : Il ne convient qu'à des comédiens de tirer vanité des habits qu' ils portent.* (It is only fitting for comedians to take pride in the clothes they wear).

Le génie n'est qu'une plus grande aptitude à la patience. (Genius is only a greater aptitude for patience.)—H. de Séchelles, *Voyage à Montbar*. An ix [1801] p. 15.

BUFFON (1707-88) in 1785, during a visit to him by H. de Séchelles (1760-94). Variously, but incorrectly quoted, as "Le génie n'est qu'une longue patience. Le génie, c'est la patience. Le génie n'est autre chose qu'une grande aptitude à la patience."—Cf. *Notes and Queries*, 9th S. xi, 373-4. Cf. " The good plan itself, this comes not of its own accord ; it is the fruit of ' genius' (which means transcendant capacity of taking trouble, first of all) :"—Carlyle, *Hist. of Frederick the Great*, bk. 4, ch. 3. " Patience is a necessary ingredient of genius." —Beaconsfield, *Contarini Fleming*. Μελέτη τὸ πᾶν. (Care is everything). —Diogenes i, 7, 6, 99. PERIANDER (fl. B.C. 625).

Le gouvernement de France est une monarchie absolue tempérée par des chansons. (The government of France is an absolute monarchy tempered by songs).

Remark made to Chamfort (1741-94) by a witty person. (Cf. Œuvres choisies, A. Houssaye's edition, p. 800). Often quoted as: "La France est un gouvernement absolu, tempéré par des chansons." (France is an absolute government, etc.) Cf. The following lines at the end of Beaumarchais' *Mariage de Figaro*, alluding to the people of France :

> " Qu'on l'opprime, il peste, il crie,
> Il s'agite en cent fa-açons;
> Tout finit par des chansons."

(Let them be oppressed, they swear, they cry,
They agitate themselves in a hundred ways ;
All ends in songs).

also Beaumarchais'*Barbier de Séville*, act. I, sc. 2. " Aujourd'hui, ce qui ne vaut pas la peine d'être dit, on le chante. (Now-a-days, that which is not worth saying is sung). Cf. the remark by a Russian magnate to Count Munster, the Hanoverian minister, after the murder in 1801 of the Emperor Paul (1754-1801) : " Le despotisme tempéré par l'assassinat, c'est notre Magna Charta." (Despotism tempered by assassination is our Magna Charta). See Liberalism is trust of the people tempered, etc.

Le gouvernement de l' ' ordre moral.' (The government of moral order).

Term applied to the government of Marshal MacMahon (1808-93) who was elected president, May 24, 1873. The words "l'ordre moral " occur in MacMahon's letter published in the *Journal Officiel* of May 25, 1873.

Le " grand Francais" (The "great Frenchman ").

Surname given to FERDINAND DE LESSEPS (1805-94) by LÉON GAMBETTA (1838-82) at a banquet in Paris, May 29, 1879, *à propos* of the Panama Canal.

Le juste milieu. (The golden mean.) *Moniteur universel*, Jan. 31, 1831, p. 1.

In a speech by LOUIS-PHILIPPE (1773-1850) in reply to an address from the town of Gaillac (Tarn) Jan. 29, 1831. " Nous chercherons "à nous tenir dans *un juste milieu*, "également éloigné des excès du " pouvoir populaire et des abus du pouvoir royal." (We shall seek to keep within an exact mean, equally removed from the excesses of popular power and the abuses of royal power). Bossuet, in his *Traité du Libre Arbitre*, ch. 4, vol. x, p. 115, also uses the phrase. Cf. " Pyrrhonisme. — " L'extrême esprit est accusé de folie, " comme l'extrême folie. Rien que " la médiocrité n'est bon . . . . " C'est sortir de l'humanité que de "sortir du milieu : la grandeur de "l'âme humaine consiste à savoir " s'y tenir ", etc. (Pyrrhonism.— Extreme wit is accused of madness, like extreme madness. Nothing but mediocrity is good. . . . . To go beyond the mean is to go beyond humanity : the greatness of the human soul consists in knowing how to keep there, etc).—Pascal, *Pensées*, art 6, 17. " Illud quod medium est atque inter utrumque probamus." (That we approve which both extremes avoids).—Martial, *Epigrams*, I, 57 (58). " In medio tutissimus ibis" (A middle course is the safest)—Ovid, *Metamorphoses*, bk. 2, l. 137 ; also Horace, *Odes*, bk. 2, x, 5 (" aurea mediocritas "). The expression " golden mean " occurs in Massinger's *Great Duke of Florence*, act 1, sc. 1 ; Pope's *Moral Essays*, epist. 3, l. 246, etc.

Le labourage et le pastourage sont deux mamelles dont la France est alimentée et les vraies mines et trésors du Pérou. (Tillage and pasturage are the two breasts by which France is nourished ; and the real mines and treasures of Peru). Sully, *Économies royales*, ch. 82.

Saying of the Duc de Sully (1560-1641).

Le manteau troué de la dictature. (Dictatorship's mantle full of holes.) *Journal Officiel.* Débats parlementaires, p. 1267.

In a speech by C.-T. Floquet (1828-96) in the French Chamber, Apr. 19, 1888, alluding to General Boulanger (1837-91).

Cf. Socrates' saying, of which the above is an application.

Le mot impossible n'est pas français. (The word impossible is not French.)

Saying of Napoleon (1769-1821). " Ce n'est pas possible m'écrivez-vous : cela n'est pas français. (It is not possible, you write : that is not French). — Napoleon's letter to Lémarois, July 9, 1813. Cf. Impossibilium nulla obligatio. (There can be no obligation to perform the impossible). Latin law maxim. " Impossible est un mot que je ne dis jamais." (Impossible is a word that I never utter). Collin d'Harleville, *Malice pour malice*, act 1, sc. 8. " En effet, j'aurais [Fouché] " dû me rappeler que Votre Majesté "[Napoleon] nous a appris que le " mot *impossible* n'est pas français." (In fact I ought to have remembered that your Majesty has taught us that the word *impossible* is not French). — *Mémoires de Joseph Fouché*, 1824, vol. 1, p. 330. It

is said that the Marquis de Feuquières (1648-1711) in the time of Louis XIV said to an officer who excused himself for not having attacked a certain post because it was "inattaquable": " Monsieur, ce mot-là n'est pas français." (Sir, that word is not French). Another version : " Im-" possible, monsieur ? sachez que " ce mot n'est pas français." (Impossible, sir, know that that word, etc). Attributed to a French general in the wars of the Republic, an officer having said that a perilous attack was impossible. Cf. Impossible ! ne me dites jamais ce bête de mot (" Impossible ! never name to me that blockhead of a word.") Carlyle, *The French Revolution* (1837, vol. 2, p. 172). Said by Mirabeau (1749-91) to his secretary : " Impossible ! dit-il en se " soulevant de sa chaise ; ne me " dites jamais ce bête de mot " (Impossible ! said he rising from his chair ; never say that stupid word to me.) Dumont, *Souvenirs sur Mirabeau* 1832, p. 218. Cf. the remark attributed to the Comte d' Auteroches (   ) *à propos* of the siege of Maestricht to someone who spoke of the town as impregnable (*imprenable*) " Ce mot-là, Monsieur, n'est pas français." (That word, sir, is not French.)—Dugast-Dubois de Saint-Just. *Paris la Cour et les Provinces*, vol. 1, p. 6. Also attributed to the Duc de Bourbon in 1744, referring to a town in Piedmont. Carlyle in his essay " Mirabeau " refers to La Fontaine's (*Contes*, bk. iv. 15) conte, " La chose impossible." See Impossible, sir ! don't talk to me of impossibilities.

L'empire, c'est la paix. (The Empire is peace). *Le Moniteur universel.* Oct. 12, 1852.

In a speech at Bordeaux, Oct. 9,

1852, by Prince LOUIS NAPOLEON (1808-73) president of the French Republic (afterwards Napoleon III).

L'empire est au flegmatique. (The Empire belongs to the calm person). E. Hamel, *Hist. de St. Just*, p. 279 (1859).

ANTOINE SAINT-JUST (1767 or 8-94) to ROBESPIERRE (1758-94) who lost his temper in a debate.

Cf. " Il mondo è de' flemmatici ", (The world belongs to the phlegmatic ones). Italian proverb.

L'empire est fait. (The Empire is a fact). *Le Moniteur*, Jan. 18, 1851, p. 187.

L.-A. THIERS (1797-1877)—Jan. 17, 1851, in the French Assembly. See Voici l'empire.

Le mur de la vie privée. (The wall of private life).

Expression originating in a phrase used in a speech by P.-P. ROYER-COLLARD (1763-1846), Apr. 27, 1819. " Voilà donc la vie privée " murée, si je puis me servir de " cette expression . . ." (Private life is therefore shut in by walls, if I may be permitted the expression.) *Le Moniteur universel*, Apr. 29, 1819, p. 529. He repeated the phrase Mar. 7, 1827 : " la vie privée doit être murée." (Private life ought to be within walls.)

TALLEYRAND (1754-1838), according to Stendhal,* is credited with the phrase in a letter to M. Colomb, Oct. 31, 1823. " La vie " privée d'un citoyen doit être " murée." (The private life of a citizen ought to be within walls).

Cf. Alphonse Karr *Les Guêpes*, p. 244.
June 1840 (Michel Lévy) vol. i,

" La vie privée doit être murée."

* *Correspondence*, 1855, pt. 1, p. 249.

L'entente cordiale. (The cordial understanding).

LOUIS-PHILIPPE (1773-1850) in a speech at the opening of Parliament, Dec. 27, 1843, said . " La " sincère amitié qui m'unit à la " reine de la Grande Bretagne et la " *cordiale entente* qui existe entre " mon gouvernement et le sien," etc. (The sincere friendship between me and the queen of Great Britain and the cordial understanding existing between my government and hers, etc. The phrase " A cordial good understanding " however, is said to have been used at an earlier date by LORD ABERDEEN (1784-1860), with regard to France and England, in a private letter to his brother, Sir Robert Gordon (1791-1847) ambassador at Vienna.—*Hist. de la Monarchie de juillet*, vol. 5, p. 207. Name adopted by an Anglo-French (non-political) Association founded 1897, with the object of promoting a " cordial understanding between the English and the French peoples," etc.

Le pauvre homme ! (Poor man !)

From Molière's (1622-73) *Tartuffe* (act I, sc. 5), but said to have been suggested to the poet by LOUIS XIV (1638-1715) alluding to a repast made by Péréfixe, bishop of Rodez, although this is disputed by (A.) Bazin, *les Dernières années de Molière*. According to Tallement des Réaux (*Historiettes*, vol. 2, p. 245) it is a Capucine monk and *not* LOUIS XIV who uttered the exclamation. The monk was enquiring after the health, etc., of père Joseph (1577-1638).

Le petit doigt d'un chasseur. (A chasseur's little finger.)

In a despatch from GENERAL BEURNONVILLE (1752-1821) to the minister of war, dated Dec. 20, 1792, he refers to the losses being

FRENCH SAYINGS

confined to the "petit doigt d'un
de nos chasseurs" (little finger of
one of our chasseurs). *Le Moniteur
universel,* Dec. 23, 1792.

**Le (petit) ruisseau de la rue du
Bac.** (The gutter stream of
the rue du Bac).

MADAME DE STAËL'S (1766-
1817) expression, to typify her
beloved Paris, from which she was
exiled (Cf. her work *Dix Années
d'Exil*) by Napoleon.

"Il n'y a pas pour moi de rivière
"qui vaille mon petit ruisseau," etc.
(There is no river which to me is
equal to my little gutter stream, etc.)
Cf. Ste-Beuve, *Portraits de femmes
et Causeries du lundi.* Another
version : "Ah! il n'y a pas pour
"moi de ruisseau qui vaille celui de
la rue de Bac." (Ah! there is no
stream which to me is worth that of
the rue de Bac).

Le premier vol de l'aigle. (The
eagle's first flight.)

Attributed to A.-M.-J.-J. DUPIN
the elder (1783-1865), Louis
Philippe's testamentary executor,
when, a few weeks after the *coup
d'État* (Dec. 2, 1851) Napoleon III
(1808-73) ordered the sale of the
Orleans family's goods. Also attributed to MME. DE RÉMUSAT
(1780-1821), but she could not have
used it in reference to the same circumstance.

Le quart d'heure de Rabelais.
(Rabelais' quarter of an hour.)

Allusion to the 'bad quarter of
an hour' passed, it is said, by
Rabelais (1483-1553). The story
as regards Rabelais is found in
Rabelaesina Elogia, by Antoine Le
Roy and elsewhere, but discredited.
(Cf. Voltaire *Lettre sur Rabelais,*
1767). Cf.
"So comes a reck'ning when the banquet's
   o'er,
"The dreadful reck'ning ; and men smile
   no more."

—Gay, *The What D'ye Call it,*
act 2, sc. ix. "Il me semble déjà que
"le quart-d'heure de Rabelais sonne,
"que la toile se lève : quelle situation !
"ah je frémis !. . .." (It seems to
me that Rabelais' quarter-of-an-hour
is striking, that the curtain is rising :
what a situation ! ah I tremble !. . .)
—Allainval, *L'Embarras des Rich-
esses*—Prologue (first played, 1725).
See (and cf.) Un mauvais quart
d'heure.

**Le roi de France ne venge pas
les querelles du duc d'Orléans**
or "les injures" instead of "les
querelles", *i.e.* insults. (The
King of France does not avenge
the quarrels of the Duke of
Orleans.)—Suard, *Notes sur
l'esprit d'imitation.*

Phrase used by LOUIS XII (duc
d'Orléans) (1462-1515) on coming to
the throne (1498) and receiving a
deputation from the town of Orleans
making their submission. He said :
"Il ne seroit décent et à honneur à
"un roi de France de venger les
"querelles, indignations et inimities,
"d'un duc d'Orléans." (It would
neither be fitting nor honourable
for a king of France to avenge the
quarrels, indignations and enmitiés
of a Duke of Orleans.) *Chronique
abrégée* published at the end of Jean
d'Auton, by Paul Lacroix, 1835, p.
224. President Hénault, in his
*Abrégé chronologique de l'histoire de
France,* 1744, affirms that the remark
refers more particularly to Louis II
de La Trémoille (1460-1525) who
had made the duc d'Orleans prisoner
at the battle of St. Aubin-le-Cormier
(July 27, 1488). Another version :
"Ce n'est pas au roi de France à
venger les injures du duc d'Orleans."
(It is not for the king of France to
avenge the insults of the duke of
Orleans). See Il serait honteux au
duc de venger les injures faites au
comte.

Le roi est le maître, il peut attendre tant qu'il lui plaira. (The king is the master, he can wait as long as it pleases him).

Said by G. B. LULLI (1633-87) referring to king LOUIS XIV (1638-1715), who arrived too soon at a ballet in which he was to take part.

Le roi est mort, vive le roi! (The king is dead, long live the king!)

Words used by the heralds to the people under the monarchical régime in France (heard for the last time in 1824), announcing at one and the same time the king's death and the coming to the throne of his successor. The words are said to have been used for the first time at the death of Charles VII (1461) and the accession of Louis XI, thus putting in practice the French legal principle "Le roi ne meurt jamais" (the king never dies). On the news reaching the Louvre of the assassination of Henry IV, Sillery, Jeannin and Villeroi, the three ministers leagued against Sully, hastened to the queen. She, on seeing them, cried : "Le roi est mort !"—"Vous vous trompez, madame," replied Sillery; "en France, le roi ne meurt pas." (You are mistaken, madam; in France the king does not die).

Le roi " et son auguste famille." (The king "and his august family.")

Saying said to have been invented by a German named CURTIUS who (abt. 1780) opened a wax-work exhibition in Paris and applied the words " et son auguste famille" to successive groups of figures.

Le roi (*or* la reine) le veult. (The king [or the queen] wills it.)

Form of royal assent made by the Clerk of Parliament to bills submitted to the Crown after passing the two Houses. The form of

dissent (Le roi s'avisera = The king will consider it) is now never used.

Le roi me reverra. (The king will see me again).

Ascribed to PRINCE BISMARCK (1815-98), at his dismissal in March, 1890 ; but the words were never uttered by him (see *Hamburger Nachrichten*, 1 Jan. 1891).

Le roi règne et ne gouverne pas (The king reigns and does not govern).

The *résumé* of the republican party's policy made by A.-L. THIERS (1797-1877) Jan. 18, 1830, in *le National*, a newspaper founded by him. See Rex regnat, sed non gubernat. Cf. also *Le National*, Feb. 19, 1830.

M. Perraud, bishop of Autun, in a speech at the reception of M. Duruy (1811-94) into the French Academy, June 18, 1885, said "Si Dieu existe, ce n'est pas assez "qu'il règne : il faut encore qu'il "gouverne." (If God exists, it is not enough that he should reign : he must also govern.)

Les affaires, c'est l'argent des autres. (Business is other people's money.) Mme. de Girardin, *Marguerite ou deux amours*, vol. 2, p. 104 (1852).

By M. DE MONTROND (   ) to BARON JAMES DE ROTHSCHILD (1844-81). The latter had declined to lend the former some money saying that altho' his house was rich the money belonged to the business. The expression occurs in Dumas fils' *la Question d'argent* (act 2, sc. 7) represented Jan. 31, 1857. Cf. also Béroalde de Verville (1558-1612) *le Moyen de parvenir* (1856 edition p. 184) " *Pétrarche*. Mais de " quoi sont composées les affaires " du monde. *Quelqu'un.* Du bien " d'autrui." *Petrarch*. (But of what is the business of the world composed? *Another*. Of the wealth of other people).

Le sang qui vient de couler était-il donc si pur? (Was the blood that has just been spilt so pure then?)

Said by BARNAVE (1761-93) July 23, 1789)—after the taking of the Bastille (July 15, 1789) referring to the indignation at the death of those who had perished in the tumult. As Barnave was on his way to execution, two men who apparently had taken up a position for the purpose, cried out: "Barnave, le sang qui coule est- "il donc si pur?" (Barnave, is the blood which is being shed so pure then?)—*Memento, ou Souvenirs inédits*, 1838, vol. 2, pp. 223-4.

Also quoted: "Le sang qui vient "de se répandre était-il donc si pur?" (Was the blood that has just been spilt so pure then?)

Le saucisson de M. Constans. (M. Constans' sausage).

Allusion to M. CONSTANS having, in the course of negotiations relative to an insurance company called "la Ville de Lyon" received from M. Baratte, one of the founders, an Arabian gun and a Lyons sausage— *Journal Officiel*, Débats parlementaires p. 608. Mentioned in reply to a question put in the Chamber of Deputies by M. Laguerre (March 16, 1889) who accused M. Constans of having received 10,000 francs and 250 fully paid shares for allowing his name to be placed on the prospectus.

Le saut périlleux. (The dangerous leap.)

Reference to his abjuration of faith made by HENRI IV (1553-1610) in a letter to GABRIELLE d'ESTRÉES (1571-99) July 23, 1593). "*Ce sera dimanche que je fairay le*

sault périlleux" (I shall take the dangerous leap on Sunday).

Les "baïonnettes intelligentes." (Intelligent bayonets.)

Phrase owing its vogue to an article in the *Journal des Débats* of Aug. 10, 1829, in which occurs the following. "Les baïonnettes aujour- "d'hui sont intelligentes; elles con- "naissent et respectent la loi." (Bayonets [i.e. soldiers] to-day are intelligent, they know and respect the law).

Les bleus sont toujours bleus, les blancs sont toujours blancs. (The blues are always blue, the whites are always white).

Remark by NAPOLEON (1769-1821) to GENERAL GERARD (1773-1852) alluding to the defection of GENERAL BOURMONT (1773-1846) June, 1815. Both were afterwards made marshals. *Blancs* and *Bleus* were names given at the time of the Revolution to the *légitimists* (or royalists) and the republican soldiers respectively.

Les bons rois sont esclaves et leurs peuples sont libres. (Good kings are slaves and their subjects are free).

Saying of QUEEN MARIE LECZINSKA (1703-68) wife of Louis XV. Cf. "The king that is not free is not a king."—G. West, *Institution of the Garter*, l. 1156). See who drives fat oxen &c.

Les chevaux du roi de France sout mieux logés que moi. (The king of France's horses are better housed than I).

Said by the DUKE OF HANOVER on seeing LOUIS XIV's stables at Versailles.

Les étrangers sont la postérité contemporaine. (Foreigners are contemporary posterity).

—*The Croker papers* (1884, vol 1, 326).

MME. DE STAËL (1766-1817), when in England, referring to the high Continental opinion of the riches, strength and spirit of this country. Mr. Croker (under date Oct. 24, 1825) says. "This striking "expression I have since found in "the journal of Camille Des-"moulins." (The exact reference is not given, and the editor has not yet been able to find it). Cf. "Byron's "European fame is the best earnest "of his immortality, for a foreign "nation is a kind of contemporaneous "posterity." *Stanley, or the Recollections of a Man of the World*, vol. 2, p. 89.

Les gens que j'ai vus à la cour m'ont forcée de m'estimer. (The people I have seen at court have forced me to esteem myself).

Said by MME. DU BARRY (1743-93), alluding to the people of quality surrounding Louis XV.

Les grands noms ne se font qu'en Orient. (It is only in the East that great names are made).

Saying of NAPOLEON (1769-1821) after his return from Italy (1797) and being desirous that the expedition to Egypt (1798) should be undertaken.

Les "hochets de la vanité." (Vanity's playthings).—*Moniteur universel*, June 3, 1848.

Term applied by CLÉMENT THOMAS ( ) general of the *garde nationale* in the National Assembly, June 2, 1848, with regard to the cross of the Legion of Honour. On May 7, 1802, when the question of the creation of the Legion of Honour was being discussed, NAPOLEON (1769-1821) said, replying to Berlier ( ), "On appelle

"cela des *hochets*; eh bien! c'est "avec des hochets que l'on mène "les hommes," etc. (They call those playthings; well, it is with playthings that men are led.) —*Mémoires sur le Consulat* (1827) p. 83.

Le silence des peuples est la leçon des rois. (The peoples' silence is the kings' lesson).—*Sermons de Messire de Beauvais*, 1807, vol. 4, p. 243.

In the funeral sermon of LOUIS XV (1710-74) preached by the ABBÉ DE BEAUVAIS (1731-90) at Saint-Denis (July 27, 1774). . . . *et son silence est la leçon des rois* (. . . and their [the peoples'] silence is the kings' lesson). Repeated by Mirabeau to the Constituent Assembly, July 15, 1789.—Thiers, *Révolution française*, vol 1, ch. 2. Cf. Silence often expresses more powerfully than speech the verdict and judgment of society.—Speech of Disraeli in House of Commons, Aug. 1, 1862.

L'esprit nouveau. (The new spirit).

Phrase used by E. SPULLER (1835-96) minister of public instruction,—in the Chamber of Deputies, March 3, 1894, alluding to an order of the mayor of St. Denis prohibiting religious ceremonies on the public highways.

Les restes d'une voix qui tombe, et d'une ardeur qui s'éteint. (The remains of a failing voice and of an expiring ardour).

Concluding words of JACQUES BOSSUET'S (1627-1704) funeral sermon on the PRINCE DE CONDÉ, March 10, 1687.

Les siècles ne sont pas à nous. (The centuries are not ours).—Thiers, *Le Consulat et l'Empire*, bk. 25.

NAPOLEON (1769-1821) in 1806

to his brother JOSEPH, KING OF
NAPLES (1768-1844) when advising
him to erect fortresses, etc., at once.

L'essai loyal.   (The loyal trial).

L.-A. THIERS (1797-1877) in his
speech of Jan. 17, 1851, said, referring to the Republic, "Faisons
"donc cette expérience, faisons-la
"loyalement, sans arrière-pensée."
(Let us then try this experiment,
try it loyally, unreservedly.)—*Discours parlementaires*, vol 9, p.
105.   On Dec. 26, 1871, he said,
"Croyez-moi, vous qui voulez faire
"un essai de la République, et
"vous avez raison, il faut le faire
"loyal."   (Believe me, you who
wish to make a trial of the Republic,
and you are right, you must make
it loyally).   *Ibid*, vol 13, p. 627.

Les souliers de M. Dupin.   (M.
Dupin's shoes.)

Saying alluding to the thick
country shoes worn by A.-M.-J.-J.
DUPIN, aîné (the elder) (1783-1865).
He was in the habit of attending
each year the agricultural meetings
at Clamecy, of which he was the
founder, dressed in country fashion,
and his "gros souliers" became quite
celebrated.

Les temps heroïques sont passés.
(The heroic times have passed
away).

LÉON GAMBETTA (1838-82).

Cf.   " Ils sont passés ces jours de fête.
      " Ils sont passés, ils ne reviendront
        pas."

(They are past, those fête-days.
They are past, they will not return).
Anseaume, *Le Tableau parlant*, sc. v.

Le style est l'homme même.
(The style is the man himself).

In the speech made by BUFFON
(1707-88) on his reception by the
French Academy (Aug. 25, 1753).
Variously misquoted

"Le style est tout l'homme."
"Le style, c'est l'homme."

L'état, c'est moi.   (I am the State.)
Voltaire, *Siècle de Louis* XIV,
ch. 24.   Dulaure, *Hist. of Paris*,
1863, p. 387.

Words attributed to LOUIS XIV
(1638-1715) in a speech to his
parliament, April 13, 1655.   The
words "*mon État*" occur in it as
reported in the *Journal d'un bourgeois de Paris*, and have probably
given rise to the expression.
Napoleon, examining his position in
1813, quoted the phrase. . . . *à
compter de ce jour*, "*l'État ce fut
moi!*" (. . . from that moment, I
was the State).—*Mémorial de Sainte-
Hélène.*

M. le duc de Noailles in his
Histoire de Mme. de Maintenon
(vol. 3, pp. 667-70) denies that the
famous phrase was ever uttered by
the king, but says the "*mot*" will
"stick to him, because it is within
"the truth, if it is taken in its true
"sense : the sentiment of the close
"relationship which exists between
"the interest of the country and
"that of royalty."   It may be noted
that in his instructions to his son he
says : "Quand on a l'État en vue, on
"travaille pour soi.   Le bien de
"l'un fait la gloire de l'autre.
"(When one has the State in view,
"it is working for one's self.   The
"good of one makes the glory of
"the other)."   Again : "La nation
"ne fait pas corps en France, elle
"réside tout entière dans la personne
"du roy." (The nation does not constitute a *corps* in France ; it resides
entirely in the king's person.)—
Monarchie de Louis XIV, etc.,
1818, p. 327.   The following is from
la Revue britannique for May, 1851,
p. 254.

"Sans nier à notre souscripteur
"qu'Elisabeth, avant Louis XIV,
"eût dit ou à peu près dit : L'État

"c'est moi! sans entrer avec lui "dans une polémique sur la politique "et la religion d'Elisabeth," etc. [the point is not pursued]. (Without denying to our subscriber that Elizabeth, before Louis XIV, had said or almost said, "I am the State," without entering into a discussion with him as to Elizabeth's politics and religion, etc.)

Le temps et moi. (Time and I.) Cardinal MAZARINS' motto (1602-61). Cf. 'Oft was this saying in our bishop's mouth,' says Lloyd, before ever it was in Philip the Second's — "Time and I will challenge any two in the world." *State Worthies* (1670, pp. 88-9). See Time is on our side.

L'étude a été pour moi le souverain remède contre les dégoûts de la vie, n'ayant jamais eu de chagrin qu'une heure de lecture n'ait dissipé. (Study has been for me the sovereign remedy against life's mortifications, never having had a chagrin that an hour's reading has not dissipated.) Saying of MONTESQUIEU (1689-1755) in his youth.

L'Europe sera républicaine ou cosaque. (Europe will be Republican or Cossack.) Prophecy usually attributed to NAPOLEON (1769-1821), but probably derived from the following remark made by him. ". . . car dans l'état actuel des "choses, avant dix ans, tout "l'Europe peut être cosaque, ou "toute en république." (. . . for in the present state of things before ten years, all Europe may be Cossack, or all Republican).—*Mémorial de Ste. Hélène*, vol. 3, p. 111 (1828).

L'exactitude est la politesse des rois. (Punctuality is the politeness of kings.)
Saying of Louis XVIII (1755-1824).—*Souvenirs de J. Laffitte*, vol. 1, p. 150.

L'exploitation de l'homme par l'homme. (The exploiting of man by man.)
Phrase used by socialists. It occurs in a letter from le PÈRE ENFANTIN (1796-1864) dated Nov. 15, 1828, ". . . l'exploitation sans travail de l'homme par l'homme." (. , . the exploiting without work of man by man.)—*Œuvres de Saint-Simon et d'Enfantin*, 1872, vol. 25, p. 109. The phrase was used in 1840 at a banquet in a speech by the banker GOUDCHAUX.—Thureau-Dangin, *Hist. de la Monarchie de juillet*, vol. 4, p. 182.

L'heure est venue de guérir toutes mes plaies par une seule. (The time has come to cure all my wounds with a single one.)
HENRI II (1595-1632) duc de Montmorency and marshal of France, when his surgeon pressed him to let his wounds be dressed. He was decapitated the same day.

L'homme malade. (The sick man.)
According to the *Annuaire historique* for 1853 (p. 66 and following) this celebrated phrase was used by the Emperor NICHOLAS I of Russia (1796-1855) in a conversation with Sir E. Hamilton Seymour at a *soirée* given by the Grand-Duchess Hélène. He said " Tenez, nous avons sur les "bras *un homme malade*." (We have on our hands a sick man.) Also said to have been used by him when in England in 1844 in conversation with the Duke of Wellington and Lord Aberdeen, referring to Turkey. " We have on our hands "*a sick man*, a very sick man. It "would be a great misfortune if one "of these days he should happen to

"die before the necessary arrange-
"ments are made." . . . —Nicholas
of Russia, to Sir George Hamilton
Seymour, British chargé d'affaires
(Jan. 11, 1844). Cf. *Blue Book*,
1854. Sir Thomas Roe (c. 1568?-
1644), ambassador of James II at
Constantinople, wrote that the
Ottoman Empire had "the body of
"a sick old man, who tried to appear
"healthy, although his end was
"near." The *Dict. of Nat. Biog.*
(vol. 49, p. 90) says that he described
the Turkish Empire as "irrecover-
ably sick" (*Negotiations*, p. 126)
and compared it (almost in the words
of the Emperor Nicholas 230 years
later) to 'an old body, crazed
'through many vices, which remain,
'when the youth and strength is
'decayed.' (*Ibid*, p. 22). Don
John, Governor-general of the
Netherlands, writing in 1577 to
Philip II of Spain, referred to the
prince of Orange as "the sick man."
He said to Philip: "Money is the
"gruel with which we must cure
"this sick man."—Motley, *The
Dutch Republic*, vol. 2. Said the
Emperor Frederick-William IV
(1795-1861) to the ambassador, on
Feb. 20, 1853: "Ich wiederhole
"Ihnen, dass der Kranke im Sterben
"liegt." (I repeat to you that the
sick man lies in death). Voltaire,
in his correspondence (XVI) with
Catherine of Russia, wrote: "Votre
"Majeste dira que je suis un malade
"bien impatient et que les Turcs
"sont beaucoup plus malades."
(Your Majesty will say that I am an
impatient sick person and that the
Turks are much more sick.) Cf.
"J'ai vu avec étonnement la faiblesse
"de l'empire des Osmanlins. Ce
"corps malade ne se soutient pas par
"un régime doux et tempéré, mais
"par des remèdes violents qui
"l'épuisent et le minent sans cesse."
(I have seen with astonishment the
weakness of the Ottoman empire.

This sick body is not supported by a
mild and temperate diet, but by
violent remedies which continually
exhaust and undermine it).—Montesquieu, *Lettres persanes*, letter 19
(first pub. 1721). Parodied by
Mr. T. Healy (born 1855) in the
House of Commons, July 24, 1902,
alluding to Ireland as "the sick
child of the British Empire."—*The
Daily Telegraph*, July 25, 1902.

**L'homme s'agite, mais Dieu le
mène.** (A man's heart de-
viseth his way; but the Lord
directeth his steps—Book of
Proverbs xiv. 9).

In a sermon by FÉNÉLON (1651-
1715), on the subject of the discovery
of America, for the feast of Epiphany
(Jan. 6, 1685). "Mais que vois-je
"depuis deux siècles ? Des régions
"immenses qui s'ouvrent tout-à-
"coup ; un nouveau monde inconnu
"à l'ancien et plus grand que lui.
"Gardez-vous bien de croire qu'une
"si prodigieuse découverte ne soit
"due qu'à l'audace des hommes.
"Dieu ne donne aux passions
"humaines, lors même qu'elles
"semblent décider de tout, que ce
"qu'il leur faut pour être les instru-
"ments de ses desseins. Ainsi
"*l'homme s'agite, mais Dieu le
"mène.*" (But what do I see in
the past two centuries? Immense
regions which suddenly open ; a
new world unknown to and larger
than the old one. Do not allow
yourselves to believe that such a
prodigious discovery is only due to
the daring of men. God only gives
to human passions, even when
they seem to decide everything,
just what is necessary for them
to be the instrumeuts of his designs. Thus, &c. Cf. "Homo pro-
ponit, sed Deus disponit." (Man
proposes, but God disposes).
Thomas à Kempis, Imitation of
Christ, bk. 1, ch. 19.

" L'homme aujourd'hui sème la cause,
" Demain Dieu fait mûrir l'effet."—
(Man to-day sows the cause,
To-morrow God ripens the effect—)
V. Hugo, *Les Chants du Crépuscule*—
Napoléon II.

Liberté, égalité, fraternité. (Liberty, equality, fraternity).

Motto of the French Republic, invented by ANTOINE-FRANCOIS MOMORO (1756-94). He was of Spanish origin, and in 1789 styled himself *premier imprimeur de la liberté.* Under the Reign of Terror the words were preceded by *Unité et indivisibilité de la République* (Unity and indivisibility of the Republic) and followed by *ou la mort* (or death). In Chamfort's (1741-94) opinion (indignant at the misuse of the word *fraternité*) the words *fraternite ou la mort* meant *Sois mon frère ou je te tue* (Be my brother or I kill thee).

Cf. " Bon Dieu ! l'aimable siècle où
l'homme dit à l'homme,
"Soyons frères—ou je t'assomme.
(Heavens, what an age ! when man to
man doth cry
Let us be brothers—for if not, you die.)
Ecouchard Lebrun.— *Epigrammes*, V, 23.

L'immobilité, c'est le plus beau mouvement de l'exercice. (Immobility is the finest movement of exercise.)—E. Blaze, *La vie militaire sous le 1er empire* (edition 1888, p. 21).

Phrase used by KUHMANN, an Alsatian, at the military school at Fontainebleau.

L'impot du sang. (The blood-tax).

Phrase used for the first time by GENERAL FOY (1775-1825) in the French Chamber, May 28, 1824, speaking against the bill for increasing the number of recruits for the army. . . . *cet impot du sang.* (. . . This blood-tax. . . .) *Le Moniteur universel,* May 30, 1824, p. 685

L'ingratitude est l'indépéndance du cœur. (Ingratitude is the heart's independence).

One of three sentences written by NESTOR ROQUEPLAN (1804-70), the author of *Nouvelles à la main,* in an album at the request of M. Philoxene Boyer. See Gratitude is a lively sense &c.

L'insurrection est le plus saint des devoirs. (Insurrection is the holiest of duties).—Mémoirs etc., du Général Lafayette 1837, vol. 2, p. 382.

In a speech by GENERAL LAFAYETTE (1757-1834) Feb. 20, 1790, to the Constituent Assembly. The context materially qualifies the sense of the phrase.
Cf. "Quand le gouvernement "viole les droits du peuple, l'insur- "rection est, pour le peuple et pour "chaque portion du peuple, le plus "sacré des droits et le plus indis- "pensable des devoirs." (When the government violates the people's rights, insurrection is, for the people and for each portion of the people, the most sacred of rights and the most indispensable of duties).— *Moniteur universel,* June 27, 1793. See Rebellion to tyrants etc.

L'Italie est un nom géographique. (Italy is a geographical name.)

PRINCE METTERNICH (1773-1859)—in corresponding with LORD PALMERSTON (1784-1865) in 1847. See Deutschland ein geographischer Begriff.

L'ordre avec le désordre. (Order with disorder).

Phrase used by M. MARC CAUSSIDIÈRE (1809-61) prefect of police and member of parliament for the Seine, May 16, 1848, in the French Assembly, when rendered responsible for the disorder of the preceding day. "J'ai maintenu l'ordre avec le désordre." (I have maintained order with disorder). — *Le Moniteur universel*, May 17, 1848, pp. 1064-5.

L'ordre règne à Varsovie. (Order reigns at Warsaw).

GENERAL HORACE SÉBASTIANI (1772-1851) on Sep. 16, 1831, communicated to the Chamber the news that Warsaw was in the hands of Russia (Sep. 8, 1831). The actual words were, *La tranquillite*, instead of *L'ordre*. Cf. *Le Moniteur universel*, Sep. 17, 1831, p. 1601, also Dumas, *Mémoires*, 2nd series, vol. 4, ch. 3.

L' "organisateur de la victoire" (The organiser of victory).

Origin uncertain, but according to the account of a sitting of the Convention on May 27, 1795, in the *Moniteur* of June 2, 1795, Carnot spoke and someone cried out "Carnot a organisé la victoire" (Carnot has organised victory). In *Mémoires sur Carnot*, by his son, (vol. 1, p. 585, 1861) a voice [some say Lanjuinais, others Bourdon] cried : "Oserez-vous porter la main "sur celui qui a organisé la victoire "dans les armées françaises ?" (Will you dare lay hands on him [Carnot] who has organised victory in the French armies?)

Madame, je vous ai fait attendre longtemps; mais vous avez tant d'amis que j'ai voulu avoir seul ce mérite auprès de vous. (Madam, I have made you wait a long time ; but you have so many friends that I wanted to be the only one to have this distinction with regard to you).

LOUIS XIV (1638-1715) when handing to MME. SCARRON (1635-1719) the brevet of her pension.
A similar compliment is said to have been paid by LOUIS XIV to

CARDINAL FLEURY (1653-1743) on his appointment as Bishop of Fréjus (cf. Noël and Planche, *Éphémérides*, April 1803, p. 144).

Madame* se meurt ! Madame est morte ! (Madam is dying ! Madam is dead !)

JACQUES BOSSUET (1627-1704)— in his sermon at St. Denis, Aug. 21, 1670, on the death of HENRIETTA OF ENGLAND, duchess of Orleans (1644-70).

Ma demeure sera bientôt dans le néant et mon nom vivra dans le Panthéon de l'histoire. (My dwelling will soon be non-existent and my name will live in history's Pantheon).

DANTON'S (1759-94) reply when asked, at his trial, his name and abode. Preceded by : "Je suis "Danton, assez connu dans la "révolution ;" (I am Danton, pretty well known in the revolution). —*Derniers momens*, p. 200.

Ma foi, j'ai vu que Votre Majesté et moi ne sommes pas grand' chose. (Faith, I saw that your Majesty and I are of little account).

Said to LOUIS XV (1710-74) by LANDSMATH, his equerry, whom he had ordered to go and see the body of the latter's confessor, in reply to the king's question, 'What did you see?'

Mais donne donc ! mais donne donc ! (Give it me then ! give it me then !) *Derniers moments et agonie de M. le comte de Buffon*, etc. Corr. inéd., vol. 2, pp. 612-4.

Last words of BUFFON (1707-88)

* "Madam" is the title given to the eldest daughter of the king or the dauphin or the wife of "Monsieur" the king's brother.

alluding to the extreme unction. Another account by one of his secretaries (Aude, pp. 53-4) says that his last words were addressed to his son : " Ne quittez jamais le " chemim de la vertu et de l'honneur, "c'est le seul moyen d'être heureux." (Never leave the path of virtue and honour, it is the only way to be happy).

Mangez un veau et soyez chrétien. (Eat a calf and be a Christian)— Racine, *Fragments historiques.*

Reply by the ABBÉ FEUILLET, (1622-93), during Lent, to MONSIEUR (the king's eldest brother). The latter took a small biscuit from the table saying : "Cela n'est pas rompre le jeûne, n'est-il pas vrai ? " (That isn't breaking the fast, is it ?)

Mangez-vous de la vache à Colas ? (Lit. Do you eat Colas's cow? but really meaning : Are you a Huguenot ?)

Saying towards the end of HENRI IV's reign. Allusion to an incident (Sep. 1605) with regard to a cow belonging to Colas Pannier, farmer at Bionne, near Orleans. " Il est de la vache à Colas," a proverbial expression used to designate Protestants. Cf. D. Lottin—*Recherches historiques sur la ville d' Orleans*, etc.

Marche! Marche! (March ! March !)

JACQUES BOSSUET (1627-1704)— in one of his sermons for Easter Day, alluding to the onward march of human life.

M. de la Rochefoucault m'a donné de l'esprit, mais j'ai réformé son coeur. (M. de la Rochefoucault has given me wit, but I have reformed his heart).

MME. DE LA FAYETTE (1634-93) of LA ROCHEFOUCAULT (1613-80). Made in the 1st edition of *Segraisiana*

(p. 28) to read thus : " Madame de " La Fayette, disoit M. de La " Rochefoucault," etc. (Mme de La Fayette, said M. de La Rochefoucault, etc.), instead of " Madame "de La Fayette disoit : M. de La " Rochefoucault m'a donné," etc. (Mme de La Fayette said : " M. "de la Rochefoucault has given me," etc.)

Mes amis, allez-vous-en et priez pour moi, afin que mon agonie s'achève en paix. (My friends, go away and pray for me, so that I may die in peace).

Last words of CHARLES V., the Wise (1337-80). The correct version, however, is : " Mes amis, alez vous "en, et priez pour moy, et me "laissiez, affin que mon traveil soit "finé en paix." Christine de Pisan, *Le livre des fais du sage roy, Charles* [V], pt. 3, ch. 71 (vol vi of the "Collection complète des Mémoires" edition Petitot, 1825, p. 44).

Mes amis, je ne vous ferai jamais pleurer autant que je vous ai fait rire. (My friends, I shall never make you weep so much as I have made you laugh).

Dying words of P. SCARRON (1610-60).

Messieurs, j'espérais avant peu vous faire sortir d'ici ; mais m'y voila moi-même avec vous, et je ne sais comment cela finira. (Gentlemen, I was hoping before long to set you free ; but here I am with you myself, and I know not how it will end).

DANTON (1759-94)—when conducted to the Luxemburg prison, to his fellow-prisoners.

Messieurs, la séance continue! (Gentlemen, the sitting is proceeding !)

CHARLES DUPUY (   ) Dec.

9, 1893, to restore calm to the Assembly immediately after the Anarchist Vaillant's bomb had exploded in the French Parliament.

Messieurs (les Anglais), tirez les premiers. (Gentlemen [the English], fire first).

At the battle of Fontenoy (May 11, 1745) LORD CHARLES HAY (died 1760) said: *Messieurs des gardes françaises, tirez!* (Gentlemen of the French guards, fire!) to which the COMTE D'AUTEROCHES replied: "Messieurs, nous ne tirons jamais "les premiers, tirez vous-mêmes." (Gentlemen, we never fire first, fire yourselves).—Voltaire, *Précis du règne de Louis XV*, edition 1769, p. 176. The *Dict. Nat. Biog.*, however, in its article on Lord Charles Hay (vol. XXV, p. 253) contradicts the statement that he uttered the above words. Cf. Also Marquis de Valfons, *Souvenirs* (1860), p. 143.

Messieurs, nous avons un maître; ce jeune homme fait tout, peut tout, et veut tout. (Gentlemen, we have a master, this young man does everything, is capable of anything, and desires everything).

Attributed to the ABBÉ SIEYÈS (1748-1836), referring to NAPOLEON (1769-1821), but denied by him. His account is that on Bonaparte asking why he would not remain consul with him, he replied, " Il "ne s'agit pas de consuls, et je ne "veux pas être votre aide de camp." (It is not a question of consuls, and I don't want to be your aide-de-camp.)

Messieurs, voilà le maréchal de Biron que je présente également à mes amis et à mes ennemis. (Gentlemen, there is marshal Biron whom I present

equally to my friends and my enemies).

HENRI IV (1553-1610)—to the deputations who came to compliment Charles de Gontaut, DUC DE BIRON (1562-1602), on his being raised to the peerage (1598), after the retaking of Amiens (Sep. 25, 1597).

Mes six sous! mes six sous! (My six sous [halfpennies]! my six sous!)

Saying of BOIELDIEU (1775-1834) —alluding to an old man's blessing in return for the above sum, given him by Boieldieu when a child at Rouen.

Mieux vaut mille fois mourir avec gloire que de vivre sans honneur. (Better a thousand times to die with glory than live without honour).

Maxim attributed to LOUIS VI (surnamed *le Gros*) (1078-1137).

Mignonne, je vous donne ma mort pour vos étrennes. (My darling, I give you my death for a New Year's gift).

LOUIS XII (1462-1515)—to his young (and third) wife (PRINCESS MARY, sister of Henry VIII) on his death-bed. He died Jan. 1, 1515.

Milord, ils sont du même alphabet. (My lord, they are of the same alphabet). *The Croker Papers*, vol. 1, p. 327.

MME. DE STAËL (1766-1817) at Lord Liverpool's (1770-1828) house at Coombe Wood (near Addiscombe) when asked whether M. de Ségur, ambassador at Berlin, was related to the old family of Ségur (meaning that they were *not* related, although of the same name). She at first said that they were related "*du côte des syllabes*" (on the side of the syllables). See L'alphabet est à tout le monde.

Misérable, tu n'empêcheras pas nos têtes de se baiser dans le panier. (Wretch, thou wilt not prevent our heads from kissing in the basket [of the guillotine].)

Last words of DANTON (1759-94) —addressed to the executioner, who prevented him embracing his friend HÉRAULT DE SÉCHELLES (1760-94) April 5, 1794.

M. le président ne veut pas qu'on le joue. (The president * will not allow it to be played).

Attributed (but erroneously—see Taschereau, *Hist. de Molière*, 2nd edit., p. 122) to MOLIÈRE (1622-73) *à propos* of *Tartuffe*.

Some have it that the meaning was that the president would not allow himself to be represented. Cf. "Nous allions vous donner le *Bon Père* ; Monseigneur ne veut pas qu'on le joue." (We were going to give you *le Bon Père ;* my lord will not allow it to be played). This announcement was made by FLORIAN (1755-94) one evening with regard to his comedy, *le Bon Père*, M. le duc de Penthièvre (1725-93) having said that he would not come to see it. The *mot* is also attributed to LOPES DE VEGA (1562-1635) or CALDERON (1600-81) with regard to a comedy entitled l'Alcade [de Zamalea]. "L'alcade ne veut pas qu'on le joue." (The alcade will not allow it [himself] to be played).

Mon ami, je mourrai aujourd'hui. (My friend, I shall die to-day).

Dying words of MIRABEAU (1749-91) to his doctor, Cabanis. Followed by : "Quand on est là, "il ne reste plus qu'une chose à "faire, c'est de se parfumer, de se "couronner de fleurs et de s'en-

* M. de Lamoignon (1617-77).

"vironner de musique, afin d'entrer "agréablement dans le sommeil "dont on ne se réveille plus." (When you are at that point, there remains only one thing more to be done, that is to scent yourself, to crown yourself with flowers, so as to enter agreeably upon that sleep from which there is no awakening). —A. Mézières, *Les Mirabeau*, vol 5, pp. 336-7.

Mon ami, veux-tu bien permettre que je finisse ma dernière douzaine d'huîtres ? (My friend, will you let me finish my last dozen of oysters ?)

General A.-L. de Gontaut, DUC DE BIRON (1747-93)—to the executioner, who came to tell him that all was ready. See also J'ai été infidèle a Dieu &c.

Mon devoir à moi, c'est de conserver. (My duty is to preserve [life.])

DESGENETTES (1762-1837) to NAPOLEON (1769-1821) at Jaffa, (May 1799)—when the former advised the use of opium for putting an end to the sufferings of the plague-stricken soldiers. Another version (perhaps less likely), in Thiers' *Histoire de la Révolution française*, is : Mon métier est de les guérir, et non de les tuer. (My profession is to cure, and not to kill them). Cf. also *la Biographie générale*, col. 252 note.

Mon Dieu ! La nation française ! Tête d'armée ! (My God ! The French nation ! Head of the army !)

Last (incoherent) words of NAPOLEON (1769-1821). He died on the island of St. Helena, May 5, 1821.

Lord Rosebery's *The last phase* gives them as : "France . . . armée . . . tête d'armée." An-

other account says: "Mon fils ! . . .
Tête d'armée. . . . France." (My
son ! . . . Head of the army. . . .
France).

**Mon pauvre La Fontaine, vous
seriez bien bête si vous
n'aviez pas tant d'esprit.**
(My poor La Fontaine, you
would be very stupid if you
hadn't so much wit).

MME. DE LA SABLIÈRE (1636-93)
to La Fontaine (1621-95). He did
not usually shine in company.

**Monseigneur, ces deux corps
vont avoir l'honneur de se
combiner devant vous.** (My
lord, these two bodies are going
to have the honour of combin-
ing before you).

Remark said to have been made
by BARON THÉNARD (1777-1857) on
the occasion of a visit of the DUC
D'ANGOULÈME (1775-1844) to the
École polytechnique. Another version is that the phrase was used to
LOUIS XVIII (1755-1824) and that
"*gaz*" was said instead of "*corps.*"

Monseigneur, vous avez tort !
(My lord, you are wrong !)

BENSERADE (1612-91) to CAR-
DINAL MAZARIN (1602-61) concerning a dispute in a game of
piquet. "What dost thou know of
it ?" rejoined the cardinal. "The
silence of these gentlemen proves
it : they would cry out louder than
you if you were right." Voltaire
credits the COMTE DE GRAMONT
(1604-78) with a similiar remark
made to LOUIS XIV (1638-1715).

Mon siège est fait. (My siege is
finished.)

Reply by ABBÉ VERTOT (1655-
1735) when some documents were
brought to him for his History of the
Order of Malta and the Siege of
Rhodes. He had already finished
his history and said, when the docu-

ments arrived, "J'en suis fâché
mais," etc. (I am sorry but, etc.)
d'Alembert *Réflexions sur l'histoire*,
read to the French Academy, Jan.
19, 1761. Cf. I have victualled
my camp.—English Saying.

Monsieur est encore tout chaud !
(Monsieur [the body of] is still
quite warm !)

Said by the DUC DE MONTFORT
—just after the death of Philip, duke
of Orleans (1640-1701)—when asked
if he would play at brelan (a game
of cards).

**Monsieur le maréchal, on n'est
pas heureux à notre âge.**
(Monsieur the marshal, one is
not lucky * at our age)

LOUIS XIV. (1638-1715) to
MARSHAL VILLEROI (1644-1730)
Their respective ages at the time
were 68 and 63.

Mort au champ d'honneur! (Dead
on the field of honour !)

Reply made by the oldest sergeant
of the regiment (46th demi-brigade)
every day when the name of LA TOUR
D'AUVERGNE (1743-1800) was
called (his name stood at the head
of the roll). This homage only
ceased to be paid to him in 1814.
Théophile-Malo Corret de la Tour
d'Auvergne, called *le premier grenadier de France* (the first grenadier of
France) was killed at Oberhausen
June 27, 1800. The ceremony has
been (1897) revived and a similar
one with regard to sergeant Blandan
(the hero of Beni-Mered) was ordered
(Dec. 5, 1881) by Col. Brugnot
commanding the 26th regt. of the
line. Cf. Washington Irving's
Sketches in Paris in 1825: *The
Field of Waterloo* (Stuyvesant edition, vol. 4. p. 251) in which mention
is made of both "Dead on the field

* Alluding to the marshal's reverses.

of honour !" and "Premier Grena-dier de France."

Mort aux tyrans, paix aux chaumines. (Death to the tyrants, peace to the cottages.)

Oath taken by the Jacobins (Jan. 21, 1794), on the anniversary of LOUIS XVI's (1754-93) death, at the foot of the statue of Liberty, *place de la Révolution.* See Guerre aux châteaux &c.

Morte la bête, mort le venin ! (Lit. The animal dead, the venom dead. Dead folks cannot bite.)

Proverb repeated by HENRI III (1551-89), after the murder of the duc de Guise (1550-88). The king's mother, Catherine de Médecis, in bed with the gout, asked the meaning of the noise caused by the murder (it took place underneath her chamber) and the king, entering the room, said : "Madame, ce matin je me suis rendu roi de France ; j'ai fait mourir le roi de Paris !" (Madam, this morning I have become king of France ; I have caused the death of the king of Paris !) Catherine, stupefied, replied : "Vous avez fait "mourir le duc de Guise ! Dieu "veuille que cette mort ne soit point "cause que vous soyez roi de rien ! "C'est bien coupé, mais saurez-vous "recoudre ?" (You have caused the death of the duc de Guise ! God grant that this death may not be the cause of your being the king of nothing ! It is well cut, but will you know how to sew it up again. See Il n'oserait !

Mort ou victorieux. (Dead or victorious).

GENERAL A. DUCROT (1817-82) addressed a proclamation to the soldiers during the siege of Paris, in which he said, "je ne rentrerai dans Paris que mort ou victorieux." (I will only re-enter Paris dead or victorious).

Moulin à paroles. (Windbag.)

Attributed to MME. CORNUEL (1605-94) applying the term to the COMTE DE FIESQUE. *Tallemant des Réaux, Historiettes,* vol. 9. p. 54 (1840).

Napoléon ! Ella ! Marie-Louise !

Last words of MARIE-JOSEPHINE-Rose Tascher de la Pagerie (1763-1814), wife of Napoleon I, referring to Napoleon's second wife, Josephine having been divorced by him.

Nation boutiquière. (Shop-keeping nation.)

BARÈRE DE VIEUZAC (1755-1841) —in a speech to the Convention (28 prairial) June 16, 1794, in defence of the Committee of Safety, but usually attributed to Napoleon. So far the editor has been unable to trace any report *in French* of the speech in question. The earliest record of the phrase seems to be that in "The Register of the Times" (pub. 1794) p. 72, which is as follows :

"Report of the arrival of the "French convoy from America and "the engagement of the 1st. of June." "28 Prairial, Monday, June 16th, "1794.—Let Pitt then boast of this "victory [Lord Howe's victory of "1st June] to his nation of shop-"keepers (*nation boutiquière*)." In a speech by Barère de Vieuzac (7 prairial) 26th May 1794, occur the words : "Nation bretonne, agio-"teuse et marchande, fière de ton "grand commerce," etc. (Speculating and trading British nation, proud of thy great commerce, etc.). Cf. "You were all greatly offended "with me [Napoleon I] for having "called you a *nation of shop-keepers* "... I meant that you were a nation "of merchants, and that all your "great riches, and your grand re-

"sources arose from commerce,
"which is true," [under date May
31, 1817].—B. E. O'Meara, Napoleon at St. Helena (ed. 1888, vol.
2, pp. 121-2); Also "To found a
"great empire for the sole purpose
"of raising up a people of customers
"may at first sight appear a project
"fit only for a *nation of shopkeepers.*
"It is, however, a project altogether
"unfit for a *nation of shopkeepers ;*
"but extremely fit for a nation
"whose government is influenced
"by shopkeepers."—Adam Smith's
Wealth of Nations, bk. 4, ch. 7,
pt. 3.

Note.—In the 1776 edition, vol. 2, p. 221,
the concluding words of the above are "a
nation that is governed by shopkeepers."
A note (p. 62 of vol. 1) in *Notes from a
Dairy,* by Sir M. E. Grant Duff, refers to
"La Nation Boutiquière and other poems"
(by Henry Lushington, 1855) as a "but
little known but most brilliant book."

**N'aurez-vous pas l'éternité entière
pour vous reposer ?** (Will
you not have all eternity in
in which to rest ?)

ANTOINE ARNAULD (1612-94) to
PIERRE NICOLE (1625-95), the latter
saying that he wanted rest. Also
quoted as "N'avez-vous pas pour
vous reposer l'éternité entière ? "
Another account says that Arnauld's
remark referred to himself and that
Nicole advised him (Arnauld) to
rest from his labours. Arnauld
replied, "Me reposer ! eh ! n'avons-
"nous pas pour cela l'éternité ? "
(Rest ! haven't we eternity for that,
eh ?)

N'avouez jamais ! (Never confess !)

The assassin AVINAIN (otherwise
Davinain), an ex-butcher, executed
at Paris, Nov. 29th, 1867, when on
the scaffold, said to the public,
"Messieurs, n'avouez jamais ! "
(Gentlemen, never confess !)—*Le
Droit,* Nov. 29th, 1867

N'ayez pas de zèle. (Don't be
zealous).

Attributed to TALLEYRAND (1754-
1838) by Sainte-Beuve (*Critiques et
portraits,* vol. 3, p. 324). Often
quoted as "Surtout, pas de zèle ! "
(Above all, no zeal !) or, "Surtout,
messieurs, point de zèle." (Above-
all, gentleman, no zeal !) "Au bas-
"d'une des lettres de Chesterfield,
"on trouve ce conseil donné à un
"résident, son ami intime : 'Pas
"de vivacité—Temper !' C'est le
"mot de M. de Talleyrand à ses-
"élèves : *Surtout pas de zèle !*"
(At the foot of one of Lord Chesterfield's letters we find this advice-
given to a resident, his intimate
friend : "No vivacity—Temper !"
It is Talleyrand's *mot* to his pupils :
Above all no zeal !)—*Revue des deux
Mondes,* Dec. 15, 1845, p. 919.
Cf. Μισεῖ γὰρ ὁ θεὸς τὰς ἄγαν
προθυμίας."—"God hateth over-
zeal."—EURIPIDES. *Orestes,* 708.
—(*Menelaus.*)

**N'écoutez ni le Père de Tourne-
mine ni moi, parlant l'un de
l'autre, car nous avons cessé
d'être amis.** (Don't listen
either to father Tournemine or
me, speaking of each other, for
we have ceased to be friends.)

MONTESQUIEU (1689-1755)—
after he had quarrelled with father
TOURNEMINE (1661-1739).

Ne me manquez pas ! (Don't
miss me !)

Last words of CH. H. COMTE DE
LA BÉDOYÈRE (1786-1815), condemned and shot, Aug, 19, 1815,
pointing to his breast. *Derniers
momens,* &c., 1818, p. 270. See-
Surtout ne me manquez pas.

**Ne parlons jamais de l'étranger,
mais que l'on comprenne que
nous y pensons toujours.**
(Let us never speak of the

foreigner, but let it be understood that we are always thinking of him.)

LÉON GAMBETTA (1838-81)—in a speech at a banquet at Saint-Quentin, Nov. 16, 1871. *La République francaise,* Nov. 18, 1871, p. 1.

Ne pouvant s'élever jusqu'à moi, ils m'ont fait descendre jusqu'à eux. (Not being able to raise themselves to my level, they have made me descend to theirs).

Inscription found attached to the statue of Napoleon, which had been removed from the top of the Vendome column at the period of the First Revolution (in 1814).

Ne soyez pas surpris si j'ai récompensé si tard votre mérite ; j'appréhendais d'être privé du plaisir de vous entendre, si je vous faisais évêque. (Don't be surprised that I have rewarded your merit so tardily ; I was afraid of being deprived of the pleasure of hearing you, if I made you a bishop.)

LOUIS XIV (1638-1715) to E. FLÉCHIER (1632-1710) made bishop of Lavaur in 1685. See Madame, je vous ai fait attendre &c.

Ne vous avais-je pas bien dit que vous n'êtes qu'une poule mouillée, et qu'avec un peu de fermeté vous retabliriez vos affaires? (Didn't I tell you how irresolute you are, and that with a little firmness you would re-establish your affairs?)

PÈRE JOSEPH (1577-1638) to RICHELIEU (1585-1642)—after energetic measures had been adopted for the defence of the Capital.

Ne vous pressez pas ; on ne saurait marcher bien vite, quand on est aussi chargé de lauriers que vous l'êtes. (Don't hurry ; it is impossible to walk very quickly, loaded with laurels as you are.)— Voltaire.

LOUIS XIV (1638-1715) to the PRINCE DE CONDÉ (1621-86) after the victory of Senef (Aug. 11, 1674). The prince suffering from gout, asked the king to excuse him for keeping him waiting on the staircase.

Ni un pouce de notre territoire, ni une pierre de nos forteresses. (Neither an inch of our territory nor a stone of our fortresses.)

Words occurring in a circular by JULES FAVRE (1809-80) to the French diplomatic agents, dated Sep. 6, 1870. " Nous ne cèderons ni un pouce," &c. (We will neither yield an inch, &c). *Journal Officiel,* Sep. 7, 1870.

Nos fusils Chassepot ont fait merveille. (Our Chassepot guns have done wonders.)

In a despatch dated Nov. 9, 1867 from GENERAL P. L. C. A. DE FAILLY (1810-92) referring to the victory over Garibaldi's army at Mentana (Nov. 3, 1867). *Le Moniteur universel,* Nov. 10, 1867.

Nous dansons sur un volcan. (We are dancing on a volcano.)

Remark made by M. DE SALVANDY (1795-1856) to the Duke of Orleans (1773-1850) afterwards LOUIS-PHILIPPE (May 31, 1830) at a ball given at the Palais-Royal. " C'est une fête toute napolitaine, monseigneur ; nous dansons," &c. (It is quite a Neapolitan fête ; we are dancing, &c.) Guizot, *Mémoires pour servir à l'histoire de mon temps*, vol. 2. p. 13. Also Salvandy, *Livre des cent et un*, vol. 1. p. 398. Cf. NAPOLEON'S (1769-1821) saying: "Vous êtes sur un volcan." (You are walking over a volcano.) Thibaudeau, *Le Consulat et l'Empire* vol 1, p. 42. The Emperor Nicholas is reported to have said to Sir Hamilton Seymour "You may speak of the throne in England as being safe, but I, you know, sit upon a volcano."—Sır M. E. Grant Duff's *Notes from a diary*, vol. 1, p. 272.

Nous l'acceptons le cœur léger . . . (We accept it [the responsibility] with light hearts. . . .)

Phrase used by M. EMILE OLLIVIER (1825-   ) keeper of the seals, July 15, 1870, *à propos* of the declaration of war between France and Germany. *Journal Officiel*, July 16, 1870.

Nous n'avons pas de marine.—Et celles de Vernet, Monsieur? (We have no navy. — And Vernet's, sir?)

The painter LA TOUR (1704-88) is said to have remarked to LOUIS XV (1710-74) "We have no navy"; and the' king replied as above, making the word "marine" mean marine subjects. (And what about those of Vernet, sir?)

According to the *Abecedario*, published by de Chenevière and de Montaiglon (article La Tour), the king made no reply.

Nous ne serions pas grands sans les petits ; nous ne devons l'être que pour eux. (We should not be great without the little ; we ought only to be so *for* them).

Saying of MARIE LECZINSKA

(1703-1768), wife of Louis XV (1710-74).

Cf. "Les grands ne nous paroissent grands que parce que nous "Sommes à genoux . . . Levons "nous. . . ."

The above was the motto of the *Révolutions de Paris*, the first No. of which is dated July 12, 1789. Composed by E.-A. de Loustalot (1762-90) its principal editor. L. Prud'homme (1752-1803) was the *directeur - propriétaire*. Fournier (L'Esprit dans l'Histoire, p. 376) quotes it thus ;—"Les grands ne "sont grands que parce que nous "sommes à genoux ; relevons-nous." Cf. also Dubosc Montandré, *Le Point de l'Ovale* (Moreau, Bibliographie des Mazarinades, vol. 2, p. 359) : "Voyons que les grands ne "sont grands qu' parce que nous 'les portons sur nos épaules. Nous "n'avons qu'à les secouer pour en "joncher la terre." (Let us see that the great are only great because we carry them on our shoulders. We have only to shake them to strew the ground with them).

Nous nous reverrons. (We shall meet again).

Last words of the abbé F.-R DE LAMENNAIS (1782-1854), the 'modern Savonarola'.

Nous nous saluons, mais nous ne nous parlons pas. (We bow, but we do not speak.)

Attributed to GUILLAUME DE BAUTRU (1588-1665) and to VOLTAIRE (1694-1778). The former, congratulated on having taken off his hat on passing a crucifix, made the above reply. The latter is said to have used the words to Piron who, seeing him take off his hat as a priest passed them bearing the *viatique*, asked him if he was reconciled to God See Tallemant des Réaux, *His-*

toriettes, 1840, vol. 3, p. 104, also
Pironiana (Avignon, 1813) p. 99.

**Nous périrons ensemble ou nous
sauverons l'État.** (We will
perish together or we will save
the state).

Said by LOUIS XIV (1638-1715)
in 1709 to VILLARS (1653-1734)
after the battle of Malplaquet.

**Nous sommes archiprêts; il ne
manque pas un bouton de
guêtre.** (We are more than
ready; there is not a gaiter
button wanting).

Phrase attributed to MARSHAL
LE BOEUF (1809-88) minister of
war, alluding to the Franco-German
war. G. Du Barrail *Mes souvenirs,*
1896, vol. 3, p. 148.

**Nous sommes assemblés par la
volonté nationale, nous ne
(*or* n'en) sortirons que par la
force.** (We are assembled by
the national will, we will only
disperse by force).

Said to have been uttered in a
speech by MIRABEAU (1749-91) to
the Constituent Assembly (June 23,
1789). *Éphémérides de Noël,* 1803.
The popular version is.—"Allez dire
"à votre maître que nous sommes
"ici par la volonté du peuple, et
"que nous n'en sortirons que par la
"force des baïonnettes." (Go, tell
your master that we are here by
the will of the people and that the
bayonet's point alone will make us
leave) Carlyle's version (*Essays,*
vol. v, p. 266—*Mirabeau*) is:
'"Go, Monsieur, tell those who
sent you, that we are here by will
of the Nation; and that nothing
but the force of bayonets can drive
us hence!"' (said to de Dreux-
Brezé.) "Cependant, pour éviter
"toute équivoque et tout délai, je
"vous déclare que si l'on vous a
"chargé de nous faire sortir d'ici,

"vous devez demander des ordres
"pour employer la force; car nous
"ne quitterons nos places que par
"la puissance des baïonnettes."
(However, to avoid any misunder-
standing and any delay, I declare to
you that if you have been commanded to turn us out from here,
you must ask for orders to use force;
for we shall only leave our place if
compelled by bayonets.) *Le Moniteur* June 20-24, 1789, p. 48, col. 1.
The President of the Assembly's
(J.-S. Bailly, 1736-93) version however is:—
"Allez dire à eux qui vous envoient,
"que la force des baïonnettes ne
"peut rien contre la volonté de la
"nation." (Go and tell those who
sent you that the bayonets' force is
of no avail against the will of the
nation).

Nouvelle couche sociale. (New
social stratum).

Expression used by L. GAMBETTA
(1838-81) in a speech at Grenoble,
Sep. 26, 1872. *La République
française,* Oct. 2, 1872, p. 1.

**Oh! c'était le bon temps, j'étais
bien malheureuse!** (Oh!
those were good times, I was
so unhappy!)

By SOPHIE ARNOULD (abt. 1740-
1803).

Quoted by Rulhière (1735-91) in
an epistle (à Monsieur de Cha——
etc.) following his poem *Les jeux de
mains* (1808, p. 43).
"Un jour une actrice fameuse,
"Me contait les fureurs de son
premier amant;
"Moitié rêvant, moitié rieuse,
"Elle ajouta ce mot charmant:
"Oh! c'était le bon temps, j'étais
bien malheureuse!"
(One day a famous actress, was
telling me of her first lover's jealousy,
Half-dreaming, half laughing, she
added this charming *mot,* etc.)

Cf. Oh! le bon temps où nous étions si malheureux. (Oh! the good times when we were so miserable!) quoted by Dumas père in *Le Chevalier d'Harmental* (vol. 2, p. 318) as by either Ninon de l'Enclos or Sophie Arnould; and the song beginning:—
"Le bon temps que c'était, le bon temps que c'était,
"Du temps que la reine Berthe filait!"
(What good times they were, what good times they were,
When Queen Bertha span!)

Oh! Oh! voilà qui s'appelle un mauvais présage. Un Romain à ma place serait rentré. (Oh! Oh! that's what is called a bad omen. A Roman in my place would have gone in again).

By C. G. DE LAMOIGNON DE MALESHERBES (1721-94), who stumbled as he was leaving the Conciergerie prison to mount the fatal cart, April 24, 1794. *Derniers momens*, p. 211. Cf. *Teneo te Africa!*

Oh! priez seulement pour le corps; il ne faut pas demander tant de choses à la fois. (Oh! pray for the body only; too many things must'nt be asked for at once).

Attributed to LOUIS XI. (1423-83) in reply to François de Paul (1416-1507) who is supposed to have said:—"Sire, je vais prier Dieu pour le repos de Votre Majesté." (Sire, I am going to pray to God for your Majesty's repose).

Oh, que non! on craint peu celui qu'on n'estime pas. (Oh no! we little fear him whom we do not esteem).

Reply of Lucien Bonaparte's eldest daughter CHARLOTTE (1796-

) when asked whether she was not afraid of the consequences of irritating her uncle (Napoleon) by refusing to marry Ferdinand VII of Spain (1784-1833).

O Liberté! O Liberté! que de crimes on commet en ton nom. (O Liberty! O Liberty! what crimes are committed in thy name!)

By MME. ROLAND (1754-93) on passing a statue of Liberty on her way to the scaffold. Lamartine, *Hist. des Girondins*, bk. 51, ch. 8.
Another version: "Ah! liberté, comme on t'a jouée! (Ah! liberty, how they have cheated thee!) Generally regarded as her last words. *Derniers momens*, p. 178.

O mon Dieu, conserve-moi innocente, donne la grandeur aux autres. (O God, keep me innocent, give greatness to others).

Words scratched with a diamond on a window of the castle of Frederiksborg by CAROLINE MATILDA (1751-75), Queen of Denmark and sister of George III.

On appelle les papes Votre Sainteté, les rois Votre Majesté, les princes Votre Gracieuseté; pour vous, madame, on devrait vous appeler Votre Solidité. (They call popes, Your Holiness; kings, Your Majesty; princes, Your Graciousness; you, madam, should be called Your Solidity).

Words said to have been uttered by LOUIS XIV (1638-1715) to Mme. de Maintenon (1635-1719), referring to her reputation for judgment and good sense.

On croirait que je vous pardonne. (One would think that I am forgiving you).

FRENCH SAYINGS

9# FRENCH SAYINGS 159

Remark made by HENRI IV (1553-1610) to Rosny (1560-1641) (afterwards duc de Sully) in the park of Fontainebleau (early in May, 1605). Relevez-vous, mon ami, on croirait que je vous pardonne. (Rise, my friend, one would think that I am forgiving you) ; or Relevez-vous, relevez-vous ; ils vont croire que je vous pardonne. (Rise, rise, they will think that I'm forgiving you.) La Harpe—*Éloge de Henri IV.*

On fait un pont d'or à un ennemi qui se retire. (We make a golden bridge for a retreating enemy).

By a FRENCH GENERAL to the Russian General count Miloradovitch (1770-1825), when meeting to propose terms of peace. Cf. "Le Comte de Pitillan, en parlant "de la guerre, souloit dire, *Quant* "*ton ennemy voudra fuyr, fay luy* "*un pont d'or.*" (The count de Pitillan, in speaking of war, used to say, *When thy enemy wishes to fly, make a bridge of gold for him.*) — Gilles Corrozet, "*Les Divers Propos Memorables,*" etc. Paris, 1557, p. 78. Rabelais (*Gargantua,* bk. I., ch. 43) makes Gargantua say :—"Ouvrez toujours "à vos ennemis toutes les portes et "chemins, et plûtôt leur faites un "pont d'argent,* afin de les renvoyer." (Always open to your enemies all gates and outlets, and rather make for them a bridge of silver, to get rid of them). Cf. "Scipio Africanus dicere solitus est, "hosti non solum dandam esse "viam fugiendi verum etiam "muniendam." (Scipio Africanus used to say that you ought to give the enemy not only a road for flight

* *i.e.* stratagem—give them a seeming advantage. The French proverb is "Il faut faire un pont d'or à son ennemi." (Make a golden bridge for your enemy).

but also a means of defending it). Frontinus, *Strateg.,* IV. 7, 16. Attributed to SCIPIO AFRICANUS (abt. 235-183 B.C.), *ut supra.*

On n'aime pas un homme par qui on a été battu. (A man is not liked by those he has beaten.)

NAPOLEON (1769-1821) referring to Wellington being sent as ambassador to France after the Restoration.

On ne gagne pas les batailles avec les mains, mais avec les pieds. (Battles are not won with the hands, but with the feet.)

Maxim of MARSHAL SAXE (1696-1750), he considering quickness of movement of more importance than actual combats.

On ne me touche pas, je suis l'arche. (They will not touch me, I am the arch.)

Saying of DANTON (1759-94) referring to his life being threatened. Cf. Il n'oserait.

On ne passe pas, quand bien meme qu'encore tu serais le petit caporal. (You cannot pass not even if you were the "little corporal" himself.)

Attributed to JEAN COLUCHE, the sentry of Ebersperg, to Napoleon, but he really only said *On ne passe pas!* (You cannot pass !) Cf. *L'Illustration* of 1846 and the *Journal du Loiret,* August 29, 1862. According to the *Mémorial de Sainte-Hélène* (vol i., p. 232), the *sobriquet* " *le petit caporal* " originated from the singular custom of the oldest soldiers giving after each battle (during the Italian campaign) a new title to their young general. He was made corporal at Lody and sergeant at Castiglione. The soldiers continued to call him " *le petit caporal.*"

On ne perd pas plus gaiement son royaume. (No one could lose a kingdom more gaily.)

Said by ETIENNE DE VIGNOLLES, surnamed La Hire (1390-1442) to Charles VI (1403-61), abt. 1428. *On n'avoit jamais veu nv ouy parler qu'aucun perdist si gayement son Estat que lui.* (No one had ever heard or seen anyone lose his kingdom so gaily as he).—Edmond Richer (early in 17th century.)

On ne prend jamais le roi, pas même aux échecs. (The king is never taken, not even at chess.)

Phrase attributed (erroneously) to Louis VI. (1078-1137), at the battle of Brémule (Brenneville) where he was beaten by Henry I of England (August 20, 1119). *Sache qu' on ne prend jamais le roi, pas même aux échecs.* (Know that the king is never taken, not even at chess.) Dreux du Radier, *Tablettes anecdotes et historiques des rois de France, depuis Pharamond jusqu'à Louis XV*, vol. I., p. 148. It is said that an English knight took hold of the horse's reins, saying " Le roi est pris " (The king is taken) ; and the king knocked him down with his war club, using the above words.

On ne ramène guère un traitre par l'impunité, au lieu que par la punition l'on en rend mille autres sages. (One traitor can scarcely be reclaimed by impunity, while a thousand others are made wise by punishment.)

Saying of CARDINAL RICHELIEU (1585-1642.) *Mercure hist. et polit.*, July, 1688, pp. 7-8.

On ne s'appuie que sur ce qui résiste. (We only lean on that which resists.)

Reply made by ANDRIEUX (1759-1833) to NAPOLEON (1769-1821) (when First Consul), who complained of the Tribunat's resistance. " Vous· êtes à l'Institut, " général, de la section de mécani- " que ; vous devez donc savoir " qu'on," etc. (You are at the Institute, general, you belong to the mechanics section ; you ought, therefore, to know that, &c.

On ne tombe jamais que du côte où l'on penche. (One never falls but on the side towards which one leans.)

By F.-P.-G. GUIZOT (1787-1874), in the Chamber of Deputies, May 5, 1837. *Moniteur*, May 5-6, 1837. Referred to by NAPOLEON III (1808-73), in a letter, dated Jan. 13, 1867, to Émile Ollivier.

On prend plus de mouches avec une cuillerée de miel, qu'avec vingt tonneaux de vinaigre. (More flies are caught with a spoonful of honey than with twenty barrels of vinegar.)

Favorite saying (proverb) of HENRY IV (1553-1610.) H. de Péréfixe, *hist du roi Henri le Grand*, vol. 2, p. 306.

On presse l'orange et on jette l'écorce. (One squeezes the orange and throws away the peel.)

FREDERICK II of Prussia (1712-86), is reported to have said to La Mettrie (1709-1751), alluding to Voltaire (1694-1778), *J'aurai besoin de lui encore un an tout au plus ; on presse,* etc. (I shall want him another year at most ; one squeezes, etc.) Cf. Also Voltaire's letter to Mme. Denis, Sept. 2, 1751. " *On presse l'orange et on en jette l' écorce.*"

On rend l'argent de tout achat qui a cessé de plaire. (Money returned for any purchase that has ceased to please.) Advertisement of a tailoring establishment at Paris, established in 1868. Abbrevated on its sign or trade-mark to "On rend l'argent" (Money returned) and often so quoted.

On reprend son bien où on le trouve. (One takes back one's property wherever one finds it.) Reply made by MOLIÈRE (1622-73) when reproached with having appropriated two scenes* from *Le Pédant joué* (Cyrano de Bergerac) in *Les Fourberies de Scapin*. Another version is as follows :— "Cette scène est bonne, elle " m'appartient de droit ; *je reprends* " *mon bien partout où je le trouve.*" (That scene is good, it belongs to me by right ; I take back my property wherever I find it.) Cf. also *La Vie de M. de Molière*, by Jacques le Febvre, 1705, pp. 13-14. De Grimarest's *Vie de Molière* (1705 edit., p. 14) says : "Il m'est permis de reprendre mon bien où je le trouve." (I am permitted to take back my property, where I find it.) Cf. "Cette culotte est mienne ; et
je prendrai
"Ce qui fut mien où je le
trouverai."
("Mine are these breeches, and
a rule I make it,
Where'er I find my property, to
take it.")
Voltaire, *La Pucelle* (1841) chant 3, l. 374. See Il est permis en littérature &c.

On retrouve des soldats, il n'y a que l'honneur qui ne se retrouve pas. (We can get

* More particularly that in which the words " Que diable allait-il faire dans cette galère ?"

other soldiers, it is only honour which cannot be regained). Said by NAPOLEON (1769-1821) to Maret (1763-1839) at Bordeaux, on learning the capitulation of Baylen (July 22, 1808).

On veut me faire mourir de plaisir. (They want to kill me with pleasure). Said by VOLTAIRE (1694-1778) March 30, 1778, referring to the public enthusiasm for him. Another account has it that the words used were : "Vous voulez m'étouffer sous les roses." (You want to stifle me with roses.)

Ostez-vous de devant moy, ne m'offusquez pas, car je veux paroistre. (Don't get in front of me, don't obscure me for I wish to be seen).— Brantôme. By HENRY IV (1553-1610), wearing long plumes, to his soldiers at the battle of Coutras (1587). See Ralliez vous à mon panache blanc.

Où est la femme ? See Cherchez la femme.

Oui, et combien les hommes sont petits. (Yes, and how little men are.) Death-bed utterance of MONTESQUIEU (1689-1755)—in reply to the question, by the Curate of Saint-Sulpice : "Monsieur, vous comprenez combien Dieu est grand ?" (You understand how great God is ?) The Jesuits were anxious to obtain his retractation of the *Lettres Persanes*, whilst the Encyclopædists were endeavouring to prevent it. Biog. universelle (Michaud), vol. xxix, pp. 519-20.

Oui, je suis Français ; je mourrai Français. (Yes, I am a Frenchman ; I shall die a Frenchman).-

11

By Marshal M. Ney (1769-1815) during his trial. Condemned by the court of peers Dec. 6, 1815. *Derniers momens*, p. 328.

Oui, sire, le moulin n'y est plus ; mais le vent y est encore. (Yes, sire, the mill is there no longer, but the wind is there still).

Reply made by the duc de Vivonne (1636-88) to Louis XIV (1638-1715) in the park at Versailles, on being asked if he remembered that a mill used to be there.

Où la vertu va-t-elle se nicher ! (Where is virtue going to nestle !) Attributed to Molière(1622-73). He gave a louis to a poor man and the latter ran after him, saying that he must have given it him in mistake. Molière gave him another, making the above exclamation. Voltaire (édit. Garnier) vol. 23, p. 95 (*Vie de Molière*). Sometimes quoted : " Où diable la vertu va-t-elle se nicher ? "

Ouvrez, c'est l'infortuné roi de France. (Open, it is the unfortunate king of France).— Froissart.

Words uttered by Philip VI (1293-1350) after the battle of Crecy (Aug. 26th, 1346) on arriving at the château de Broye. Generally misquoted " *Ouvrez, c'est la fortune de la France.*" (Open it is the fortune of France).

Note.—In the earliest edition of Froissart's *Chronicles* (abt. 1495) the words are *la fortune de France*, but in that of 1840, edited by J. A. C. Buchon, the error has been corrected and noted. " *Ouvrez, ouvrez, châtelain, c'est l'infortuné roi de France,*" (Cf. *Froissart*, bk. 1, pt. 1, ch. 292, p. 240, 1840 edition).

Panat fait tache dans la boue. (Panat makes even mud dirtier.) Saying of Rivarol (1753-1801) alluding to the untidy personal appearance of the Chevalier de Panat.

Pardon, Sire, il n'en a tué qu'une ; c'est votre Majesté qui a tué les vingt autres. (Pardon, Sire, he has only killed one ; it is your Majesty who has killed the twenty others).

Saying attributed to the duc de Montausier (1610-90), governor to the eldest son of Louis XIV. The king said that he had let justice take its course with regard to an assassin whom he had pardoned after his first crime, but who had since killed twenty people.

Paris vaut bien une messe. (Paris is indeed worth a mass).

Expression generally attributed to Henri IV (1553-1610), but probably invented after his death.

The phrase *Sire, sire, la couronne vaut bien une messe* (Sire, sire, the crown is indeed worth a mass),* is in the *Caquets de l'accouchée*, ascribed to the duc de Rosny, (Sully) (1560-1641) the king having asked him why he didn't attend mass like himself. Cf. " A la vue " de Gênes la superbe et de ses en-" virons pittoresques, il [Napoleon] " s'écria : ' cela vaut bien une " guerre.' " (At the sight of Genoa the superb and its picturesque surroundings, he cried : ' that is indeed worth a war.') This was on his journey through Italy after his coronation in Milan.—J. Fouché, *Mémoires*, 1824, pt. 1, p. 332.

Pas encore, mon fils, pas encore. (Not yet, my son, not yet.)

Attributed to Louis XIII (1601-43) when on his death-bed, after asking the dauphin his name (he had just been baptised) and receiving the reply " Je m'appelle Louis XIV." (My name is Louis XIV).

* Dentu's edition (Bibliothèque elzévirienne) pp. 172-3.

Peine forte et dure. (The strong and hard pain).

Punishment (now abolished) inflicted when a person indicted for felony refused to plead. A method of torture, ending in death, consisting of the pressure of a weight of iron and semi-starvation. Nowadays, if any one refuses to plead, the Court may order a plea of "Not guilty" to be entered. Cf. Wharton's *Law Lexicon ;* also F. Watt, *The Law's Lumber Room,* 1895, vol. 1, p. 10).

Pends-toi, brave Crillon. (Hang thyself, brave Crillon).

Voltaire relates (in a note to *La Henriade,* chant viii, l. 97, 1730 edition) that HENRI IV surnamed *Le Grand* (1553-1610) wrote : "Pends-toi, brave Crillon, nous "avons combattu à Arques, et tu "n'y étais pas. . . . Adieu, brave "Crillon, je vous aime à tort et à "travers." (Hang thyself, brave Crillon, we have fought at Arques, and thou wert absent. . . . Adieu, brave Crillon, I love you through all.) The only foundation for the above seems to be a letter from the king to GRILLON (1541-1615) (so called by Henri IV) from the camp at Amiens, dated Sept. 20, 1597 : "Brave Gryllon, pandes vous de "navoyr esté ycy pres de moy lundy "dernyer à la plus belle occasyon "quy ce soyt james veue et quy "peut estre ce verra james." . . . (Brave Crillon, hang yourself for not having been here with me on Monday last at the finest opportunity that ever was seen and which perhaps may never happen again). *Collection des documents inédits sur l'histoire de France,* vol. 4, p. 848, (Berger de Xivrey).

Pendu jusqu'à ce que mort s'ensuive. (Hanged until death ensues).

Formula decreed April 24, 1524, by the Bordeaux parliament to be inserted in all condemnations to hanging. See Let him be hanged by the neck.

Périsse notre mémoire, et que la France soit libre ! (Perish our memory, and let France be free !)

P. V. VERGNIAUD (1753-93) concluded his speech to the National Assembly (Sep. 17, 1792,) by saying : "Périssent l'assemblée nationale et "sa mémoire, pourvu que la France "soit libre !" (Perish the National Assembly and its memory, provided that France is free !), after quoting the words : "Périssent mon nom et "ma mémoire, et que la Suisse soit "libre" (Perish my name and memory, and let Switzerland be free !) as if uttered by William Tell, whereas he was really quoting a line from Lemierre's tragedy of *Guillaume Tell* (act 1, sc. 1) : "Que la Suisse soit libre, et que "nos noms périssent." (Let Switzerland be free, and let our names perish.) At the conclusion of Vergniaud's speech all the members rose and exclaimed : "Oui, oui, "périssons tous et que la liberté "reste ! Oui, oui, périsse notre "mémoire et que la France soit "libre !" (Yes, yes, let us all perish and liberty remain ! Yes, yes, perish our memory and let France be free !) Cf. DANTON'S (1759-94) phrase in his *Discours à la Convention Nationale,* March 10, 1793 : "Que la France soit libre et que mon nom soit flétri." (Let France be free and my name be dishonoured.) Cleopatra, in Corneille's *Rodogune* (1644), says (act 5, sc. 1) : "Tombe sur moi le ceil, pourvu que je me venge !" (Let the heavens fall on me, so that I avenge myself.) See Périssent les colonies &c.

Périssent les colonies plutôt qu'un principe! (Perish the colonies rather than a principle!)

The above is the *résumé* of two phrases from speeches in the Constituent Assembly (May 13, 1791) by DUPONT DE NEMOURS * (1739-1817)and ROBESPIERRE‡(1758-94).

Plus ma qualité de roi me peut donner de facilité à me satisfaire, plus je dois être en garde contre le péché et le scandale. (The more my rank of king renders it easy to satisfy my desires, the more I must be on my guard against sin and scandal.)

LOUIS XIII (1601-43) to Saint Simon (1607-93) when talking of Mlle. de Hautefort (1616-91). "... *mais plus ma qualité de roi* " *me peut donner plus de facilité à* " *me satisfaire qu'a un autre, plus* " *je dois, etc.* (... but the more my rank of king renders it easier for me to satisfy my desires than for another, the more I must, etc.) Saint Simon, *Mémoires.* Cf. "In maxima fortuna minima licentia est" (The higher your station, the smaller your liberty). — Sallust, *Catilina*, lvi.

Plutôt la mort que l'esclavage, C'est la devise des Français. (Rather death than slavery, is the motto of the French.)

Refrain sung at the foot of the scaffold, Oct. 31, 1793, by J.-P. BRISSOT (1754-93) and his companions. *Derniers momens*, p. 169.

* *Il vaudrait mieux sacrifier les colonies qu'un principe.* (It is better to sacrifice the colonies rather than a principle.)—*Le Moniteur*, May 15, 1791, p. 558.

‡ *Périssent les colonies s'il doit vous en coûter votre bonheur, etc.* (Perish the colonies if they are to cost you your happiness, etc.) See Périsse notre mémoire etc.

Cf. "Plutôt souffrir que mourir, C'est la devise des hommes." (Rather suffer than die, is man's motto).—La Fontaine, *La Mort et le Bûcheron.*

Politique de "fous furieux." (Enraged madmen's policy).

L.-A. THIERS(1797-1877)—in his speech at Versailles, June 8, 1871, on the abrogation of the laws of exile. He alluded to the efforts of Gambetta to continue the war as follows:—"Oui, messieurs, nous "étions tous révoltés, je l'étais "comme vous tous, contre cette "politique de *fous furieux* qui "mettait la France dans le plus "grand péril." (Yes, gentlemen, we were all opposed, myself like you all, to this enraged madmen's policy, which exposed France to the greatest danger). *Discours Parlementaires*, vol. 13, pp. 313-4.

Pour Colin, c'est un bon garçon qui ne dira jamais de mal de personne.

BOILEAU - DESPRÉAUX'S father, alluding to his son Nicolas (1636-1711).

Pour être heureux, il faut avoir un bon estomac et un mauvais cœur. (To be happy we must have a good stomach and a bad heart.)

Saying attributed to FONTEN-ELLE (1657-1757), also to the physician J. MOLIN (1666-1755) substituting in the latter case "long life" for "happiness." *Journal de Paris*, Mar. 9, 1778, pp. 269-70.

Pour faire la guerre avec succès, trois choses sont absolument nécessaires: premièrement, de l'argent; deuxièmement, de l'argent; troisièmement, de l'argent. (To make war successfully, three things are absolutely necessary; firstly, money; secondly, money; thirdly, money).

FRENCH SAYINGS

165

MARÉCHAL GIAN JACOPO DE TRIVULZI, called the *Grand Tri-vulce* (1448-1518) to LOUIS XII (1462-1515) when about to surround the Milanese (1499). See Quand on combat à lances d'argent, on a souvent la victoire—an earlier saying. Cf. the proverbial saying " L'argent est le nerf de la guerre." (Money is the sinews of war).

Pourquoi le grondez-vous? Croyez-vous qu'il ne soit pas assez affligé de m'avoir fait attendre? (Why do you scold him? Don't you think he is sorry enough for having kept me waiting?) LOUIS XIV (1638-1715) when a park gatekeeper was being reprimanded for not being at his post to open the gate for him. Racine, *Fragments historiques.* See J'ai failli attendre.

Pourquoi pleurez-vous? m'avez-vous cru immortel? (Why do you weep? did you think me immortal?). Death-bed utterance of LOUIS XIV (1638-1715). H. Martin, *Hist. de France*, vol. 14, bk. 91.

Pourtant j'avais quelque chose là! (Yet I had something there!) Words uttered by the poet A. CHÉNIER (1762-94) on the scaffold, July 25, 1794. Chénier said to his friend the poet J. A. ROUCHER (1745-94), who was executed the same day, "Je n'ai rien fait pour la postérité.., (I have done nothing for posterity..) and, striking his forehead, added the above words. *Œuvres posthumes* d'André Chénier (1839, p. xxxi of Introduction). Another version : "J'avais pourtant quelque chose là."—*Derniers momens*, p. 232. See Why should we legislate for posterity?

Prendre la paille. (To take the straw.) Mlle. DE MONTPENSIER, surnamed La Grande Mademoiselle (1627-93), when Condé's troops were approaching Paris during the Fronde, walked through the streets with a bundle of straw in her hands crying : " Que ceux qui ne sont pas pour " Mazarin [*i.e.*, on the king's side] " prennent la paille, sinon ils seront " saccagés!" (Let those who are not for Mazarin, take some straw, if not their houses will be pillaged !)

Puisque l'armée n'a pu voir Villars mourir en brave, il est bon qu'elle le voie mourir en chrétien. (Since the army has not been able to see Villars die a brave man's death, it is right that it should see him die like a Christian.) MARÉCHAL DE VILLARS (1653-1734) when badly wounded at Malplaquet (1709), referring to the sacrament being administered to him.

Puisse mon sang cimenter votre bonheur! (May my blood cement your happiness!) Last words of LOUIS XVI (1754-93) on the scaffold. Another account gives his last words as follows: " Je meurs innocent de tous les " crimes dont on m'accuse, je par- " donne à mes ennemis, je désire " que mon sang soit utile aux " Français, et qu'il apaise la " colère de Dieu. Et toi, peuple " infortuné . . ." (I die innocent of all the crimes of which I am accused, I forgive my enemies, I desire that my blood be of service to the French, and that it may appease God's anger. And thou, unfortunate people . . .). The rest was inaudible, as Santerre ordered the drums to be beaten.—*Derniers momens*, p. 119. See also Faites, sire, ce sacrifice &c.

Quand ferons-nous cesser ces mascarades? Nous n'avons pas voulu détruire la superstition pour établir l'athéisme. (When shall we cease these masquerades? We did not want to destroy superstition in order to establish atheism.)

DANTON (1759-94) referring to the saturnalias called " Fêtes de la Raison " (Feasts of Reason.)

Quand j'ai pris une résolution, je vais droit à mon but et je renverse tout de ma soutane rouge. (When I am resolved, I go straight to my goal and I overthrow everything with my red robe).

Saying of CARDINAL RICHELIEU (1585-1642). Often misquoted, and a different meaning given to the phrase. (Cf. Victor Hugo's *Marion Delorme*, act 2, sc. 1.) Michelet, *Précis de l'hist. de France*, p. 237) quotes the saying : " Je n'ose rien " entreprendre que je n'y aie bien " pensé ; mais quand une fois j'ai " pris ma résolution, je vais droit " à mon but, je renverse tout, je " fauche tout, et ensuite je couvre " tout de ma robe rouge." (I dare undertake nothing unless I have well considered it ; but once I have made up my mind, I go straight to my goal, I overthrow everything, I cut down everything, and then I cover everything with my red robe).

Quand je faisais le métier de satirique, que j'entendais assez bien, on me menaçait de coups de bâton ; à présent, on me donne une pension pour faire le métier d' historien que je n'entends pas. (When I played the part of satirist, which I understood pretty well, I was threatened with the stick ; now I am given a pension for playing the part of an historian, which I don't understand).

Remark made by BOILEAU-DESPRÉAUX (1636-1711) on his appointment as king's historiographer.

Quand je mourrai, l'univers fera un grand ouf ! (When I die, the world will utter a great *ouf!* [of relief]).

NAPOLEON'S (1769-1821) remark after hearing the compliments paid him on his asking what would be said of him after death. "L'homme " vraiment heureux est celui qui se " cache de moi au fond d'une pro- " vince, et quand," etc. (The truly happy man is he who hides from me in the heart of the country, and when, etc).—Mme. de Rémusat. ʹ

Quand je secoue ma terrible hure, il n'y a personne qui osât m'interrompre. (When I shake my terrible locks, there is no one who dares to interrupt me.)

Saying of MIRABEAU (1749-91). *Les Mirabeau*, vol. 5, p. 364 ; also E. Dumont, *Souvenirs de Mirabeau*, 1832, p. 197. Cf. " Ἡ κόμη τοὺς μὲν καλοὺς εὐπρεπεστέρους ὁρᾶσθαι ποιεῖ, τοὺς δὲ αἰσχροὺς φοβερωτέρους." (The hair makes the handsome look more comely, and the ugly more frightful.)— *Plutarch, Lysander I.*

LYCURGUS (fl. c. 850 B.C.)

Quand la justice a parlé, l'humanité doit avoir son tour. (When justice has spoken, humanity must have its turn).

In a speech by P. V. VERGNIAUD (1753-93) in pronouncing sentence of death (Jan. 17, 1793) on king LOUIS XVI (1754-93).

Quand le feu est à la maison, on ne s'occupe pas des écuries. (When the house is on fire, one does not trouble about the stables).

Said by BERRIER ( ) minister of the navy, to BOUGAINVILLE, (1729-1811) Montcalm's (1712-59) lieutenant. Bougainville replied : *On ne dira pas du moins que vous parlez en cheval.* (It will not be said that you speak as a horse.)— Charles de Bonnechose, *Montcalm et le Canada français.*

Quand le feu roi votre père, de glorieuse mémoire, me faisait l'honneur de m'appeler auprès de sa personne, pour s'entretenir avec moi sur ses grandes affaires, au préalable il faisait sortir les bouffons. (When the late king your father, of glorious memory, did me the honour of sending for me, to consult with me on his important affairs, he first of all sent away the buffoons). The DUC DE SULLY (1560-1641) to LOUIS XIII (1601-43).

Quand le phénomène que vous venez de constater s'est produit, toute chance est perdue et la mort n'est plus qu'une question de secondes. En effet, vous le voyez : je vais mourir, je meurs. (When the phenomenon which you have just observed is produced, all hope is lost and death is only a question of seconds. In fact, you see it : I am about to die, I *am* dying). Dying words of DR. RICHET (1816-92). On his death-bed he was explaining to his son and another doctor friend the evolution of pulmonary congestion, from which he was suffering, analyzing its symptoms and indicating the progress of the disease.

Quand on combat à lances d'argent, on a souvent la vic-toire. (When one fights with lances of silver, victory often follows). LOUIS XI (1423-83). Cf. Rabelais, *Gargantua,* 1, 46. "Les nerfs des batailles sont les pecunes." (Coin is the sinews of war.) See Pour faire la guerre avec succès &c.

Quand orgueil chevauche devant, honte et dommage le suivent de bien près. (When pride goes before, shame and misfortune follow close behind).— Philippe de Commines, *Mémoires,* bk. 2, ch. 4. Favourite maxim of LOUIS XI (1423-83).

Quand vous m'aurez tué, il ne me faudra que six pieds de terre. (When you have killed me, I shall only require six feet of earth.) President MATHIEU MOLÉ, (1584-1656) Feb. 27, 1649, to one of the angry crowd who held a gun to his head, threatening to shoot him. — *Biographie universelle : art.* Molé (Mathieu), p. 289, note. Chateaubriand, in his *Mélanges Littéraires,* says : " Six pieds de " terre feront toujours raison au plus " grand homme du monde." (Six feet of earth will always conquer the greatest man in the world).

Quant aux injures, on ne les élèvera jamais au-dessus de mon dédain. (As for insults, they will never be raised above my contempt). F.-P.-G. GUIZOT (1787-1874) replying to the attacks upon him in the Chamber of Deputies, Jan 26, 1844, spoke as follows : " Et quant " aux injures, aux calomnies, aux " colères extérieures, on peut les " multiplier, les entasser tant qu'on " voudra, on ne les élèvera jamais " au-dessus de mon dédain." (And as for insults, calumnies, outside anger, they may be multiplied, and heaped up as much as may be desired, but they will never be raised above my contempt.)—*Moniteur*, Jan. 27, 1844.

Qu'a-t-on décidé ? (What has been decided ?)
ISAAC CASAUBON (1559-1614)—on seeing the Sorbonne for the first time (it had not been rebuilt) and when told that there was a *salle* where discussions had taken place for 400 years.

Que celui qui a peur s'en aille ! (Let him who is afraid go away !)
Reply made by the DUC DE GUISE (1550-88) on being advised by some of his people to accept peace and pardon for his friends if he consented to quit Paris (1588).

Que d'eau ! que d'eau ! (What a quantity of water ! what a quantity of water !)
Attributed to MARSHAL MAC MAHON (1808-93)—on seeing the inundations caused by the overflow of the Garonne. The abbé Berry (MACMAHON, 1895, p. 65) says that the Marshal made the remark to cut short a long speech by the mayor of Toulouse.

Que de choses dans un menuet ! (What a number of things in a minuet !) — Helvétius, *de l'Esprit*, 1758, Discours 2, ch. I.
MARCEL, a celebrated dancing-master of the 17th century, when admiring the dancing of one of his pupils.

Que de sang et de meurtres ! Ah ! que j'ai suivi un méchant conseil ! (What a quantity of blood and murders ! Ah ! what bad advice have I followed !)—Th. Lavallée, *Hist. des Français*.

Last words attributed to CHARLES IX of France (1550-74), but authenticity disputed. In A. Sorbin de Sainte-Foy's *Hist. contenant un abrégé de la vie, etc.*, *de Charles IX* (Paris, in-8°, 1574) Archives curieuses, 1ère série, vol. 8, pp. 273-331, the king is reported to have said " Oui," in reply to Sorbin's question, " Sire, m'entendez-vous pas bien?" (Sire, do you not hear me well?)

Que Dieu ne m'abandonne jamais ! (May God never forsake me !)
Last words of BLAISE PASCAL (1623-62).—See *Life of Pascal*, by Mme Périer.

Que mon sang soit le dernier versé. Le bon Pasteur donne sa vie pour ses brebis. (May my blood be the last shed. The good Shepherd giveth His life for His sheep).
Dying words of D.-A. AFFRE, Archbishop of Paris (1793-1848), hit by a stray shot at the barricades of the Faubourg St.-Antoine, June 25, 1848. Died two days after.

Qu' est-ce que cela prouve? (What does that prove?)
A geometrician who witnessed a performance of Racine's *Phèdre*, while the rest of the audience were moved to tears at the pathetic parts, simply said : " Qu'est-ce que cela " prouve?" Attributed by Dumont (*Souvenirs sur Mirabeau*, 1832, p. 314) to JEAN TERRASSON (1670-1750).

Qu'est-ce que la raison avec un filet de voix, contre une gueule comme celle - là ? (What is reason with a weak voice against a mouth like that?)
MOLIÈRE (1622-73) to BOILEAU (1636-1711), at table, of his friend Furcroi, a barrister with powerful lungs.

Qu' est-ce que le tiers état ? tout ; qu'a-t-il été jusqu' à présent dans l'ordre politique ? rien ; que demande-t-il ? à devenir quelque chose. (What is the Third Estate ? — Everything. What has it been until now in regard to politics ?—Nothing. What does it want ?—To become something).

Words forming the title of the ABBÉ SIEYÈS' (1748-1836) famous pamphlet (Jan. 1789), said to have been suggested to him by CHAM-, FORT (1741-94). Also quoted as follows: "Qu'est-ce que le Tiers "État ? Rien ! Que doit-il être ? "Tout !" (What is the Third Estate ?—Nothing ! What should it be ?—Everything !) and attributed to L.-L.-F. DE LAURAGUAIS (1733-1824)—Cf. *Lettres de L.-B. Lauraguais à madame * * * an X* (1801) pp. 161-2.

Que vouliez-vous qu'il fît contre trois ? (What did you expect him to do against three ?)

ABBÉ SIEYÈS (1748-1836) to Dr. J. - N. CORVISART - DESMARETS (1755-1821), who deplored the death of a friend who had been attended by two physicians besides himself. The phrase is a quotation from *Horace* (act 3, sc. 6): Julie says, "Que "vouliez-vous qu'il fît contre trois?" Le vieil Horace replies, "Qu'il mourût." — (To die !) Delavigne uses words in a similar manner to Sieyès in his *Comédiens*.

Qui a peur des feuilles n'aille pas au bois. (He who is afraid of the leaves let him not go to the wood).

Said by the young nobles (July 2, 1431) to BARBAZAN, a valiant captain who proposed deferring the attack on the Burgundians owing to their strong strategic position. He replied "that he had lived without

reproach until then ; and that day would prove whether he had so spoken through fear or wisdom." The issue of the fight, as he had foreseen, proved disastrous to the French, and Barbazan was mortally wounded (1431). Also a proverb.

Qu'il doit en coûter cher à un bon cœur pour remporter des victoires ! (How dearly it must cost a good heart to gain victories !)

Reply made by the dauphin LOUIS DE FRANCE (1729-1765) to his father, LOUIS XV (1710-74), whom he accompanied to Fontenoy (May 11, 1745) when the latter visited the battle-field with him, and called his attention to the horrors of war.

Qui m'aime me suive ! (Let those who love me follow me !)

PHILIP IV of Valois (1293-1350). His barons wished to postpone the war against the Flemish until the following year, but GAUTIER DE CHATILLON, Constable of France, on being asked his opinion, replied : "Qui a bon cœur trouve toujours "bon temps pour la guerre." (He who has a stout heart is always ready to fight). Thereupon Philip exclaimed : "Qui m'aime me "suive !"—*Chronique de Saint-Denis.* Also attributed to FRANCIS I (1494-1547) at Marignan (1515), and CYRUS, King of Persia (died about 529) is credited with a similar saying to his soldiers. Cf. Qui te, Pollio, amat veniat quo te quoque gaudet. (He who loves thee, Pollis, would go to a place which delights thee too)---Virgil, 3rd eclogue. The expression was also used by LA BÉDOYÈRE (1786-1815) at Grenoble. At the news of Napoleon's approach he assembled his regiment, and cried "Vive l'Empereur !" adding, "Qui m'aime me suive !" —Thiers' *Histoire du Consulat.*

Qui ne sait pas dissimuler ne sait pas régner ; si mon chapeau savait mon secret je le brûlerais. (Who knows not how to dissimulate knows not how to reign ; if my hat knew my secret, I would burn it).

Favourite saying of Louis XI (1423-83). Cf. Sir Walter Scott, *Quentin Durward*, ch. i. The French proverb "Ta chemise Ne "sache ta guise," (Let not thy shirt know thy mind) is said to be founded on a *mot* attributed to the wise Captain Metellus, to Peter III, King of Arragon, and to Pope Martin IV : " Si ma chemise savait "mon dessein, je la brûlerais." (If my shirt knew my design, I would burn it.) See Qui nescit dissimulare &c.

Qui quitte la partie la perd. (Who leaves the game loses it).—Also a proverbial expression.

Remark made by the Arch-bishop of Lyons to the Duc de Guise (1550-88) when he seemed to have decided to leave Blois. He replied : " Mes affaires sont réduites "en tels termes que quand je "verrois la mort entrer par la "fenêtre, je ne sortirois point par la "porte pour la fuir." (My affairs are reduced to such a state that if I saw death enter by the window, I should not go out at the door to avoid it.)

Qui sait si je ne serai pas obligée de donner du pain à tous ces rois. (Who knows whether I shall not be obliged to give bread to all these kings).

Saying of Mme Laetitia Bona-parte (1750-1836) Napoleon's mother, alluding to the dignities conferred upon her children and sons-in-law and her own economy.

Qui t'a fait comte ?—Qui t'a fait roi ? (Who made thee count ? Who made thee king ?)

Adalbert,   comte de Périgueux, who had usurped the titles of comte de Poitiers and de Tours, received a message from the king, Hugues Capet (d. 996) "Qui t'a fait comte ?" to which he replied "Qui t'a fait roi ?"

Ralliez-vous à mon panache blanc. (Rally to my white crest).

Words used by Henri IV (1553-1610) in his harangue to his troops before the battle of Ivry (Mar. 14, 1590). Wearing a plume of white feathers in his helmet, so as to be recognised by all, enemies as well as friends, he said : " Mes com-"pagnons, Dieu est pour nous ! "Voici ses ennemis et les nôtres ! "Voici votre roi ! A eux ! Si vous "perdez vos cornettes, ralliez-vous "à mon panache blanc : vous le "trouverez au chemin de la victoire "et de l'honneur !" (Companions, God is on our side ! Here are his enemies and yours ! Here is your king ! Upon them ! If you lose your standards rally to my white crest, you will find it in the path of victory and honour).

At one time the king was believed to be dead and the leaguers having seen an officer bearing, like the king, a white crest, fall, deemed the victory theirs. Suddenly Henri reappeared, covered with blood and dust, and cried out to his wavering troops : " Tournez visage, afin que "si vous ne voulez combattre, pour "le moins vous me voyiez mourir." (Turn your faces, so that if you will not fight, you may at least see me die). See Ostez-vous de devant moi &c.

Rendez-moi mon père et mes enfants, et vous me guérirez.

(Give me back my father and my children [6] and you shall cure me).

Marie-Leczinska (1703-68) wife of Louis XV (1710-74) when dying, —to the doctors who sought a remedy for her ills.

Revanche pour Speierbach. (Revenge for Speierbach.) The Germans were defeated at the battle of Speierbach, Nov. 14, 1703 ; but they were victorious at Hochstedt (Blenheim), Aug. 13, 1704.

When Marshal Tallard (1652-1728), a prisoner at the latter battle, was taken before the Erbprinzen von Hessen, he said :— "Ah, monsieur le maréchal, vous "êtes très bien venu, voilà de là "revanche pour Speierbach." (Ah, *monsieur le maréchal*, you are very welcome, there is some revenge for Speierbach.)

Rien ne manque à sa gloire, il manquait a la nôtre: (Nothing is wanting to his glory, he was wanting to ours.)

Inscription on a statue of Molière (1622-73) at the French Academy (1773) and suggested by B.-J. Saurin (1706-81). Cf.

"Intrépide, et partout suivi de la victoire,
Charmant, fidèle ; enfin rien ne manque à sa gloire."

(Intrepid, and everywhere followed by victory,
Charming, faithful ; in short nothing is wanting to his glory).

Andromaque, act 3, sc. 3, ll. 21-2.
— Racine.

Racine's line probably suggested part of the inscription.

Rien ne prépare mieux à la diplomatie que l'étude de la théologie. (There is no better preparation for diplomacy than the study of theology).

Saying of Talleyrand (1754-1838).

Rien n'est plus adroit qu'une conduite irréprochable. (Nothing is more adroit than irreproachable conduct.)

Maxim of Madame de Maintenon (1635-1719).

Rien ! rien ! rien ! (Nothing nothing ! nothing !)

Words used by M. Desmousseaux de Givré, deputy for Eure-et-Loir, April 27, 1847, in the French Chamber, alluding to the Conservative policy of L.-A. Thiers.

Saint-Arnaud de café-concert. (Saint-Arnaud of the music-halls).

Words by which Jules Ferry (1832-93) alluded to General Boulanger (1837-91) in a speech at Épinal, July 24, 1887. —*Le Matin,* July 26, 1887.

Note.—St. Arnaud was a famous French general (1798-1854).

Sans peur et sans reproche.

See Le chevalier sans peur &c.

Santé, donc elle peut ; gaieté, donc elle veut. (Health, then she can ; gaiety, then she wishes to).

Remark made by d'Orléans de La Mothe, (1683-1774), bishop of Amiens, three years before his death, to a young woman who had just taken the vows.

Seigneur, je vous demande pardon, je ne l'avais pas fait pour vous. (Lord, forgive me, I did not do it for you).

G.-B. Lulli (1633-87) on hearing sung at a mass an air that he had composed for the opera.

Se soumettre ou se démettre. (Submit or demit [resign].)

Journal des Débats, Aug. 18, 1877.

Phrase used by Leon Gambetta (1838-82) at a banquet at Lille, Aug. 15, 1877, alluding to the government of Marshal MacMahon.

Se tenir le plus près possible du roi. (To keep as near as possible to the king.)
Advice given to the MARÉCHAL DE VILLARS (1653-1734) by his mother.

Si ce n'est pas là Dieu, c'est du moins son cousin germain. (If that is not God, it is at least his cousin german).— Carlyle, *The French Revolution*, 1837, vol. 2.
Last words of MIRABEAU (1749-91)—referring to the sun. He afterwards wrote a request for opium, and on the doctor shaking his head wrote " Dormir ! " (to sleep), pointing to the word. Carlyle refers to " *Fils adoptif*, viii, 450. *Journal de la maladie et de la mort de Mirabeau*, by P. J. G. Cabanis, 1803."

Si ces messieurs qui causent ne faisoient pas plus de bruit que ces messieurs qui dorment, cela accommoderoit fort ces messieurs qui écoutent. (If those gentlemen who are talking made no more noise than those who are asleep, it would be a great convenience to those gentlemen who are listening.)
Rebuke by ACHILLE DE HARLAY, (1639-1712) comte de Beaumont (great nephew of the *grand* Harlay), chief president of the Paris Parliament, to those councillors who were sleeping and those who were talking.

Si c'est possible, c'est fait ; si c'est impossible, cela se fera. (If it is possible, it is done ; if it is impossible, it shall be done).
C.-A. DE CALONNE (1734-1802) to MARIE ANTOINETTE (1755-93) on being asked to obtain a large sum of money for her. The exact words, however, were : " Madame, " si cela n'est que difficile, c'est fait ; " si cela est impossible, nous ver-

" rons." (Madame, if that is only difficult, it is done ; if that is impossible, we will see).

Si cette canaille n' a pas de pain, elle mangera du foin (*or* qu'elle mange du foin). (If the rascals have no bread they will eat hay [*or* let them eat hay]).
Saying attributed to J.-F. FOULON (1715-89)—alluding to the people during the famine. See Si le peuple n'a pas de pain &c.

Si, dans le siècle dernier, on eût fait enfermer Luther and Calvin, on aurait épargné bien des troubles et bien du sang à l'Europe. (If, in the last century, Luther and Calvin had been imprisoned, Europe would have been spared many troubles and much bloodshed).
Answer made by CARDINAL RICHELIEU (1585-1642) to the DUCHESSE D'AIGIULLON (died 1675) and others who interceded for the abbé de Saint-Cyran, arrested in 1638 as a Jansenist.

Si Dieu n'existait pas, il faudrait l'inventer. (If God did not exist, it would be necessary to invent him.)—Voltaire, *A l'auteur du livre des Trois Imposteurs*, l. 22.
Phrase quoted in a speech by ROBESPIERRE (1758-94) Nov. 21, 1793.—*Le Moniteur universel*, Nov. 26, 1793, p. 508. Mentioned by Carlyle in his essay " Voltaire " (Critical and Miscellaneous Essays, vol. 2, p. 146, 1888 ed.)

Si j'avais connu un plus homme de bien et un plus digne sujet, je l'aurais choisi. (If I had known a better man and a worthier subject, I should have chosen him).
LOUIS XIV (1638-1715) to GUILLAUME DE LAMOIGNON (1617-77) on his being selected to replace

Bellièvre as chief president of the Paris parliament (1658).

Si j'avance, suivez-moi ; si je recule, tuez-moi ; si je meurs, vengez-moi. If I advance, follow me ; if I retreat, kill me ; if I die, avenge me).

COUNT HENRI DE LA ROCHE-JAQUELEIN (1772-94) to the men who had placed themselves under his orders during the insurrection of La Vendée (1793). See Tibi istum ad munimentum &c.

Si j'avois fait pour Dieu ce que j'ai fait pour cet homme-là, je serois sauvé dix fois, et maintenant je ne sais ce que je vais devenir. (If I had done for God what I have done for that man, I should be saved ten times over, and now I don't know what will become of me.) J. B. COLBERT (1619-83) on his death-bed—referring to LOUIS XIV (1638-1715). "Je ne veux plus "entendre parler du roi ; qu'au "moins il me laisse mourir tran-"quille. C'est au roi des rois que "j'ai maintenant à répondre. . . "Si j'avois fait pour Dieu ce que "j'ai fait pour cet-homme-là, je "serois sauvé dix fois, et maintenant "je ne sais ce que je vais devenir." (I don't want to hear the king spoken of ; let him at least leave me to die in peace. It is to the king of kings that I now have to answer. . . . If I had done &c.)—Racine, *Œuvres diverses*. See Had I served God &c.

Si je me courbais, c'est que je cherchais les clefs du paradis. (If I stooped, it was because I was looking for the keys of Paradise.) Attributed (but denied) to POPE SIXTUS-QUINT (1521-90)—who is said to have thrown away his crutches on being elevated to the papacy—speaking to the CARDINAL DE MÉDICIS (1551-1609). — Cf. Gregorio Leti, also V. Ranke, *Hist. of the Popes*, Bk. 4, sec. 4. The crutches of Sixtus-Quint are often spoken of in connection with the idea of all further disguise being thrown aside when an object is attained.

Si je n'y suis pas, Dieu veuille m'y mettre ; et si j'y suis, Dieu veuille m'y retenir. (If I am not, may God make me so ; and if I am, may God keep me so.) Reply of JOAN OF ARC (1412-31) at her trial, to the question "Savez-vous être en la grâce de Dieu ?" (Are you in God's grace ?) Another version : "Si je n'y suis, Dieu m'y "mette ! et si j'y suis, Dieu m'y "maintienne !" (If I am not, God make me so ! and if I am, God keep me so.)

Si j'étais accusé d'avoir volé les tours de Notre-Dame, je commencerais par me cacher. (If I were accused of having stolen the towers of Notre-Dame, I should begin by hiding myself.) ACHILLE DE HARLAY, comte de Beaumont (1639-1712)—to show what little protection there was for an accused person. Another version : "Si j'étais accusé d'avoir "volé les tours de Notre-Dame, et "que j'entendisse crier derrière moi "'au voleur' je me sauverais à "toutes jambes." (. . . and I heard "stop thief" called out after me, I should run away as fast as I could.)

Si je tenais toutes les vérités dans ma main, je me donnerais bien de garde de l'ouvrir pour les découvrir aux hommes. (If I held all the truths in my hand, I should take good care not to open it to discover them to mankind.)

FONTENELLE (1657-1757)—not because he disdained truth, but because he did not like his peace disturbed. Alluded to by Grimm, *Correspondance littéraire*, Feb. 15, 1757. Another version : " Si j'avais la main remplie de vérités, je me garderais bien de l'ouvrir." (If I had my hand full of truths, I should take care not to open it.) Voltaire (édition Garnier, vol. xlii, p. 570) in his letter to Helvetius, Sep. 15, 1763, explains the reason of Fontenelle's *mot* as being that he had let truths escape him and been made to suffer for it.

Si l'abbé nous avait parlé un peu de religion, il nous aurait parlé de tout.

LOUIS XVI (1754 93) — after hearing a sermon by the ABBÉ MAURY (1746-1817). Grimm's *Mémoires*.

Si la bonne foi était bannie du reste de la terre, elle devrait se retrouver dans le cœur et dans la bouche des rois. (If good faith was banished from the rest of the earth, it ought still to remain in the hearts and mouths of kings.)

Attributed to JEAN II, surnamed le Bon (1319-64)—on the occasion of the return of his son, the Duke of Anjou, to France, having escaped from Calais (1363) without waiting for the ratification of a treaty (1362). Authenticity doubtful, and Froissart makes no mention of the phrase in connection with the event. (Cf. Froissart, bk. 1, pt. 2, ch. 159.) A similar saying is attributed, perhaps justly, to FRANÇOIS Ier (1494-1547)— *Recueil d'apophthègmes et bons mots*, 1695, pp. 83-4.

Si l'argent est, comme on dit, le nerf de la guerre, il est aussi la graisse de la paix. (If money is, as they say, the sinews of war, it is also the grease of peace.)

Attributed to CARDINAL RICHE-LIEU (1585-1642). See Pour faire la guerre avec succès &c. Cf. ". . . . mais entreprendre des "dépenses considérables, sans "savoir où trouver le nerf de la "guerre ; mon enfant, cela n'appar-"tient qu'à vous," &c. (. . . but to undertake considerable expense, without knowing where to find the sinews of war ; my child, that only belongs to you, &c.)— Mme. de Sévigné, Lettres, Feb. 19, 1690. (1836 edit., vol. 2, p. 582.) " Les nerfs des batailles sont les pécunes." (The sinews of war is money.) — Rabelais, *Gargantua*, bk. 1, ch. 46. ". . . Victuals and ammunition, "and money too, the sinews of "the war, are stored up in the "magazine."—Fletcher, *The Fair Maid of the Inn*, Act 1, sc. 2. (Licensed 1625-6, after the death of Fletcher). " I would wish that everything I touched might turne to gold : this is the sinews of war, and the sweetnesse of peace.—John Lyly, *Midas*, act 1, sc. 1. " Moneys are the sinews of war ;"—T. Fuller. *The Holy State* (*The Good Soldier*), 1642-58. " Neither is money the "sinews of war, (as it is trivially "said,) where the sinews of men's "arms in base and effeminate "people are failing."— Bacon's *Essays*, On the true greatness of kingdoms and estates (1813, p. 131). " Primum nervos belli, pecuniam "infinitam, qua nunc eget." (In the first place the sinews of war, unlimited money, which is now wanting.)—Cicero, *Phil.* v, ch. 2. " Pecuniæ belli civilis nervi sunt." (Money is the sinews of civil war.) —Tacitus, *Hist.*, bk. ii, ch. xxiv. "'Εν μὲν εἰρήνῃ παρέχω τὰ τέρπνα, ἐν δὲ πολέμοις νεῦρα τῶν πράξεων

γίνομαι." (" In peace I provide
enjoyment, and in war become the
sinews of action.") CRANTOR.
(*Sextus Empiricus, Adversus
Ethicos, XI.*, 53.) "Ὁ πόλεμος
οὐ τεταγμένα σιτεῖται." (" War
cannot be maintained by allotting
funds as one allots rations.")
Archidamus (d. 338 B.C.) *Plutarch, Cleomenes, XXVII.* "Ὑπο-
τέτμηται τὰ νεῦρα τῶν πραγμάτων."
(The sinews of affairs are severed.)
Aeschines, In Ctesiphontem, 166.
DEMOSTHENES (abt. 382--322 B.C.)
" I danari non sono il nervo della
" guerra, secondo che è la comune
"opinione," etc. (Money is not
the sinews of war, according to the
popular belief, etc.) Machiavelli,
*Discorsi sopra la prima Deca di T.
Livie*, bk. 2, ch. x, (written about
1516).

**Si le cardinal est en paradis, il
faut que le diable se soit
laissé escamoter en chemin.**
(If the cardinal is in Paradise,
the Devil must have allowed
himself to be cheated on the
road.)
Said by the COMTE DE TRÉVILLE,
captain of the guards, to LOUIS XIII
(1601-43), speaking of Richelieu.
See Ah! che se gli è un Dio &c.

**Si le peuple n'a pas de pain,
qu'il mange de la brioche.**
(If the people have no bread,
let them eat *brioche*.)*
Attributed to MARIE ANTOIN-
ETTE (1755-93), also to her friend
the DUCHESS OF POLIGNAC (died
1793, aged 44). See Si cette canaille
n'a pas de pain &c. The following
extract from J.-J. Rousseau's *Les
Confessions* (pt. 1, bk. vi.) which
were written 1737-41, shews that at
all events Marie Antoinette did not
originate the saying :—" Enfin je
"me rappelai le pis-aller d'une
"grande princesse à qui l'on disoit
A sort of cake.

" que les paysans n'avoient pas de
"pain, et qui répondit : 'Qu'ils
"mangent de la brioche.'' (At
last I remembered the resource of a
great princess who was told that the
peasants had no bread, and who
replied : Let them eat *brioche*. (Cf.
also Louis XVIII, *Relation d'un
voyage à Bruxelles et à Coblentz*
(Paris 1823, p. 59). " Aussi en
" mangeant la croûte avec le pâté,
"nous songeâmes à la reine Marie-
" Antoinette, qui répondit un jour
"que l'on plaignait devant elle les
"pauvres gens qui n'ont pas de
" pain : ' Mais, mon Dieu, que ne
"' mangent-ils de la croûte de
"' pâté?'" (Also when eating the
crust with the pasty, we thought of
queen Marie Antoinette, who one
day, when poor people who have
no bread were pitied in her presence
replied : " But goodness me, why
don't they eat .pie-crust.) And :
" Le hasard m'a fait, un de ces jours
" derniers, rencontrer un livre daté
" de 1760—où l'on raconte le même
" mot d'une duchesse de Toscane
"ce qui me paraît prouver, à peu
" près, que le mot n'a pas été dit
" par Marie-Antoinette, mais re-
"trouvé et mis en circulation par
"elle." (Chance has brought to
my notice a book dated 1760—
where a duchess of Tuscany is
credited with the same *mot*, which
seems to me to almost prove that
it did not originate with Marie-
Antoinette, but that she merely
found and put it into circulation.)
—Alphonse Karr, *Les Guêpes*,
April, 1843.

**Si le roi mange une seconde fois,
nous n'aurons plus personne.**
(If the king eats a second time,
we shall have nobody.)
DUKE OF ORLEANS (1674-1723)
—alluding to the diminution in the
number of courtiers round him when
LOUIS XIV (1638-1715) rallied and

176 FRENCH SAYINGS

ate after taking an elixir shortly before his death.

S'il faut périr, périons [*i.e.* périssons]. (If we must perish, let us perish !)

Favourite saying of the celebrated clown AURIOL (1808-81), parodying certain tragic lines, such as :
". . . S'il faut périr, nous périrons ensemble." (If we must die, we will die together). — Corneille, *Nicomède*, act I, sc. I.

S'il vous arrive quelque chose d'heureux, ne manquez pas d'aller le dire à vos amis, afin de leur faire de la peine.
(If anything lucky happens to you, don't fail to go and tell it to your friends, in order to annoy them).

A saying of COUNT MONTROND. Capt. Gronow's *Recollections and Anecdotes*—Count Montrond. Byron is supposed to have alluded to him, on his first visit to England, as the ". . . Preux chevalier de la Ruse."

Sinon, non ! (If not, no !)

Generally quoted in French, but really said in Spanish as under :
"Nos ostros que cada uno por si
"somos tanto como os, y que
"juntos podemos mas que os, os
"hacemos nuestro Rey, contanto
"que guardareis nuestros fueros ;
"si no, no !" (We who separately are worth as much as thou, and who united are worth more, make thee our king, on condition that thou preservest the priviléges of the nation ; if not, not !)

Formula used by the chief magistrate of the kingdom of Aragon to the sovereign at his coronation in the presence of the Cortès.

Si Poulle revient vous lui direz que je n'y suis pas. (If Poulle returns you will tell him that I am not at home).

The ABBÉ SIEYÈS (1748-1836) to his servant, on returning home after the trial of the ABBÉ POULLE (1703-81) who had discharged a pistol at Sieyès, fracturing his wrist (an III of the Republic—1794-5). The sympathies of the judges were with the accused.

Sire, je vous dois tout, mais je crois m'acquitter en quelque manière en vous donnant Colbert. (Sire, I owe everything to you, but I think I can in some measure repay you by giving you Colbert).

CARDINAL MAZARIN (1602-61), when dying—to LOUIS XIV (1638-1715).

Sire, que cette vue vous apprenne à ménager le sang de vos sujets. (Sire, let this spectacle teach you to take care of the blood of your subjects).

MARSHAL SAXE (1696-1750) — when visiting the battle-field of Fontenoy the day after the battle (fought May 11, 1745) to LOUIS XV (1710-74).

Sire, rien n'est impossible à Votre Majesté ; elle a voulu faire de mauvais vers et elle a réussi. (Sire, nothing is impossible for Your Majesty ; you wanted to write bad verses and you have succeeded).

Reply made by BOILEAU (1636-1711)—to LOUIS XIV (1638-1715) on being asked his opinion of some lines he had written.

Sire, voici un pauvre aveugle qui aurait besoin d'un bâton (Sire, here is a poor blind man, who requires a *bâton* [staff]).

Remark made by the DUKE OF BURGUNDY (1682-1712) in presenting lieutenant-general de Laubanie (after the siege of Landau in which he lost his sight) to LOUIS XIV.

Si vous voyez que la couronne soit mieux employée en l'un de vous qu'en moi, je m'y octroie volontiers et le veut de bon cœur. (If you think that the crown would be borne better by one of yourselves than by me, I will willingly and with all my heart resign it).— Words used by PHILIP-AUGUSTUS (Aug. 27, 1214) before the battle of Bouvines. M. L. Paris, *Chronique de Rains* (Reims) 1837, pp. 146-8. A popular, but incorrect, version is : " S'il est quelqu'un parmi vous qui se juge plus capable que moi de la porter [the crown], je la mets sur sa tête et je lui obéis." (If there is anyone among you who deems himself more capable of wearing it than I, I place it on his head and will obey him). Cf. A similar anecdote in the *Alexiade*, bk. 4, ch. 5, concerning Robert Guiscard (1015-85) before the battle of Dyrrachium (now Durazzo), 1082.

Soldats, c'est le soleil d'Austerlitz ! (Soldiers, it is the sun of Austerlitz !) NAPOLEON (1769-1821)—to his army (Sep. 7, 1812) on arriving at the battle-field of Moscow, the sun rising in a clear sky, although it had rained a great deal the previous day. Allusion to the brilliant sunrise the day of the battle of Austerlitz (Dec. 2, 1805). Ségur (*Hist. de Napoléon et de la Grande Armée*, bk. 7, ch. 9, vol. 1, p. 380, 1826 edit.) gives the phrase as : " Voilà le soleil d'Austerlitz !" (There is the sun of Austerlitz !)

Soldats, droit au cœur! (Soldiers, straight at my heart !) Last words of MARSHAL M. NEY (1769-1815), shot Dec. 7, 1815. After declaring that he had never betrayed his country. Another version : " Soldats ! hâtez-vous, et tirez-là !" (Soldiers ! make haste,

and aim there !) putting his hand to his heart.—*Derniers momens*, p. 333.

Soldats ! M. l'abbé veut dire qu'il n'y a pas de salut pour les lâches ! Vive le roi ! et en avant ! (Soldiers ! M. l'abbé means that there is no salvation for cowards ! Long live the king ! and forward !) Said by LIEUTENANT-COLONEL DE CHAMOUROUX before the battle of Rocoux (1746), losing patience at the length of the almoner of the Auvergne regiment's exhortation.

Sonate, que me veux-tu? (Sonata, what dost thou want with me ?) FONTENELLE (1657-1757),—tired of sonatas, much in vogue in his day. Cf. *Canon, que me veux-tu?* —Victor Hugo, *Les Misérables*.

Songez que du haut de ces pyramides quarante siècles vous contemplent ! (Remember that forty centuries are looking down at you from the summit of these pyramids !) NAPOLEON'S (1769-1821) words to his soldiers (July 21, 1798) after landing in Egypt.—Thiers, *Hist. de la Révolution française*. Other authorities quote the famous phrase as follows : " Français, songez que " du haut de ces monuments quar-"ante siècles ont les yeux fixés sur " vous." (Frenchmen, remember that from the summit of these monuments forty centuries have their eyes fixed upon you.)—P. Martin, *Histoire de l'expédition française en Egypte*, 1815, vol. 1, p. 199. " Soldats, quarante siècles vous regardent." (Soldiers, forty centuries are looking at you.)—Napoléon's Mémoirs—Guerre d'Orient, vol. 1, p. 160 (dictated at St. Helena to General Bertrand). " Du haut de ces Pyramides," &c. (From the summit of these Pyramids, &c.)—Mémoires,

12

&c., 1823, by General Gourgaud, vol. 2, p. 239.

"Vingt siècles, descendus dans l'eternelle nuit,
"Y sont sans mouvement, sans lumière et sans bruit."
(Twenty centuries fallen into eternal night
Are there motionless, without light and noiseless)
Chateaubriand, *Mémoires d'Outre-Tombe*, vol v, p. 306, 1849-50 ed.
The second line appears to have been taken by Chateaubriand from Pierre La Moyne's *Saint Louys, ou la Sainte Couronne reconquise (Poème héroïque)* bk. v, p. 145, 1658 ed.
"Là sont les Devanciers joints à leurs Descendants ;
"Tous les Règnes y sont ; on y voit tous les Temps ;
" Et cette Antiquité si célèbre en l'Histoire
"Ces Siècles si fameux par la voix de la Gloire
"Réunis par la Mort, en cette obscure nuit,
"Y sont sans mouvement, sans lumière et sans bruit."
(These are the Ancestors joined to their Descendants ;
All Reigns are there ; there are seen all Ages ;
And that Antiquity so celebrated in History
Those Centuries so famous by the voice of Glory
Reunited by Death, in this dark night,
Are there motionless, without light and noiseless.)

Songez que le soleil ne se couche jamais dans l'immense hérit-age de Charles-Quint— (Remember that the sun never sets on the immense empire of Charles V.)
NAPOLEON (1796-1821) to J. FOUCHÉ (1763-1820) c. 1808. Followed by (completing the sentence) "et que j'aurai l'Empire des deux Mondes," (and that I shall have the Empire of the two Worlds.) Fouché *Mémoires*, 1824, pt. I, p. 366; Scott, *Life of Napoleon*, 1827, vol. vi, p. 141.

Sorti de la légalité pour rentrer dans le droit. (Departed from legality to return to justice.)
Formula used by PRINCE LOUIS-NAPOLEON (1808-73), then president of the republic, referring to the *coup d'état* of Dec. 2, 1851. " Elle "[France] a compris que je n'étais " sorti de la légalité que pour rentrer "dans le droit." (She [France] has understood that I only departed from legality to return to justice). —*Le Moniteur universel*, Jan. 1, 1852, p. 2. It is said (Cf. *L'Inter-médiaire des Chercheurs et Curieux* vol. xxvii, cols. 91-2) that the *mot* was suggested by a poor curate to his superior who passed it on to the bishop who used it in his letter of congratulation to Napoleon III. The latter at once appropriated it. See La légalité nous tue.

Soutiens ma tête, Joseph, c'est la plus forte tête du monde ! (Support my head, Joseph, it is the strongest head in the world !)
Last words attributed to MIRA-BEAU (1749-91), to his valet, who was standing at his bedside.

Souvenez-vous, mon fils, que la royauté n'est qu'une charge publique, dont vous rendrez un compte rigoureux dans un autre monde. (Remember, my son, that royalty is only a public office, of which you will render a strict account in another world.)
Dying words of LOUIS VI. sur-named "le Gros" (the Fat) (abt. 1078-1137) to his son.

Souvenez-vous que je m'appelle Arcole. (Remember that my name is Arcole).
Attributed to a young man (whose name, however, was JEAN FOURNIER) who with a flag in his hand rushed on the *pont de la Grève*, July 28, 1830. He fell dead immediately.

Souvent femme varie. (A woman is often capricious).
The following couplet is said to

have been written with a diamond on a window-pane at the château of Chambord by FRANCIS I (1494-1547), but the incident is of doubtful authenticity.

> "Souvent femme varie,
> "Malhabil qui s'y fie."

(A woman is often capricious. Foolish is he who trusts her). —Bernier's *history of Blois*, middle of 17th century.
The second line is often quoted as "Bien fol qui s'y fie," but the sense is the same. Brantôme (Vie des Dames galantes, Discours IV) refers to the writing as simply, "Toute femme varie." (Every woman is capricious) and as being by the *side* of a window. This is more probable. V. Hugo introduces the couplet in *Le roi s'amuse* (act 4, sc. 2). Cf.

> "Mais quoi? le naturel des femmes est volage,
> "Et à chaque moment se change leur courage.
> "Bien fol qui s'y abuse, et qui de loyauté
> "Pense jamais trouver compagne une beauté."

(But what? women are fickle by nature,
And their fidelity changes every instant.
Whoever is hoodwinked by them, or who seriously thinks
That in a beauty he will find a companion is mad).
—R. Garnier, *Marc Antoine*, act I.
"Often change doth please a woman's mind."—Sir T. Wyatt, *The Deserted Lover*.
"Φυὴν δ' ὡς πόντος ἀλλοίην ἔχει."
"Uncertain as the sea is woman's nature."
—Simonides of Amorgos, *De Feminis*, 42.
"Varium et mutabile semper Femina."
"A woman's will Is changable and uncertain still."—(*Conington*).—Virgil, *Æneid, IV.* ll. 4, 569-70
"'—*Varium et mutabile*, Philip.'"

—Sir W. Scott, *Quentin Durward*, ch. xxx, (Louis to Des Comines).
Surtout ne me manquez pas.
(Above all, don't miss me).
Last words of LOUIS ANTOINE HENRI DE BOURBON, DUC D'ENGHIEN (1772-1804) to the gendarmes, just before being shot at Vincennes, Mar. 21, 1804. See C'est plus qu'un crime, c'est une faute. Also, Ne me manquez pas!
Tant que je te la serrerai, je serai vivant. . . . Après cela je ne saurai plus où je serai. (As long as I press your hand, I shall be alive. . . . After that I shall no longer know where I am).
Dying words of PROFESSOR A. TROUSSEAU (1810-67), taking hold of his daughter's hand at the time. —*Nouveaux mémoires de Goncourt.*
Tant que je vivrai. je règnerai comme je l'entends; mais mon fils sera forcé d'être libéral. (As long as I live, I will reign as I like; but my son will be compelled to be liberal).
NAPOLEON (1769-1821), referring to the tendencies of the time.
Ta religion est bien malade, les médecins l'abandonnent. (Thy religion is very ill, the doctors give it up.)
Attributed to HENRY IV (1553-1610) and said to SULLY (1560-1641) à propos of a Huguenot doctor turned Catholic.
Tenez, citoyen ministre, mon rôle est d'être pendu et non d'être bourreau. (Look here, citizen minister, my *rôle* is to be hanged and not to be hangman).
Reply by ANDRIEUX (1759-1833) to FOUCHÉ (1763-1820), who offered him a post of censor.
Tire la ficelle, ma femme! (Pull the string, wife!)

Saying popularised by LEVASSOR at the *Variétés* (Paris) in 1839. In a comic sketch a showman uses the phrase to his wife every time he requires the scene of the panorama to be changed.

Tirer vanité de son rang, c'est avertir qu'on est au-dessous. (To be vain of one's rank, is to show that one is beneath it). Saying of MARIE LECZINSKA (1703-68), wife of Louis XV.

Tirez, chasseurs ce sont les ennemis. (Fire, men, they are the enemy). Said to have been uttered by the CHEVALIER D'ASSAS (born 1738) at Clostercamp in the night of Oct. 15-16, 1760, when he was killed.— Comte de Rochambeau, *Mémoires*, 1809, vol. 1, p. 162. See A moi, Auvergne, voilà les ennemis.

Note.—Facing the title-page of P. Baillot's *Récit de la bataille de Marathon* (Dijon 1791), are the following words : "Si tu parles, tu es mort.—Auvergne ! "feu, c'est l'ennemi.
    Le chevalier d'Assas."
(If you speak, you are a dead man.— Auvergne, fire, it's the enemy.
    The chevalier d'Assas.)

Tirez le rideau, la farce est jouée. (Draw the curtain, the comedy is ended). Usually regarded as RABELAIS' (1495-1553) last words. "Je m'en "vais chercher un grand peut-être ; "tirez le rideau, la farce est jouée." (I am going to seek a great "per-haps" ; draw the curtain, the comedy is ended). Another anecdote is also told of Rabelais when dying. His *curé* in bringing him the Host is reported to have said : " *Voilà votre Sauveur et votre maître, qui veut bien s'abaisser jusqu'à venir vous trouver ; le reconnaissez-vous.*"— " *Hélas ! oui, je le reconnais à sa monture.*" (There is your Saviour and Master, who is kind enough to stoop to come and see you ; do you recognise him ?—Alas ! yes, I

recognise him by his steed). The authenticity of both the above sayings is, however, denied. See Je vais quérir &c. Cf. The grand Perhaps ! R. Browning—Bishop Blougram's Apology. The phrase is also attributed to PIERRE BAYLE, (1647-1706).

Toujours Grétry. (Still Grétry). Reply by ANDRÉ GRÉTRY (1741-1813), to NAPOLEON (1769-1821), being tired of the latter asking his name week after week. Mme. de Rémusat. *Mémoires* vol. 2, ch. 10.

Tous empires, royaulmes et provinces sans justice sont forests pleines de brigands. (All empires, realms and provinces without justice are forests full of robbers.) Saying of the CHEVALIER BAYARD (1475-1524). When asked what a good man should leave to his children, Bayard replied : " Ce "qui ne craint ni la pluie, ni la "tempeste, ni la force des hommes, "ni la justice humaine : la sagesse "et la vertu." (That which fears neither rain, nor storm, nor man's might, nor human justice : wisdom and virtue.)

Tous les changements que j'ai trouvés dans le monde depuis douze ans, c'est que les hommes n'ont plus de barbe et les chevaux plus de queue. (All the changes I have found in the world since twelve years ago are that men no longer have beards and that horses have longer tails). The MARÉCHAL DE BASSOMPIERRE (1579-1646)—imprisoned in the Bastille for 12 years and liberated Jan. 20, 1643.

Tous les Français sont mes complices, et vous-mêmes l'auriez été si j'eusse réussi. (All Frenchmen are my accomplices, and you would your-

selves have been, if I had succeeded).

GENERAL C.-F. DE MALET (1754-
1812)—replying to the question as
to the names and number of his
accomplices.—*Derniers momens*, p.
257.

Tout à l'huile ! tout à l'huile !
(Oil with all of it ! oil with all
of it !)
Order given by FONTENELLE
(1657-1757) to the cook as to some
asparagus. The ABBÉ TERRASSON
(1670-1750), who only liked butter
with it, had a fit before sitting down
to dinner and the instructions previously given were for half to be
served with butter and half with oil.
—Grimm. *Corresp. littéraire, Feb.,
1757.* An intimate acquaintance of
Fontenelle, writing to the *Journal de
Paris* (see March 16 and 17, 1778,
pp. 297-9 and 301-2 respectively)
denies that Fontenelle was the hero
of the anecdote and asserts that being
very fond of asparagus, he used to
tell the story to his friends.

**Tout appartient à la patrie quand
la patrie est en danger.**
(Everything belongs to the
country when the country is in
danger.)
DANTON (1759-94)—in his speech
in the Legislative Assembly, Aug.
28, 1792.

Tout arrive en France. (In
France, all things come to
pass).
The DUC DE LA ROCHEFOU-
CAULT (1613-80), Oct. 4, 1650,
CARDINAL MAZARIN (1602-61)
having remarked that no one would
have thought, a week before, that
they would all four [the other 2
were the duc de Bouillon and Pierre
Lenet] be in the same carriage.
P. Lenet, *Mémoires*, p. 413.
The saying has been attributed to
TALLEYRAND (1754-1838).

**Tout beau, Jean le Blanc, vou-
drais-tu faire mourir en eau
douce un général des
galères ?** (Gently, Jean le
Blanc, do you want to drown
in fresh water a general of the
galleys ?)
Remark made by the DUC DE
VIVONNE (1636-88) to the white
horse (Jean le Blanc) he rode at the
passage of the Rhine (1672). The
horse nearly threw him into the
river and he received a shot in the
shoulder at the same moment.
Another version is, " Au moins ne
" t'avise pas de faire mourir un
" amiral dans l'eau douce ! (At all
events don't take it into your head
to drown an admiral in fresh water.)
—*Intermédiaire des Chercheurs*, vol.
xxxiii, col. 362.

**Toute nation a le gouvernement
qu'il mérite.** (Every nation
has the government it deserves.)
COUNT J. DE MAISTRE (1753-
1821) in a letter from St. Peters-
burg, dated August 27, 1811, *à
propos* of the new constitutional laws
of Russia. J. de Maistre, *Lettres et
Opuscules*, Lettre 76.

**Toutes les fois que je donne une
place vacante je fais cent
mécontents et un ingrat.**
(Every time I fill a vacant post
I make a hundred people discontented and one ungrateful.
LOUIS XIV (1638-1715).—
Voltaire, *Siècle de Louis XIV*,
ch. 26. See The gratitude of
place-expectants &c.

**Tout est fini pour moi. Le
roi de Prusse se charge de
moi.** (All is ended with me.
The king of Prussia will take
care of me).
NAPOLEON III (1808-73), Sept 2,
1870,—the day after Sedan.
Tout est perdu fors l'honneur.
(All is lost save honour.)

The form in which an expression used by FRANCIS I (1494-1547) in a letter to his mother after the defeat at Pavia (Feb. 24, 1525), has come down to us. The letter begins, "Madame, pour vous faire sçavoir "comme se porte le reste de mon infortune, de toutes choses ne m'est demeuré que l'honneur et la vie qui est saulve." (Madam, to let you know how I fare in my misfortune, nothing is left to me but honour and my life, which is safe).—A. Champollion-Figeac, *Captivite du roi François* I er, p. 129. Three centuries later, another great personage was to repeat the phrase in all its brevity. When NAPOLEON, after the defeat of Waterloo, returned to Paris (June 21, 1815), the first person he met at the Elysée was M. de Caulaincourt; they shook hands in silence, but Drouot, who accompanied the Emperor, could not refrain from saying to those present : "Tout est perdu !" Napoleon added quickly, "Excepté l'honneur." Cf.

"Charles Quint portait envie
"A ce roi plein de valeur,
"Qui s'écriait a Pavie
"'*Tout est perdu fors l'honneur.*'"
("That mighty monarch Charles of Spain,
"Was envious of the valrous king,
"Who at Pavia did complain,
"'Save honour, I've lost everything.'")
Béranger, *Le bon Français.*

Tout est perdu, madame, et j'ai le malheur d'avoir conservé la vie ! (All is lost, madam, and I have the misfortune to have preserved my life !)
JOACHIM MURAT (1767-1815) May 19, 1815, embracing his wife, having visited his capital secretly. *Derniers momens* p. 289. He was shot Oct. 13 (?Sept. 29) in the same year.

Tout est possible à Paris parce qu'il y a la comédie et du pain. (Everything is possible in Paris, because the theatre and bread are there).
MME. DE MAINTENON (1635-1719) during a time of famine in 1710.

Tout par raison. (Everything by reason).
Saying attributed to CARDINAL RICHELIEU (1585-1642).

Tout solda` `français porte dans sa gi` `ne la bâton de maréch (Every French soldier c` `ies in his knapsack a marsha`` ``s *bâton*).
LOUIS XVIII (1755-1824), after witnessing some manœuvres by the students of the Ecole de Saint-Cyr, addressed them as follows : "Mes "enfants, je suis on ne peut "plus content ; rappelez-vous bien "qu'il n'est aucun de vous qui "n'ait dans sa giberne le bâton de "maréchal du duc de Reggio, c'est "à vous à l'en faire sortir."
(My children, I could not be more pleased, remember that there is not one of you who has not the marshal's *bâton* of the duc de Reggio in his knapsack, it is for you to bring it out). *Moniteur universel,* Aug. 10, 1819.

Note.—The title of duc de Reggio was conferred upon Marshal Oudinot (1767-1849) after the battle of Wagram.

The famous phrase has also been attributed to NAPOLEON, but apparently without any justification. See La carrière ouverte aux talents &c.

Tout vieillit ici, Monsieur, il n'y a que votre éloquence qui ne vieillit pas. (Everything ages here, Monsieur, there is only your eloquence which does not grow old).
LOUIS XIV (1638-1715) to BISHOP MASCARON (1634-1703), who preached a last sermon to the Court in 1694.

Très peu quand je me considère ; beaucoup quand je me compare. (Very little when I look at myself ; much when I compare myself [with others]).

Reply of the ABBÉ MAURY (1746-1817) to Regnault (or Regnaud) de SAINT-JEAN-D'ANGÉLY (1736-1820) when asked by the latter if he did not think a great dea¹ of himself. Œuvres de A.-V. Arna *Mélanges,* p. 431.

Trois tronçons. (Three fragments).

In a speech by EUGÈNE ROUHER (1814-84) in the Corps législatif, March 16, 1867, alluding to the alliance of Austria, Prussia and Germany. " Au lieu de cette " cohésion puissante qu'avaient " créée les traités de 1815, nous " n'avons plus en face de nous qu'une " confédération divisée en trois "tronçons." (Instead of this powerful coalition which the treaties of 1815 had created, we have now before us only a confederation divided into three fragments). *Le Moniteur universel,* March 17, 1867, p. 309.

Tuez-les tous, car le Seigneur connaît ceux qui sont à lui. (Kill them all, for the Lord knows his own).

Attributed (but contested) to the legate ARNAULD AMALRIC (died 1225) or MILON, when asked by the Crusaders how they should distinguish heretics from the faithful ones, at the massacre of Béziers (1209). " Caedite eos, novit enim " Dominus qui sunt ejus." (Kill them, for the Lord knows who are his).—Pierre-Césaire d'Heisterbach. *Dialogimiraculorum distinctio* 5, ch. 21, p. 139 (edition B. Tissier). *Bibliotheca Patrum Cistercensium,* vol. 2. Another version. " Tuez-les tous ; Dieu reconnaîtra les siens." (Kill them all ; God will know his own).

Tu montreras ma tête au peuple ; elle en vaut la peine. (Thou wilt show my head to the people ; it is worth the trouble).

Request made by DANTON (1759-94) on the scaffold to the executioner (April 5, 1794). Preceded by : " Oh, ma femme ! oh, ma bien " aimée ! oh ! mes enfans ! je ne " vous reverrai donc plus ! " (Oh, my wife ! oh, my beloved ! oh, my children ! I shall never see you more then !) Then, interrupting himself, he said, "Danton, point de faiblesse." (Danton, no weakness). *Derniers momens,* p. 202. See Allons, Danton &c.

Tu trembles, Bailly ?—J'ai froid. (Thou tremblest, Bailly?—I am cold).

Question asked of JEAN SYLVAIN BAILLY (1736-93) by one of his executioners (Nov. 12, 1793) and his reply. See If I tremble with cold &c. L. A. Thiers, in his *Hist. de la Révolution* (vol. 5, p. 411, 1832) says : " Tu trembles, " lui dit un soldat. Mon ami, " répond le vieillard, c'est de froid." (Thou tremblest, said a soldier to him. My friend, replied the old man, it is with cold).

Un ancien Grec avait une lyre admirable ; il s'y rompit une corde ; au lieu d'en remettre une de boyau, il en voulait une d'argent, et la lyre, avec sa corde d'argent, perdit son harmonie. (One of the ancient Greeks had an admirable lyre ; he broke one of the strings ; instead of replacing it with one of catgut he wanted a silver one, and the lyre, with its silver string, lost its harmony).

OLIVIER PATRU, (1604-81) in 1675, at the Academy, when a candidate presented himself, whose only title to consideration was his noble birth.

Un courtisan doit être sans humeur et sans honneur. (A courtier must be without temper and without honour). Definition by the Regent PHILIP OF ORLEANS (1674-1723).

Une cour sans femme est un printemps sans roses. A court without a woman is a spring without roses). Attributed to FRANCOIS Ier. (1494-1547).

Une idée par jour. (One idea per day). Saying attributed to ÉMILE DE GIRARDIN (1806-81), and appearing as a heading in "*la Presse*" of Feb. 29, 1848.

Une révolution ne peut se faire géométriquement. (A revolution cannot be made geometrically). Saying of DANTON (1759-94).

Une seule loi, une seule langue, une seule croyance. (One law, one language, one belief). Maxim of NICHOLAS I of Russia (1796-1855). See One country, one constitution &c.

Une tempête dans un verre d'eau. (A storm in a glass of water). PAUL I of Russia (1754-1801)— with reference to the troubles in Geneva towards end of 18th century. Dutens, *Dutensiana*, 40. See A tempest in a tea-pot.

Un je ne sais quoi, qui n'a plus de nom dans aucune langue. (An "I don't know what," which has no name in any language). JACQUES BOSSUET (1627-1704)— in his funeral sermon on HENRIETTE D'ANGLETERRE (1644-70), Aug. 21, 1670. The words : "Madame se meurt ! Madame est morte !" (q.v.) occur in the same sermon.

Un jour vous regretterez de ne pas mourir comme moi au champ des braves. (One day

you will regret not having died like me on the battle-field). Said to NAPOLEON (1769-1821) July 27, 1799, at the battle of Aboukir, by COLONEL FUGIÈRES, when dying.

Un mauvais quart d'heure. See Je voudrois bien voir &c.

Un prince est le premier serviteur et le premier magistrat de l'Etat. (A prince is the first servant and the first magistrate of the State). Motto (written in French) of FREDERICK THE GREAT'S (1712-86) political testament. *Mémoires de Brandebourg*, p. 234 (1751). The expression also occurs several times in his works. Cf. "Ce n'est "pas le souverain, c'est la loi, Sire, "qui doit regner sur les peuples. "Vous n'en êtes que le ministre et le "premier dépositaire." (It is not the sovereign, but the law, sire, [Louis XV] which should govern nations. You are only its minister and first depository).—Massillon, *Le Petit Carême, Sermon pour le jour de l'Incarnation.* "[Rex] pro-"bavit, non rempublicam suam esse, "sed se reipublicæ." ([The king] declared that he belongs to the state, not the state to him.)—Seneca, *De Clementia I*, 19.

Un roi de France peut mourir ; il n'est jamais malade. (A king of France may die ; he is never ill). Reply of LOUIS XVIII (1755-1824) to those who begged him to take care of himself. He insisted on performing the official functions of royalty to the last, although in a deplorable state of health. *Hist. des deux Restaurations* (1858) vol. 7, pp. 73-4. Another version gives the words as : "Un "roi de France meurt, mais il ne "doit pas être malade ;" (A king of France dies, but he must not be

FRENCH SAYINGS 185

ill) and says that they were used to the COMTE D'ARTOIS(1757-1836), his brother (afterwards Charles X) Aug. 25, 1824. See Decet imperatorem stantem mori.

Un roi non lettré est un âne couronné. (An illiterate king is a crowned donkey). Written by FOULQUES II (died 958), sovereign Count of Anjou, to LOUIS IV D'OUTRE-MER, king of the Franks. The latter one day surprised the Count occupied in musical composition, which provoked a smile. Foulques wrote: "Sachez, Seigneur, qu'un roi non lettré est un âne couronné. Cf. also Philippe de Comines (1445-1509) Mémoires, bk. 2, ch. 6. Cf. "Roy sanz lettre est comme asne couronné. (An unlettered king is like a donkey crowned).—Eustache Deschamps, Balades, mccxliv. Cf. the saying of DIOGENES (c. 412-323 B.C.) "Τὸν πλούσιον ἀμαθῆ πρόβατον (εἶπε) χρυσόμαλλον." ("A rich man without instruction is a sheep with a golden fleece.") Diogenes Laertius, VI., 2, 6, 47.

Un soldat qui a bien dormi en vaut deux. (One soldier who has slept well is worth two). A saying of GENERAL DE VENDÔME (1654-1712), beloved by his soldiers.

Venez voir comment meurt un maréchal de France sur le champ de bataille. (Come and see how a marshal of France dies on the battle field). MARSHAL NEY (1769-1815) at Waterloo, June 18, 1815. V. Hugo, Les Misérables: Cosette, bk. 1, ch. 12. Condemned to death and shot Dec. 7, same year. See I have sent for you that you may see &c. Also Come, my son, and see how &c.

Vive la nation! (Long live the nation!)

THE ABBÉ SIEYÈS (1748-1836) who was the first one to use the phrase, he said.

Vive la Pologne! (Long live Poland!) Cry uttered by several barristers on the occasion of the visit of the Czar Alexander II (1818-81) to the Palais de Justice, Paris, June 4, 1867. Charles Floquet was said to have been one of them. Attributed to L. GAMBETTA (1838-82) in Le Temps of Jan. 23, 1896.

Vive la République! (Long live the Republic!) Reply made by JOSEPH BARRA, (1780-93) a child of thirteen, when told that his life would be spared if he would say Vive le roi! (Long live the King!) According to the report by Admiral J. F. Renaudin (1750-1809), then commanding the Vengeur, these words were uttered by the sailors as the vessel sank, June 1, 1794, but cf. Carlyle's essay On the sinking of " The Vengeur." Renaudin was taken a prisoner to England.

Vivre libre ou mourir. (Live free or die). Motto of Le Vieux Cordelier, a journal (1st No. appeared Dec. 5, 1793) edited by CAMILLE DESMOULINS (1762-94).

Voici l'Empire. (Here is the Empire). COMTE DI CAVOUR (1810-61)—as soon as he heard of the French Revolution.—Sir M. E. Grant Duff, Notes from a diary, vol. 1, p. 303. Authority of Charles Lever.

Voilà bien du bruit pour une omelette! (What a noise about an omelette!) Attributed to the poet DES BARREAUX (1602-73) when throwing an omelette out of window during a storm on a Good Friday. —Voltaire, Letter to M. Thiriot, Dec. 24th, 1758. The words "au lard" are sometimes added. The phrase has also been attributed to GENERAL MONTECUCULLI (1608-81). Cf.

"Du tonnerre dans l'air bravant les vains carreaux,
"Et nous parlant de Dieu du ton de Des Barreaux?"

(Braving the vain thunderbolts of the air, and speaking of God to us in des Barreaux' tone?) Boileau— *La Satire des Femmes*, l. 79 from end. Another version : " Violà " bien du bruit là-haut pour une " omelette" (What a noise up above about an omelette).—Tallement des Réaux, *Historiettes*, vol. 9, p. 37 (1840).

Voilà ce que c'est l'histoire ! (That's what history is !)

Exclamation of HENRI IV (1553-1610)—after the battle of Aumale (1592) in which he was wounded, on finding that no two of the generals agreed in their accounts of the engagement in which they had taken part. See Anything but history, for history must be false.

Voilà donc le prix de ce que j'ai fait pour la liberté. (This then is the price of what I have done for liberty).

ANTOINE BARNAVE (1761-93)— on the scaffold, Nov. 18, 1793. Sometimes attributed, erroneously, to CAMILLE DESMOULINS (1762-94).

Voilà le premier chagrin qu'elle m'ait causé. (This is the first grief she has caused me).

LOUIS XIV (1638-1715)—on the death of his wife, MARIE-THÉRÈSE (born 1638) July 30, 1683, but of doubtful authenticity. Another version is. " Le ciel me prive " d'une épouse qui ne m'a jamais " donné d'autre chagrin que celui de " sa mort." (Heaven deprives me of a spouse who has never caused me any other grief than her death). Cf. the following lines by F.

Maynard (1582-1646) (*Œuvres*, p. 25) :
" La morte que tu plains fut exempte de blâme,
" Et le triste accident qui termina ses jours,
" Est le seul déplaisir qu'elle a mis dans ton âme."

(The dead for whom you weep was blameless,
And the sad accident that ended her days,
Is the only chagrin that she has ever caused you).

Voilà le seul jour heureux de ma vie. (This is the only happy day of my life).

Dying words of MARIE-THÉRÈSE (1638-83) wife of LOUIS XIV.

Voulez-vous donc qu'on vous fasse des révolutions à l'eau rose. (Would you have revolutions made with rose-water, then ?)

SÉBASTIEN ROCH NICOLAS CHAMFORT (1741-94) to MARMONTEL (1723-99), the latter regretting the excesses of the French Revolution. — Marmontel, *Mémoires*.

Vous allez voir comment on meurt pour vingt-cinq francs par jour ! (You shall see how one dies for 25 francs * a day !)

Attributed (but contradicted) to J. B. V. BAUDIN (1811 51) just before being shot dead at a barricade, Dec. 3, 1851.

Vous avez bien fait, sire. (You have done well, sire).

Reply made by JEAN BART (1651-1702) to Louis XIV (1638-1715), on being appointed vice-admiral.

Vous avez donc parole d'épouser Dieu le père ? (You have been told then to marry God the father ?)

* The pay of members of the *Corps Législatif*.

Said to MME. DE MAINTENON (1635-1719) by her brother, the COMTE D'AUBIGNÉ, on the former wishing that she were dead.

Vons avez fait, monsieur, trois fautes d'orthographe. (You have made, sir, three mistakes in spelling)

Remark made Feb. 18, 1790, by the MARQUIS DE FAVRAS (1745-90) to the official who brought the order for his execution. (Cf. V. Hugo's *Marion Delorme*, act 5, sc. 7). See your warrant is written in fair characters &c.

Vous avez la plaie et moi la douleur. (You have the wound and I the pain).

Words used to ADMIRAL COLIGNY (1517-72) by CHARLES IX (1550-74), when visiting him after being informed of the wounds inflicted by his assailants (Aug. 22, 1572). Two days later the assassins effected their object, and the admiral's mutilated remains were hanged by the populace to the gibbet at Montfaucon. It is said that the king remarking that some courtiers stopped their noses owing to the odour, alluded to the *mot* of Vitellius * saying : "Je ne le bousche comme vous "autres, car l'odeur de son ennemi "est très bonne." (I don't hold my nose like you, for the odour of one's enemy is very good.) Brantôme, *Hommes illustres*, &c., Bk. IV, Charles IX. On hearing of the crime Charles said that it was 'he himself who was wounded.' On seeing Coligny, he said, " Mon "père, vous avez la plaie et moi la "douleur ; mais je renie mon salut "que j'en ferai une vengeance si "horrible que jamais la mémoire "s'en perdra." (. . . but I'll forfeit my salvation if I do not wreak such a terrible revenge that the memory

* See Optime olera occisum &c.

of it will never die). One account (de Thou) gives "La blessure est pour vous, la douleur est pour moi." (The wound is yours, the pain is mine). Another (Le Laboureur) : "Vous avez reçu le coup au bras, et moy je le ressens au cœur." (You have received the wound in the arm, and I feel it in my heart.) A third : "A vous la douleur de la blessure ; à moi l'injure et l'outrage." (The pain of the wound is yours ; mine the insult and the outrage.) Cf. " ' If you live to be an honest " 'and loyal servant of your Prince, " ' my good youth,' answered the Frenchman, " ' you will know there " ' is no perfume to match the scent " ' of a dead traitor.' " Sir W. Scott, *Quentin Durward*, ch. 3. Cf. also "Et sur le Carrousel, au monarque Bourbon "Porté ces corps pourris qui sentent toujours bon." ("And at the Carrousel, to the Bourbon monarch Carried those dead bodies which always smell good.) —Barthélemy *Douze Journées de la Révolution*.

Vous avez quatre mots contre une idée. (You have four words against one idea)

ANTOINE RIVAROL (1753-1801), to a stupid person who boasted of knowing four languages. "Je vous en félicite : vous avez," &c. (I congratulate you : you have, &c.) Cf.

"He that is but able to express "No sense at all in several languages, "Will pass for learneder than he that's known "To speak the strongest reason in his own." —S. Butler, *Satire upon Human Learning*, pt 1, l. 65.

See In sieben Sprachen schweigen. Cf. " C'est Charles-Quint lui-même "qui a dit qu'un homme qui sait "quatre langues, vaut quatre "hommes" (It is Charles V himself who said that *a man who knows four languages is worth four men*.)

—Mme. de Staël, *Corinne*, VII, I.
Also "Charles Quint, qui parloit
"cinq ou six langues, disoit souvent,
"quand il tomboit sur leurs différ-
"entes beautés, que selon l'opinion
"des Turcs, autant de langues que
"l'homme sçait parler, autant de
"fois est-il homme;" &c. (Charles
V, who spoke five or six languages,
often said, when he encountered
their different beauties, that according to the opinion of the Turks
a man was as many times a man
as he knew languages ; &c. —Brantôme, *Capitaines étrangers*. Cf.
the saying of HERACLITUS (probably c. 535-475 B.C.) "Πολυμαθίη
νόον οὐ διδάσκει." ("Great learning
will not produce mental capacity.")
Diogenes Laertius, *IX*., 1, 2, 1.

**Vous aviez promis de m'épargner
des souffrances inutiles.** (You
promised to spare me useless
suffering).
Last words of H.-G. Riquetti,
COMTE ‚ DE MIRABEAU (1746-91)
alluding to his request for laudanum.

**Vous êtes cause de ma mort,
vous m'aviez promis de me
rendre à l'Église, et vous me
livrez à mes ennemis.**—(You
are the cause of my death, you
had promised to give me up to
the Church, and you deliver me
to my enemies.)
JOAN OF ARC (1412-31) to
PIERRE CAUCHON (died 1443)—
after he had read her sentence to
her. *Derniers momens*, p. 39.

**Vous m'avez souvent ouï dire des
impiétés ; mais dans le fond
je croyois tout le contraire
de ce que je disois. Je ne
contrefaisois le libertin et
l'athée que pour paraître plus
brave.** (You have often heard
me say blasphemous things ;
but at heart I believed the
contrary of what I said. I only

imitated the libertine and the
atheist to appear more brave.)
Attributed to the GRAND CONDÉ
(1621-86)—when about to die
(1686).—Cizeron-Rival.

Vous m'en direz tant ! (You will
say so much !)
Attributed to ANNE OF AUSTRIA
(1602-66) by president Jean Bouhier
in his *Recueil de particularités*, *bons
mots*, &c. (Biblio. Nat. ms. Fr.
25645, pp. 34-5). "*Ah! vous en
diriez tant* :. . . (Ah ! you would
say so much [use such a strong
argument, mention such a large
sum]. Said by her to G. BAUTRU
(1588-1665) whose argument was
that no woman was proof against
money. He mentioned such an
enormous sum that the queen made
the reply mentioned. The ABBÉ
J. TERRASSON (1670-1750) is
credited with a similar reply
to a question by MARIE
LESCZINSKA (1703-68). "Votre
Majeste m'en dira tant !" (Your
Majesty will say so much [will say
such large amounts]). (Cf. *Suite au
Mémorial de Sainte Hélène*, 1824,
vol. I, p. 108).

**Vous me voyez, messieurs,
occupé à faire manger
Molière que mes valets de
chambre ne trouvent pas
assez bonne compagnie pour
eux.** (You see me, gentlemen,
busy handing food to Molière,
whom my valets do not consider good enough company
for them).—Mme. Campan,
Mémoires (1823) (1622-73).
Words attributed to LOUIS XIV
(1638-1715) when helping Molière
to a portion of his own *en-cas de
nuit* to teach some of his officers a
lesson ; but authenticity doubtful.

**Vous ne voulez pas faire de la
France une caserne ; prenez
garde d'en faire un cimetière.**
(You do not want to make of

France a barracks ; take care that you do not make a cemetery of it.)
MARSHAL NIEL (1802-69)—*à propos* of the difficulties he met with in organising the *garde mobile*. —General du Barrail, *Souvenirs*, 1896, vol. 3, p. 86.

Vous pleurez, et vous êtes le maître. (You weep, and you are the master).
Words said to have been uttered by MARIE MANCINI (1640-1715), a niece of Cardinal Mazarin, on parting from LOUIS XIV (1638-1715), June 21, 1659.—Mme. de Motteville's *Mémoires*, 2nd series p. 11 (vol. 40 of the Collection Petitot). Other versions give the exact words as, "Vous pleurez, "vous êtes le maître et je pars!" (You weep, you are the master and I am going away !) — Chéruel— *Histoire de France sous le ministère de Mazarin.* "Vous êtes fâché de "mon départ, et moi de même. "Vous êtes roi et cependant je "pars!"—(You are grieved at my departure, and I also: You are king and yet I go.)—Montglat (who fixes the date as in 1661). "Ah! sire, vous êtes roi et je pars !" (Ah! sire, you are king and I depart !)— Abbé de Choisy. Mme. de Motteville quotes the phrase, but without confirming it, as "Vous êtes roi, vous pleurez et je pars !" (You are king, you weep and I depart !) Another form is : "Vous m'aimez, vous êtes roi, et je pars." (You love me, you are the king, and I depart). Cf. "Vous êtes empereur, seigneur, et vous pleurez !" (You are emperor, lord,

and you weep !)—Racine, *Bérénice*, Act 4, sc. 5. "Et cependant je pars ; et vous me l'ordonnez !" (And yet I depart, and you command me to).—Racine, *Bérénice*, Act 5, sc. 5.

Vous viendrez donc m'embrasser, monsieur de Mirabeau ? (You will come and embrace me then, Monsieur de Mirabeau ?)
Reply made by the ABBÉ MAURY (1746-1817) to MIRABEAU (1749-91), when the latter announced his intention of enclosing him in a 'vicious circle' (of argument).

Voyez le beau rendez-vous qu'il me donne ; cet homme-là n'a jamais aimé que lui-même.—(There's a fine rendezvous he is giving me ; that man has never loved anyone but himself.)
Attributed (but denied) to MME. DE MAINTENON (1635-1719)—at the death-bed of LOUIS XIV (1638-1715), he having said to her, "Nous nous reverrons bientôt." (We shall meet again soon). St. Simon, *Mémoires*, vol. 24, p. 39, edit. Delloye. Cf. Voltaire's *extraits du Journal de Dangeau*, pp. 162-3.

Voyez-moi tous, je vis et je vaincrai, Dieu aidant! (Look at me all, I live, and, with God's help, will conquer.)
By WILLIAM THE CONQUEROR (1026-87), taking off his helmet so that his face might be seen, at the battle of Hastings (1066), a cry having arisen that he was slain. Guizot. Cf. Dict. of Nat. Biog., vol. lxi, p. 296.

GERMAN SAYINGS.

Allein die Dupe einer ehrlichen Ueberzeugung zu sein, kann man Deutschland auf die Dauer nicht zumuten. (But one cannot expect that Germany should for ever be the dupe of an honest conviction). PRINCE BISMARCK (1815-98)—in the Reichstag, May 2, 1879.

. . an die Wand drücken. (To press against the wall). PRINCE BISMARCK (1815 98)—is credited with having used the phrase to Prince Putbus, a member of the Senate, but on three occasions he denied having said it : in July, 1890, in a conversation with Jul. Rittershaus, editor of the *Frankfurter Zeitung;* in May, 1891, in an answer made to him ; and in a speech to the National Liberal Reichstag deputies, April 20, 1894. The phrase refers to the proposition of the Graf zu Lippe, Oct. 7, 1869, against the Bundesoberhandelsgericht.

. . angenehme Temperatur. (Agreeable temperature). COUNT ALBRECHT TH. E. VON ROON, Prussian minister of War, (1803-79)—in a speech, Jan. 23, 1862, in connection with the modification of the statutes of Sept. 3, 1814, relating to military service : (Ich habe bereits zweimal Gelegenheit gehabt, die angenehme Temperatur, welche in diesem Hause in Betreff jener grossen Massregel [der Organisation des preuss. Heeres]

herrscht, zu fühlen. (I have already twice had the opportunity of feeling the agreeable temperature which ruled in this House with regard to that great order [the organisation of the Prussian army]).

Angstprodukt. (Anxious product). EUGEN RICHTER (b. 1838) in the Reichstag, March 9, 1887, referring to the Reichstag elected on Feb. 27, 1887, for the grant of the military proposals demanding the Septennat : Die Mehrheit dieses Reichstages ist ein Angstprodukt der Wähler. (The majority of this Reichstag is an anxious product of the voters).

. . auf den breitesten Grundlagen. (On the broadest foundations). FRIEDRICH WILHELM IV (1795-1861)—to a deputation of the states of Breslau and Liegnitz, March 22, 1848) : Nachdem ich eine konstitutionelle Verfassung auf den breitesten Grundlagen verheissen habe. . . (After I have promised a constitutional authority on the broadest foundations. . .)

. . auf einem Prinzip herumreiten. (To ride on one principle). HEINRICH LXXII, Prince Reuss zu Lobenstein und Ebersdorf—in an edict of Oct. 12, 1844 : Seit zwanzig Jahren reite Ich auf einem Prinzip herum, d.h. Ich verlange, dass ein jeglicher bei seinem Titel genannt wird. (For twenty years I have ridden [stood] on one principle, that is, I demand that each man be called by his title). The edict is printed in the *Adorfer Wochenblatt*, and copied by the *Vossische Zeitung* of Sept. 18, 1845. The expression *Prinzipienreiter* (Rider on principle) is derived from the above.

Autorität, nicht Majorität. (Authority, not majority). F. J. STAHL (1802-61)—at the 11th sitting of the Volkshause of the Erfurt Parliament, April 11, 1850. A cup was presented to him by his adherents with the above words engraved upon it. See Die Wissenschaft bedarf der Umkehr.

Baukunst—eine erstarrte Musik. (Architecture—frozen music). J. W. VON GOETHE (1749-1832) —in a conversation with Johann Peter Eckermann : Ich habe unter meinen Papieren ein Blatt gefunden, wo ich die Baukunst eine erstarrte Musik nenne. (I have found among my papers a sheet in which I call architecture frozen music). Cf. La vue d'un tel monument est comme une musique continuelle et fixée (The sight of such a monument is like a continual permanent music). — Mme. de Staël, *Corinne*, bk. iv., ch. 3.

Bei allen den Knochenbrüchen denen Deutschland im Laufe der Jährhunderte ausgesetzt gewesen ist und deren Heilung noch versucht ist. (With all the fractures to which Germany has in the course of centuries been exposed, the cure of which is still to seek. .) PRINCE BISMARCK (1815-98)—in the Reichstag, Nov. 22, 1875.

Bei uns kann nur parteilos regiert werden. (With us government without party can alone succeed). PRINCE BISMARCK (1815-98)—in the Reichstag, June 12, 1882.

. . berechtigte Eigentümlichkeiten zu schonen. (. . .to spare privileged property).

EMPEROR WILHELM I (1797-1888)—a promise made at the affiliation of Hanover, Kurhessen, Nassau, and Frankfurt, in a document dated at Castle Babelsberg, Oct. 3, 1866.

. . best-gehasste Persönlichkeit in diesem Lande. . . (. . the best-hated personage in this land. . .). PRINCE BISMARCK (1815-98)—in the Chamber of Deputies, Jan. 16, 1874, alluding to himself : Gehen Sie, von der Garonne. . . bis zur Weichsel, von dem Belt bis zur Tiber, suchen Sie an den heimischen Strömen, der Oder und dem Rhein umher, so werden Sie finden, dass ich in diesem Augenblicke wohl die am stärksten und—ich behaupte stolz ! — die am besten gehasste Persönlichkeit in diesem Lande bin. (Travel from the Garonne. . . to the Weichsel, from the Belt to the Tiber, search on our native rivers, the Oder and the Rhine, and you will find that at this moment I am the most powerful and—I maintain it proudly !—the best-hated personage in this land).

Beunruhigungsbazillus. (bacillus of unrest). CHANCELLOR G. L. VON CAPRIVI (1831-99)—in the Reichstag, Nov. 27, 1891 : Es geht durch das Land ein Pessimismus der mir im höchsten Grade bedenklich ist. . . Es ist, wie wenn ein Beunruhigungsbazillus in der Luft läge, der epidemisch geworden ist, und selbst manche angesehene Zeitungen, die sich sonst für die Bannerträger nationaler Gefühle halten, scheinen mir Reinkulturen für dies Wesen zu. (A pessimism is passing through the land, which seems to me in the highest degree serious. . . It is as if a bacillus of unrest were lodged in the air, and had become epidemic ; and many respectable journals, which were once regarded as standard-bearers of the national sentiment, seem to me to be mere propagandists for this creature). The word was also used by PRINCE VON ZEDLITZ-TRUETZSCHLER, in the Chamber of Deputies, Jan. 21, 1892.

. . bis ans Ende aller Dinge. (. . until the end of all things). GEORGE V, of Hanover (1819-78) —in a proclamation, 1865, on the anniversary of fifty years' possession of East Friesland. Cf.

But the end of all things is at hand : be ye therefore sober, and watch unto prayer. 1 Peter, iv, 7.

Catilinarische Existenzen (Catilinarians).

PRINCE BISMARCK (1815-98)—at an evening sitting of the Budget Commission of the Prussian Diet, Sept. 30, 1862 : Es gäbe zuviel catilinarische Existenzen, die ein Interesse an Umwälzungen haben. (There are too many Catilinarians who have an interest in revolutions). *Eine catilinarische Existenz* had previously formed the title of a novel by Theodor König (Breslau, 1854).

Das Ausländische hat immer einen gewissen vornehmen Anstrich für uns. (The foreigner always has a certain aristocratic bearing in our eyes). PRINCE BISMARCK (1815-98)— in the (Prussian) Second Chamber, Nov. 15, 1849.

Das Bier, das nicht getrunken wird, hat seinen Beruf verfehlt. (Beer that is not drunk has missed its vocation). MEYER BRESLAU — in the Chamber of Deputies, Jan. 21, 1880.

Das Bier ist ein Zeittöter. (Beer is a time-killer). PRINCE BISMARCK (1815-98)— in the Reichstag, Mar. 28, 1881 :

Es wird bei uns Deutschen mit wenig so viel Zeit totgeschlagen, wie mit Biertrinken. Wer beim Frühschoppen sitzt, oder beim Abendschoppen, und gar noch dazu raucht und Zeitungen liest, hält sich wohl ausreichend beschäftigt, und geht mit gutem Gewissen nach Haus in dem Bewusstsein, das Seinige geleistet zu haben. (There is more time killed amongst us Germans by beer-drinking than by anything else. The man who sits at breakfast or at supper, and at the same time smokes and reads his newspapers, considers himself amply employed, and goes home with the consciousness that he has done his duty.

Das deutsche Heer ist das deutsche Volk in Waffen. (The German army is the German people in arms). PRINCE REGENT WILHELM OF PRUSSIA [William I] (1797-1868) —in the speech from the throne at the opening of the Diet, Jan, 12, 1860.

Das ist das Unglück der Könige, dass sie die Wahrheit nicht hören wollen. (That is the misfortune of kings, that they · will not hear the truth). JOHANN JACOBY (1805-77)— when envoy of the Berlin National Assembly, to King Friedrich Wilhelm IV, Nov. 2, 1848.

Das lässt tief blicken, sagt Sabor. (That enables us to look deep, says Sabor.) SABOR — when deputy, in the Reichstag, Dec. 17, 1884 : " Der Herr Reichskanzler will nicht, dass das Wahlrecht in dem Umfange, wie es jetzt besteht, gelten bleibe, und wenn man ihm darin nachgiebt, ist er bereit, in eine Verfassungs-Aenderung zu willigen, ist sogar bereit, die Diäten zu bewilligen. Das lässt tief blicken in die Maschine, —lässt einen Einblick thun in die geistige Werkstatt, in der die soziale Reform bereitet wird. (The Chancellor does not wish the franchise to hold good as widely as is now the case ; and if we concede this to him, he is prepared to acquiesce in a change in the constitution—is even ready to agree to the Diets. That enables us to look deep into the machine—affords us an insight into the spiritual workshop in which Social Reform is prepared). — *Stenographische Berichte*, *I*, 435.

Das Mittel wäre schlimmer als das Uebel selbst. (The remedy would be worse than the disease itself). PRINCE BISMARCK (1815-98)— in the Chamber of Deputies, Jan. 29, 1863.

Das nenne ich eben die Woche mit dem Sonnabend anfangen, oder das Ziel und das Ergebnis, das durch mühsame und langjährige Arbeit zu erreichen ist, vorwegnehmen wollen. (I call that beginning the week on Saturday, or wishing to forestall the object and result, which can be reached only by laborious years of toil). PRINCE BISMARCK (1815-98)—in the Reichstag, Jan. 15, 1889, with reference to impatience and premature expectations in Colonial politics.

Das Recht muss seinen Gang haben, und sollte die Welt darüber zu Grunde gehen. (Justice must take its course, even though the world should perish). FERDINAND I (1503-64). See Fiat justitia &c.

Das Schlimmste, was uns passieren könnte, wäre wenn einer uns ganz Afrika schenkte. (The worst that

could happen to us would be for the whole of Africa to be given to us). GEORG LEO VON CAPRIVI (1831-99)—in the German Reichstag, Nov. 27, 1891, and again 17 Feb., 1894, having previously expressed the thought in connection with his attempt to justify the Anglo-German Agreement of 1890, in the Reichstag, 5 Feb, 1891.

Das steht nicht in meinem Lexikon. (That is not in my dictionary).

DR. JULIUS FRIEDRICH STAHL (1802-61) — in the Erfurt Union-Parliament, April 15, 1850 : "Dieser Spruch — mit dem die Democraten 1848 die Wogen des Aufstandes hätten bannen können— stand nicht in ihrem Lexikon, denn dieser Spruch heiszt Autorität. Da wollen sie die Gewässer besprechen mit einem Zauberspruch ihres Systems : Majorität, Majorität !" (This word—with which the democrats of 1848 could have exorcised the waves of the revolution —did not exist in their vocabulary, for this word is Authority. They want to conjure the waters with the magic word of their philosophy : Majority, Majority !). L. Börne had written :

Das Wort Friede steht nicht in meinem Wörterbuche. (The word Peace is not in my dictionary)—*Briefe aus Paris*, 45, March 25, 1831.

. . den gestrigen Tag suchen. (To seek for yesterday).

CLAUS, the Court-jester (d. 1515) —in reply to the Kurfürst Johann Friedrich, who was lamenting that he had "lost the day" : Morgen wollen wir alle fleissig suchen, und den Tag, den du verloren hast, wohl wieder finden. (To-morrow we will all diligently seek for the day you have lost, and no doubt we shall find it again). (Wolf Büttner,

13

627 *Historien von Claus Narren,*
1572, 21, 51). See Diem perdide!
. . den Schwerpunkt nach Ofen
verlegen. (To remove the
centre of gravity to Ofen).
By the anonymous author
[Kertbeny, *i.e.* Benkert] of *Spiegel-
bilder der Erinnerung* (in the
Geschichte eines Stiefgrossvaters,
1869, III, p. 189) ; but first used
by FRIEDRICH VON GENTZ (1764-
1832), in 1820, in Metternich's
cabinet ; later by Count Széchényi
in the Hungarian Parliament ; in
1840 applied to Austria by Massimo
d'Azeglio ; and in 1857 by Count
Camillo Cavour in Compiègne ; and
by Count Bismarck-Schönhausen in
1863.

Der Fürst ist der erste Diener
seines Staats. (The king is
the first servant of his State).
See Un prince est le premier
serviteur &c.

Der Karnickel hat angefangen.
(The kettle [lit. the rabbit]
began it).
See C'est le lapin qui a commencé.

Der katholische Priester ist von
dem Augenblick wo er
Priester ist, ein einregi-
mentierter Offizier des
Papstes. (The Catholic priest
—from the moment he is a
priest—is an enrolled officer
of the Pope).
PRINCE BISMARCK (1815-98)—
in the Prussian Senate, April 12,
1886.

Der Kreig wird durch Zeitung-
sartikel niemals herbeige-
führt. (War is never brought
about by newspapers).
PRINCE BISMARCK (1815-98)
—in the Reichstag, Feb. 9, 1876.
The speech continued :
". . . die Majorität hat gewöhnlich keine
Neigung zum Kriege, der Krieg wird
durch Minoritäten, oder in absoluten

Staaten durch Beherrscher oder Kabin-
ette entzündet. (The majority has usually
no inclination for war : war is kindled
through the minority, or in absolute states
through the ruler or cabinet).

Der kühne Griff. (The bold
grasp).
PRESIDENT H. W. A. VON
GAGERN (1799-1880)—at the 22nd
sitting of the National assembly
June 24, 1848. Supposed to be
derived from Schiller's *Geschichte
des 30-jährigen Krieges,* vol iii last
paragraph but one.

Der Liberalismus gerät immer
weiter, als seine Träger
wollen (Liberalism always
thrives more than its supporters
desire).
PRINCE BISMARCK (1815-98)—in
the Reichstag, Nov. 29, 1881.

Der preussische Schulmeister hat
die Schlacht bei Sadowa
gewonnen. (The Prussian
schoolmaster won the battle of
Sadowa [July 3, 1866]).

Derived from a phrase used by DR.
PESCHEL (1826-75), professor of
geology in Leipzig in an essay in
Ausland (*Die Lehren der jüngsten
Kreigsgeschichte,* no. 29, July 17,
1866, S. 695, col 1). Referred to
by Count von Moltke (1800-91) in
the German Reichstag, Feb. 16,
1874. The phrase is sometimes
attributed to the Emperor William
(1817-90) and quoted as :
"Ce sont (*or* C'est) nos maîtres d'école
qui ont vaincu la France. (It is our
schoolmasters who have defeated France)
See The Battle of Waterloo was won &c.

Der russische Nihilismus ist
mehr eine klimatische Abart
des Fortschritts als des
Sozialismus. (Russian Nihil-
ism is a climatic degeneracy of
progress rather than of Socialism).

PRINCE BISMARCK (1815-98)—
in the Reichstag, May 9, 1884.

Derselbe Faden, nur eine andere

Nummer. (The same thread, only another number).
PRINCE BISMARCK (1815-98)—at a Parliamentary soirée instituted by him, on May 4, 1880, referring to the resignation of the Kultusminister Falk and the Kulturkampf [see this heading].

Der sogennannte arme Mann. (The so-called poor man).
COUNT BALLESTREM—in the Reichstag, July 5, 1879.

Der Starke weicht einen Schritt zurück. (The strong man retreats a step).
BARON TH. VON MANTEUFFEL, Minister for Foreign Affairs (1805-82)—at the 8th session of the Prussian Second Chamber, Dec. 3, 1850. Cf. Martial, *De Spectaculis*, 31.

Der Weg nach Konstantinopel führt durch das Brandenburger Thor. (The way to Constantinople leads through the Brandenburger's gate).
Quoted by GEORG LEO VON CAPRIVI (1831-99)—in the Reichstag-Commission of the Militärvorlage, Jan. 11, 1893 — from Bismarck and Russland's *Orientpolitik von einem dreibundfreundlichen Diplomaten* (p. 30).

Der Volksgeist Preussens ist durch und durch monarchisch (The national spirit of Prussia is monarchical to the backbone).
PRINCE BISMARCK (1815-98)—in the Prussian Chamber of Deputies, Jan. 22, 1864.

Der Weg den ein preuszisches Ministerium überhaupt gehen kann ist so sehr breit nicht. (The path along which a Prussian ministry can, in the main, go is not so very wide after all).
PRINCE BISMARCK (1815-98)—in the Prussian Chamber of Deputies, Jan. 29, 1863.

. . deutsche Normaluhr. (German normal time).
PRINCE BISMARCK (1815-98)—in the Reichstag, Mar. 14, 1885 : Es ist doch fast in jedem Jahrhundert einmal ein grosser deutscher Krieg gewesen, der die deutsche Normaluhr richtig gestellt hat für hundert Jahre (There has been in almost every century a great German war, which has fixed German time for a hundred years).

Deutschland, ein geographischer Begriff. (Germany, a geographical conception).
PRINCE METTERNICH (1773-1859)—in a letter to Count Prokesch Osten, Nov. 19, 1849 (Cf. *Correspondenz von Metternich mit Gentz*, Vienna, 1881, vol. ii, p. 343). The letter describes the disunited condition of Germany at that time. See L'Italie est un nom géographique.

Die Basis des konstitutionellen Lebensprozesses ist überall der Kompromiss. (The basis of constitutional life is everywhere compromise).
PRINCE BISMARCK (1815-98)—in the Prussian Senate, Jan. 24, 1865. See Verfassungsleben eine Reihe von Kompromissen.

Die Deutschfreisinnigen halte ich weder für deutsch, noch für freisinnig. (The German liberal I regard neither as German nor as liberal).
PRINCE BISMARCK (1815-98)—in the Reichstag, Nov. 26, 1884.

Die europäische Revolution ist solidarisch in allen Ländern. (The European Revolution is solid in all lands).
PRINCE BISMARCK (1815-98)—in the Prussian Chamber of Deputies Feb. 26, 1863.

Die Flinte schiesst, und der Säbel haut. (The gun shoots and the sword strikes).

Count Eulenburg — in the Reichstag, Jan. 27, 1876. Cf. "The bayonet pierces and the sabre cleaves And human lives are lavished everywhere." Byron, *Don Juan*, can. viii, st. 88, ll. 1-2.

Die grossen Städte müssen von Erdboden vertilgt werden. (Great towns must be obliterated from the earth). Prince Bismarck (1815-98)— in his reply to Deputy Harkort, Mar. 20, 1852.

Die Gründe der Regierung kenne ich nicht, aber ich muss sie missbilligen. (I am not acquainted with the bases of the government, but I must disapprove of them). Julius Kell—in the Second Saxon Chamber, Feb. 15, 1849.

Die Politik der freien Hand. (The politics of the free hand). Prince Bismarck (1815-98)—in the Prussian House of Delegates, Jan. 22, 1864. The phrase was used, however, in 1859 by von Schleinitz, the Prussian minister, referring to the Franco-Austrian War.

Die Politik ist keine exakte Wissenschaft. (Politics is not an exact science). Prince Bismarck (1815-98)—in the Prussian Senate, Dec. 18, 1863. He made a similar remark in the Prussian Chamber of Deputies, Jan. 15, 1872. In the Reichstag, Mar. 15, 1884, and in the Prussian Chamber of Deputies, Jan. 29, 1886, he added, "sondern eine Kunst" (but an art).

Die Presse ist nicht die öffentliche Meinung. (The press is not public opinion). Prince Bismarck (1815-98)—in the Budget Commission of the Prussian Chamber of Deputies, Sept. 30, 1862.

Die Regierung muss der Bewegung stets einen Schritt voraus sein. (The government should always be a step in advance of a popular movement). Count Armin-Boytzenburg (1803-68)—at the first Session of the United Diet of 1848, April 2.

Die Religion muss in dem Volke erhalten werden. (Religion must be preserved in the people). William I (1797-1888)—to the the Protestant Ministry on the station at Züllichem, 23 Aug., 1876 : "Sie haben im Vaterlande eine grosse und wichtige Aufgabe. Sie müssen die Religion im Volke erhalten und kräftigen. (You have in the Fatherland a great and weighty task. You must preserve and strengthen religion in the people.)

Die Wissenschaft bedarf der Umkehr. (Science needs reversing). F. J. Stahl (1802-61)—when returning thanks for a cup presented to him by his adherents, Dec. 12, 1852. The phrase was afterwards altered to "die Wissenschaft muss umkehren." (Science must turn round). See Autorität, nicht Majorität.

Die Zeiten, wo Bertha spann, sind nicht mehr ! (The times when Bertha span are no more). Prince Bismarck (1815-98)—in the North German Reichstag, May 24, 1870. Cf. the French provrebial expression : "Au temps où Berthe filait " (in the days when Bertha span), *i.e.* the good old days.

Die Zentralisation ist mehr oder weniger eine Gewaltthat. (Centralization is more or less an act of violence). Prince Bismarck (1815-98)—in the North German Reichstag, April 16, 1869.

Ein Appell an die Furcht im deutschen Herzen niemals ein Echo findet. (A call to fear never finds an echo in German hearts). PRINCE BISMARCK (1815-98)—in the Customs Parliament, May 18, 1868.

Ein braves Pferd stirbt in den Sielen. (A brave horse dies in the ditch). PRINCE BISMARCK (1815-98)—in the Prussian Chamber of Deputies, Feb. 4, 1881.

. . ein frischer, fröhlicher Krieg. (. . a fresh, joyous war). HEINRICH LEO (1799-1878)—see Skrophulöses Gesindel. He had previously used the phrase in his *Volksblatt für Stadt und Land*, 1859, no. 35 : Ein langer Friede häuft nach der Verfassers Argument eine Menge fauler Gährungsstoffe auf. Darum thut uns ein frischer, fröhlicher, die Nationen, namentlich die die europäische Bildung tragenden Nationen tiefer beruhrender Krieg bitter Not . . (a long peace, according to the argument of the author, heaps up a mass of ferments. On that account a fresh, joyous war, which deeply moves nations, especially those nations which possess European culture, is a bitter need).

Ein Tropfen demokratischen Oels. (A drop of democratic oil). LUDWIG UHLAND (1787-1862)—in a speech in the Frankfort Parliament, Jan. 22, 1848 ; also used by Prince Bismarck (1815-98), in the German Reichstag, July 9, 1879.

Eine Kammer ist leichter mobil zu machen, als eine Armee. (A Chamber is easier to put in motion than an army). PRINCE BISMARCK (1815-98)—in the Prussian Chamber of Deputies, Dec. 3, 1850.

. . einen Blick in die Sonne ! (One look at the sun !) SCHILLER (1759-1805) — Last words ; but see " Liebe, gute. "

. . einen Stein zwischen die Räder werfen. (To throw a stone between the wheels). PRINCE BISMARCK (1815-98—in Prussian Senate, Mar. 7, 1872.

. . eines ehrlichen Maklers. (. . of an honest broker). PRINCE BISMARCK (1815-98) —in the Reichstag, Feb. 19, 1878.

Eisen und Blut. (Iron and blood). PRINCE BISMARCK (1815-98)— in a speech in the Prussian House of Delegates, Sep. 30, 1862. In a letter, May 12, 1859, to Baron von Schleinitz he said : " Ich sehe in unserm Bundesverhältnisse ein Gebrechen Preussens, welches wir früher oder später ' ferro et igne ' erwden heilen müssen." (I see in our relations a breach of Prussia's which sooner or later we must heal ' by iron and by fire.' . . .' Cf. Zwar der Tapfere nennt sich Herr der Länder Durch sein Eisen, durch sein Blut. (The brave man is called lord of the land by his iron and his blood). E. M. Arndt, *Lehre an den Menschen*, (1811, pp. 39-41). Denn nur Eisen kann uns retten, Und erlösen kann nur Blut. (For iron alone can save us, Blood alone can release). — Schenkendorf, *Das eiserne Kreuz.* Cædes videtur significare sanguinem et ferrum. (The slaughter seems to signify blood and iron).— Quintilian, *Declamationes*, 350.

Erbweisheit. (Hereditary wisdom). FREDRICH WILHELM IV (1795-1861)—in the address from the Throne before the Union Diet, Apr. 11, 1847. G. FREIHERR VON VINCKE afterwards, on the 15th April, in reference to Mecklenburg, alluded to " die Erbweisheit der Engländer " (the hereditary wisdom of the English) according to Eberty's *Geschichte des preussischen Staates*, vii, 265.

Er lügt wie telegraphiert. (He lies like telegraphing). PRINCE BISMARCK (1815-98)— Feb. 13, 1869. Cf. " . . the fiend, That lies like truth." Shakspere, *Macbeth*, act v, sc. 5, ll. 43-4 (Macbeth).

Erst wägen und denn wagen.
(First weigh, then venture).
COUNT VON MOLTKE'S [1800-91]
favourite maxim. Cf.
Deliberate slowly, execute promptly
(English Proverb).
Βουλεύου μὲν βραδέως, ἐπιτέλει δὲ
ταχέως τὰ δόξαντα.
(Take counsel deliberately, but carry
your plan out expeditiously). Isocrates.
Ad Demonicum, 34.

Es gehört zum deutschen Bedürfnis, beim Biere von der Regierung schlecht zu reden. (It is a necessity for the German to speak badly of the beer of the Empire).
PRINCE BISMARCK (1815-98)—
in the Reichstag, June 12, 1882.

Es giebt Zeiten, wo man liberal regieren muss, und Zeiten wo man diktatorisch regieren muss ; es wechselt alles, hier giebt es keine Ewigkeit. (There are times when liberals must rule, and times when dictators must rule ; everything changes, there is no eternity in these matters).
PRINCE BISMARCK (1815-98)—
in the Reichstag, Feb. 24, 1881.

Es ist gut. (It is good).
IMMANUEL KANT (1724-1804)—
Last words, declining a refreshing draught.

Es muss ein eigentümlicher Zauber in dem Worte Deutsch liegen. (There must lie a peculiar charm in the word "German.")
PRINCE BISMARCK (1815-98)—
in the Prussian Chamber of Deputies, Jan. 22, 1864.

Für Gott und ihr. (For God and her).
Device on the standard of
CHRISTIAN, DUKE OF BRUNSWICK,
(1599-1626). In the Thirty Years War (1618-48) he supported the Elector's cause, rather because of his love for the Electress than any other motive.

.. Garantien, die das Papier nicht wert sind, auf dem sie geschrieben stehen. (. . Guarantees which are not worth the paper on which they are written.)
COUNT VON RECHBERG, Austrian minister—in his despatch to Berlin, referring to the recognition of Italy (1861).

Gazetten müssen nicht geniert werden (Newspapers must not be fettered).
FREDERICK (II), THE GREAT (1712-86)—reply to Graf Podewil the Cabinet Minister, who was inquiring as to his wishes with regard to the Editor of the *Berliner Zeitung*. (J. D. E. Preuss, *Friedrich der Grosse*, vol. iii, p. 251).

.. Gefühl der staatlichen Verantwortlichkeit. (. . feeling of the State's responsibility).
PRINCE BISMARCK (1815-98)—
in the Reichstag, May 1, 1872.

Gegen die Regierung mit allen Mitteln zu kämpfen, ist ja ein Grundrecht und Sport eines jeden Deutschen (To fight against the Empire with all means at his disposal is indeed the right and sport of every German).
PRINCE BISMARCK (1815-98)—
in the Reichstag, May 8, 1880.

Gesetze sind wie Arzeneien ; sie sind gewöhnlich nur Heilung einer Krankheit durch eine geringere oder vorübergehende Krankheit. (Laws are like medicines ; they are usually but a cure of one disease by means of a lesser or passing disease).
PRINCE BISMARCK (1815-98—in the Pussian Senate, March 6, 1872.

Geschmuggelt wird in fast allen Ständen, besonders vom weiblichen Theil der Bevölkerung. (Smuggling exists

almost everywhere, especially in the female portion of the population).
PRINCE BISMARCK (1815-91)—in the Prussian Chamber of Deputies, June 1, 1865.
. . **Hecht im Karpfenteich.**
(. . Pike in the carp-pond).
PRINCE BISMARCK (1815-98)—in the Reichstag, Feb. 16, 1888.
From Dallmer, *Fische und Fisherei im süssen Wasser* (1871), p. 81. Prof. H. Leo had referred to Napoleon III as a 'Pike in the civilisation carp-pond of Europe.' *Volksblatt für Stadt und Land,* 1859, no. 69.
Hepp! hepp! (Hepp! hepp!)
A derisive cry shouted against the Jews, derived (according to Schrader's *Bilderschmuck der deutschen Sprache,* p. 249) from the initial letters of Hierosolyma est perdita (Jerusalem is lost): H. E. P., which was the inscription on the banners with which recruits for the crusades were acquired.
Hier stehe ich! Ich kann nicht anders. Gott helfe mir! Amen. (Here I stand! I can do naught else. God help me! Amen).
MARTIN LUTHER (1483-1546—when asked in the Reichstag at Worms if he wished to reply to the question at issue, he concluded his answer with the above words: Apr. 15, 1521.
Hie Welf, hie Waiblingen! (Here Welf, here Waiblingen.)
Battle-cry used at Weinsberg, 1140 (Jaffé, *Geschichte d. deutsch. Reich. unter Conrad III,* 1845, p. 35).
Hunde, wollt ihr ewig leben? (Hounds, would ye live for ever?)
FREDERICK THE GREAT (1712-86)—to his wavering troops at Kolin, June 18, 1757, wishing to make them charge for the seventh time.

(Martin, *Hist. of France,* vol. xv, ch. xcviii); or at Kunersdorf, Aug, 12, 1759. Carlyle (*French Revolution,* pt. ii, bk., 1. ch. 4) quotes the phrase as " R—— wollt ihr ewig leben." (Unprintable offscouring of scoundrels, would ye live for ever !).
Ich bin dankbar für die schärfste Kritik, wenn sie nur sachlich bleibt. (I am grateful for the severest criticism if it only remain real).
PRINCE BISMARCK (1815-98)—in the Reichstag, Nov. 30, 1874.
Ich bin es müde, über Sklaven zu herrschen. (I am weary of ruling over slaves).
FREDERICK (II), THE GREAT (1712-86)—to President von der Goltz, in 1785, in one of his orders. (Ed. Vehse, *Preussen,* iv, 175). Another version is:
Ich bin es satt über Sklaven zu herrschen. (I have had my fill of ruling over slaves), and derives the phrase from a letter to Baron v. d. Goltz, dated Aug. 1, 1786.
Ich bin stolz darauf, eine preussische Sprache zu reden (I' am proud of speaking a Prussian language).
PRINCE BISMARCK (1815-98)—in the Prussian Chamber of Deputies, Dec. 18, 1863.
Ich dien. (I serve).
Tradition has it that this motto was adopted by Edward, the Black Prince, in memory of the great battle of Cressy (Aug. 26, 1346), in which the blind king of Bohemia took part and was killed. His crest was three ostrich feathers and the motto as above (Hume, *Hist. of Engl.*); but see an essay by Sir H. Nicolas in *Archaeologia,* vol. 32.
Ich glaube, dass die Börse hier als ein Giftbaum wirkt. (I believe the Exchange here acts like a poison-tree).
MINISTER MAYBACH—in the Prussian Chamber of Deputies, Nov. 12, 1879.

Ich habe genug : rette dich, Bruder. (I have enough ; save thyself, brother). GUSTAVUS ADOLPHUS King of Sweden (1564-1632)—Last words ; to the Duke of Lauenburg, on the field of Lützen (Nov. 16, 1632).

Ich habe keine Zeit, müde zu sein. (I have no time to become tired). WILLIAM I (1797-1888)—in reply to the question, during his last illness, whether he felt tired.

Ich hoffe es noch zu erleben, dass das Narrenschiff der Zeit au dem Felsen der christlichen Kirche scheitert. (I hope it will not happen in my time that the "fools'-ship" of time founders on the rock of the Christian Church). PRINCE BISMARCK (1815-98—in the Prussian Second Chamber, Nov. 15, 1849.

Ich lasse mir von der Majorität des Reichstags nicht imponieren. (I do not allow myself to be imposed on by the majority of the Reichstag). PRINCE BISMARCK (1815-98—in the Reichstag, Nov. 26, 1884.

Ich liebe eine gesinnungsvolle Opposition. (I like a candid Opposition). FRIEDRICH WILHELM IV (1795-1861)—the words with which he received the young poet Herwegh in 1842.

Ich will Frieden haben mit meinem Volke. (I wish to have peace with my people). KING MAXIMILIAN II, of Bavaria (1811-64)—in his answer to von Neumayr (printed in no. 137 of the *Neue Münchener Zeitung*, 1859). Cf.

Nicht eine Welt in Waffen fürchtet sie,
So lang' sie Frieden hat mit ihrem Volke.
(It's not a world in arms she fears,
Have she but peace, with her own people).
—Schiller, *Maria Stuart*, act i, sc. 6.

In Geldsachen hört die Gemütlichkeit auf. (In money matters friendliness has no place). DAVID HANSEMANN — June 8, 1847 (*Der erste Preuss. Landt. in Berlin*, 1847, abt. ii, Heft 3, p. 1507), the precise words being " Bei Geldfragen hört, etc."

In meinem Staate kann jeder nach seiner Façon selig werden. (In my State everyone can become blessed in his own way).

On the 22nd June, 1740, Statesminister von Brand and Konsistorialpresident von Reichenbach reported to Frederick II that the schools for the children of Roman-Catholic soldiers had, in opposition to the King's express command, induced Protestants to be educated as Catholics ; on the inquiry whether these schools should be allowed to remain, they received the reply : All religions must be tolerated and the Solicitor to the Treasury has only to see to it that no injury be done by one to the others, for each must in these matters be blessed after his own manner.

. . in sieben Sprachen schweigen. (. . to be silent in seven languages). F. E. D. SCHLEIERMACHER (1768-1834) —in reference to Immanuel Bekker (1785-1871) : Nun muss ich schweigen, wie unser Philologus Bekker, den sie den Stummen in sieben Sprachen nennen." (Now I must be silent, like our philologist Bekker, whom people call the man who is dumb in seven languages)— Letter from Zelter to Goethe, Mar. 15, 1830. Sir M. Grant Duff (in his *Notes from a Diary*, vol. i, p. 318), however, attributes the phrase to B. G. Niebuhr(1776-1831). See Vous avez quatre mots contre une idée.

On disait d'un érudit, que c'était le plus grand ennemi qu'eût la raison depuis

Calais jusqu' à Bayonne, et qu'il était fou en deux sciences et quatre langues. (It was said of a learned man, that he was the greatest enemy that reason had from Calais to Bayonne, and that he was mad in two sciences and four languages). *Ducatiana.*

Ist kein Dalberg da? (Is no Dalberg there?) Saying derived from the question put by the heralds at the crowning of the German emperors. The Dalberg present is the first knight created by the newly-crowned emperor. The custom dates from the coronation, in 1452, of the emperor Frederick III (1415-93) as king of Rome. *Zeitschrift für deutsche Kulturgeschichte,* Neue Folge I, p. 101). The legend runs that a relation of our saviour who became a Roman soldier settled at Herrn sheim, near Worms, and was the ancestor of the Dalbergs. The family was long regarded as one of the most illustrious in Germany. Cf. *The Times,* June 20, 1902, p. 12 : article on the death of Lord Acton (John Emerich Edward Dalberg Acton).

Ja, wenn das Berliner Kammergericht nicht wäre. (Yes, if we had no judges in Berlin).

A miller is credited with having made the reply to Frederick the Great (1712-86), or to his minister. Generally quoted in French, as *Il y a des juges à Berlin* (q. v.) The miller refused to sell his mill, and, on being told that the king could take it without paying anything for it, he made the above reply.

. . jeden Mann und jeden Groschen. (. . every man and every groschen).

DR. WINDTHORST, Delegate for the Centre, maintained at the Commission to inquire into the governmental proposals for a "septennium," Dec. 16, 1886, that the Government should be granted the above, and repeated the words in

the Reichstag, Jan. 11, 1887. On 28 Nov. 1888, Liebknecht, the Socialist, said in the Reichstag: Diesem System keinen Mann und keinen Groschen. (Not a man nor a groschen for this system).

. . juristische Zwirnsfäden. (. . legal threads).

PRINCE BISMARCK (1815-98) in the Prussian Chamber of Deputies, Jan. 30, 1869. See Mit juristischen Theorien.

Kathedersocialisten. (Pulpit Socialists). *Nationalzeitung,* April 20, 1872.

H. B. OPPENHEIM (1819-80)— applied this term to the young professors of Political Economy, and in 1872 published a pamphlet entitled *Kathedersocialismus* (pulpit Socialism), which called forth a flood of controversial literature.

Kein deutscher Offizier lässt seinen Soldaten im Feuer im Stich und holt ihn mit eigener Lebensgefahr heraus, und umgekehrt, kein deutscher Soldat lässt seinen Offizier im Stich, das haben wir erfahren. (No German officer leaves his soldier in the lurch, but helps him out at the peril of his own life, and *vice versâ* no German soldier of whom we have had experience leaves his officer in the lurch.)

PRINCE BISMARCK (1815-98)—in the Reichstag, Feb. 6, 1888.

Kolonialbummler. (Colonial loafers).

COUNT VON CAPRIVI (1831-99)— in the Reichstag, Mar. 5, 1882, said that military loafers have often been a nuisance in the army, but not harmful, as they did not interfere with routine : ob aber die Thätigkeiten von Kolonialbummlern eben so unschädlich bleiben könnte, ist mir zweifelhaft (but whether the doings of colonial loafers could remain equally harmless is a matter of doubt to me).

Kommen Sie 'rein in die gute Stube! (Come into the parlour!)

Said by a Leipzig lady to Prince Frederick Charles of Prussia, on the occasion of the Emperor William the First's visit to Leipzig in Sept., 1876 ['*rein* (abbrev. of *herein*) means 'hither,' *rein* means 'clean,' hence the *faux pas*].

Kommt es zum Aeussersten, so ist mir das Hemd näher als der Rock. (In the last resort my shirt is nearer to me than my coat).

PRINCE BISMARCK (1815-98)—in the Prussian Chamber of Deputies, Jan 22, 1864. Cf

Tunica propior palliost. (My shirt is nearer than my cloak). Plautus, *Trinummus*, act v, sc. 2, 30. (Callicles) La chemise est plus proche que le pourpoint (The shirt is nearer than the doublet)— French Proverb; Near is my kirtle, but nearer is my smock. —English Proverb.

Kulturkampf. (War of civilization.)

PROF. VIRCHOW claims that this word, which has met with such wide adoption as describing the conflict between Church and State in Germany, was invented by him. *Speech in Magdeburg*, Oct. 16, 1876, referring to his *Programm der Fortschrittspartei* (1873), in which occurs the following passage :

Aber obwohl sie dabei nur zu oft unterlegen ist, so hat sie es doch als eine Notwendigkeit erkannt, im Verein mit den andern liberalen Parteien die Regierung in einem Kampfe zu unterstützen, der mit jedem Tage mehr den Charakter eines grossen Kulturkampfes der Menschheit annimmt. (But although it [the Progressive Party] is only too often defeated by it, yet it has recognized it as a necessity to support, in conjunction with the other liberal parties, the government in a conflict which daily assumes more the character of a great war of civilization).

Virchow, however, had been anticipated by FERDINAND LAS-SALE, the Socialist, who in an essay entitled *Gotthold Ephraim Lessing* (on Adolf Stahr's *Leben Lessings*), composed in 1858 and published in *Demokratische Studien*, vol. ii, p.505, Hamburg, 1861, had written :

Die Katharsis, welche dieses Werk in jedem eines geistigen Eindrucks nur einigermassen fähigen Gemüt hinterlassen wird, ist die, es zu erheben über die Qualen und Konflikte, die ihm selber zustossen. Eines edlen, eines nur irgend *wahrhaft* bescheiden Gemüts wird sich eine edle Gleichgültigkeit bemächtigt gegen Alles, was uns selbst widerfahren kann in einem Kulturkampf, in welchem die Grössten und Besten langsam und qualvoll verblutet sind. (The catharsis which this work will leave behind it in every mind that is at all capable of a spiritual impression is to raise it above the torments and conflicts which befall it. A noble mind, a mind with a grain of *true* modesty in it, will be possessed by a noble indifference towards all that may happen to it in a war of civilization in which the greatest and the best are slowly and painfully bled to death).

Landgraf! werde hart! (Landgrave! grow hard!)

Saying of the smith of Ruhla—alluding to Ludwig der Eiserne, second Landgrave of Thuringia (1140-72). (Cf. John Rothe, *Düringische Chronik*, ed. by Liliencron, 1859, p. 292). At the beginning of his rule Ludwig had been so easygoing that the nobles had increased in insolence and oppressed the poor. On one occasion, he lost his way in the Thuringian forest, and met the smith of Ruhla, to whom he was unknown. The smith worked all night, and at each blow of the hammer grumbled at the Landgrave's lenient ways, addressing the iron on which he was working. "Nun werde hart." (Now grow hard!) This so impressed the Landgrave that he straightway restored order throughout the land.

Lerne zu leiden ohne zu klagen. (Learn to suffer without complaining).

FRIEDRICH III (1831-88)—advice to his son, the present Emperor, at the castle of Charlottenburg, April 1888. The full sentence was: "Lerne zu leiden, ohne zu klagen, das ist das einzige, was ich dich lehren kann." ("Learn to suffer without complaining, that is the only thing which I can teach you.") Cf.

O fear not in a world like this,
    And thou shalt know ere long,
Know how sublime a thing it is
    To suffer and be strong.

Longfellow, *The Light of Stars*, last verse.
Licht! mehr Licht! (Light! more light!)
GOETHE (1749-1832) — on his death-bed. Generally considered his last words, but really uttered three days before his death. The words were uttered in a literal and not a figurative sense. J. A. Froude (in his *Life of Carlyle*, vol. ii p. 241) says that Mrs. Austin wrote to Carlyle (as he says in a letter to his brother, July 2, 1832) that Goethe's last words were:

"Macht die Fensterladen auf, damit ich mehr Licht bekomne." ("Open the shutters, that I may have more light.")
Variants are: "Macht doch den zweiten Fensterladen auch auf, damit mehr Licht hereinkomme." ("Pray open the second shutter so that more light may come in.") "Macht doch den Fensterladen im Schlafgemach auf, damit mehr Licht hereinkomme," ("Open the shutters in the bedroom so that more light may come in.")

Liebe, gute! (Dear, good one!)
SCHILLER (1759-1805) — Last words. (Düntzer, *Life of Schiller*). Carlyle (*Life of Schiller*, pt. 3, People's Edn. p. 166) gives his last words as: "Many things are growing plain and clear to me!" following his words, "calmer and calmer" when asked how he was feeling.

Lieber ein Ende mit Schrecken, als ein Schrecken ohne Ende! (Rather an end with terror, than terror without an end).
SCHILL—in the market-place of

Arneburg (on the Elbe), May 12, 1809, to the enthusiastic crowd who followed him from Berlin. Cf.
βέλτιον θανεῖν ἅπαξ ἢ διὰ βίου τρομέειν. (Better to die once for all than to spend your life in trembling).
Macht geht von Recht. (Might before right).
Attributed by Count von Schwerin (Mar. 13, 1863) to PRINCE BISMARCK (1815-98) in his speech in the Chamber of Deputies, Jan. 23, 1863, but denied by Bismarck the same day (see *Discours de M. le Comte de Bismarck*, vol. i, p. 26). Also in 1869, 1870 and 1871. Cf. the French proverb:
Force passe droit. (Might overcometh right).
Φημὶ γὰρ ἐγὼ εἶναι τὸ δίκαιον οὐκ ἄλλο τι ἢ τὸ τοῦ κρείττονος ξυμφέρον.
("I proclaim that might is right, justice the interest of the stronger." *Jowett*).
PLATO, *Republic*, I., 12 (Thrasymachus.)
La raison du plus fort est toujours la meilleure. (The reason of the stronger is always the best). La Fontaine, *le Loup et l'Agneau*.
"O, that right should thus overcome might!"
Shakspere, 2 *Henry IV*, act v. sc. 4. (Hostess Quickly).

Man kann nur aus nationalen Gründen Krieg führen. (War can be conducted only on national grounds).
PRINCE BISMARCK (1815-98)—in the North German Reichstag, April 22, 1869.

Meine Wiege stand am Webstuhl meines Vaters. (My cradle stood on my father's loom).
DEPUTY HERMANN VON BECKERATH (1801-70)—June 5, 1847, (*Der erste Preuss. Landt. in Berlin*, 1847, p. 1387.)

Meine Zeit in Unruhe, meine Hoffnung in Gott! (My time in trouble, my hope in God).
Motto of FRIEDRICH WILHELM

204   GERMAN SAYINGS

III (1797-1840). Previously of Elizabeth, Margravine of Branc burg (d. 1578), and Cathe Electress of Brandenburg (d. 1602). **Mir ist sehr schlecht.** (I feel very ill.) RICHARD WILHELM WAGNER (1813-83)—Last words.

Mit Gott für König und Vaterland. (With God for King and Fatherland.) FRIEDRICH WILHELM III (1770-1840)—from *Beilage* 3, sec. 5 of an order dated Mar. 17, 1813, concerning the organization of the militia. All the men had white tin crosses, with the above inscription, fastened in front of their caps.

Mit juristischen Theorien lässt sich auswärtige Politik nicht treiben. (Foreign politics cannot be run for legal theories.) PRINCE BISMARCK (1815-98)—in the Reichstag, Dec. 3, 1875.) See Juristische Zwirnsfäden.

Mögen die Federn der Diplomaten nicht wieder verderben, was das Volk mit so grossen Anstrengungen errungen! (May the diplomatists' pen not again spoil what the people won with such great efforts.) BLÜCHER (1742-1819)—toast at Waterloo, June 18, 1815. Alluded to by von Treitschke (*Hans von Gagern*, 1861, in *Hist. und polit. Aufs.*, 4th ed., 1871, vol. I, p. 171): "Man kennt Blüchers Toast nach Waterloo, etc." ("One knows Blücher's toast at Waterloo.")

. . **moralische Eroberungen** (. . moral conquests) *Nationalzeitung*, Nov. 25, 1858, evening edn.). EMPEROR WILHELM, when Prince Regent of Prussia (1797-1888)—to his first ministry of Hohenzollern-Auerswald, Nov. 8,

1858. The full sentence is: In Deutschland muss Preussen moralische Eroberungen machen durch die Weisheit seiner eignen Gesetzgebung und durch die Ergreifung von Einigungselementen, wie z. B. den Zollverein. (In Germany, Prussia must make moral conquests through the wisdom of its own legislation and by the adoption of measures which make for unity, such as, for example, the Zollverein. Similarly to a Deputation from Hanover, Aug. 30, 1866.

Nach Canossa gehen wir nicht (We shall not go to Canossa). PRINCE BISMARCK (1815-98)—in the Reichstag, May 14, 1872, meaning that they would not yield to the clerical party. An allusion to the penance of Henry IV, Emperor of Germany, at the Castle of Canossa (Italy), 1077. During the famous struggle (See Kulturkampf) the relations between the German government and the Vatican became somewhat strained.

Passiver Widerstand. (Passive resistance). VON UNRUH, President of the National Assembly, Nov. 10, 1848, at Berlin, when the national guard and the guilds of Berlin offered armed protection to the National Assembly. "Ich werde entschieden der Meinung dass hier nur passiver Widerstand geleistet werden könne." ("I am decidedly of opinion that only passive resistance should be rendered in this case.")

Politik von Fall zu Fall. (Policy from case to case, *i.e.*, as new issues arise). COUNT ANDRASSY (1823-90)—explaining to the Delegates that the Powers had at the Berlin Congress of 1878 decided to mutually determine their Eastern policy as each new issue arose.

Politische Brunnenvergiftung bei den Wahlen. (Political well-poisoning at Elections.) PRINCE BISMARCK (1815-98)— in the Reichstag, Jan. 24, 1882. Cf.:

Solche Skribenten schaden so viel, als wann sie die öffentlichen Brunnen vergifteten (Such scribblers do as much harm as if they were to poison the public wells) Harsdörfer, *Gesprächspiele* (1643) iv, 120.

Preussen geht fortan in Deutschland auf. (Henceforth Prussia will rise in Germany.) FREIDRICH WILHELM IV (1795-1861)—in the proclamation " An mein Volk, an die deutsche Nation," (To my people, to the German Nation), Mar. 21, 1848.

. . reine Wäsche . . (clean washing). PRINCE BISMARCK (1815-98)—in the Reichstag, Dec. 4, 1874. "Wir haben in unsern auswärtigen Beziehungen recht reine Wäsche." (In our foreign relations our washing is perfectly clean.)

Reptilienfonds. (Reptile funds, referring to Secret-Service money). PRINCE BISMARCK (1815-98)—in an answer to the president of the Reichstag, Jan. 30, 1869. In a speech in the Reichstag, February, 9, 1876, he said, " Ich nannte Reptile die Leute, die im Verborgenen gegen unsere Politik, gegen die Politik des Staates intriguieren." (I called reptiles those people who secretly intrigue against our politics, against the politics of the State).

. . rettende That. (. . saving deed).

FRIEDRICH CRISTOPHER DAHLMANN (1785-1860) is, on the authority of Von Treitschke (*Histor. u. polit. Aufsätze*, 4th ed., 1871, vol. i. 429) said to have used these words.

Revanche für Speierbach. See Revanche pour Speierbach.

Revolutionäre in Schlafrock und Pantoffeln. (Revolutionists in dressing-gown and slippers). FREIHERR VON MANTEUFFEL, Foreign Minister of Prussia, (1805-82)—in the Prussian Senate, Jan. 8, 1851. Börne (*Briefe aus Paris*, 56, Nov. 4, 1831) called Salvandy one of those easy-going Carlists who waited the return of Heinrich V in dressing-gown and slippers.

Ruhe ist die erste Bürgerpflicht. (Quiet is the first duty of a citizen). In a placard dated Oct. 17, 1806, posted in Berlin by Count von Schulenberg-Kehnert, the Monday after the battle of Jena. A copy is in the Märkisches Provinzial-Museum zu Berlin.

. . rühmlichst abwesend. (. . most honourably absent). GEO. WILHELM VON RAUMER, Director of the Prussian Archives, a member of the Council of State (1781-1873)—in the official notice (cf. Varnhagen's Tagebücher, III, 18th. & 22nd. Apr. 1846) with reference to the absence of Prince Waldemar of Prussia, who, because he was in the East Indies, could not attend the funeral of his mother on Apr. 18, 1846.

Sehe er hier, mit solchem Gesindel muss ich mich herumschlagen. (Just look here, it is with such a mob that I have to fight!) FREDERICK THE GREAT (1712-86)—to the garde-major of Wedell, before the battle of Zorndorf (Aug. 25, 1758), when the first ragged Cossacks were brought before him as prisoners of war. (Archenholz, *Geschichte d. siebenjähr Krieges*, vol. i, p. 168).

Setzen wir Deutschland, so zu sagen, in den Sattel! Reiten wird es schon können. (Put

Germany, so to speak, in the saddle, and you will find that she can ride).

PRINCE BISMARCK (1815-98)—concluding words of a speech in the Reichstag, March 11, 1867.

. . sich rückwärts zu concentrieren. (. . to concentrate oneself backwards).

GYULAI, seeing that his only chance of safety lay in a hasty passage of the Tessin, gave this order, after the battle of Palestro (1859). It has since become proverbial.

. . skrophulöses Gesindel! (Scrofulous mob!)

HEINRICH LEO (1799-1878) (*Volksblatt für Stadt und Land*, 1853, no. 61.) "Gott erlöse uns von der europäischen Völkerfäulnis und schenke uns einen frischen, fröhlichen Krieg, der Europa durchtobt, die Bevölkerung sichtet und das skrophulöse Gesindel zertritt, was jetzt den Raum zu eng macht, um noch ein ordentliches Menschenleben in der Stickluft führen zu können. (May God rescue us from the corruption of Europe, and grant us a fresh, joyous war, which shall rage through Europe, winnow the population, and crush out the scrofulous mob which now makes space too narrow for us to lead a decent human life in the stuffy atmosphere.") *Volksblatt für Stadt und Land*, 1859, no. 35. See . . ein frischer fröhlicher Krieg.

So fluscht et bater ; *or* **Dat fluscht bäter.** (Now it goes better!)

The Pommeranian militia shouted the above at the battle of Grossbeeren, Aug. 23, 1813, turning their rifles round to use the butt-ends since the rain had moistened the powder.

So lange ich lebe, wird es einen Royalisten und einen sichern Diener des Kaisers geben.

(So long as I live the Emperor will have a loyal and a true servant).

PRINCE BISMARCK (1815-98)—in the Reichstag, Nov. 29, 1881.

. . Steine in den Garten des Reiches werfen. (. . to throw stones into the garden of the Empire).

PRINCE BISMARCK (1815-98)—in the Reichstag, Jan. 15, 1889.

Unsere Politik ist, dass kein Fuss breit deu. ꞏr E꞉ . ꞏ ꞏore꞉ gehen s. kein Tit꞉ geopfert

politics ꞉ ꞏ ꞉ ꞏ ꞏ ꞏ ꞏ ꞏ of German s꞉ꞏꞏ small be lost, and that no item of German rights shall be sacrificed).

PRINCE BISMARCK (1815-98)—in the Prussian Chamber of Deputies, Dec. 18, 1863.

Unvorbereitet wie ich bin. . . (Unprepared as I am . . .)

MATTHIAS — Consulting Architect—his toast at a dinner in Halle on the completion of the new University Buildings, 1834. Cf. Unaccustomed as I am &c.

Verfassungsleben eine Reihe von Kompromissen. (Governmental life [is] a series of compromises).

PRINCE BISMARCK (1815-98)—in the Prussian Chamber of Deputies, Jan. 27, 1863 ꞏceded by "Ein konstitutioneller erfahrener Staatsmann hat gesagt, dass das ganze. (A constitutional Statesman of experience has said that all . .)." Also in the Prussian Senate, Jan. 24, 1865, and Dec. 22, 1866. See Die Basis des konstitutionellen &c.

. . Volk in Waffen. (. . nation under arms).

KAUNITZ—to Joseph II. (1741-90). "Ein ganzes Volk in Waffen ist an Majestät dem Kaiser ebenbürtig." (A whole nation under arms is equal in birth to his majesty the Emperor.)—(Georg Weber, *Weltgeschichte*, 12th. edit, vol. I, p. 819).

. . . Vorfrucht der Sozialdemokratie. (. . foretaste of social democracy).

PRINCE BISMARCK (1815-98) applied these words to the Progressive Party.

Vor Paris nichts Neues. (From Paris no news).

. . . . IELSKI—in . . . . m Ferrières . . . . rsailles, Oct. . . . . 26, 1871. Vorwärts. . . . .).

Motto and nickname (Marschall Vorwärts) of MARSHAL BLÜCHER (1742-1819). Treitschke, *Deutsche Gesch. im 19 ten. Jahrh.* (1879, vol. i., p. 504). The title is now used by a leading German socialistic journal.

Was gemacht werden kann, wird gemacht. (What can be done, shall be done).

COUNT WALLIS, Austrian Minister of Finance—in 1811, defending the order by which he reduced the bank-note by one-fifth of its face value.

. . weibliches Gepäck. (. . female baggage).

PRINCE BISMARCK (1815-98)—in the Reichstag, Ma . . . . 877 : " Es ist ein ausserordentlicher Vorzug für die Karriere, wenn Jemand ohne alles weibliche Gepäck sich durch die Welt schlagen kann." (It is a great advantage to a man to be able to fight his way through the world without female baggage). Cf. " He that hath a wife and children hath hostages to fortune, for they are impediments to great enterprises, either of virtue or mischief."— Bacon, *Essay VIII* (Of Marriage &c.).

Wenn ich keinen Widerspruch ertragen könnte, dann könnte ich ja schon gar nicht mehr leben. (If I could bear no contradiction, then I could not live any longer).

PRINCE BISMARCK (1815-98) in the Reichstag, Nov. 26, 1884.

Wenn ich König von Frankreich wäre, so dürfte ohne meine Erlaubniss kein Kanonenschuss in Europa fallen. (Were I king of France, not a shot should be fired in Europe without my permission).

Attributed to FREDERICK II, OF PRUSSIA (1712-86).

Wenn nicht, dann nicht ! (If not, then not !)

VON KOLLER, Prussian Minister, at the debate Dec. 15, 1894, in the Reichstag, as to the criminal prosecution of Liebknecht (b. 1826), in *lèse-majesté* (remaining seated while the Emperor was being cheered). Cf. Sinon, non !

Widerlegen kann ihn (Herrn Eugen Richter) Niemand, er behält doch Recht ! (Nobody can refute him [Mr. Eugen Richter] ; he is right).

PRINCE BISMARCK (1815-98)—in the Prussian Chamber of Deputies, Feb. 4, 1881.

. . wie Gott in Frankreich. (. . like God in France).

MAXIMILIAN I (1459-1519)—on the authority of Zincgref-Weidner, *Apophthegmata*, (1693, p. 10). Maximilian, in familiar conversation with some of his courtiers about other lands and kingdoms, remarked, " If it were possible that I could be God and have two sons, the eldest would have to be God after me, and the second King of France."

Wir Deutsche fürchten Gott, aber sonst nichts in der Welt ! (We Germans fear

God, but nothing else in the world!)

PRINCE BISMARCK (1815-98)—at the conclusion of his speech on the treaty between Germany, Austria, nd Hungary, Oct. 7, 1879, delivered in the Reichstag Feb. 6, 1888. Cf.

" Je crains Dieu, cher Abner, et n'ai point d'autre crainte." (I fear God, dear Abner, and have no other fear).— Racine, *Athalie.* act 1, sc. 1 (Joad). We fear the Lord, and know no other fear. —Goldsmith, *The Captivity.*

Wir können das Reifen der Früchte nicht dadurch beschleunigen, dass wir eine Lampe darunter halten ; und wenn wir nach unreifen Früchten schlagen, so werden wir nur ihr Wachstum hindern und sie verderben. (We cannot hasten the ripening of fruit by holding a lamp underneath it, and if we cut the unripe fruit, we prevent its growth, and it spoils).

PRINCE BISMARCK (1815-98)—in the North German Reichstag, May 21, 1869.

Wir färben echt, wir färben gut, Wir färben's mit Tyrannenblut. (We colour true we colour good, we colour it * with tyrants' blood).

From a political song of the year 1848, by August Brass, quoted in the Reichstag, May 10, 1895.

Wir wollen die Waffen auf dem Fechtboden niederlegen, aber weggeben wollen wir sie nicht. (We will lay down our arms in the fencing-school, but we will not give them up).

PRINCE BISMARCK (1815-98)—at

* i.e. the banner of liberty.

soirée, May 4, 1880, with reference to the " Kulturkampf."

Zeitungsschreiber, ein Mensch, der seinen Beruf verfehl that. (The journalist, a man who has missed his vocation).

Attributed to PRINCE BISMARCK (1815-98), but no confirmation of it in this form has so far been discovered. The phrase seems to rest upon a sentence of his in a speech (Nov. 10, 1862) made on the occasion of the visit to the King of a deputation from Rügen, when Bismarck stated that the Government would offer every facility for arriving at an understanding with the House of Delegates, "aber die oppositionelle Presse diesem Streben zu sehr entgegenwirke, indem sie zum grossen Teil in Händen von Juden und unzufriedenen, ihren Lebensberuf verfehlt habenden Leuten sich befinde" (but the Opposition press was working too strongly against this effort, inasmuch as it consisted in great part of Jews and discontents, people who had missed their vocation in life).

Zwischen mich und mein Volk soll sich kein Blatt Papier drängen. (Between me and my people not a sheet of paper shall intrude).

Derived from a speech of FRIEDRICH WILHELM IV (1795-1861), Apr. 11, 1847 :

Es drängt mich zu der feierlichen Erklärung . . ., dass ich nun und nimmermehr zugeben werde, dass sich zwischen unsern Herr Gott im Himmel und dieses Land ein beschriebenes Blatt, gleichsam als eine zweite Vorsehung eindränge. . . . (I am impelled to declare . . ., that neither now nor ever will I allow a written leaf to intrude, like a second Providence, between our Lord in heaven and this land).

GREEK SAYINGS

Ἄγγελλε τοίνυν, ὅτι Γάϊον Μάριον ἐν τοῖς Καρχηδόνος ἐρειπίοις φυγάδα καθεζόμενον εἶδες. (Go tell him that you have seen Caius Marius sitting in exile among the ruins of Carthage).

CAIUS MARIUS (157-86 B.C.)—to an officer of the governor of Libya, Sextilius, who forbade him to land there (Plutarch, *Lives*: *Marius*, xl).

Ἀληθῆ λέγεις · εἰ μὴ γὰρ σὺ τὴν πόλιν ἀπέβαλες, οὐκ ἂν ἐγὼ παρέλαβον. (Very true ; for if you had not lost the city, I could never have recaptured it).

FABIUS MAXIMUS (275-202 B.C.) —to Marcus Livius, who had been in command of Tarentum when Hannibal obtained possession of it. The latter held it until recaptured by the Romans. Marcus Livius told the Senate that he, and not Fabius, was the real author of the recapture of the town (Plutarch, *Lives*: *Fabius Maximus*, xxiii).

Ἀλλ᾽ αὐτὸ τοῦτο μάλιστα φιλοσοφίας ἴδιον, τὸν καιρὸν ἑκάστων ἐπίστασθαι. ('Tis the special province of philosophy to know the due season for everything).

ARCESILAUS (B.C. 438-360)—(Diogenes Laertius, *Lives*: *Arcesilaus*, § 41).

Ἄλλος ἐγώ. (A second self).

ZENO (d.c. 260 B.C.)—on being asked who was a true friend. (Diogenes Laertius, *Lives*: *Zeno*, § 23). Commonly quoted in the Latin form, "alter ego."

Ἀλλ᾽ ἐγὼ οὐ καταγελῶμαι. (But I am not derided).

DIOGENES, the Cynic (412-323 B.C.)—reply to one who told him that he was being derided ; meaning that only those are really derided who are affected by ridicule. (Plutarch, *Lives*: *Fabius Maximus*, X.)

Ἀλλ᾽ οὐχ οὗτος πολέμιος ὤν ἡμέτερος ἐνταῦθα ἔστηκεν ; (Is not he that has his stand there my enemy ?).

EMPEROR AUGUSTUS (63 B.C.-14 A.D.)—referring to a brazen statue of Brutus in the city of Milan (Plutarch, *Lives*: *Dion & Brutus*, V).

Ἄν ἔτι μίαν μάχην Ῥωμαίους νικήσωμεν, ἀπολούμεθα παντελῶς (One more such victory over the Romans and we are utterly undone).

PYRRHUS (318-272 B.C.)—when congratulated on his victory over the Romans at Asculum (Plutarch, *Lives*: *Pyrrhus*, xxi ; *Apophthegmata*: *Pyrrhus*, 3). Hence the

14

GREEK SAYINGS

Wellington's words immediately
after the battle (June 18, 1815) of
Waterloo:

I have never fought such a battle; and I
hope never to fight such another.—Lt. Col.
Williams, *Life and Times of Wellington*,
vol. ii, p. 266.

Amurath (Murad) II (d. 1451)
replied to those who congratulated
him on the victory of Varna (1444)
that 'two such victories would
destroy his empire.'

Ανθρωπε πολλὰ ἔχοντι τῷ γήρᾳ
τὰ αἰσχρὰ μὴ προστίθει τὴν ἀπὸ
τῆς κακίας αἰσχύνην. (My good
fellow, old age is quite ugly
enough without your adding
the deformity of wickedness to
it).

CATO MAJOR (234-149 B.C.)—to
an old man who was acting wrongly
(Plutarch, *Lives*: *Cato Major*, 9).

Ἄνθρωπον ζητῶ. (I am looking
for a man).

DIOGENES (412-323 B.C.)—having
lighted a candle at noon, and being
asked the reason why he did so
(Diogenes Laertius, *Lives*: *Diogenes*,
§ 41). Phaedrus (*Fabulae*, bk. III,
xix) attributes this saying to Æsop,
who, when a busybody in the
market place asked him what he
was doing with a lighted torch at
noon (which he was hurriedly
carrying to light his master's fire)
answered, "Hominem quaero,"
meaning that, had his interrogator
been "a man," he would not have
unseasonably made mirth of him."

Cf.: Which yet my soul seeketh, but I
find not: one man among a thousand have
I found; but a woman among all those
have I not found.—*Ecclesiastes*, ch. 7, v.
28.

'Ανίκητος εἶ, ὦ παῖ. (You are
invincible, my son).

DELPHIC ORACLE—reply to
Alexander the Great (356-323 B.C.)
before he started on an expedition

to Asia. As she refused to mount
the prophetic tripod, the young
hero dragged her thither (Plutarch,
Lives: *Alexander*, xiv).

Αὐτᾶς ἄκουκα τήνας. (I have
heard the originals).

A SPARTAN—when invited to
hear a man imitate the nightingale
(Plutarch, *Lives*: *Lycurgus*, xx).
The same reply to the same question
is attributed to Agesilaus (*id.*,
Agesilaus, xxi).

Αὐτὸς ἔφα. (Himself said it).

Saying among the DISCIPLES OF
PYTHAGORAS ZACYNTHIUS (6 cent.
B.C.), referring to him. (Diogenes
Laertius, *Lives*: *Pythagoras*, § 46).
Commonly quoted in the Latin form
"Ipse dixit."

Βασιλικῶς. (Like a king).

PORUS (fl. 4th cent. B.C.)—to
Alexander the Great, on the former
being captured and asked how he
wished to be treated (327 B.C.).
Alexander then enquired if he had
nothing else to ask, and Porus replied that everything was comprised
in these words (Plutarch, *Lives*:
Alexander, lx).

Βέλτιον· πλείονας γὰρ νικήσομεν.
(So much the better, for then
we shall conquer more).

PELOPIDAS (d. 364 B.C.)—when
told that Alexander, the tyrant, was
advancing to meet him with a great
force (Plutarch, *Lives*: *Pelopidas*,
32).

. . . βέλτιόν ἐστιν ἅπαξ ἀποθανεῖν
ἢ ἀεὶ προσδοκᾶν. (It is better
to die once for all than constantly to live in expectation of
death).

JULIUS CÆSAR (100-44 B.C.)—
Plutarch, *Lives*: *Cæsar*, lvii). Cf.

"Cowards die many times before their
deaths;
The valiant never taste of death but
once"—Shakspere, *Julius Cæsar*, act
ii, sc. 2. (Cæsar)

GREEK SAYINGS

211

Βραδέως ἐγχείρει τοῖς πραττομένοις· ὃ
δ' ἂν ἕλῃ, βεβαίως τηρῶν διάμενε.
(Be slow to put your hand to
an undertaking, but, when you
have done so, maintain it and
persevere with it to the end).
BIAS, one of the Seven Wise Men
of Greece (fl. c. 550 B.C.) (Diogenes
Laertius, *Lives*: *Bias*, § 87).

Γίνεται τοίνυν ὃ βούλομαι· βούλομαι
γὰρ Ἀθηναίους τοῦτο λαλεῖν, ἵνα
μή τι χεῖρον περὶ ἐμοῦ λέγωσι.
(Just what I wanted has happened, then ; for I wish the
Athenians to gossip about this,
that they might not say something worse about me).
ALCIBIADES (450-404 B.C.)—
when reproached by his friends for
having cut off his dog's tail, and
told that all Athens was sorry for the
dog (Plutarch, *Lives* : *Alcibiades*,
ix).

Γλώττης κρατεῖν, καὶ μάλιστα ἐν
συμποσίῳ. (Rule your tongue,
especially at a feast).
CHILO (d. B.C. 597)—(Diogenes
Laertius, *Lives* : *Chilo*, § 69).

Γνῶθι σαυτόν. (Know thyself).
THALES (636-546 B.C.)—(Diogenes Laertius, *Lives* : *Thales*, §
40). Also attributed to Chilo, and
to Phemonoes.

Διὰ τοῦτο δύο ὦτα ἔχομεν, στόμα δὲ
ἕν, ἵνα πλείω μὲν ἀκούωμεν,
ἥττονα δὲ λέγωμεν. (The
reason of our having two ears
but only one mouth is that we
may hear the more and speak
the less).
ZENO (d. c. 260 B.C.)—(Diogenes,
Laertius, *Lives* : *Zeno*, § 23).

Διὰ τούτων ἔξω λόγος οὐκ ἐκπορεύεται.
(Through this no words go out.)
At the Spartan public dinners it
was the custom for the oldest person
present, pointing to the door, to say

the above words to each man on
entering. Plutarch, *Lives*: *Lycurgus*,
xii. Cf. "Tell no tales out of
school." (*English Proverb*).

Δός μοι ποῦ στῶ καὶ κινῶ τὴν γῆν.
(Give me a standpoint, and I
can move the earth).
ARCHIMEDES (c. 287-212 B.C.)
referring to the immense power of
the lever. (*Pappus Alexandrinus,
Collectio lib. viii.*, 11, *Prop.* 10).
Another version of Archimedes'
saying is given in Plutarch's *Life of
Marcellus* (§xiv) : εἰ γῆν εἶχεν ἑτέραν,
ἐκίνησεν ἂν ταύτην μεταβὰς εἰς
ἐκείνην (if he had another earth, by
going into it he could remove this
one). The 'lever of Archimedes'
is hence used proverbially.

Δοτέον Φωκίωνι ταύτην τὴν χάριν.
(We must grant this favour to
Phocion).
ANTIPATER (390-319 B.C.) to
Craterus, taking him by the hand.
Phocion's request to the first-named
was that he should remain where he
was and arrange terms of peace.
Craterus did not approve of this.
(Plutarch, *Lives* : *Phocion*, xxvi).

Ἐγὼ γὰρ καὶ ταύτην εὐτυχῆ ποιήσω
Ῥωμαίοις τὴν ἡμέραν. (Well,
I will make it a happy day for
the Romans !)
LUCULLUS (c. 109-c. 57 B.C.) re-
ferring to the 6th October, which
was considered an unlucky day.
(Plutarch, *Lives* : *Lucullus*, xxvii).

Ἐγὼ δὲ πολλῷ χρόνῳ. (I take a long
time.)
ZEUXIS (b. c. 450 B.C), hearing
Agatharchus, the painter, boast
how rapidly he could produce a
picture. (Plutarch, *Lives* : *Pericles*,
xiii).

Ἐγὼ μὲν ἐβουλόμην παρὰ τούτοις
εἶναι μᾶλλον πρῶτος ἢ παρὰ
Ῥωμαίοις δεύτερος. (I would

212 GREEK SAYINGS

rather be the first man here
than the second man in Rome).
JULIUS CAESAR (100-44 B.C.)—
when crossing the Alps on his way
to Spain. Plutarch, *Lives*: *Caesar*,
xi). Cf.
Tel brille au second rang qui s'éclipse
au premier. (One shines in the second
rank who is outshone in the first).—
Voltaire, *La Henriade*, Chant i.
Ἔζησαν. (They have lived).
CICERO (106-43 B.C.) to the
conspirators, who were waiting for
the night, thinking that those who
had been killed were still alive and
might be rescued. He meant that
they were alive no more, and so
avoided a word of ill-omen, 'dead.'
(Plutarch, *Lives*: *Cicero*, xxii).
There is no Latin authority for the
original word, 'vixerunt.'

Εἰ γάρ τι καλὸν ἔργον πεποίηκα,
τοῦτό μου μνημεῖον ἔσται · εἰ
δὲ μηδὲν, οὐδ᾽ οἱ πάντες ἀνδρι-
άντες. (If I have done any
good work, that will keep my
memory green ; but, if not, all
the statues in the world will
not do it).

AGESILAUS (438-360 B.C.)—on his
death-bed, desiring that no statue
should be raised to him. (Plutarch,
Apophthegmata: *Agesilaus*, 12). See
Ἐμοῦ δὲ ἐρωτᾶν βούλομαι μᾶλλον &c.

Εἴ γε βασιλεῖς ἔμελλον ἕξειν
ἀνταγωνιστάς. (Yes, if I were
going to have kings for my
opponents).

ALEXANDER THE GREAT, (356-
323 B.C.)—when asked whether he
would contend in the foot-race at
Olympia, for he was a remarkably
swift runner. (Plutarch, *Lives*:
Alexander, iv.)

Εἰ μὲν ὡς πρεσβευταὶ πολλοὶ
πάρεισιν, εἰ δ᾽ ὡς στρατιῶται,
ὀλίγοι. (If they have come as
ambassadors, they are too
many—if as soldiers, too few).

TIGRANES II (89-36 B.C.)—
referring to Lucullus's army
(Plutarch, *Lives*: *Lucullus*, xxvii).

Εἰ μὴ 'Αλέξανδρος ἤμην, Διογένης ἂν
ἤμην. (If I were not Alexander
I would be Diogenes).

ALEXANDER THE GREAT (356-
323 B.C.)—to express his admiration
of Diogenes, whom he visited at
Corinth (Plutarch, *Lives*: *Alexander*,
xiv). See Μικρὸν ἀπὸ τοῦ ἡλίου
μετάστηθι.

. . εἰ χαλεπὸν οὕτως ἐστὶν, ὥστε
μηδὲ ὄνον προσελθεῖν χρυσίον
κομίζοντα. ([He asked] if it
was so difficult that an ass
laden with gold could not get
in).

PHILIP OF MACEDON (382-336
B.C.) to his scouts who repeated
that a stronghold he wished to
capture was impregnable. (Plutarch *Apophthegmata*: *Philip*, 14).
Ἐρρέθη γοῦν, ὅτι τὰς πόλεις αἱρεῖ τῶν
Ἑλλήνων οὐ Φίλιππος, ἀλλὰ τὸ
Φιλίππου χρυσίον. (It was said that
the cities of Greece were captured
not by Philip, but by Philip's gold).
Cf. The advice given by the DEL-
PHIC ORACLE to Philip (382-336 B.C.)
" Arm yourself with arms of silver,
and nothing shall resist you." One
of Diogenianus' *Proverbs* (II, 81) is
Ἀργυραῖς λόγχαις μάχου, καὶ πάντων
κρατήσεις. (Fight with spears of
silver, and thou wilt overcome all
thy foes).
Cf. Fight thou with shafts of silver, and
o'ercome,
When no force else can get the masterdom.
Herrick, *Hesperides*, *Aphorism* 271.
In eo neque auctoritate neque gratia
pugnat, sed quibus Philippus omnia castella
expugnari posse dicebat, in quae modo
asellus onustus auro posset ascendere.
(His weapons are neither authority nor
popularity, but rather those referred to in
the saying of Philip of Macedon, that no
city was impregnable so long as it could be
entered by an ass laden with gold.) Cicero,
Ad Atticum, i, 16, 12). Often referred to as
" Philip's Ass."

Nihil esse tam sanctum (dictitat) quod non violari, nihil tam munitum quod non expugnari pecunia possit. (There is no sanctuary so holy that money cannot profane it, no fortress so strong that money cannot take it by storm.) (Cicero, *In Verrem*, i, 2, 4). See Quand on combat à lances d'argent &c.

Εἰδέναι μὲν μηδὲν, πλὴν αὐτὸ τοῦτο, εἰδέναι. (He knew nothing, excepting that he knew it [*i.e.*, that he knew nothing]).

SOCRATES (B.C 468-399)—to the Delphic Oracle, which had told him that he was the wisest man in all Greece. (Diogenes Laertius, *Lives*: *Socrates*, § 32).

Εἰς αὔριον τὰ σπουδαῖα. (Business to-morrow).

ARCHIAS, governor of Thebes (fl. c. 4th cent. B.C.) on receiving a letter which he was desired to read instantly (it was to warn him of a conspiracy to murder him). The delay cost him his life. (Plutarch, *Lives* : *Pelopidas*, 10).

Εἷς οἰωνὸς ἄριστος ἀμύνεσθαι περὶ Πύρρου. (The best of omens is king Pyrrhus' cause).

PYRRHUS (318-272 B.C.) in reply to a remark by Lysimachus, who regarded Pyrrhus' dream as to Sparta as a bad omen (Plutarch, *Lives*: *Pyrrhus*, xxix). Adapting Homer's line (*Iliad*, xii, 243) : Εἷς οἰωνὸς ἄριστος, ἀμύνεσθαι περὶ πάτρης. (The best of omens is our country's cause.—*Lord Derby's Translation*).

Εἶτα οὐκ ἀγαπᾷς ὅτι μετὰ Φωκίωνος ἀποθνήσκεις ; (Are you not content, then, to die in Phocion's company ?)

PHOCION (c. 400-317 B.C.) to Thodippus, who was in prison and bewailing his fate, when he saw the hemlock being prepared. (Plutarch, *Lives* : *Phocion*, xxxvi).

Εἶτα γράμματα διδάσκεις "Ομηρον ἐπανορθοῦν ἱκανὸς ὤν ; οὐχὶ τοὺς νέους παιδεύεις ; (Do you, you who are able to correct Homer, teach children to read ? Why do you not employ your time in instructing *men ?*)

ALCIBIADES (450-404 B.C.)—to a schoolmaster who said he had a copy of Homer corrected by himself. (Plutarch, *Lives* : *Alcibiades*, vii).

Ἐκείνη ἐν ᾗ τῶν ἀδικουμένων οὐχ ἧττον οἱ μὴ ἀδικούμενοι προβάλλονται καὶ κολάζουσι τοὺς ἀδικοῦντας. (That in which those who are not wronged espouse the cause of those who are, and punish the wrong-doers).

SOLON (638-558 B.C.)—when asked what city he thought was the best modelled. (Plutarch, *Lives: Solon*, xviii).

Ἐλλυχνίων ὄζειν αὐτοῦ τὰ ἐνθυμήματα. (His impromptu smell of the lamp).

PYTHEAS (fl. 4th cent. B.C.)—of Demosthenes' orations, ridiculing his habit of not making a speech without preparation. Demosthenes replied :

Οὐ ταὐτὰ γὰρ ἐμοὶ καὶ σοὶ, ὦ Πυθέα, ὁ λύχνος σύνοιδε. (My lamp, Pytheas, sees very different work from yours). —Plutarch, *Lives: Demosthenes*, viii. Cf. :

Whence is thy learning? Hath thy toil O'er books consum'd the midnight oil? —John Gay, *The Shepherd and the Philosopher*.

Ἐμὲ δὲ αὐτὸν πρὸς πόσας ἀντιστήσεις ; (And for how many then do you reckon me?).

ANTIGONUS (d. 242 B.C.)—as he was about to begin a sea-fight off Andros, someone having said that the enemy's fleet was the more numerous. (Plutarch, *Lives: Pelopidas*, 2).

214 GREEK SAYINGS

Ἐμὲ Δημοσθένης, ἡ ὗς τὴν Ἀθηνᾶν.
(To compare Demosthenes with me is like comparing a sow with Minerva). DEMADES (d. 318 B.C.) an opponent of Demosthenes.— (Plutarch, *Lives: Demosthenes*, xi).

Ἐμοῦ δὲ ἐρωτᾶν βούλομαι μᾶλλον τοὺς ἀνθρώπους, διὰ τί ἀνδριὰς οὐ κεῖται Κάτωνος ἢ διὰ τί κεῖται.
I would much rather that men should ask why I have no statue than why I have one). CATO MAJOR (234-149 B.C.)— (Plutarch, *Apophthegmata Catonis*, 10; *Lives*: *Cato Major*, xix).

Ἐμοῦ μὲν, ὦ παῖ, τὴν σὴν μητέρα γαμοῦντος οὐδὲ ὁ γείτων ἤσθετο τοῖς δὲ σοῖς γάμοις καὶ βασιλεῖς καὶ δυνάσται συγχορηγοῦσιν.
(My boy, when I married your mother not even our neighbours heard of it: but kings and princes are contributing to your wedding). DEMADES (d. 318 B.C.)—to his son Demeas, on the occasion of the latter's marriage.—(Plutarch, *Lives: Phocion*, xxx).

Ἐνταῦθά εἰσιν οἱ πολέμιοι. (Here are the enemy!) JULIUS CAESAR (100-44 B.C.)— to a man bearing the eagle and running away. Caesar seized him by the neck and turned him round saying as above.—(Plutarch, *Lives: Caesar*, lii).

Ἔοικεν, ὦ ἄνδρες, ὅτε Δαρεῖον ἡμεῖς ἐνικῶμεν ἐνταῦθά, ἐκεῖ τις ἐν Ἀρκαδίᾳ γεγονέναι μυομαχία.
(It appears, my friends, that while we were conquering Darius here in Asia, there was a battle of mice across the seas in Arcadia.) ALEXANDER THE GREAT (356-323 B.C.)—referring to a battle

between Agis and Antipater (Plutarch, *Lives: Agesilaus*, xv).

Εὕρηκα, εὕρηκα. (I have found it, I have found it). ARCHIMEDES (287-212 B.C.)—on discovering the law of specific gravity. (Vitruvius Pollio, *De Architectura*, ix, 3). Generally quoted as 'Eureka,' or, more correctly, 'Heureka.'

Ἡ τῶν ἐμῶν λόγων κοπὶς πάρεστιν.
(Here comes the pruning-knife of my periods). DEMOSTHENES (385-322 B.C.)— when Phocion rose to speak used to whisper to his friends as above. (Plutarch, *Lives: Phocion*, v).

Ἡράκλεις, ὡς ψυχρὸν ὑμῶν τὸ βαλανεῖον. (By Hercules, how cold this bath of yours is!) JUGURTHA (154-104 B.C.)—when thrust naked into a dungeon, his clothes having been torn off him. (Plutarch, *Lives: Marius*, xii). Cf. also Sallust Jugurtha, ch. cxxii. and Longfellow, *Jugurtha.*

Θαρρεῖ· τοιοῦτον ἐστι τῆς ἀρετῆς τὸ χρῶμα. (Cheer up—that is the colour of virtue!) DIOGENES (B.C. 412-323)—on seeing a young man blush. (Diogenes Laertius, *Lives: Diogenes*, § 54).

Ἴθι, γενναῖε, τόλμα καὶ δέδιθι μηδέν. Καίσαρα φέρεις καὶ τὴν Καίσαρος τύχην συμπλέουσαν. (Come, good sir, have courage and fear nothing: you have Caesar and Caesar's fortune on board with you). JULIUS CAESAR (100-44 B.C.)—to the frightened pilot on board a vessel going from Dyrrachium to Brundisium. (Plutarch, *Lives: Caesar*, xxxviii). Cf. :

"Je réponds de la barque, en dépit de Neptune ! Songe donc qu'elle porte un poëte et sa fortune !"

("I'll answer for the barque, in spite of Neptune! Remember that it bears a poet and his fortune.")—Piron, *La Métromanie*, act iv., sc. 2.

Κἀγώ, νὴ Δί', εἰ Παρμενίων. (So would I too, indeed, if I were Parmenio).

ALEXANDER THE GREAT (356-323 B.C.)—to Parmenio, when the latter advised accepting the brilliant offers of Darius after the battle of Issus, saying 'I should accept them if I were Alexander.' (Plutarch, *Lives*: *Alexander*, xxix).

.. καθεύδειν αὐτὸν οὐκ ἐῴη τὸ τοῦ Μιλτιάδου τρόπαιον. (.. the trophy of Miltiades would not let him sleep).

THEMISTOCLES (514-449 B.C.)—when asked the cause of his reserve and his sleeplessness after Miltiades' victory at Marathon (490 B.C.)

Καὶ μὴν μάλιστα ἡμεῖς ἐφικνούμεθα τοῖς ἐγχειριδίοις τῶν πολεμίων. (And yet we generally reach our enemies with these little daggers).

KING AGIS (d. 239 B.C.)—replying to an Athenian who jeered at the small Spartan swords, saying that the jugglers on the stage swallowed them with ease. (Plutarch, *Lives*: *Lycurgus*, xviii).

Καὶ ποῦ τότε ἤμην ἐγώ; (And where was I all the time?)

LYSIMACHUS (c. 362-282 B.C.)—when Onesicritus was reading aloud to him the fourth book of his *History of Alexander* after Lysimachus had made himself king. (Plutarch, *Lives*: *Alexander*, xlvi).

Καὶ σύ, τέκνον; (And thou, too, my son?)

JULIUS CAESAR (100-44 B.C.)—Dying words, to Marcus Brutus, on his stabbing him in the Roman senate. (Suetonius, *Twelve Caesars*,

i, 82; Dio Cassius, xliv, 19; Shakspere, *Julius Caesar*, act iii, sc. 1: "et tu, Brute").—See Ista quidem vis est.

Καιρὸν γνῶθι. (Mark the fitting moment).

PITTACUS (B.C. 652-569).—Diogenes Laertius, *Lives*: *Pittacus*, § 79).

Κάκιστον δὲ ἄρχοντα εἶναι τὸν ἄρχειν ἑαυτοῦ μὴ δυνάμενον. (The worst ruler is the man who cannot rule himself).

CATO MAJOR (234-149 B.C.) — (Plutarch, *Apophthegmata Catonis*, 8: the Latin original does not occur). Cf.: "Melior est longanimus robusto; et qui dominatur in animum suum, eo qui capit civitatem" (He that is slow to anger is better than the mighty; and he that ruleth his spirit than he that taketh a city).—Prov. xvi, 32.

Καλὰ τὰ διδασκάλια παρὰ Θηβαίων ἀπολαμβάνεις, μὴ βουλομένους αὐτοὺς μηδὲ εἰδότας μάχεσθαι διδάξας. (The Thebans pay you well for having taught them to fight, whether they would or no).

ANTALCIDAS (fl. 4th cent. B.C.)—when he saw King Agesilaus wounded, alluding to the latter having, by his frequent and long-continued invasions of Boeotia, made the Thebans a match for the Spartans in the art of war. (Plutarch, *Lives*: *Lycurgus*, xiii).

Κοινὰ τὰ φίλων. (Friends have all things in common).

BION (fl. c. 250 B.C.)—(Diogenes Laertius, *Lives*: *Bion*, § 53).

Κρεῖττον εἶναι τοῖς ποσὶν ὀλισθεῖν, ἢ τῇ γλώττῃ. (Better a slip of the feet than of the tongue).

ZENO (d. c. 260 B.C.)—(Diogenes Laertius, *Lives*: *Zeno*, § 26).

Λήγει μὲν ἀγὼν τῶν καλλίστων ἄθλων ταμίας, καιρὸς δὲ καλεῖ μηκέτι μέλλειν. (The play, that has dispensed fairest prizes, is over, and the time summons us from further tarrying).
DEMONAX (2nd century A.D.) —Dying words (Lucian, *Life of Demonax*, 65). See Acta est fabula ; Tirez le rideau &c.

Μᾶλλον διὰ τοὺς πολίτας πειθαρχικοὺς γεγονότας. (Nay, rather in her citizens knowing how to obey).
KING THEOPOMPUS (fl. 770-724 B.C.)—in reply to the remark that Sparta's safety lay in her kings knowing how to rule. (Plutarch, *Lives*: *Lycurgus*, xxx).

Μεμαστίγωσο ἂν, εἰ μὴ ὠργιζόμην. (Had I not been angry, I should have beaten you).
PLATO (B.C. 428-347)—to a child. Similarly, when Xenocrates entered the room once, he asked him to beat the child, as he could not himself, because he was angry. αὐτὸν γὰρ μὴ δύνασθαι διὰ τὸ ὠργίσθαι. (Diogenes Laertius, *Lives*: *Plato*, § 39.)

. . μέχρι τοῦ βωμοῦ φίλος εἶναι ([he said that] he was his friend as far as the altar).
PERICLES (470-429 B.C.)—when asked to bear false witness for someone (Plutarch, *Apophthegmata*: *Pericles*, iii,) Francis I (1494-1547) when writing to Henry VIII. of England, in 1534, used the words :
Je suis votre ami, mais jusqu' aux autels. (I am your friend, but only as far as the altars).
Henry had advised him to separate himself from the Church of Rome as he himself had just done. Cf. :
Well and wisely said the Greek,
Be thou faithful, but not fond ;
To the altar's foot thy fellows seek,
The Furies wait beyond.
– R. W. Emerson, Quatrains, Pericles
See Usque ad aras amicus.

Μὴ βασίλευε. (Be not a king).
AN OLD WOMAN—to Demetrius (337-283 B.C.), who replied to her entreaty for a hearing that he had no leisure to attend to her (Plutarch, *Lives* : *Demetrius*, xlii).

Μηδὲν ἄγαν · καιρῷ πάντα πρόσεστι καλά. (Nothing in excess : all good things depend on due proportion).
THALES (B.C. 636-546)–(Diogenes Laertius, *Lives* : *Thales*, § 41 ; also attributed by him to Solon, Socrates, and Cleobulus). Usually quoted in the latin form of Terence : "Ne quid nimis."

Μηδέποτε εἰς τοῦτον ἐγὼ καθίσαιμι τὸν θρόνον, ἐν ᾧ πλέον οὐδὲν ἕξουσιν οἱ φίλοι παρ᾽ ἐμοὶ τῶν ἀλλοτρίων. (Never may I bear rule if my friends are to reap no more benefit from it than anyone else).
THEMISTOCLES (c. 533—c. 465 B.C.)—when told that he, if he were impartial, would make a very good governor of Athens (Plutarch, *Lives* : *Aristides*, ii).

Μιαρώτατε Κάσκα, τί ποιεῖς ; (You villain, Casca, what are you doing ?)
JULIUS CAESAR (100-44 B.C.)— when stabbed by Casca, who was followed by the other conspirators, Caesar is said to have received three and twenty wounds (Plutarch, *Lives* : *Caesar*, lxvi).
There is no Latin authority for the saying, though Plutarch states that it was said in Latin. Cf. :
"See, what a rent the envious Casca made :"—Shakspere, *Julius Caesar*, act iii, sc. 2.

Μικρὸν ἀπὸ τοῦ ἡλίου μετάστηθι. (Stand a little way out of my sunshine).
DIOGENES (fl. B.C. 412-323)—to Alexander the Great, when invited

by him to ask a favour, which would be at once granted. (Plutarch *Lives* : *Alexander*, xiv, Another version :
'Αποσκότησόν μου.
(Stand out of my light).—Diogenes Laertius, *Lives* : *Diogenes*, 38.

Μισῶ σοφιστὴν ὅστις οὐχ αὑτῷ σοφός.
(I hate a philosopher who is not wise in his own interest).
ALEXANDER THE GREAT (356-323 B.C.)—alluding to the behaviour of Kallisthenes in society. (Plutarch, *Lives* : *Alexander*, liii). A quotation from Euripides—*Fragment* 930.

Μόνον συνενέγκαι ταῦτα τῇ Σπάρτῃ.
(I only pray that this may redound to the good of Sparta).
AGESISTRATA, mother of King Agis, who had been hanged (399 B.C.), offering her neck to the halter. (Plutarch, *Lives* : *Agis*, xx).

.. τοῦτο τῇ Σπάρτῃ λῷόν ἐστι
(.. this is best for Sparta).
Words heard in a dream by an Ephor and communicated to Cleomenes (d. 220 B.C.) Referring to the removal of the Ephors (Plutarch, *Lives*: *Cleomenes*, vii). Kratesiclea, Cleomenes' mother, on hearing that Ptolemy, king of Egypt, had offered him assistance on condition of receiving her and his children as hostages, said :

Οὐ θᾶττον ἡμᾶς ἐνθέμενος εἰς πλοῖον ἀποστελεῖς ὅπου ποτὲ τῇ Σπάρτῃ νομίζεις τοῦτο τὸ σῶμα χρησιμώτατον ἔσεσθαι πρὶν ὑπὸ γήρως αὐτοῦ καθήμενον διαλυθῆναι.

(Will you not place us on board as soon as possible, and send us wherever this body of mine will be useful to Sparta, before it be consumed by old age after remaining idle at home)—(Plutarch, *Lives: Cleomenes*, xxii).

Galba's litter was overturned near the Lake of Curtius, and, as he fell to the ground, many ran and stabbed

him. He, offering his throat to them, said :—
Δρᾶτε εἰ τοῦτο τῷ δήμῳ 'Ρωμαίων ἄμεινόν ἐστι.
(Do it, if it be best for the Roman people). See Puisse mon sang &c.

Ναὶ μὰ τὸν Δία, σκέπτομαι εἴ τι δύναμαι τοῦ λόγου ἀφελεῖν ὃν μέλλω λέγειν πρὸς τοὺς 'Αθηναίους. (Yes, indeed, I am considering whether I can shorten the speech which I am about to deliver to the Athenians).

PHOCION (c. 400-318 B.C.)—on his friends remarking that he seemed thoughtful (Plutarch, *Lives* : *Phocion*, v).
Cf. " Je n'ai fait celle-ci plus longue que parce que je n'ai pas eu le loisir de la faire plus courte." (I have only made this [letter] longer because I have not had the leisure to make it shorter).—B. Pascal, *Lettres Provinciales*, letter 16 (near end).

.. νεκρὸς οὐ δάκνει (.. a dead man does not bite).

THEODOTUS CHIUS—(Plutarch, *Lives* : *Pompeius*, lxxvii). Another version is : Οἱ τεθνηκότες οὐ δάκνουσιν (Dead men do not bite)—*Erasmus*, *Chiliades adagiorum*, " *Obtrectatio*."

Νικᾷς, ὦ Καῖσαρ (Thou conquerest, Cæsar).
CAIUS CORNELIUS (fl. 1st cent. B.C.)—reputed to be skilled in divination, watching the birds in Patavium, while the battle of Pharsalia (48 B.C.) was going on. Observing the signs he called out as above (Plutarch, *Lives* : *Cornelius*, xlvii).

Ο ἂν αὐτῶν ποιήσῃς, μεταγνώσῃ.
(Whichever you do, you will repent).
SOCRATES (B.C. 468-399)—when asked whether it was best to marry or not (Diogenes Laertius, *Lives* : *Socrates*, § 33). See Τοὺς μὲν νέους μηδέποτε, τοὺς δὲ πρεσβυτέρους μηδεπώποτε.

Ὁ ἂν ὑμῶν τὴν μάχαιραν ὀξυτέραν
ἔχῃ. (To him whose sword is
the sharper).

PYRRHUS (318-272 B.C.)—when
asked by one of his sons to which of
them he would leave his empire.
(Plutarch, *Lives* : *Pyrrhus*, ix).

Ὁ ἀπροσδόκητος [θάνατος] (That
[death] which is unexpected).

JULIUS CÆSAR (100-44 B.C.)—
the conversation turning in his presence, on what was the best kind
of death. (Plutarch, *Lives* : *Caesar*,
lxiii).

Ὁ εἰδὼς λόγον καὶ καιρὸν οἶδεν. (He
who knows how to speak knows
also when).

ARCHIDAMIDAS (d. 328 B.C.)—
remark when Hecatæus, the sophist,
having been invited to the public
table, was blamed for having said
nothing during the whole of the
supper-time. (Plutarch, *Lives* :
Lycurgus, xx).

Οἱ λόγοι σου, ὦ ξένε, πόλεως δέονται.
(This language, my friend,
requires a state to back it).

LYSANDER (d. 395 B.C.)—to a
Megarian who used considerable
freedom of speech towards him.
[Megara was always treated by the
Greeks as a negligible quantity]
(Plutarch, *Lives* : *Lysander*, xxii).

Ὁ ταύτης κρατῶν βέλτιστα περὶ γῆς
ὅρων διαλέγεται. (He that is
master of this, is in possession
of the best argument as to
frontier lines).

LYSANDER (d. 395 B.C.)—drawing his sword at the same time,
referring to a dispute between the
Argives and the Lacedæmonians
about their frontier (Plutarch, *Lives*:
Lysander, xxii). See Ultima ratio
regem.

Οἱ μὲν ἄνδρες γεγόνασί μοι γυναῖκες·
αἱ δὲ γυναῖκες ἄνδρες. (My men
have become women, and my
women men).

XERXES (d. 465 B.C.)—after the
battle of Salamis, referring to the
bravery of Artemisia (Herodotus,
Histories, viii, 88).

Ὅπου γὰρ ἂν τῆς Ἰταλίας ἐγὼ κρούσω
τῷ ποδὶ τὴν γῆν, ἀναδύσονται καὶ
πεζικαὶ καὶ ἱππικαὶ δυνάμεις.
(For in whatever part of Italy
I stamp the earth with my foot,
there will spring up forces, both
footsoldiers and horsemen).

POMPEY (c. 106-48 B.C.)—to
those who said that there were not
sufficent troops to repulse Cæsar,
(Plutarch, *Lives* : *Pompey*, lvii ;
Apophthegmata : *Pompey*, xi).

Ὅπου γὰρ ἡ λεοντῆ μὴ ἐφικνεῖται,
προσραπτέον ἐκεῖ τὴν ἀλωπεκῆν.
(Where the lion's skin will not
reach, we must sew the fox's
skin on to it).

LYSANDER (d. 395 B.C.)—those
who said that Hercules' posterity
ought not to make use of deceit in
war, (Plutarch, *Lives* : *Lysander*,
vii ; *Apophthegmata Laconica* :
Lysander, 3). Cf. Coudre la peau
du renard à celle du lion.—French
saying.
    If the lion's skin cannot, the fox's
shall.—Eng. Prov.
    Si leonina pellis non satis est,
assuenda vulpina,—Latin Prov.
    Also Lytton, *Richelieu*, act i, sc. 2.

Οὐ γὰρ δὴ χώρην γε οὐδεμίαν κατόψεται
ὁ ἥλιος ὅμουρον ἐοῦσαν τῇ ἡμετέρῃ.
(Never shall the sun shine on
any country whose frontiers
march with ours).

XERXES (d. 465 B.C.)—in a speech
to the Persian nobles. (Herodotus,
Histories, vii, 8).

Οὐ δή πού τι κακὸν λέγων ἐμαυτὸν
λέληθα; (Can I have said
something bad without knowing
it?)
PHOCION (c. 400-317 B.C.)—when
making a remark in a speech which
was vociferously applauded, turning
to some of his friends. (Plutarch,
Lives: Phocion, viii). See Il m'arrive
un grand malheur &c.

Οὐ δοκεῖ ὑμῖν ἄξιον εἶναι λύπης εἰ
τηλικοῦτος μὲν ὢν 'Αλέξανδρος
ἐθνῶν τοσούτων ἐβασίλευεν ἐμοι
δὲ λαμπρὸν οὐδὲν οὔπω
πέπρακται; (Do you not think
it is a matter for sorrow that,
whilst Alexander was king of
so many nations at so early an
age, I have not yet done anything that is glorious?)
JULIUS CÆSAR (100-44 B.C.)—
when reading the history of Alexander. He burst into tears, and
made the above reply on being
asked the reason. (Plutarch *Lives*:
Caesar, xi)

Οὐ δύναται γὰρ 'Αντίπατρος ἅμα μοι
καὶ φίλῳ καὶ κόλακι χρῆσθαι. (I
cannot be Antipater's friend
and toady at the same time).
PHOCION (c. 400-317 B.C.)—when
Antipater asked him to perform
some disgraceful service for him.
(Plutarch, *Lives*: *Phocion*, xxx).
Cf. "I can't be your friend and your
flatterer too."—English Saying.

Οὐ κλέπτω τὴν νίκην. (I do not
steal my victories).
ALEXANDER THE GREAT (356-
323 B.C.)—when his officers tried
to persuade him to fall upon the
Persians by night. (Plutarch, *Lives*:
Alexander, xxxi).

Οὐ μόνον δ' ἦν ἄρα τὸ φίλων πεῖραν
λαβεῖν οὐ σμικρὸν κακόν, ἀλλὰ
καὶ τὸ φρονίμων στρατηγῶν. (It

is no less an evil for a man to
have to make trial of his friends,
than it is for a state to have
occasion to put her generals to
the test).
EURIPIDES (481-406 B.C.)—
quoted by Plutarch, *Lives*: *Fabius
Maximus*, xvii.

Οὐ παύσεσθε ἡμῖν ὑπεζωσμένοις ξίφη
νόμους ἀναγιγνώσκοντες; (Won't
you stop citing laws to us, who
are girded with swords?)
POMPEY (c. 106-48 B.C.)—when
the Mamertini protested that the
introduction of Roman administration was illegal. (Plutarch, *Lives*:
Pompey, x).

Οὔτε τὰ πολλά γ' ἔπη φρονίμην
ἀπεφήνατο δόξαν. ('Tis not a
multitude of words that shows
a prudent judgment).
THALES (B.C. 636-546)—(Dio-
genes Laertius, *Lives*: *Thales*, § 35).

Οὔ τοι ἀπόβλητ' ἐστὶ θεῶν ἐρικυδέα
δῶρα. (The glorious gifts of
the gods are not to be cast away).
DIOGENES (B.C. 412-323)—being
twitted with having received a
mantle of Antipater. (Diogenes
Laertius, *Lives*: *Diogenes*, § 66). Cf.:
Take the good the gods provide thee.—
Dryden, *Alexander's Feast*, l. 107.
See . . χρῶ δεξάμενος ἣν ὁ θεὸς
δίδωσιν.

Οὐ τοιαῦτά μοι ὁ λασανοφόρος σύνοιδεν.
(The carrier of my nightstool
has not so good an opinion of
me).
ANTIGONUS (380-301 B.C.) King
of Sparta—when Hermodotus in a
poem referred to him as a 'child of
the Sun.' (Plutarch, *De Iside et Osire*
24 ; *Apophthegmata Antigoni*, 7).
See Il n'y a point de héros &c.

Οὐ τοὺς Λακεδαιμονίους ἐρωτᾶν πόσοι
εἰσὶν, ἀλλὰ ποῦ εἰσὶν οἱ πολέμιοι.
(The Spartans do not ask how
many the enemy are, but where
they are).

KING AGIS (d. 399 B.C.)—(Plutarch, *Apophthegmata Agidos*, 1).
CLEOMENES (d. 220 B.C.) quoted,
or rather parodied, this saying when
he said to his countrymen μάτην
Λακεδαιμόνιοι πυνθάνονται περὶ τῶν
πολεμίων, οὐ πόσοι εἰσὶν, ἀλλὰ ποῦ
εἰσὶν (It is useless for the Spartans
to ask not how many their enemies
are, but where they are), alluding to
the flight of the Achaeans near
Pallantium. (Plutarch, *Lives*: *Cleomenes*, iv). Cf. :

Tant de victoires avaient donné aux
Suédois une si grande confiance, qu'ils ne
s'informaient jamais du nombre de leurs
ennemis, mais seulement du lieu où ils
étaient. (So many victories had given such
great confidence to the Swedes, that they
never asked the number of their enemies,
but only asked where they were.)—Voltaire.

Οὐδεὶς γὰρ δι' ἐμὲ τῶν ὄντων Ἀθηναίων
μέλαν ἱμάτιον περιεβάλετο. (For
no Athenian ever wore mourning
through my means).

PERICLES (494-429 B.C.)—on his
death-bed, overhearing his friends
enumerating his many claims to
fame, and reminding them that they
did not mention his greatest and
most glorious claim (Plutarch, *Lives*:
Pericles, 38).

Οὐδὲν ἀνδρείας χρήζομεν ἐὰν πάντες
ὦμεν δίκαιοι. (We should have
no need of courage, if justice
were universal).

AGESILAUS (438-360 B.C.)—being
asked which was the better, justice
or valour (Plutarch, *Apophthegmata*:
Agesilai, 3).
Οὐδὲν ἄρα δυνατὸν γενέσθαι ἄκοντος
θεοῦ. (It is impossible, it seems,
to do anything against the will
of heaven !)

HANNIBAL (247-182 B.C.)—on
hearing that the bones of Marcellus,
which he had sent in a silver urn to
his son, had been scattered on the
ground in a struggle between their
escort and some Numidians. (Plutarch, *Lives* : *Marcellus*, xxx).

Οὐδὲν αὕτη ὑμᾶς λελύπηκεν ἡ ὀφρὺς,
ὁ δὲ τούτων γέλως πολλὰ κλαῦσαι
τὴν πόλίν πεποίηκεν. (Yet his
frown has never done you any
harm ; but the laughter of these
men has brought great sorrow
upon the State).

CHARES (fl. *c.* 367-338 B.C.)—the
Athenians laughing when he mentioned Phocion's gloomy brow in a
speech. (Plutarch, *Lives*: *Phocion*, v)

Οὐδὲν ἦν ἄρα θαυμαστὸν ἄρχειν
γυναῖκας ἀνθρώπων φευγόντων
τὴν ἐλευθερίαν. (No wonder
women bear rule in a city where
men fear to be free).

CLEOMENES (d. 220 B.C.)—
referring to Alexandria, whose
inhabitants were afraid to join in
his conspiracy. (Plutarch, *Lives* :
Cleomenes, xxxvii).

Οὐδὲν· οὐδὲ γινώσκω τὸν ἄνθρωπον,
ἀλλ' ἐνοχλοῦμαι πανταχοῦ τὸν
Δίκαιον ἀκούων. (None at all,
neither know I the man ; but
I am tired of everywhere hearing him called ' the Just ').

A GREEK PEASANT—to Aristides
(d. 469 B.C.), not knowing who
he was, on being asked whether
Aristides had ever done him any
harm.

Οὐκ Ἀθηναῖος οὐδ' Ἕλλην ἀλλὰ
κόσμιος. (I am a citizen, not
of Athens or of Greece, but of
the world).

SOCRATES (468-399 B.C.)—
(Plutarch, *De Exilio*, v.) Cf. the
saying of Marcus Aurelius (*Quod
sibi ipsi scripsit*, vi, 44) :

Πόλις καὶ πατρὶς, ὡς μὲν 'Αντωνίνῳ, μοι ἡ 'Ρώμη, ὡς δὲ ἀνθρώπῳ, ὁ κόσμος. (My city and country, as Antoninus, is Rome, but as a man, the world).

Οὐκ αἰσχύνῃ καλῶς οὕτω ψάλλων ; (Are you not ashamed to play so well ?)

PHILIP OF MACEDON (382-336 B.C.)—to his son, who played brilliantly on the harp at an entertainment. (Plutarch, Lives: Pericles, i.) Antisthenes (fl. 366 B.C.) said, on hearing that Ismenias was an excellent flute-player :

'Αλλ' ἄνθρωπος μοχθηρός· οὐ γὰρ ἂν οὕτω σπουδαῖος ἦν αὐλητής. (But he must be a poor sort of a man, for otherwise he would not have been such an excellent piper). Id., ibid., i.

. . οὐκ ἂν ἡ Ἑλλὰς δύο Λυσάνδρους ἤνεγκε. (Greece could not have borne two Lysanders).

ETEOKLES, the Lacedæmonian —alluding to Lysander's cruelty (Plutarch, Lives: Lysander, xix). Archestratus is said to have made a similar remark about Alcibiades. Cf. Alexander's reply to Darius :

. . μήτε τὴν γῆν ἡλίους δύο μήτε τὴν 'Ασίαν δύο βασιλεῖς ὑπομένειν. (. . the earth could not brook two suns, nor Asia two masters). (Plutarch, Apophthegmata, Alexandri, 11).

Οὐκ ἔλεγον ὅτι Ξανθίππη βροντῶσα καὶ ὕδωρ ποιήσει ; (Did I not say that when Xanthippe thundered, she would afterwards also rain ?)

SOCRATES (B.C. 468-399)—when his wife lectured him and then threw·water in his face. (Diogenes Laertius, Lives: Socrates, § 36).

Οὐκ ἔστιν ἐν πολέμῳ δὶς ἁμαρτεῖν. (In war it is not permitted to make a second mistake).

LAMACHUS (d. 414 B.C.)—to one of his captains whom he was reprimanding for some fault he had committed, the captain having said that he would not do it again. (Plutarch, Apophthegmata : Lamachi, 1).

Οὐκ εὐτρεπὴς οὗτος ; οὐ νεουργής ; ἀλλ' οὐκ ἂν εἰδείη τις ὑμῶν, καθ᾽ ὅ τι θλίβεται μέρος οὑμὸς πούς᾽ (Is it not a fine [shoe]? Is it not a new one ? and yet none of you can say where my foot is pinched).

A ROMAN put away his wife, and, on his friends blaming him, saying :' " Is she not chaste ? is she not beautiful ? is she not fruitful ? " he held out his shoe, making the above remarks. (Plutarch, Lives : Æmilius Paulus, v). Cf. " But I wot best wher wryngith me my scho."—Chaucer, Marchandes Tale, l. 399.

Οὗτός ἐστιν ὁ Πλάτωνος ἄνθρωπος. (Here is Plato's ' man ').

DIOGENES (B.C. 412-323)—on bringing into the school a cock, which he had previously plucked. Plato had defined man as 'a two-legged animal without feathers.' 'With flat nails' was afterwards added.

Ἄνθρωπος ζῶον ἄπτερον, δίπουν, πλατυώνυχον. (Man is a wingless animal, with two feet and flat nails). —Plato, Definitions (ed. Stephens, p. 415, A ; Cf. Diogenes Laertius, Lives : Diogenes, vi., 2, 6). Cf. : Homo est animal bipes rationale. (Man is a two-footed reasoning animal).—Boëthius, De Consolatione Philosophiae, v, Prosa, iv.

Πάντα λίθον κίνει. (Turn every stone).

DELPHIC ORACLE—advice given to Polycrates (d. 522 B.C.) as the best means of finding a treasure buried by Mardonius, Xerxes' general, on the field of Plataea (Corpus, *Parœmiograph Grœc.*, i, p. 146). It is the origin of the expression "To leave no stone unturned." Cf. :

Πάντα κινῆσαι πέτρον. (To leave no stone unturned). — Euripides *Heraclidae*, l. 1002 ; and

'Tis good for us to live in gravel-pits,* but not for gravel-pits to live in us ; a man in this case should leave no stone unturned. —Swift, *Journal to Stella*, letter 34.

Πανταχόθεν ὁμοία ἐστὶν ἡ εἰς ᾅδου κατάβασις. (The descent to Hades is alike from every side).

ANAXAGORAS (B.C. 499-427)—to one who was grieved that he should die in a foreign country. (Diogenes Laertius, *Lives*: *Anaxagoras*, § 11).

Πάνυ μὲν οὖν · λέγω μὴ μνησικακεῖν τοῖς ᾿Αθηναίοις. (Certainly, my message is that he bear no malice against the Athenians).

PHOCION (c. 400-317 B.C.)— when asked shortly before his death, if he had any message for his son, Phocus. (Plutarch, *Lives*: *Phocion*, xxxvi).

Παραπλήσια ἔργα εἶναι νομέως ἀγαθοῦ καὶ βασιλέως ἀγαθοῦ. (The functions of a good shepherd and those of a good king are much the same).

CYRUS (d. 529 B.C.)—(Xenophon, *Cyropaedia*, viii, 2, 14).

Πάταξον μὲν, ἄκουσον δέ. (Strike, but hear me).

* Patients were sent to Kensington gravel-pits for the sake of air.

THEMISTOCLES (514-449 B.C.)— to Eurybiades, the Spartan, who had raised his staff as if to strike him. (Plutarch, *Lives*: *Themistocles*, xi). Cf. :

"Tenez, monsieur, battez-moi plutôt, et me laissez rire tout mon soûl ; cela me fera plus de bien." (Look, sir, beat me rather, and let me laugh my fill ; that will do me more good).—Molière, *Le Bourgeois gentilhomme*, act 3, sc. 2. See Frappe, mais va-t-en.

Παῦσαί με, ὦ ἄνθρωπε, κλαίων · καὶ γὰρ οὕτω παρανόμως καὶ ἀδίκως ἀπολλύμενος κρείττων εἰμὶ τῶν ἀναιρούντων. (Stay your tears, friend ; for in my unlawful and wrongful death I am better than those that are murdering me).

KING AGIS (d. 399 B.C.)—on being led to execution, to one of the prison officers who was weeping. (Plutarch, *Lives*: *Agis*, xx).

Πλεῖν ἀνάγκη, ζῆν οὐκ ἀνάγκη. (It is necessary to sail : it is not necessary to live).

POMPEY (c. 106-48 B.C.)—when about to sail for Sicily, &c., to collect grain, the ships' masters being unwilling to start. (Plutarch, *Lives*: *Pompey*, xi). See Je n'en vois pas la nécessité.

. . πλείονα δ᾿ ἂν ἔτι τούτων εἰρήκειν, εἰ πλείων παρῆν οἶνος ἡμῖν. (. . and we should have said more [evil] of you, if we had had more wine).

A YOUTH—to PYRRHUS (d. 272 B.C.). The youth, with others, had been speaking ill of Pyrrhus over their wine (Plutarch, *Lives*: *Pyrrhus*, viii).

Ποιητὰ δὲ νόμιμα εἶναι. (Whatever is, is right).

DEMOCRITUS (B.C. 460-357)— Diogenes Laertius, *Lives*: *Democritus*, § 45). Cf. :

Whatever is, is right.—Pope, *Essay on Man*, Ep. i, l. 294.

Πολὺ δὲ μεῖζον τὸ ἐπιθυμεῖν ὧν δεῖ. (Yes, a much greater ; for a man to desire no more than is necessary).

MENEDEMUS (b.c. 385 B.C.)— on hearing another maintain that there could be no greater good than for a man to get what he desired. (Diogenes Laertius, *Lives* : *Menedemus*, § 136).

Πόσων ἐγὼ χρείαν οὐκ ἔχω. (How many things are there of which I have no need ?)

SOCRATES (B.C. 468-399)—(Diogenes Laertius, *Lives* : *Socrates*, § 25.

.. πότε ἄρα παυσόμεθα νικῶντες ; (I wonder when we shall leave off being victorious !)

* PHOCION (c. 400-317 B.C.)— when despatch after despatch arrived from the camp announcing fresh successes (Plutarch, *Lives* : *Phocion*, xxiii). See *Ω τύχη &c.

Πρὶν δ᾽ ἂν τελευτήσῃ, ἐπισχέειν, μηδὲ καλέειν κω ὄλβιον ἀλλ᾽ εὐτυχέα. (Wait till a man's life be ended ; till then call him not happy, but lucky).

SOLON (639-558 B.C.), one of the Seven Sages of Greece—to Crœsus, who asked if he did not consider him happy. (Herodotus, *Histories*, i, 32). This saying, in various forms, became a commonplace of classical literature.

.. ᾧ δ᾽ εἰς τέλος ὁ δαίμων ἔθετο τὴν εὐπραξίαν, τοῦτον εὐδαίμονα νομίζομεν. (. . him only we call happy to whom the deity has vouchsafed happiness to the end.) (Plutarch, *Lives* : *Solon*, xxvii). Generally quoted

as 'Call no man happy till his death.'

Πρότερόν ἐστι τοῦ πρωρατεῦσαι τὸ φυρᾶσαι. (Before setting the watch we must think of provisioning the ship—*Harbottle*).

DEMADES (d. 318 B.C)— (Plutarch, *Lives* : *Cleomenes*, xxvii).

Πῦρ μαχαίρᾳ μὴ σκαλεύειν. (Do not poke fire with a sword).

PYTHAGORAS (6th cent. B.C.)— (Diogenes Laertius, *Lives* : *Pythagoras*, § 19.

Πῶς δ᾽ ἂν οὐκ εἴη Χαρίλαος ἀνὴρ ἀγαθὸς, ὃς οὐδὲ τοῖς πονηροῖς χαλεπός ἐστι ; (How can Charilaus be anything but a good man?—he is not harsh even to the wicked).

KING ARCHELAUS (d. 405 B.C.) —when hearing King Charilaus, his brother-king, extolled for his goodness. (Plutarch *Lives* : *Lycurgus*, v.)

Πῶς δ᾽ οὐ μέλλω φέρειν βαρέως ἀπολιπὼν, πόλιν ἐχθροὺς τοιούτους ἔχουσαν οἵους ἐν ἑτέρᾳ φίλους εὑρεῖν οὐ ῥᾴδιόν ἐστιν ; (How can I help being grieved at leaving a city where my very enemies are such that it were hard to find their like to be my friends in any other country).

DEMOSTHENES (c. 382-322 B.C.) —bursting into tears on his political opponents begging him to accept money for his journey after his escape from Athens (Plutarch, *Lives* : *Demosthenes*, xxvi).

Ῥεῖν τὰ ὅλα ποταμοῦ δίκην. (All things flow onward, like a river).

HERACLITUS (fl. B.C. 513.)— Diogenes Laertius, *Lives* : *Heraclitus*, § 6). Commonly quoted as πάντα ῥεῖ.

. . σήμερον παρὰ Λουκούλλῳ δειπνεῖ Λούκουλλος. (Lucullus will sup to-day with Lucullus).

LUCULLUS (c. 115-c.56 B.C.)— when supping alone and being angry at only a moderate repast having been prepared (Plutarch, *Lives* : *Lucullus*, xli).

Σκαιοὺς φύσει καὶ ἀγροίκους εἶναι Μακεδόνας, καὶ τὴν σκάφην λέγοντας. (The Macedonians are uncouth in nature and boorish, and call a tub a tub).

PHILIP OF MACEDON (382-336 B.C.)—(Plutarch, *Apophthegmata Philippi*, 15). Cf. :
Ἀγροικός εἰμι τὴν σκάφην σκάφην λέγων. (I am a countryman and call a tub a tub).
(Meineke, *Fragmenta Comic. Anon.*, 199 ; and
Τὰ σῦκα, σῦκα, τὴν σκάφην σκάφην λέγων. (Calling figs figs, and tubs tubs).
(ANONYMOUS, in Lucian, *Quomodo Historia sit conscribenda*, 41).

Σπεῦδε βραδέως. (Hasten slowly).

AUGUSTUS (63 B.C.-14 A.D.)— a common expression of his (Suetonius, *Twelve Caesars*, ii, 25). Usually quoted in its Latin form ' Festina lente.'

Σὺ γὰρ πρῶτος ἐν τῇ οἰκίᾳ σου ποίησον δημοκρατίαν. (Begin by establishing a democracy in your own household).

LYCURGUS (fl. c. 850 B.C.)—to one who proposed to establish a democracy in Sparta. (Plutarch, *Lives* : *Lycurgus*, xix).

Σὺ δὴ τολμᾷς, ἄνθρωπε, Γάϊον Μάριον ἀνελεῖν ; (Fellow, dost dare kill Caius Marius?).

CAIUS MARIUS (c. 153-86 B.C.) —to a soldier who entered his apartment in the dark, sword in hand, intending to assassinate him. The soldier, terrified, took to flight crying :
Οὐ δύναμαι Γάϊον Μάριον ἀποκτεῖναι. (I cannot kill Caius Marius) —Plutarch, *Lives* : *Marius*, xxxix.

Σὺ μὲν οὖν, εἰ μέγας εἶ στρατηγὸς, ἀνάγκασόν με διαγωνίσασθαι μὴ βουλόμενον. (Nay, if you are a great general, do you force me to fight against my will !)

CAIUS MARIUS (c. 153-86 B.C.) —to Publius Silo, leader of the Marsi, who taunted him by saying :
Εἰ μέγας εἶ, ὦ Μάριε, διαγώνισαι καταβάς (If you are a great general, Marius, come down and fight me). (Plutarch, *Lives* : *Marius*, xxxiii).

Σὺ νικᾶν οἶδας, νίκη δὲ χρῆσθαι οὐκ οἶδας. (You know how to gain a victory, but not how to use it).

HAMILCAR BARCAS, the Carthaginian (d. 229 B.C.)—to Hannibal. (Plutarch, *Lives* : *Fabius Maximus*, xvii). The saying is also attributed to Maharbal.

Συμβούλευε μὴ τὰ ἥδιστα, ἀλλὰ τὰ κάλλιστα. (Consider not what is most pleasant, but what is best).

SOLON, (B.C. 638-558)—(Diogenes Laertius, *Lives* : *Solon*, § 60).

Ταῦτα, ὦ Κεφάλων, ἐπίχειρα τῆς βασιλικῆς φιλίας. (These, Cephalon, are the wages of my friendship with the king).

ARATUS (c. 272-213 B.C.)—to one of his friends who noticed that he spat blood. His illness was

caused by drugs administered to him
by order of Philip of Macedon.
(Plutarch, *Lives*: *Aratus*, lii).

Τέκνον, ἢ τὰν ἢ ἐπὶ τᾶς (My son,
with it [your shield], or upon
it !)
SPARTAN MOTHER, to her son—
(Plutarch, *Apophthegmata Lacae-
narum*, 15).

Τὴν φιλαργυρίαν μητρόπολιν πάντων
τῶν κακῶν. (Love of money is
the fountain-head of all evils).

DIOGENES (B.C. 412-323)—(Diogenes Laertius *Lives*: *Diogenes*, §
50). Stobaeus attributes the saying
to Bion.

. . τὴν ψυχὴν ἐν ἀλλοτρίῳ σώματι
ζῆν (. . the soul of a lover in-
habits the body of his beloved).

CATO MAJOR (234-149 B.C.)—
(Plutarch, *Lives* : *Cato Major*, ix).

. . τῆς πίστεως μηδενὶ λογισμῷ χώραν
διδούσης. (. . a promise leaves
no room for deliberation).

SERTORIUS (*c.* 121-73 B.C.)—to
Cinna, referring to the latter's in-
vitation to Marius. (Plutarch, *Lives*:
Sertorius, v).

Τί γὰρ ἄλλο ἢ τοῖς νενικημένοις ὀδύνη :
(What should it mean but woe
to the conquered !)

BRENNUS, chief of the Gauls (fl.
c. 390 B.C.)—in reply to Sulpicius,
the Roman tribune, who asked the
meaning of the former taking off his
sword and belt and throwing them
into the scale in which the gold to
be paid by the Romans was being
weighed. (Plutarch, *Lives* : *Camillus*, xxviii). The Gauls tampered
with the scales, at which the
Romans became angry. Camillus,
arriving, took the gold from the
scales, and ordered the Gauls to

depart, saying that it was the
custom of the Romans to deliver
their country, not with gold, but
with iron. (Plutarch, *Ibid.*, xxix).
Cf. Vae Victis. (Woe to the conquered).—Livy, *Hist.* v, 48.

Τί λέγεις ; οὐδὲ ποτήριον ἔχεις οὐδὲ
ἱμάτιον ; (What ! haven't you
got a cup or a coat of mine ?)

PHILOTAS (fl. 4th cent. B.C.) son
of Parmenio—his purse-bearer having told him that he had no money,
a friend having come to borrow
some. (Plutarch, *Lives*: *Alexander*,
xlviii).

Τί οὖν εἴ σε Τιβέριος ἐκέλευσεν
ἐμπρῆσαι τὸ Καπετώλιον ; (What
then, if Tiberius had told you
to burn the Capitol ?)

PUBLIUS SCIPIO NASICA (fl. 2nd
cent. B.C.)—asked of Blossius of
Cumae, who admitted that he had
done everything at the bidding of
Tiberius. (Plutarch, *Lives*: *Tiberius
Gracchus*, xx). The question is,
however, attributed by Cicero
(*Laeluis*, c. 11) and by Valerius
Maximus (iv, c. 7) to Laelius.

Τὸ γὰρ ἄπραγμον οὐ σῴζεται μὴ
μετὰ τοῦ δραστηρίου τεταγμένον.
(Indolence is not secure unless
it be ranged beside activity, *i.e.*,
if indolent persons wish to come
out of the struggle safe, they
had better take sides with the
active).

PERICLES (494-406 B.C.)—Thucydides, *Histories*, ii, 63, 3).

Τὸ μὲν ἐμὸν ἀπ' ἐμοῦ γένος ἄρχεται,
τὸ δὲ σὸν ἐν σοὶ παύεται. (My
family begins with me, and
yours ends with you).

IPHICRATES (d. 380 B.C.)—to
Harmodius, the latter having reproached him with his humble
15

extraction (Plutarch, *Apophtheg-mata*: *Iphicrates*, 5)—Cf.

From yon blue heaven above us bent,
The gardener Adam and his wife
Smile at the claims of long descent.
Howe'er it be, it seems to me,
'Tis only noble to be good.
Kind hearts are more than coronets,
And simple faith than Norman blood.

Tennyson, *Lady Clara Vere de Vere*, ll. 50-6.

See C'est nous qui sommes des ancêtres;
La seule différence entre eux et moi &c.

Τὸ παρὸν εὖ ποιεῖν. (Do well the duty that lies before you).

PITTACUS (B.C. 652-569).—(Diogenes Laertius, *Lives*: *Pittacus*, § 77).

. . τὸ τοιοῦτον ἄριστον οὐ χωρεῖ προδοσίαν. (Treason and a dinner like this do not keep company together).

EPAMINONDAS (411-363 B.C.)— alluding to the absence of luxury at his own (Spartan) dinner-table. (Plutarch, *Lives*: *Lycurgus*, xiii).

Τὸν βίον οὕτω δεῖν μετρεῖν, ὡς καὶ πολὺ καὶ ὀλίγον χρόνον βιωσομένους. (We should so mete out our life as though we had both a short time and a long time to live).

BIAS (fl. *c*. 550 B.C.)—(Diogenes Laertius, *Lives*: *Bias*, § 87).

Τὸν ἥλιον ἀνατέλλοντα πλείονες ἢ δυόμενον προσκυνοῦσιν (. . more men worship the rising than the setting sun).

POMPEY (c. 106-48 B.C.)—referring to himself and Sulla. Sulla, when told of this, said Θριαμβευσάτω (Let him triumph!) (Plutarch, *Lives*: *Pompey*, xiv). Cf. .

"Men shut their doors against a setting sun."—Shakspere, *Timon of Athens*, act I, sc. 2.
    Let others hail the rising sun,
    I bow to that whose race is run.
David Garrick, *On the Death of Mr. Pelham*.

Τὸν κόρον ὑπὸ τοῦ πλούτου γεννᾶσθαι, τὴν δὲ ὕβριν ὑπὸ τοῦ κόρου. (Satiety is born of wealth, insolence of satiety).

SOLON (B.C. 638-558)—(Diogenes Laertius, *Lives*: *Solon*, § 59).

Τὸν λόγον εἴδωλον εἶναι τῶν ἔργων. (The word is the image of the deed).

SOLON (638-558 B.C.)—(Diogenes Laertius, *Lives*: *Solon*, § 58). Cf. : Λόγος ἔργου σκιή. (Speech is the shadow of action).

DEMOCRITUS (B.C. 460-357)— (Diogenes Laertius, *Lives*: *Democritus*, § 5).

Τὸν πλοῦτον νεῦρα πραγμάτων. (Riches are the sinews of business).

BION (fl. c. 250 B.C.)—(Diogenes Laertius, *Lives*: *Bion*, § 48). Cf. : Τὰ χρήματα νεῦρα τῶν πραγμάτων. (Money is the sinews of business).

CLEOMENES (d. 220 B.C.)—(Plutarch, *Lives*: *Cleomenes*, § 27).

Τὸν τεθνηκότα μὴ κακολογεῖν. (Speak no evil of the dead).

CHILO (d. B.C. 597.)—(Diogenes Laertius, *Lives*; *Chilo*, § 70). The above is the origin of the saying "De mortuis nil nisi bonum." Cf. :

Τὸν τελευτηκότα μὴ κακολόγει, ἀλλὰ μακάριζε. (Speak not evil of the dead, but call them blessed).

CHILO—(Stobaeus, *Florilegium*, *CXXV*., 15.)

Τὸν γὰρ οὐκ ὄντα ἅπας εἴωθεν ἐπαινεῖν. (All men are wont to praise him who is no more). Thucydides, *Histories*, *II*, 45, 1.

Τὸν φίλον δεῖν εὐεργετεῖν, ὅπως ἢ μᾶλλον φίλος, τὸν δὲ ἐχθρὸν, φίλον ποιεῖν. (We should do good to our friend to make him more friendly, and to our enemy to make him a friend).

CLEOBULUS (fl. c. 560 B.C.)—(Diogenes Laertius, *Lives*: *Cleobulus*, § 91). Cf. :

Ἀλλήλοις ὁμιλεῖν, ὡς τοὺς μὲν φίλους ἐχθροὺς μὴ ποιῆσαι · τοὺς δ' ἐχθροὺς, φίλους ἐργάσασθαι. (We ought so to behave to one another as to avoid making enemies of our friends, and at the same time to make friends of our enemies).

PYTHAGORAS (c. 582-c. 500 B.C.) —(Diogenes Laertius, *Lives*: *Pythagoras*, § 23).

Τοῦ πλουτεῖν τὸ πλουτίζειν εἶναι βασιλικώτερον. (It is more kingly to enrich others than to be wealthy one's self).

PTOLEMY LAGUS (c. 367-283 B.C.)—(Plutarch, *Apophthegmata* : *Ptolemy Lagus*, 1).

Τοὺς ἀγαθοὺς ἄνδρας θεῶν εἰκόνας εἶναι. (Good men are images of the gods).

DIOGENES (B.C. 412-323)—Diogenes Laertius, *Lives*: *Diogenes*, § 51).

Τοὺς μὲν ἄλλους ἀνθρώπους ζῆν, ἵν' ἐσθίοιεν · αὐτὸν δὲ ἐσθίειν, ἵνα ζῴη. (Other men live to eat, but I eat to live).

SOCRATES (B.C. 468-399)—(Diogenes Laertius, *Lives*: *Socrates*, § 34).

Another version :

Οἱ μὲν λοιποὶ ζῶσιν ἵν' ἐσθίωσιν, αὐτὸς δὲ ἐσθίω ἵνα ζῶ. (Other men live to eat, but I eat to live).

(Stobaeus, *Florilegium*, xvii, 22). Cf. :

".. et que, suivant le dire d'un ancien, il "faut manger pour vivre, et non pas vivre "pour manger" (".. and that, according to the saying of an ancient sage, one must eat to live, and not live to eat.")—Molière, *L'Avare*, act iii, sc. 5.

Τοὺς μὲν νέους μηδέποτε, τοὺς δὲ πρεσβυτέρους μηδεπώποτε. (Young men should never marry, old men never at all.)

DIOGENES (412-323 B.C.)—in reply to the question what he thought the best time to marry. Diogenes Laertius, *Lives*: *Diogenes*).

See Ὁ ἂν αὐτῶν ποιήσῃς, μεταγνώσῃ.

Τοὺς μὲν οἰκέτας δεσπόταις, τοὺς δὲ φαύλους ἐπιθυμίαις δουλεύειν. (Servants are ruled by their masters, weak men by their passions).

DIOGENES (B.C. 412-323)—(Diogenes Laertius, *Lives*: *Diogenes*, § 66).

Τοὺς μὲν παῖδας ἀστραγάλοις, τοὺς δὲ ἄνδρας ὅρκοις ἐξαπατᾶν. (. . cheat boys with dice, and men with oaths).

LYSANDER (d. 395 B.C.—recorded by Androclides, as an example of his great indifference to the obligations of an oath. (Plutarch, *Lives*: *Lysander*, viii; *Apophthegmata Laconica*: *Lysander*, 4). Also attributed to DIONYSIUS THE TYRANT (Plutarch, *De Fortuna Alexandri*, i, 9).

Τοὺς πρεσβυτέρους τιμᾶν δεῖν. (We should reverence our elders).

PYTHAGORAS (6th cent. B.C.)— Diogenes Laertius, *Lives*: *Pythagoras*, § 23).

.. τοὺς χρηστοὺς μὴ δεῖσθαι βοηθείας (.. good men do not need any intercessor).

PHOCION (*c.* 400 317 B.C.)—when reproached by his friends for having interceded in court for some worthless man who was being tried. (Plutarch, *Lives* : *Phocion*, x).

Τοῦτο μὲν ἀναγκαῖόν ἐστιν, ὦ Θεμιστόκλεις, καλὸν δὲ καὶ στρατηγικὸν ἀληθῶς ἢ περὶ τὰς χεῖρας ἐγκράτεια. (That, Themistocles, is very true ; but it is also the part of an honourable general to keep his hands clean).

ARISTIDES (d. 469 B.C.)—to Themistocles, the latter saying that he thought it the most valuable quality for a general to be able to divine beforehand what the enemy would do. (Plutarch, *Lives* : *Aristides*, 24).

Τοῦτο μὲν, ὦ φίλοι, τὸ ῥέον αἷμα καὶ οὐκ ἰχώρ, οἷός. πέρ τε ῥέει μακάρεσσι θεοῖσιν. (This, my friends, that flows from my wound is blood, and not ' Ichor that flows through the veins of the gods ').

ALEXANDER THE GREAT (356-323 B.C.)—when wounded by an arrow (Plutarch, *Lives* : *Alexander*, xxviii).

Τούτῳ νίκα. (By this conquer).— See In hoc signo vinces.

Ὑμεῖς ἐμοί, ὦ ἄνδρες ᾿Αθηναῖοι, συμβούλῳ μὲν κἂν μὴ θέλητε, χρήσεσθε συκοφάντῃ δὲ οὐδὲ ἂν θέλήτε. (Men of Athens, I shall always give you my advice, whether you wish it or not ; but I will not accuse men falsely even if you wish it.)

DEMOSTHENES (*c.* 382-322 B.C.) —when called upon to impeach someone, the Athenians becoming

riotous because he refused. (Plutarch, *Lives* : *Demosthenes*, xiv).

Ὑπόκρισις · ὑπόκρισις · ὑπόκρισις. (Delivery ! delivery ! delivery !)

ANDRONICUS (*c.* 284-*c.* 204 B.C.) —to Demosthenes, who asked him what were the three chief essentials of rhetoric. The passage in Plutarch runs :᾿ "Οθεν ἐρομένου αὐτὸν τί πρῶτον ἐν ῥητορικῇ, εἶπεν, Ὑπόκρισις· καὶ τί δεύτερον, Ὑπόκρισις · καὶ τί τρίτον, Ὑπόκρισις. (Accordingly when he [Demosthenes] asked him [Andronicus] what was the first thing in rhetoric, he said Delivery ; and the second, Delivery ; and the third, Delivery)—*Lives of the Ten Orators* : *Demosthenes*, 345. Cf. Boswell's *Life of Johnson* [1824 ed. vol. ii, p. 195], 1773.

Φιλήκοον εἶναι, μᾶλλον ἢ φιλόλαλον. (Be fond of listening, rather than fond of chattering).

CLEOBULUS (fl. *c.* 560 B.C.)— (Diogenes Laertius *Lives* : *Cleobulus*, § 92). Cf. :
.. be check'd for silence, But never tax'd for speech.— Shakspere. *All's Well that Ends Well*, act I, sc. I, ll. 76-7 (Count of Rousillon). Cf. :

Χρὴ σιγᾶν ἢ κρείσσονα σιγῆς λέγειν. (Keep silence or let thy words be worth more than silence).

PYTHAGORAS—(Stobaeus, *Florilegium XXXIV.*, 7).

Ἢ σιγὴν καίριον ἢ λόγον ὠφέλιμον ἔχε. (Keep timely silence, or say something profitable).

PYTHAGORAS—(*Id., Ibid.*, xxxiv, 8).

Φίλους μὴ ταχὺ κτῶ · οὓς δ' ἂν κτήσῃ, μὴ ἀποδοκίμαζε. (Do not make friends quickly, but do not cast them off when made).

SOLON (B.C. 638-558)—(Diogenes Laertius, *Lives*: *Solon*, § 60).

Φίλων παρόντων καὶ ἀπόντων μεμνῆσθαι. (Bear in mind your friends, whether present or absent).

THALES (B.C. 636-546)—(Diogenes Laertius, *Lives*: *Thales* § 37).

Φοβερώτερόν ἐστιν ἐλάφων στρατόπεδον ἡγουμένου λέοντος ἢ λεόντων ἐλάφου. (An army of stags led by a lion is more to be feared than an army of lions led by a stag).

CHABRIAS (d. 358 B.C.)—(Plutarch, *Apophthegmata*: *Chabrias*, 3). Also attributed by Stobaeus (*Florilegium*, LIV, 61) to PHILIP OF MACEDON (383-336 B.C.)

. . χαλεπὸν ἐλεεῖν ἅμα καὶ φρονεῖν. (. . it is hard to have pity and be wise).

AGESILAUS (438-361 B.C.)—when leaving a sick friend behind in spite of his entreaties, the camp being suddenly broken up (Plutarch, *Lives*: *Agesilaus*, xiii).

Χαλεπὸν ἐσθλὸν ἔμμεναι. (It is difficult to be good).

PITTACUS (B.C. 652-569)— Diogenes Laertius, *Lives*: *Pittacus*, § 76).

Χαλεπὸν μὲν ἐστιν, ὦ πολῖται, πρὸς γαστέρα λέγειν ὦτα οὐκ ἔχουσαν. (It is a difficult task, fellow-citizens, to make the stomach hear reason, seeing that it has no ears).

CATO MAJOR (234-149 B.C.)— beginning of a discourse to the Roman people, dissuading them from an unreasonable clamour for largesses and distributions of corn, (Plutarch, *Lives*: *Cato Major*, 8).

Cf.: The belly hath no ears.—English Proverb.
Ventre affamé n'a point d'oreilles.— French Proverb.

. . χρῶ δεξάμενος ἦν ὁ θεὸς δίδωσιν (. . take the gift the gods provide you).

THEOCRITUS, the prophet (*c.* 290-*c.* 210 B.C.)—to Pelopidas, alluding to a filly escaped from some horses at pasture, and which was used as a sacrifice (Plutarch, *Lives*: *Pelopidas*, 22). See Οὔ τοι ἀπόβλητ᾽ ἐστὶ θεῶν ἐρικυδέα δῶρα.

Ὢ Ἀθηναῖοι, ἆρα γε πιστεύσετε ἂν ἡλίκους ὑπομένω κινδύνους ἕνεκα τῆς παρ᾽ ὑμῖν εὐδοξίας; (Do you believe, Athenians, how great are the dangers I face to win a good name at Athens?)

ALEXANDER THE GREAT (356-323 B.C.)—after crossing the Hydaspes, the passage of which was disputed by Porus. (Plutarch, *Lives*: *Alexander*, lx).

Carlyle (in his essay on Voltaire), alluding to Voltaire, says, "At all "hours of his history, he might "have said with Alexander: 'O "Athenians, what toil do I undergo "to please you!' and the last "pleasure his Athenians demand of "him is, that he would die for "them." (Critical and Miscellaneous Essays 1888 ed., vol. 2, p. 155).

Ὢ γύναι, Ἀθηναῖοι μὲν ἄρχουσι τῶν Ἑλλήνων, ἐγὼ δὲ Ἀθηναίων, ἐμοῦ δὲ σύ, σοῦ δὲ ὁ υἱός, ὥστε φειδέσθω τῆς ἐξουσίας, δι᾽ ἥν, ἀνόητος ὢν πλεῖστον Ἑλλήνων δύναται. (Woman, the Athenians govern the Greeks, I govern the Athenians, you govern me, and your son governs you: so let him not abuse his power, which, simple as he is, enables him to do more than all the Greeks put together).

THEMISTOCLES (*c*. 533-*c*. 465 B.C.)—to his wife, in reference to his son, who used to take advantage of his mother's weakness. (Plutarch, *Lives*: *Cato Major*,8). A saying of Cato Major's, (234-149 B.C.) when discoursing of the power of women was πάντες ἄνθρωποι τῶν γυναικῶν ἄρχουσιν, ἡμεῖς δὲ πάντων ἀνθρώπων, ἡμῶν δὲ αἱ γυναῖκες (all men rule their wives ; we rule all men ; and we are ruled by our wives)—*ibid.*, 8. Cf. :

Les Français gouvernent le monde, et les femmes gouvernent les Français. (The French govern the world, and women govern the French).

Ὦ Ἡράκλεις, ὡς πολλοὺς ὁρῶ στρατηγούς, ὀλίγους δὲ στρατιώτας. (By Hercules, how many generals I see—and how few soldiers !)

PHOCION (c. 400-317 B.C.)—alluding to those who pestered him with advice as to what he should do, Mikion having landed at Rhamnus with a large force of Macedonians and mercenaries. (Plutarch, *Lives*: *Phocion*, xxv). Cf. : Who can direct when all pretend to know?—Goldsmith, *The Traveller*, l. 64.

Ὦ καλῆς ἡμέρας. (Oh happy day !)

ANTIGONUS (d. 239 B.C.)—words shouted after a victory, when he vomited a quantity of blood, fell sick of a fever, and died. (Plutarch, *Lives*: *Cleomenes*, xxx).

Ὦ Κάτων, φθονῶ σοι τοῦ θανάτου καὶ γὰρ ἐμοὶ σὺ τῆς σαυτοῦ σωτηρίας ἐφθόνησας. (Cato, I grudge thee thy death, for thou hast grudged me thy safety).

JULIUS CAESAR (100-44 B.C.)—referring to Cato (95-46 B.C.) Plutarch, *Lives*: *Cato*, xxii).

Ὦ Κρίτων, τῷ Ἀσκληπιῷ ὀφείλομεν ἀλεκτρυόνα. (Crito, I owe a cock to Æsculapius : will you remember to pay the debt ?)

SOCRATES (468-399 B.C.)—Last words (Plato, *Dialogues* : *Phædo*, 118 A).

Ὦ Λιγάριε, ἐν οἵῳ καιρῷ νοσεῖς. What an unseasonable time you have found for your illness, Ligarius).

BRUTUS (86-42 B.C.)—to Caius Ligarius, when the conspiracy was being formed against Caesar. Ligarius replied :

Ἀλλ᾽ εἴ τι, ὦ Βροῦτε, σεαυτοῦ φρονεῖς ἄξιον, ὑγιαίνω. (Yes ; but if you, Brutus, contemplate anything worthy of yourself, I am well.) (Plutarch, *Lives*: *Marcus Brutus*, xi).

"I am not sick, if Brutus have in hand any exploit worthy the name of honour."—Shakspere, *Julius Caesar* act ii, sc. 2 Ligarius.

Ὦ μακάριε Ξενόκρατης, θῦε ταῖς Χάρισιν. (Happy Xenocrates, sacrifice to the Graces !)

PLATO (B.C. 428-347)—constantly said to Xenocrates, who was always very solemn and grave (Diogenes Laertius, *Lives*: *Xenocrates*, § 7 ; also Plutarch, *Lives* : *Marius*, ii). Cf. Sacrifice to the Graces (Lord Chesterfield, *Letters* : *9th March* 1748).

"Nay, then, we must sacrifice to the Muses ourselves," said Elizabeth—Sir W. Scott, *Kenilworth*, ch. xvii.

Ὦ μῆτερ, τήμερον ἢ ἀρχιερέα τὸν υἱὸν ἢ φυγάδα ὄψει. (Mother, you shall to-day see your son either Pontifex Maximus or an exile).

JULIUS CAESAR (100-44 B.C.)—on the day of his election. (Plutarch, *Lives*: *Caesar*, vii). See Aut Caesar, aut nihil.

GREEK SAYINGS

Ὦ ξένε, οὐκ ἐν δέοντι χρῆ τῷ δέοντι.
(You speak, my good sir, of what is much to the purpose—elsewhere).
KING LEONIDAS (fl. *c.* 492-480 B.C.)—rebuking one who was discoursing about a matter which was itself opportune though the occasion and place were inopportune (Plutarch, *Lives* : *Lycurgus*, xx).

Ὦ παῖ, ζήτει σεαυτῷ βασιλείαν ἴσην, Μακεδονία γάρ σε οὐ χωρεῖ.
(My son, seek out a kingdom worthy of thyself, for Macedonia will not hold thee).
PHILIP OF MACEDON (382-336 B.C.)—to Alexander the Great, after the latter had successfully ridden the horse Bucephalus. (Plutarch, *Lives* : *Philip*, vi).

Ὦ παῖδες, πάντα προλήψετα ιὸ πατήρ· ἐμοὶ δὲ οὐδὲν ἀπολείψει μεθ᾽ ὑμῶν ἔργον ἀποδείξασθαι μέγα καὶ λαμπρόν.
(My father will forestall us, boys, in everything: he will leave no great and glorious exploit for me to achieve with you).
ALEXANDER THE GREAT (356-323 B.C.)—as a lad, whenever he heard of his father's victories. (Plutarch, *Lives* : *Alexander* v).

Ὦ Περίκλεις, καὶ οἱ τοῦ λύχνου χρείαν ἔχοντες ἔλαιον ἐπιχέουσιν.
(Pericles, even those who have occasion for a lamp supply it with oil).
ANAXAGORAS (499-427 B.C.)—when Pericles besought him to live. Anaxagoras was in want and had determined to starve himself to death. (Plutarch, *Lives* : *Pericles*, xvi).

Ὦ Σόλων, τοῖς βασιλεῦσι δεῖ ὡς ἥκιστα ἢ ὡς ἥδιστα ὁμιλεῖν. . . Μὰ Δί᾽ ἀλλ᾽ ὡς ἥκιστα ἢ ὡς ἄριστα. (Solon, one ought to say either very little to kings

or else say what they wish most to hear. . . Nay, rather, one should say either very little or what it is best for them to hear.)
ÆSOP (fl. 570 B.C.)—to Solon, when vexed at Crœsus' ungracious reception of the latter ; with Solon's reply. (Plutarch, *Lives* : *Solon*, xxviii).

Ὦ τύχη, μικρόν τί μοι κακὸν ἀντὶ τῶν τοσούτων καὶ τηλικούτων ἀγαθῶν ποίησον. (O ! fortune, for so many and such great benefits, send me some small evil !)
PHILIP OF MACEDON (382-336 B.C.)—on receiving news that a son had been born to him, a great victory gained by his general, Parmenion, and that he had been crowned at the Olympian games. (Plutarch, *Apophthegmata* : *Philip*, 3). See πότε ἄρα παυσόμεθα νικῶντες ; Æmilius (c. 229-160 B.C.)—addressing the people after burying his second child, referred to the fickleness of Fortune in similar terms, " knowing that she never bestows any great kindness unalloyed and without exacting retribution for it."

. . . ὠδίνειν ὄρος, εἶτα μῦν ἀποτεκεῖν (. . . the mountain was in labour, and lo ! it brought forth a mouse).
AGESILAUS (438-360 B.C.)—(Plutarch, *Lives* : *Agesilaus*, xxxvi). Cf.
" Quid dignum tanto feret hic promissor hiatu ? Parturiunt montes, nascetur ridiculus mus."
(What's coming, pray, that thus he winds his horn ? The mountain labours, and a mouse is born.—*Conington*).
—HORACE. *De Arte Poetica*, 138.
" The mountain has brought forth a mouse."—English saying.

ITALIAN SAYINGS.

Ah! che se gli è un Dio, ben tosto lo paghèra ; ma veramente se non e'è Dio, è galant' huomo. (If there is a God, he will be well punished ; but, really, if there is no God, he is a clever man.)

Attributed to POPE URBAN VIII (1568-1644), referring to Cardinal Richelieu (1585-1642). See Si le cardinal est en paradis &c.

Anch' io sono pittore! (I, too, am a painter.)

Attributed to CORREGGIO (1494-1534), standing before Raphael's picture of St. Cecilia at Bologna, but its authenticity is doubtful. Another version is "Son pittore anch' io." (I am a painter also.)— P. Luigi Pungileoni, *Memorie istoriche di Antonio Allegri detto il Correggio* (Parma, 1817, vol. 1, p. 60.)

Ancora imparo! (I am still learning!)

INSCRIPTION accompanying a favourite device of MICHAEL ANGELO (1474-1563) of an old man in a go-cart, with an hourglass upon it.

Chiesa libera in libero Stato. See Libera Chiesa in libero Stato.

Ci siamo e ci resteremo. (Here we are, and here we will remain.)

VICTOR EMMANUEL II (1820-78), when receiving a deputation at the Quirinal Palace after entering Rome (June 2, 1871), is said to have uttered the following words : "A Roma ci siamo e ci resteremo" (We are at Rome, and there we will remain.) See J'y suis, j'y reste.

Economie sino all' osso. (Economies right down to the bone, *i.e.*, thorough retrenchment.)

QUINTINO SELLA, in a speech to the Chamber of Deputies, Dec. 15, 1869.

Eppur si muove! (Nevertheless it moves !)

Attributed to GALILEO GALILEI (1564-1642), after his recantation of his *Dialogue* on Sun-spots and the sun's rotation, before the Inquisition in 1632 ; but authenticity doubtful (see J. J. Fahie, *Galileo : his life and work*, 1903.)

ITALIAN SAYINGS 233

Fango che sale. (Dregs which rise to the top.)

GUISEPPE COLOMBO, Minister of Finance, at a conference at Milan, Nov. 7, 1889, referring to the administrative elections. "La "popolazione bassa approfitta di "questa inerzia, e il fango sale, "sale e sale." (The lower orders of the population take advantage of this indulgence, and the dregs rise, rise, and keep rising.) Cf. :

Sopra il fango che sale or non mi resta
    Che gittare il mio sdegno in vane carte
E dal palco mortale un dì la testa
(Over the dregs that rise, there but remains to me to fling my scorn in empty words, and one day raise the scaffold's frame above them.)—Carducci, *Rime nuove*, pt. 2, sonnet xxxiii, last lines.

Fuori i barbari! (Away with the barbarians!)

Attributed to POPE JULIUS II, otherwise Giuliano della Rovare (1441-1513), who held the Apostolic See from 1503 to 1513 ; referring to the Spanish army and all foreigners. According to Guiccardini (*Istoria d' Italia*, bk. ii) the Pope was continually hoping that "Italia rimanesse libera dai Barbari." (Italy should remain free from the barbarians.)

Godiamoci il papato, poichè Dio ce l'ha dato. (Let us enjoy the papal office, since God has given it to us.)

POPE LEO X (1475-1521) was in the habit of using this phrase to his brother Giuliano.

Governo negazione di Dio. (The negation of God erected into a system of government.)

PROVERBIAL PHRASE, said to be derived from the first of two letters to the Earl of Aberdeen on the state prosecutions of the Neapolitan Government (under date April 7, 1851) from the Rt. Hon. W. E. Gladstone (1809-98.) " I have

" seen and heard the strong and " too true expression used, This is " the negation of God erected into " a system of Government."

Il nostro è secolo di transizione e, quel che è peggio, di transazione. (Our century is one of transition, and what is worse, of [compromising] transactions.)

Saying of GIOVAN BATTISTA NICCOLINI (1765-1861), recorded by Vanucci in his *Ricordi della vita e delle opere di G. B. Niccolini*, vol. i, p. 382.

In Italia il potere non ha arricchito nessuno. (In Italy power has brought riches to none.)

Written by G. B. GIORGINI, on a draft bill for a pension to Luigi Carlo Farini (1822-66) brought before the Chamber of Deputies, April 16, 1863. " . . in Italia le " vicendep olitiche sono state per " molti una causa di rovina : il " potere non ha arricchito nessuno." (In Italy the vicissitudes of politics have been a cause of ruin to many ; power has enriched no one.) *Atti Parlam. Legisl.* VIII, *Sessione 1861-3, Camera dei Deputati*, p. 4622.

Io non credo alla geografia. (I do not believe in geography).

Attributed to PRINCE ONORATO CAETANI DI TEANO, better known as the Duke of Sermoneta, during his presidency of the Società Geografica Italiana. In allusion to the Duke Michelangelo, who, when a troublesome man was pressing upon him in an indiscreet manner a very expensive geographical work, replied : " Mi dispiace proprio tanto, ma io non credo alla geografia." (Indeed I am exceedingly sorry, but I have no faith in geography).

La monarchia ci unisce, la
repubblica ci dividerebbe.
(Monarchy unites us, the republic would divide us).

FRANCESCO CRISPI (1819-1901),
in the Italian Parliament, May 1,
1864.

L' aritmetica non è un' opinione
(Arithmetic is not an opinion).

Attributed to the Deputy BER-
NARDINO GRIMALDI, in a speech
in parliament, Nov. 27, 1879. The
phrase occurred in the course of a
personal explanation, after resigning
the post of minister of finance. "La
"seconda dichiarazione che tengo a
"fare è questa, che per me tutte
"le opinioni sono rispettabili, ma
"ministro o deputato ritengo che
"l' aritmetica non sia un' opinione."
(The second declaration that I wish
to make is this, that all opinions
are respectable, in my view, but,
whether minister or deputy, I maintain that arithmetic is not an
opinion.) *Atti Parlam., Discussioni
della Cam. dei Dep., Sess.* 1878-9,
(vol. x, col. 8707). But it really
originated with Filippo Mariotti in
a speech at Serrasanquirico. (Cf.
D. Gaspari *Memorie storiche*, 1883,
p. 259).

Lente dell 'avaro.   (The miser's
[dish of] lentils).

GIOVANNI LANZA, in a speech to
the Chamber of Deputies, Dec. 15,
1869. Quoted by Antonio Star-
rabba Di Rudini, (1839-   )in a
speech at Milan, Nov. 9, 1891.

Libera Chiesa in libero Stato·
(A free Church in a free State).

CAMILLE BENSO, Conte di Ca-
vour (1810-61)—his dying words.
Massari, *Il Conte di Cavour, Ricordi
biografici* (2nd edit., 1875, p. 434).
"Frate, frate, libera Chiesa in libero
Stato." (Brother, brother, &c.).

He had often repeated the phrase,
and notably in parliament, Mar. 27,
1861, on the occasion of a discussion
on the whole question of Rome.

Libero io nacqui, e vissi, e morrò
sciolto.   (Free I was born,
have lived, and will die also).
Words on a medal struck at Rome
by QUEEN CHRISTINA, of Sweden
(1626-89).

L'Italia è fatta, ma chi farà ora
gl' Italiani?   (Italy is made,
but who will now make the
Italians?)

MASSIMO D'AZEGLIO (1798-1866),
at the first meeting of the Italian
Parliament at Turin, in 1860.

L' Italia farà da sè.   (Italy will
make its own way).

CARLO ALBERTO (1798-1849), in
his proclamation to the people, Mar.
23, 1848.

Nè elettori nè eletti.   (Neither
electors nor elected).

Saying used on the occasion of
the abstention of the Catholics from
voting at the election of Giacomo
Margotti, director of the *Unità
Cattolica* of Turin, in 1860. He
replied in his paper by using the
phrase "Nè apostati nè ribelli"
(Neither apostates nor rebels).

Obbedisco.   (I obey).

GIUSEPPE GARIBALDI (1807-82),
writing from Bezzecca, Aug. 9,
1866, replied to an order received
from general La Marmora to retreat
(upsetting his plans when on the
point of success) as follows: "Ho
"ricevuto dispaccio 1072. Obbe-
"disco. Garibaldi." (I have received your despatch, no. 1072. I
obey).

Per Dio, l'Italia sarà!   (By God,
Italy shall be!).

VICTOR EMMANUEL II (1820-78) is reported to have said these words, pointing with his sword to the Austrian camp, soon after the defeat of Novara, March 23, 1849.

Piace a me e basta. (It pleases me and that is enough).

AGOSTINO DEPRETIS (1831-88), in parliament, when replying to the honourable Bosdari, to defend his own measures.

Più santi che uomini da bene. (More holy than good men themselves).

FLORENTINE SAYING—applied to hypocrites who affect outward holiness of life, but are in their hearts worse than other men. Dati, *Lepidezze* (Firenze, 1829, p. 41). Cf.

"Malus ubi bonum se simulat, tune est pessimus. Publilius Syrus, *Sententiæ*, 284. ("An ill man is always ll ; but he is worsti of all when he pretends to be a saint"— Bacon.)

Re galantuomo. (King Honestman).

Surname given to VICTOR EMMANUEL II (1820-78) by the people (*La vita e il regno di Vittorio Emanuele*, vol. 1, p. 160.)

Rispondo che non rispondo. (I reply that I do not reply.)

GIOV. FILIPPO GALVAGNO, Minister of Agriculture (afterwards Minister of the Interior)`, in Parliament.

Roma o morte. (Rome or death.)

BATTLE-CRY used in the unfortunate expedition of Aspromonte ; also, some years later, in the equally unfortunate one of Mentana. The order of the day drawn up by Guiseppe Civinini, Garibaldi's secretary, on Aug. 1, 1862, and read by the general, began as follows : "Italia e Vittorio Emanuele, Roma o Morte"

(Italy and Victor Emmanuel, Rome or death).

Se non è vero è ben trovato. (If it isn't true, it is well discovered.)

Attributed to the CARDINAL D'ESTE (1479-1520), referring to Ariosto's *Orlando Furioso.* Cf. :

Se non è vero è molto ben trovato. (If it isn't true, it is marvellously well discovered.)—Bruno, *Gli Eroici Furori*, pt. ii, dialogue 3.

Cf. " Fatti pure in là, non mi toc-"car con essa ; se non è vero, egli è "stato un bel trovato." (Go on ahead; don't trouble me with that matter ; if it is not true, it was right well discovered.) Cf. A. F. Doni, *Marmi* (1863 ed., p. 76.) (The work was first pub. 1552, but probably the phrase was then already proverbial.)

Se son piene le carceri, son vuote le sepolture. {If the prisons are full, the graves are empty.)

CARDINAL LUIGI LAMBRUSCHINI, Secretary of State under Gregory XVI (1765-1846), to someone who one day said to him that the prisons were not capable of accommodating any more political prisoners.

Tu sei piu rondo che l'O di Giotto. (Thou art rounder than Giotto's O.)

PROVERBIAL SAYING, alluding to a circle drawn with a pencil by G. di Bondone Giotto (1276-1336) as a specimen of his work to be submitted to pope Benedict XI about 1304. Another account says that the circle was drawn for Pope Boniface VIII, his predecessor. Cf. Carlyle's essay on *Mirabeau.*

Videre Napoli et Mori. (See Naples and Mori).

Mori is a little village near Naples. Said to be the origin of the expression. " See Naples and die." (a *jeu de mots*).

Viva Verdi! (Long live Verdi!)
Cry of the ITALIAN PATRIOTS
(1859), really referring to V(ictor-
E(mmanuel) R(e) D'I(talie) (1820-
78), under cover of the name of the
composer (Guiseppe) Verdi.

Zone grigie. (Gray Zones).
FRANCESCO CRISPI (1819-1901),
in a conversation with M. Saint-Cère,
editor of the Paris *Figaro* in 1890 ;
it was published in that journal, on
the 29th of September in the same
year. "La question des nation-
"alités se meurt. Il n'y a puls de
"divisions marquées, tranchées ; il
"y a sur toutes les frontières de tous
"les pays des *zones grises* où les
nationalités se mêlent." (The
question of nationalities is dying.
There are no longer any distinct,
defined divisions, there are on the
frontiers of all countries gray zones
where the nationalities mix).

LATIN SAYINGS.

Abiit, excessit, evasit, erupit. (He is gone, he has fled, he has escaped, he has burst through us).

CICERO (106-43 B.C.) at the beginning of his second oration against Catiline, referring to Catiline's flight. (Cicero, *In Catilinam II*, i, 1).

Acta est fabula. (The play is over).

DEMONAX (2nd cent. A.D.), Greek philosopher and contemporary of Hadrian and Marcus Aurelius, who lived 100 years and allowed himself to die of hunger.—Last words (in their Latin form): but see λήγει μὲν ἀγὼν τῶν καλλίστων. The phrase "Acta est fabula" was used in ancient times to inform the people that they might go home, the spectacle being ended. Augustus, (63 B.C.-14 A.D.) on his death-bed, asked his friends around him whether they thought he had played his part in life well, and quoted the following two lines from a Greek poet:

Εἰ δὲ πᾶν ἔχει καλῶς, τῷ παιγνίῳ
Δότε κρότον, καὶ πάντες ὑμεῖς μετὰ
χαρᾶς κτυπήσατε

(In loud applause to the actor's praise
If all be right, with joy your voices raise).
—Suetonius, *Twelve Caesars*, 99. See
Tirez le rideau &c.

. . **ad Kalendas Graecas.** (. . at the Greek Calends).

AUGUSTUS (63 B.C.-14 A.D.)—a common expression of his in connection with debts owing to him, which he expected would never be paid, seeing that there were no calends in the Greek months. (Suetonius, *Twelve Caesars* : *Augustus*, 87.) Cf.

"Ad Graecas, bone rex, fient mandata Kalendas." (Your commands, noble king, shall be obeyed at the Greek Kalends),

QUEEN ELIZABETH (1533-1603) — message sent to Philip II of Spain, through his envoys.

Ad usum Delphini. (For the use of the Dauphin).

Motto applied to the editions of Latin authors executed by order of LOUIS XIV (1638-1715) for his son, the Dauphin.

Alea jacta est.—See Jacta alea esto.

Amicus Plato, sed magis amica veritas. (Plato is dear to me, but dearer still is truth).

ARISTOTLE (384-322 B.C.)—referring to Plato (428-347 B.C.), from whose opinions he sometimes differed. (Ammonius, *Life of Aristotle :* the Greek original is not preserved). The saying of Aristotle is a paraphrase of Socrates' words to Simmias and Cebes (Plato, *Dialogues : Phaedo*, xci).

238

LATIN SAYINGS

**An nescis, mi fili, quantilla pru-
dentia mundus regatur?**
(Dost thou not know, my son,
with how little wisdom the
world is governed?)

AXEL, COUNT OXENSTIERN
(1583-1654) Swedish chancellor—
when his son hesitated to represent
Sweden at the Peace Congress of
Westphalia at the end of the Thirty
Years War, in 1648, alleging his
ignorance and inexperience. The
correct version is:

An nescis, mi fili, quantilla prudentia
regitur orbis?—Woodhead, *Memoirs of
Queen Christina*, vol. 1, p. 225. Cf.
also Lundblad, *Svensk Plutark*, ii,
(Stockholm, 1826, p. 95). Ap-
parently written by the chancellor
in a letter to his son in 1641, but
the expression had previously appeared in print (in German):
Florilegium Christopheri Lehman,
Frankfort, 1640: " Die Welt wird
mit wenig Witz regiert." (The
world is ruled with little wisdom).
The words are attributed to POPE
JULIUS III (1487-1555) by Pedro
Jos. Suppico de Moraes, *Colecçion
Politica de Apophthegmes Memorav.*,
Lisbon, 1733, t. II, vol. ii, p. 44.
Lord Chesterfield is also said to
have used (or quoted) the phrase
to his son, after a Ministerial
dinner:
"Behold with what little wisdom the
"world is governed." Cf. ". . . for
thou little thinkest what a little foolery
governs the whole world."—(John Selden,
Table Talk: Pope).

Aut Cæsar, aut nihil. (Either
Cæsar, or nothing).

CÆSAR BORGIA (c. 1457-1507)—
his motto. See Ὦ μῆτερ, τήμερον ἢ
ἀρχιέρεια &c. Cf. " Either a man
or a mouse" (Proverb).

**Ave, Imperator, morituri te salu-
tamus!** (Hail, Cæsar! we
who are about to die salute
you).

Formula used by the ROMAN
GLADIATORS, when defiling past the

imperial box in the circus before
fighting. Cf. Suetonius, *Twelve
Cæsars: Claudius*, 21. Often quoted
" Ave, Cæsar, etc."

Bis dat qui cito dat. (He gives
twice who gives quickly).

FRANCIS BACON (1561-1626)
Lord Verulam—in his speech, May
7, 1617, on taking his seat as Lord
Keeper. Cf.
Bis dat qui dat celeriter. (He gives
twice who gives quickly)(PUBLILIUS SYRUS,
Sententiae, 225); and Ὡς μέγα τὸ μικρόν
ἐστιν ἐν καιρῷ δοθεν. (How great the
small gift is when given in season)—
MENANDER, *Monosticha*, 752.

**Cæsarem se non regem esse [re-
spondit].** (I am no king, but
Cæsar).

CAIUS JULIUS CÆSAR (100-44
B.C.)—on declining the title of king
(Suetonius, *Twelve Cæsars*, 79).

Castigat ridendo mores. (He
corrects morals by ridicule).

JEAN SANTEUL (1630-97)—
Motto given to the harlequin
Joseph Biancolelli, called Domini-
que (1640-88).

Cave ne cadas! (Beware lest you
fall!)

In ancient Rome it was the
custom, when honouring a victorious general, to place behind the
chariot in which he rode to the
Capitol a slave who repeated the
above words amid the shouts of the
people. See Hominem memento
te.

Civis sum romanus. (I am a
Roman citizen).

Said by the Romans under certain
circumstances, when wishing to
recall the privileges attaching to the
title. Lord Palmerston (1784-1865)
used the phrase as "Civis Romanus
sum" in the House of Commons,
June 25, 1850:

. . and whether, as the Roman in days
of old held himself free from indignity,
when he could say *Civis Romanus sum*,
so also a British subject, in whatever land

he may be, shall feel confident that the watchful eye and the strong arm of England will protect him against injustice and wrong (Sir W. Reid, *Life of W. E. Gladstone*, 1899, p. 357).

Consule tibi! (Look to thyself!)

St. Augustine (354-430)—in his first sermon, *In natali Cypriani martyris*, in which he recounts the first dialogue between St. Cyprian and the pro-consul before whom the bishop of Carthage appeared :

Cum enim ejus immobilem mentem videret, quando ei dixit : ' Jusserunt te principes cæremoniari,' responditque ille : ' Non facio, adjecit et ait : Consule tibi !' (When he saw that his mind was not to be shaken, after he had said to him ' Your rulers have given orders that you shou d worship,' he replied, ' I will not do it,' and added ' Look to thyself !'

Cui adhæreo præest. (He whom I favour wins).

Motto on the tent of Henri VIII. (1491-1547) at the Field of the Cloth of Gold, June 1520.

Cum dignitate otium. (Ease with dignity).

Cicero (106-43 B.C.)—alluding to literature practised by statesmen retired from affairs of state (Cicero, *Pro Sestio*, xlv., 98). The phrase occurs also in *Ad Familiares* i, 9, 21, and in *De Oratore*, i, 1, 1. Cf.

Quid est enim dulcius otio literato? (What is more delightful than lettered ease?)—Cicero, *Tusculanæ Disputationes* ; *V.*, 36, 105. The phrase is usually quoted as ' Otium cum dignitate.'

Decet imperatorem stantem mori. —See Imperatorem stantem mori oportere.

Delendam esse Carthaginem. (Carthage must be blotted out).

Cato Major (234-149 B.C.): he is said to have often added these words to his speeches when giving his opinion on any subject whatever. On the other hand, Publius Scipio, called Nasica (fl. 2nd cent. B.C.), used to end all his speeches by saying : " And I further am of opinion that Carthage should be left alone."

(Florus, *Epitome Rerum Romanarum*, ii, 15, § 4 ; Plutarch, *Lives : Cato Major*, 27).

De mortuis nil nisi bonum—See Τὸν τεθνηκότα μὴ κακολογεῖν.

Deo erexit Voltaire. (Voltaire erected it to God).

Voltaire (1694-1778 — inscription placed over a church he had built at Ferney ; altered from *Deo soli* (To God alone), a common dedication. Cf.

Nor his, who for the bane of thousands born,
Built God a Church, and laugh'd his word to scorn.—Cowper, *Retirement*, ll. 687-8.

(Evidently an allusion to the church at Ferney, erected by Voltaire.)

Desponsamus te, mare, in signum veri perpetuique dominii. (We wed thee, O sea, in sign of a true and perpetual dominion).

Formula in use by the Venetian Doges at the annual ceremony of ' wedding' the Adriatic.

Diem perdidi! (I've lost a day !)

The Emperor Titus (40-81)— on recalling the fact that he had not benefited anyone that day (Suetonius, *Twelve Cæsars : Titus*, 8). Cf.

" I've lost a day," the prince who nobly cried
Had been an emperor without his crown ;
Of Rome? say, rather, lord of human race :
He spoke, as if deputed by mankind.—
Young, *Night Thoughts*, ii, 99 ;
" Count that day lost whose low descending sun
Views from thy hand no worthy action done."—
Stamford, *Art of Reading*, 1803, 3rd. edit. p. 27 ;
" Good Titus could, but Charles could never say,
Of all his royal life, he ' lost a day.' "—
Duke, *Poem on the Death of Charles II ;*
" This world, 'tis true,
Was made for Cæsar, but for Titus, too ;
And which more blest? Who chain'd his country? say,
Or he whose virtue sigh'd to lose a day ?"—
Pope, *Essay on Man*, Ep. iv, st. 1 ;

" Tel fut cet empereur sous qui Rome
　　adorée
Vit renaître les jours de Saturne et de
　　Rhée ;
Qui rendit de son joug l'univers amoureux ;
Qu'on n'alla jamais voir sans revenir
　　heureux ;
Qui soupirait le soir, si sa main fortunée
N'avait par ses bienfaits signalé la journée "
(Such was this emperor under whom adored
　　Rome—
Saw renewed the days of Saturn and of
　　Rhea ;
Who released the amorous universe from
　　its yoke ;
Who was never visited without a happy
　　return ;
Who sighed at evening, if his favored hand
Had not by his benefits crowned the day.)
Boileau, *Épître Ière. (au Roi)*, l. 109;
" La plus perdue de toutes les journées est
celle où l'on n'a pas ri." (The most wasted
of all days is the one when we have not
laughed)—Chamfort, *Maximes et Pensées*,
ch. I. (ed. 1824, vol. i, p. 355). See Den
gestrigen Tag suchen.

**Domine ! Domine ! fac finem !
　fac finem !** (Lord ! Lord !
make an end ! make an end !)
DESIDERIUS ERASMUS (1465 or
7-1536)—Last words.

Ego et meus rex (I and my King.)
CARDINAL WOLSEY (1471-1530)
—Formula when chancellor of Eng-
land.) Cf.

" Then, that, in all you writ to Rome, or
　else
To foreign princes *Ego et Rex meus*
Was still inscribed ; in which you brought
　the King
To be your servant.—
Shakspere, *King Henry VIII*, act 3, sc. 2,
(Duke of Norfolk).

**Ego sum rex Romanus et super
　grammaticam.** (I am king of
the Romans and above grammar).

The EMPEROR SIGISMUND (1368-
1437)—at the Council of Constance
in 1414, on a grammatical error, in
his speech to the assembled prelates,
being pointed out to him. (Wolf-
gang Menzel's *Geschichte der Deutschen*, ch. 325 (1837 ed., vol. ii, p.
477) ; also Carlyle, *Frederick the
Great*, ch. xiv.) Cf.

" La grammaire, qui sait régenter, jusqu'aux rois,
Et les fait, la main haute obéir a ses lois !"
(Grammar which knows how to govern
　even kings,
And with a high hand makes them obey
　its laws !)—Molière, *Les Femmes
Savantes*, act 2, sc. 6. Cf. Cæsar
non supra grammaticos. (Cæsar is
not above the grammarians)—Latin
Proverb.

**Erravi cum Petro, sed non flevi
cum Petro.** (Like Peter, I
have erred, unlike Peter, I have
not wept).

STEPHEN GARDINER (1483-
1555), bishop of Winchester—Last
words.

Et tu quoque, mi fili. (And thou
also, my son).
JULIUS CÆSAR (100-44 B.C.)—
dying words, but generally quoted
as : Et tu Brute ?—See Καὶ σὺ
τέκνον.

Evasisti. (Thou art saved.)
The EMPEROR HADRIAN (76-
138)—the day he came into power,
meeting an old enemy and noticing
his embarrassment.

Ex luce lucellum. (Out of light a
little gain).
Motto jokingly suggested by
ROBERT LOWE, Viscount Sherbrooke (1811-92) for the new label
when he proposed a tax of ½d. per
box on lucifer matches. Owing to
the opposition the proposal was
withdrawn (Dict. Nat. Biogr., vol.
xxxiv, p. 200.) Cf. also Reed,
Life of Gladstone, p. 572.

Festina lente—See Σπεῦδε βραδέως.

Fiat justitia, et pereat mundus.
(Let justice be done, though
the world perish).
Motto of FERDINAND I of Germany (1503-64)—(Johannes Man-
lius, *Loci Communes*, 1563, vol. ii,
p. 290).

Fiat justitia, ruat cælum. (Let
justice be done, though the
skies fall).

LORD MANSFIELD (1704-93)—phrase used (quoted) in the case of Rex. *v.* Wilkes, Wilkes having been sentenced to outlawry for publication of No. 45 of *The North Briton* in his absence from the court, (Burrows, *Reports*, A.D. 1770, vol. iv, 2562), and to be found in Ward's *Simple Cobbler of Agawam in America*, 1647. In a work called *Fovre Treatises*, &c, by Iohn Downame, London, 1609, p. 67, occur the words :

"For better it is that a private man should perish, than that the publike administration of law and justice should be stayed and hindered," and opposite is printed in italics "Fiat justitia et ruat cælum."

Cf. William Watson, *Decacordon of Ten Quodlibeticall Questions* (1602), pp. 8 & 338 :

Do well and right, and let the world sink—George Herbert, *Country Parson*, ch. 29. Ruat cælum, fiat voluntas tua—Sir T. Browne, *Religio Medici*, p. ii, sec. 11—". . if that cannot be, I say again the same that I wrote, fiat justitia," said by Charles I (1600-49), referring to the Earl of Strafford (*Percy Anecdotes*, vol. i. p. 120). See Périssent les Colonies &c. (note) ; Das Recht muss seinen Gang haben &c.

Finis Poloniæ. (The end of Poland).

Said to have been uttered by KOSCIUSKO (1756-1817), at Maciejowice, Oct. 10, 1794 (*Südpreussische Zeitung* Oct. 25, 1794) ; but denied by him in a letter dated Nov. 12, 1803, to Count de Ségur, in the first edition of whose *Histoire des Principaux Événements du règne de Frédéric-Guillaume* II, it appeared : later editions do not contain it. Cf.

"Hope, for a season, bade the world farewell,
And Freedom shriek'd—as Kosciusko fell!"—Campbell, *Pleasures of Hope*, l. 381, and *Ode on the Fall of Poland*, by Francis Hastings Doyle (*Miscellaneous Verses*, 1834 ed., pp. 23-9).

Flavit, et dissipati sunt. (He blew, and they were scattered).

Inscription on a medal struck by order of QUEEN ELIZABETH (1533-1603), to commemorate the defeat of the Spanish Armada, 1588. It was struck at Middleburg, in Holland. Flavit. et. dissipati. sunt. 1588. 'The Spanish fleet dispersed and wrecked ; above, in clouds, the name of Jehovah in Hebrew.' —*Medallic Illustrations of Brit. Hist.*, vol. i, p. 145. Cf. "Thou didst blow with thy wind, the sea covered them : they sank as lead in the mighty waters "—*Exodus*, xv, 10. " Gott der Allmächtge blies, Und die Armada flog nach allen Winden. (God the Almighty remained And the Armada flew to all winds)—Schiller, *Die unüberwindliche Flotte.*

Fortis dura coquit. (The brave man digests hard things).

A favourite motto of RICHELIEU (1585-1642)—an ostrich with the above inscription.

Habes . . . . . confitentem reum. (You have a defendant who pleads guilty).

CICERO (106-43 B.C.)—in his speech for Ligarius, exiled by Cæsar for having borne arms against him in Africa (*Pro Ligario*, i, 1, § 2).

Haec est fides? (Is this your fidelity ?)

The EMPEROR NERO (37-68)—Last words.

Haec ornamenta mea sunt. (These are my jewels).

CORNELIA (2nd cent. B.C.), mother of the Gracchi—when presenting her children to a lady who had been showing her her jewels, &c. (*Valerius Maximus*, bk. iv, ch. 4).

"Pointing to such, well might Cornelia say,
"When the rich casket shone in bright array,
"'These are my jewels?'"—Samuel Rogers, *Human Life.*

Hannibal ad portas. (Hannibal is at the gates.)

The Romans' cry of alarm after the battle of Cannes (216 B.C.) Sometimes Catiline's name is substituted for Hannibal's, alluding to the revolt of that person in the time of Cicero. Alluded to by Mirabeau

16

in one of his speeches in the Constituent Assembly when opposing Necker's financial proposal. " Catiline est aux portes, et l'on délibère. (Catiline is at the gates, and we are deliberating.") A combination of the first-named Latin phrase (substituting Catiline for Hannibal) and the following : Dum Romae consulitur, Saguntum expugnatur. (While Rome deliberates, Saguntum is stormed).—Livy, *Hist.* xxxi, 7. Cf.

Hannibal, credo, erat ad portas (Hannibal, I believe, was at the gates)— Cicero, *Philippica*, i, 5, 11 : *De Finibus*, v. 9, 22 ; Livy, *Hist.* xxiii, 16.

Hannibal, peto pacem. (I, Hannibal, ask for peace).

HANNIBAL (c. 247-183 B.C.)—in a speech in favour of peace, to Scipio, the Roman general, on Hannibal's recall to Carthage at the end of the second Punic War. (Livy, *Histories* xxx, 30).

Hoc age. (Do this.)

Cry of the herald who walked before the magistrates or priests when engaged in any religious rite, with the object of warning the people to apply their minds wholly to the religious ceremony. Cf. Plutarch, *Lives : Coriolanus*, xxv. ("Οκ ἄγε).

Hoc est signum Dei. (This is a sign from God).

CHARLES LE TÉMÉRAIRE (1433-77) — exclamation before beseiging Nancy, (Jan., 1477), a golden lion surmounting his helmet having fallen off. He threw himself into the *mêlée* and was killed.

Hoc unum scio, me nihil scire.— See Εἰδέναι μὲν μηδὲν, πλὴν αὐτὸ τοῦτο εἰδέναι.

Hic vobis bellum et pacem portamus ; utrum placet sumite. (In this I bring you war and peace, take which you please).

FABIUS CUNCTATOR (275-202 B.C.)—when demanding reparation from the Carthaginians for having taken possession of Saguntum, as he made a lap with the folds of his toga. (Livy, *Histories*, xxi, 19.)

Hoc voluerunt. (They would have it so).

JULIUS CAESAR (100-44 B.C.)—on entering the camp of Pompeius and seeing the dead bodies and slaughter still going on. He added that they brought him into such a critical position that he, Caius Caesar, who had been successful in the greatest wars, would have been condemned, if he had disbanded his troops, (Suetonius, *Caesar*, 30 ; Plutarch. *Lives : Caesar*, xlvi). Cf.

"Vous l'avez voulu, vous l'avez voulu, George Dandin, vous l'avez voulu " (You would have it so, you would have it so, George Dandin, you would have it so)— Molière, *George Dandin*, act 1, sc. 9.

Hominem memento te. (Remember thou art a man).

According to Tertullian, a public slave was placed in the chariot of a successful general when awarded the honour of a public triumph, who whispered the above words into his ear.

"I think that Amy is the slave in the chariot who is placed there by my evil fortune to dash and to confound my triumph, evenwhen of the highest.—Sir W. Scott, *Kenilworth*, ch. xxi. See Cave ne cadas.

Ignorabimus. (We shall never know it).

EMIL DU BOIS-REYMOND, German scientist (1818-96)—conclusion of a speech at Leipzig in 1872.

Illi in extremis prae timore imbellis sudor ; ego imperturbatus morior. (A dastard sweat accompanies his last moments ; I die at peace).

LUCILIO VANINI (1584-1619) philosopher of the Italian Renaissance—Last words. He was hanged, and then burned, after having his tongue cut out. (Gramont, *Hist. Gal.*, iii, 211).

Imperatorem stantem mori oportere. . (An Emperor should die standing. .).

VESPASIAN, Roman Emperor (9-79)—Last words. He died in making the effort to raise himself. (Suetonius, *Twelve Caesars: Vespasianus*, 24). Cf. "Un amiral francais doit mourir sur son banc de quart. (A French admiral should die at his post)—Dying words of Vice-Admiral Francois Paul de Brueys d'Aigalliers (1753-98) on board *L'Orient* at the battle of the Nile, Aug. 1, 1798. See Un roi de France peut mourir &c. ; A Bishop ought to die on his legs ; and While there is life there is will.

Imperium et libertas (Empire and liberty).

BENJAMIN DISRAELI [Earl of Beaconsfield] (1804-81)—in a speech at the Guildhall, Nov. 9, 1879. "One of the greatest of Romans, "when asked what were his politics, "replied, *Imperium et Libertas*. "That would not make a bad pro-"gramme for a British ministry." Cf. Tacitus, *Agricola*, ch. 3, in which he says of Nerva : . . res olim dissociabiles miscuerit, principatum ac libertatem (. . he combined two things hitherto incompatible—empire and liberty).

Disraeli had previously made use of the phrase, in his speech on Agricultural Distress, Feb. 11, 1851.

Ingrata patria, ne ossa quidem habebis! (Ungrateful country, thou shalt not possess even my bones !)

Words uttered by SCIPIO AFRICANUS, MAJOR (c. 234-183 B.C.) to be placed on his tomb in Campania. He had left Rome in disgust, after his trial for having received bribes, although he had been acquitted (Valer. Maximus, *De Dictis Factisque*, bk. v., ch. 3, § 2. Luis de Camoens (c. 1525-79), the Portuguese poet, on leaving his

native country, is credited with having said : Ingrata patria, non possidebis ossa mea ! (Ungrateful country, thou shalt not possess my bones !)—*Percy Anecdotes*, iii, p. 135.

In hoc signo vinces. (In this sign thou shalt conquer).

These words (in their Greek original, τούτῳ νίκα) inscribed by CONSTANTINE THE GREAT (272-337) on his standards, &c. He is said to have seen in the heavens a luminous cross with the inscription, when marching against Maxentius (Eusebius, *Vita Constantini*, i, 28).

In manus, Domine, tuas commendo animam meam. (Into thy hands, O Lord, I commend my spirit).

MARY QUEEN OF SCOTS (1542-87)—Last words (Froude, *History of England*). "Domine, in manus tuas commendo spiritum meum" were also said to be the dying words of Charlemagne (742-814); and "In manus, Domine, commendo spiritum" were the last words of Louis XIII (1601-43), according to the *Memoirs* of Mlle. de Montpensier (p. 20). See Lord into thy hands &c.

Ipse dixit—See αὐτὸς ἔφα.

Ista quidem vis est. (This indeed is compulsion).

JULIUS CÆSAR (100-44 B.C.)—on being assassinated (Suetonius, *Twelve Cæsars*, 82). According to Mérimée (*Mélanges Historiques*) Cæsar uttered his last words in Greek. See καὶ σὺ τέκνον.

Jacta alea esto. (Let the die be cast).

JULIUS CÆSAR (100-44 B.C.)—as he crossed the river Rubicon on his return from Gaul (Suetonius, *Twelve Cæsars*, 32). The phrase 'to cross the Rubicon' is commonly used in English to indicate the taking of some decisive step. Plutarch, *Lives: Pompeius*, 60) also quotes the saying : 'Ανερρίφθω κύβος. (Let the die be cast !) which occurs also in Menander (fl. B.C. 322), *Arrephoros*,

1 (Koch, *Com. Attic. Fragm.*, iii, p. 22).

Laboremus. (Let us be doing). EMPEROR SEPTIMUS SEVERUS (146-211). Last words, at York.

Legatus est vir bonus peregrè missus ad mentiendum reipublicæ causâ. (An ambassador is an honest man sent abroad to lie for the commonwealth). SIR HENRY WOTTON (1568-1639)—written in the album of his friend Fleckamore, as he was passing through Augsburg on his way to Venice. In a letter to Velserus (1612) Wotton says : "This merry definition of an "Ambassador I had chanced to "set down at my friend's Mr. "Christopher. Fleckamore, in his "Album." Cf.

'Twas for the good of my country that I should be abroad—G. Farquhar, *The Beaux' Stratagem*, act iii, sc. 2. True patriots all ; for be it understood We left our country for our country's good.—*Prologue written for the Opening of the Play-house at New South Wales, Jan 16, 1796.* (G. Barrington, *New South Wales*, p. 152) ; And bold and hard adventures t'undertake leaving his country for his country's sake—Fitzgeffray, *Life of Drake* (1600).

Τοῖς ἄρχουσι δὴ τῆς πόλεως, εἴπερ τισὶν ἄλλοις, προσήκει ψεύδεσθαι ἢ πολεμίων ἢ πολιτῶν ἕνεκα ἐπ' ὠφελείᾳ τῆς πόλεως.

(The rulers of the state are the only persons who ought to have the privilege of lying, either at home or abroad ; they may be allowed to lie for the good of the state.—*Jowett*). Socrates, in Plato, *Republic*, iii, 3.

See Ever speak the truth &c.

. . Mirari se . . quod non rideret haruspex, haruspicem cum vidisset. (. . he wondered that one soothsayer did not laugh when he saw another soothsayer). CATO (234-149 B.C.)—(Cicero, *De Divinatione*, ii, 24, 51).

Mitis depone colla Sicamber : adora quod incendisti, incande quod adorasti. (Bend thy neck, meek Sicambrian ; adore what thou hast burnt, burn what thou hast adored). Attributed to ST. REMY (437-533)—when baptizing Clovis in 496. (Gregory of Tours, *Hist. ecclesiastica Francorum*, bk. ii, ch. 31).

Multa agendo nihil egi. (By undertaking many things I have accomplished nothing.) HUGO GROTIUS (1583-1645)—Dying words (quoting Phaedrus, *Fabulae*, ii, 3) : contradicted, however, by P. Bayle in his *Dict. Historique* (1720, 3rd edition, vol. ii, p. 1324) : "Qu'on a inséré un mensonge dans un petit Livre Anglais [a note says : *Sentimens de quelques Théologiens de Hollande* p. 402], lorsqu'on y a mis que Grotius dit en mourant, 'multa agendo nihil egi,' en entreprenant beaucoup de choses je n'ai rien avancé." (That a lie has been inserted in a little English book, when it has been said in it that Grotius said, when dying,' 'multa agendo nihil egi,' in undertaking many things I have not advanced at all).

Another version is :—Ah, vitam perdidi operose nihil agendo (I have spent my life laboriously doing nothing.) Cf. Strenua nos exercet inertia (Busy idleness wearies us)—Horace, *Épist.* I. xi, 28 ; and Seneca, *De Tranquillitate*, xii, 2 (inquieta inertia), *De Brevitate*, xi, 3 (desidiosa occupatio). Bayle gives the last words as, "Vocem tuam. audio, sed quæ singula dicas difficulter intelligo (I hear your voice, but I scarcely understand all that you say).

Nec pluribus impar. (A match for many). LOUIS DOUVRIER—Motto composed for Louis XIV (1638-1715) (le Roi Soleil). The emblem accompanying it was a sun throwing its rays on a globe. The words had been adopted more than a century previously by Philip II of Spain.

Nemo ante mortem beatus. (Nobody before death is happy)— See Πρὶν δ'ἂν τελευτήσῃ &c.

Ne supra crepidam sutor judicaret. ([The cobbler] should not venture an opinion beyond his last).

APELLES, Greek painter (c. 330 B.C.)—to a shoemaker who had already criticised a sandal and who was venturing to find fault with something else (Pliny, *Hist. Nat.*, bk. xxxv, ch. x, § 36). A similar story is told by Lucian of Phidias, the Greek sculptor (c. 490-432 B.C.). The phrase is often misquoted, "Ne sutor ultra crepidam." See Faites des perruques.

Nolite confidere in principibus, in filiis hominum, in quibus non est salus. (Put not your trust in princes, nor in the son of man, in whom there is no help).

Thomas Wentworth, EARL OF STRAFFORD (1593-1641) — when condemned to death, alluding to his master Charles I. Cf. *Book of Psalms* cxlvi, 3. See, Put not your trust in princes, &c.

Non Angli, sed Angeli! (Not Angles, but Angels!)

POPE GREGORY I (c. 550-604), before he was made pope (c. 574)— on seeing some English children in the slave-market at Rome. The full sentence was "Non Angli sed Angeli forent si fuissent Christiani" (They would be Angels, not Angles, if had they been Christians).

Non expedit. (It is not expedient).

Words usually employed be the Cancelleria Apostolica to any pressing demand when refusing compliance. A decree of the Holy Office June 3, 1886, threw light on the phrase by adding that *non expedit* implies prohibition.

Non olet. (It [gold] has no smell).

THE EMPEROR VESPASIAN (9-79) —to his son Titus, who was blaming him for having imposed an unpopular tax on urinals. The emperor raised the money received from the tax to his nose, and inquired "Num odore offenderetur" (whether he was offended by the smell). On Titus, saying "No," he added "Atqui e lotio est" (And yet it comes out of urine). (Suetonius, *Twelve Caesars*, xxiii). There is thus no classical authority for the phrase as commonly quoted "non olet." Cf. :

Lucri bonus est odor ex re
Qualibet (Gain smells sweet, from what soe'er it springs) — JUVENAL, *Satires*, *XIV.*, 204.

Non possumus. (We are unable to do so).

POPE CLEMENT VII (d. 1534)— in reply to the demand of Henry VIII for his consent to the divorce from Queen Catherine of Aragon. Since that time these words have been the regular formula of refusals by the supreme pontiff. Cf. "Non enim possumus nos quæ vidimus et audivimus, non loqui" (For we cannot but speak the things which we have seen and heard).—*Acts* iv, 20).

Nulla dies sine linea. (No day without its line.)

Form in which a habit of APELLES (fl. c. 332 B.C.) is now expressed. "Apelli fuit alioquin perpetua con-"suetudo nunquam tam occupatam "diem agendi, ut non lineam "ducendo exerceret artem." (It was Apelles' constant habit never to allow a day to be so fully occupied that he had not time for the exercise of his art, if only to the extent of one stroke of the brush). Pliny, *Hist. Nat.*, bk. xxxv, ch. x, 36. In recent times Emile Zola (1840-1902) adopted the words as his motto.

. . **nullum esse librum tam malum ut non aliqua parte prodesset.** (No book is so bad

but benefit may be derived from some part of it.)
PLINY THE ELDER (23-79)—a saying of his (Pliny the Younger, *Epistolae*, iii, 5.)
Nullum quod tetigit non ornavit. (He touched nothing which he did not adorn).
DR. JOHNSON (1709-84)—a line from his epitaph on Oliver Goldsmith (Boswell's *Life of Johnson*, 1888 ed., vol. ii, p. 153). Usually quoted "Nihil tetigit quod non ornavit," both being equally bad Latin. Cf.

"Il embellit tout ce qu'il touche." (He embellishes all that he touches).—Fénelon, *Lettre sur les occupations de l'Acad. franç.* iv.

. . **nunquam se minus otio͏sum esse, quam cum otiosus, nec minus solum, quam cum solus esset.** ([he used to say that] he was never less idle than in idleness, or less alone than in solitude).
SCIPIO AFRICANUS MAJOR (234-183 B.C.)—(Cicero, *De officiis*, iii, 1, 1). Plutarch (*Apophthegmata: Scipio Presb.*) reports this saying at less length: Ὅποτε σχολάζοι πλεονα πράττειν ([he used to say that] when he was at leisure he did most work.)

A wise man is never less alone than when he is alone—Swift. *Essay on the Faculties of the Mind.*
In solitude where we are least alone—Byron, *Childe Harold*, iii, 90. Then, never less alone than when alone—Rogers, *Human Life.*

Nutrimentum spiritus. (Food of the spirit).
The (unclassical) inscription of the Berlin Royal Library (finished in 1780). Derived from a lecture by Frederick the Great (1712-86).
Omnia mea porto mecum. (All my property is with me).
BIAS, the Greek philosopher (fl. 550 B.C.)—in reply to those who fled

from the town of Priene (besieged by Cyrus's generals) taking that which they valued most with them, and expressing their astonishment at his calmness and want of preparation for his flight (Cicero, *Paradoxa*, i. 8). Quoted by Carlyle (*French Revolution*, p. 250). Seneca (*De Constantia Sapientis*, v, 6) says that when STILPO, the Greek philosopher (fl. 310 B.C.), was asked, at the taking of Megara, whether he had lost anything, he replied "Nihil: omnia namque mea mecum sunt" ("nothing: for everything I own is with me").

Omnia mutantur, nos et mutamur in illis;
Illa vices quasdam res habet, illa vices. (All things are changed, and with them we, too, change; Now this way and now that turns fortune's wheel).
LOTHAIR I OF GERMANY (c. 795-855)—(Matthias Borbonius, *Deliciæ Poetarum Germanorum*, I, 685. Generally quoted "Tempora mutantur," &c.

Optime olere occisum hostem et melius civem. (An enemy killed always smells good, especially when it is a citizen).
AULUS VITELLIUS (c. 15-69)—when visiting the battle-field of Bedriacum, April, 69. (Suetonius, *Twelve Cæsars*: *Vitellius*, x). See Vous avez la plaie &c.
O sancta simplicitas! (O holy simplicity!)
JOHN HUSS (1373-1415)—at the stake, an old woman busying herself in heaping up the wood (Milman, *Latin Christianity*, bk. 13, ch. 9, 1864 ed., vol. viii, p. 296). Cf. *The Death of Huss*, a poem by Alfred Austin. Büchmann, *Geflügelte Worte*, 16th ed., p. 395, states that one of the faithful at the Council of Nice silenced a pertinacious

opponent by using these words, and refers to Rufinus in his version of Eusebius, *Eccles. Hist.*, bk. x, ch. 3.

O tempora, O mores! (What times! what morals!)

MARCUS TULLIUS CICERO (106-43 B.C.)—(*In Catilinam*, I, i, 2).

Otium cum dignitate—See Cum dignitate otium.

Pæte, non dolet. (This [wound] hurts me not, Pætus).

ARRIA (? -42), wife of Cæcina Pætus—after stabbing herself, presenting the dagger to her husband, who then followed her example. Martial's epigram (i, 13) is:

Casta suo gladium cum traderet Arria Pæto,
Quem de visceribus strinxerat ipsa suis,
' Si qua fides, vulnus quod feci non dolet, inquit,
'Sed quod tu facies, hoc mihi, Pæte, dolet.'
(When to her husband Arria gave the steel, Which from her chaste, her bleeding breast she drew ;
She said—" My Pætus, this I do not feel, But, oh ! the wound that must be given by you !")

. . pater patriae. (. . the father of his father-land.)

Title conferred by CATO (234-149 B.C.) upon Cicero, who is said to be the first person so styled (Plutarch, *Lives*: *Cicero*, xxiii), " πατέρα πατρίδος." Cf.

". . our father—the friend, I may say the father of his country . ."—Sir W. Scott, *The Pirate*, ch. 38 (Brenda Troil). "Madam," he said, "remember that you are a Queen—Queen of England—mother of your people."—Sir W. Scott, *Kenilworth*, ch. xl (Burleigh, to Queen Elizabeth).

Peccavi! (I have sinned [Scinde]!)

SIR CHARLES NAPIER (1782-1853)—in a dispatch announcing the victory of Hyderabad in 1843, after he had entered upon the war without official sanction.

Perdicca interrogante quando cælestes honores haberi sibi vellet, dixit tum velle cum ipsi felices essent. Suprema

hæc vox fuit regis. (When Perdicca asked him when he wished to have divine honours paid to him, he said that he wished them to be paid when they were lucky. These were the last words of the king).

ALEXANDER THE GREAT (356-323 B.C.)—Last words (Quintus Curtius, *De Rebus Alexandri*, x, 5, 6).

Princeps qui delatores non castigat, irritat. (The prince who does not punish informers encourages them).

EMPEROR DOMITIAN (52-96)—(Suetonius, *Twelve Caesars : Domitianus*, viii, 9).

Pro lege, rege, grege. (For law, king, and people).

WILLIAM OF ORANGE, surnamed " the Silent," (1533-84)—motto.

Provocarem ad Philippum, sed sobrium. (I would appeal to Philip, but when he is sober).

A MACEDONIAN WOMAN — to Philip of Macedon (382-336 B.C.), who had condemmed her when he was intoxicated after leaving a feast. She was successful in her appeal. (Valerius Maximus, vi, 2, *Externa* 1). The passage runs:

Inserit se tantis viris mulier alienigeni sanguinis, quae a Philippo rege temulento immererent damnata, Provocarem ad Philippum, inquit, sed sobrium. (Among these great men, there is also a woman of foreign origin, who, on being unjustly condemned by King Philip in his cups said, ' I would appeal to Philip, but when he is sober').

Qualis artifex pereo! (What an artist the world is losing in me !)

EMPEROR NERO (37-68)—shortly before his death (Suetonius, *Twelve Caesars : Nero*, vi, 49).

Quam vellem me nescire literas! (How I wish that I did not know my letters !)

EMPEROR NERO (37-68)—in the early years of his reign, on being requested to sign a writ for the execution of a malefactor. (Suetonius, *Twelve Caesars : Nero*). Cf.

" Je vondrais, disiez-vous, ne savoir pas écrire." *(*Would that I knew not how to write ; you * said).—Racine, *Britannicus*, act iv, c. 4. (Burrhus).

Joachim Gersdorff, a Danish deputy, when signing the treaty between Denmark and Sweden (1658) is reported to have said. ' Vellem me nescire litteras.' (I could wish that I was unable to write.)— *Percy Anecdotes*, vol. 1, p. 155.

Quando hic sum, non jejuno Sabbato ; quando Romae sum, jejuno Sabbato. (When I am here, I do not fast on Saturday ; when I am at Rome, I fast on Saturday).

ST. AMBROSE (340-97).—Reply to St. Augustine, who had consulted him with regard to fasting. At Rome they fasted on Saturday, and at Milan they did not. (St. Augustine, *Epistolae*, xxxvi, § 32 : *To Casulanus*). This is supposed to be the origin of the saying ' When in Rome, do as the Romans do.' Cf.

When they are at Rome, they do there as they see done.—Burton, *Anatomy of Melancholy*, pt. iii, sec. 4, mem. 2, subs. 1.

Quicquid laudat vituperio dignum est ; quicquid cogitat, vanum ; quicquid loquitur, falsum ; quicquid improbat, bonum ; quicquid extollit, infame est. (Whatever they praise deserves blame ; whatever they think is vain ; whatever they say is false ; whatever they disapprove is good ; whatever they glorify is infamous).

POPE JOHN XXII (1244-1334)— alluding to the common people. (Bzovius, *Ad ann.* 1334, No. 2).

* Nero.

Quid times ? Caesarem vehis. (What do you fear ? Caesar is your passenger).
See Καῖσαρα φέρεις &c.

Qui facit per alium est perinde ac si faciat per seipsum. (He who does a thing through an agent is as responsible as if he were to do it himself).

POPE BONIFACE VIII (c 1225-1303)—(*Sexti Decretalium Liber*, x, *tit.* 20, *de Regulis Juris* 72). Usually quoted as " Qui facit per alium facit per se " (He who acts through another acts himself), a legal maxim.

Quinctili Vare, legiones redde ! (Quintilius Varus, give me back my legions !)

EMPEROR AUGUSTUS (63 B.C.-14 A.D.)—alluding to the defeat of the Romans by Arminius, when Varus lost three whole legions. (Suetonius, *Twelve Caesars ; Augustus*, 23). Cf.

O mort ! épargne ce qui reste !
Varus, rends-nous nos légions.
(O death ! spare what remains !
Varus, give us back our legions.)

Casimir Delavigne's, *Messénienne* on Waterloo. See Give me back my youth.

Qui nescit dissimulare, nescit regnare (Who knows not how to dissimulate, knows not how to reign).

LOUIS XI. (1423-83)—referring to his son, asserting that he would know enough if he knew the five words above (De Thou, *Histoire Universelle*, vol. iii, p. 293). Cf. Sir Walter Scott, *Quentin Durward*, ch. i ;

Savoir dissimuler est le savoir des rois. (To know how to dissimulate is the knowledge of kings)—Richelieu, *Mirame* (tragedy); also Montaigne's *Essays*, bk. 2. ch. xvii, and note ; Qui ne sçait dissimuler ne peut régner. (Who knows not how to dissimulate cannot reign)—XVIth century proverb ; and . . . . . vivere nescit, Ut bene vulgus ait, qui nescit dissimulare. (He knows not how to live, As says the saw, who knows not how to feign) Palingenius, *Zodiaeus Vita* " Cancer," 683.

Qui tacet consentire videtur.
(Silence gives consent).
POPE BONIFACE VIII (1225-1303)—(*Sexti Decretalis Liber*, bk. v, tit. xii, *de Regulis Juris*, 43). Cf. Qui ne dit mot consent. (Silence gives consent)—French Proverb.

Quoniam meos tam suspicione quam crimine judico carere oportere. (Because the members of my household should be free not only from crime, but from the mere suspicion of it). JULIUS CÆSAR (100-44 B.C.)—when asked why he had put away his wife, after Clodius (in love with her) had introduced himself into Cæsar's house disguised as a woman (Suetonius, *Twelve Cæsars* : *Julius Cæsar*, 74). Plutarch (*Lives. Cæsar*, 10) quotes the saying as : "Ὅτι τὴν ἐμὴν ἠξιοῦν μηδὲ ὑπονοηθῆναι. (Because I considered that my wife should not even be the object of suspicion). In his *Apophthegmata* (*Cæsar*, 3) the words are given as : Τὴν Καίσαρος γυναῖκα καὶ διαβολῆς δεῖ καθαρὰν εἶναι (Cæsar's wife should be above suspicion). Cf. . . τὸν Καίσαρος ἔδει γάμον οὐ πράξεως αἰσχρᾶς μόνον, ἀλλὰ καὶ φήμης καθαρὸν εἶναι (Cæsar's marriage should be free not only from a shameful act, but even from the report of it).—Plutarch, *Lives* : *Cicero*, 29.

Quousque tandem abutere, Catilina, patientia nostra? (How far then, Catiline, will you abuse our patience ?). CICERO (106-43 B.C.)—at the beginning of the first oration against Catiline (*In Catilinam*, I, i, 1).

Rex regnat, sed non gubernat. (The king reigns, but does not govern). JAN ZAMOISKI (1541-1605)—in a speech at the Diet of 1605, reproaching King Sigismund III

(1568-1632). See Le roi règne et ne gouverne pas.

Sancte Pater, sic transit gloria mundi. (Holy Father, thus passeth away the glory of the world). Formula used at the crowning of the popes, and said as the lighted bunches of tow extinguish themselves. See Sic transit gloria mundi.

Sanitas sanitatum, omnia sanitas. (Sanity of sanities, all is sanity).
BENJAMIN DISRAELI [Earl of Beaconsfield] (1804-81)—in a speech at Manchester, April 3, 1872, he said :

A great scholar and a great wit, 300 years ago, said that, in his opinion, there was a great mistake in the Vulgate...... and that instead of saying, 'Vanity of vanities, all is vanity,'— *Vanitas vanitatum, omnia vanitas* *—the wise and witty king really said *Sanitas*, &c.

The views expressed in that speech were called "a policy of sewage" by a leading Liberal member of Parliament, and the phrase was referred to by Disraeli in his speech at the Crystal Palace, June 24, 1872. Beaconsfield probably was referring to Gilles Ménage (1613-92), for in a postscript to a letter from G. G. Leibnitz (1646-1716) to the abbé Nicaise, dated Hanover, Sept. 29, 1693, the philosopher mentions that he was in the habit of using the phrase without knowing that Ménage used it also, as he learns from *Ménagiana* is the case :

Comme nous [*i.e.* Ménage and M. de Balzac] nous entretenions de ce qui pouvoit rendre heureux, je luy dis ; *Sanitas sanitatum, & omnia sanitas*. Il me pria cependant de ne point publier cette pensée, parce qu'il vouloit luy donner place en quelque endroit. En effet il s'en est servy dans quelqu'un de ses "ouvrages." ("As we were talking of what could make any-one happy, I said to him : *Sanitas sanitatum, et omnia sanitas*. He begged me, however, not to publish this idea,

* The Vulgate, *Ecclesiastes* I, 2.

because he wanted to use it in some place. In fact he has made use of it in some one of his works.")— *Ménagiana*, p. 166, Amsterdam, 1693.

Sat celeriter fieri, quidquid fiat satis bene. (Whatever is done well enough is done quickly enough).

EMPEROR AUGUSTUS (63 B.C.— 14 A.D.)—Suetonius, *Twelve Cæsars: Augustus*, xxv).

Si ad naturam vives, nunquam eris pauper : si ad opiniones, nunquam eris dives. (If you live according to nature, you will never be poor : if according to fancy, you will never be rich).

EPICURUS (342-270 B.C.)—(Seneca, *Epistolae*, xvi, 7).

Sic transit gloria mundi. (Thus passeth away the glory of the world).

It is said that, as the Roman emperors passed in state through the streets of the Imperial city, they were preceded by an officer who carried burning flax and who from time to time uttered the above words. See Sancta Pater, sic transit gloria mundi.

Sint ut sunt, aut non sint. (Let them be as they are, or let them be not at all).

LORENZA RICCI, general of the Jesuits (1703-75) — reply, when it was proposed to him that the order should be preserved on condition that some of its rules should be altered. The Order was abolished, by Clement XIV, on July 21, 1773. Also attributed to CLEMENT XIII (1693-1769).

Sub hoc signo vinces.—See In hoc signo vinces.

Tandem aliquando surge, carnifex? (Are you ever going to rise, you butcher?)

MAECENAS — written on his tablets, and thrown to the Emperor

Augustus (27 B.C.-14 A.D.), as the latter was about to pass sentence of death on a number of persons. Cæsar rose without condemning anyone to death.

Tempora mutantur, nos et mutamur in illis. (Times change and with them we too, change).

—See Omnia mutantur &c.

Teneo te, Africa ! (I hold thee fast, Africa).

CÆSAR (100-44 B.C.)—who fell on landing in Africa, turning in his favour what would otherwise have been looked upon as a bad omen. (Suetonius, *Twelve Cæsars*, 59). See J'ai saisi cette terre de mes mains, &c. ; Oh ! oh ! voilà qui s'appelle, &c.

Tibi istum ad munimentum mei committo, si recte agam ; sin aliter, in me magis. (I hand it over to you as a defence for myself, if I do right ; if I do wrong, as a defence against myself).

EMPEROR TRAJAN (c. 52-117)— to Subarranus when appointed captain of his guards, referring to a drawn sword (Dio Cassius). Another version is ' Pro me ; si merear, in me,' (For me ; if I deserve it, against me)—*Percy Anecdotes*, vol. iii., p. 343.

Ubi tu, Caius, ego, Caia. (Where you are, M, there will I, N, be).

Formula pronounced by a bride at marriage ceremonies, according to Roman tradition.

Ultima ratio regum. (The last argument of kings).

CARDINAL RICHELIEU (1585-1642)—maxim adopted by him, who even had it engraved on cannons. He derived it from Cardinal Francisco Ximenès (1436-1517), who, when asked for reasons for certain acts of authority on his part, commanded a discharge of artillery,

saying ' Hæc est ratio ultima regis '
(' There is the king's last argument '). Cf.

'—the gag—the rack—the axe—is the
ratio ultima Romæ'—Sir W. Scott,
Monastery, ch. xxxi (Henry Warden).

**Urbem . . marmoream se re-
linquere, quam lateritiam
accepisset** (. . I found Rome
brick, and left it marble).

AUGUSTUS (63 B.C.-14 A.D.)
—referring to the improvements he
had made in the city (Suetonius,
Twelve Cæsars, ii, 29; cf. Dio
Cassius, lvi, 589). The saying was
alluded to by Lord Brougham
(1778-1868) in his speech on
Law Reform in the House of
Commons, Feb., 1828. He spoke
for six hours. " Urbem venalem et
mature perituram, si emptorem
invenerit " (the city was for sale, and
would come to an untimely end if
a purchaser could be found).
JUGURTHA (d. 106 B.C.)—apostro-
phizing Rome (Sallust, *Jugurtha*,
35).

Urbi et orbi. (On the city and the
world).

Formula accompanying the papal
benediction given from the balcony
of St. John de Latran on Holy
Thursday, Easter Day and Ascen-
sion Day. Cf. also Mme. de Staël,
Corinne, bk. x, ch. v, end.

Usque ad aras amicus. (I am a
friend right up to the altar.)—
See Μέχρι τοῦ βωμοῦ φίλος
εἶναι

**Utinam populus Romanus unam
cervicem haberet!** (Would
that the people of Rome had
but one neck!)

CAIUS CALIGULA (12-41)—when

incensed at the applause at the
Circensian games in opposition to
him. Suetonius, IV., 30.

Vae! puto deus fio. (Alack! I
think I am becoming a God).

EMPEROR VESPASIAN (9-79)—
shortly before his death (Suetonius,
Twelve Cæsars: Vespasianus, xxiii).

Veni, vidi, vici. (I came, I saw,
I conquered).

JULIUS CÆSAR (100-44 B.C.)—
in a note to Amantius, at Rome,
after his victory over Pharnace, King
of Pont, near Zela. The note is,
however, probably not authentic.
There is no Latin authority for the
words, but Plutarch (*Lives: Julius
Cæsar*, 50) quotes them as Ἦλθον,
εἶδον, ἐνίκησα. Cf.

" But what of that? he saw me, and
yielded; that I may justly say with the
hook-nosed fellow of Rome,—I came, saw
and overcame "— Shakespeare, II *King
Henry IV.*, act IV., sc. 3.
" Cæsar himself could never say
" He got two victories in a day,
" As I have done, that can say, Twice I,
" In one day, *Veni, Vidi, Vici.*"—S.
Butler, *Hudibras*, pt. 1. can. 3, l. 733.

Vicisti, Galilæe! (Thou hast conquered, Galilæan).

Attributed to the EMPEROR
JULIAN, " the Apostate " [331-63].
The story is that he was mortally
wounded by a javelin, and that he
threw some blood from the wound
against heaven, exclaiming as above
(Theodoret, *Eccles. History*, bk, iii,
ch. 25). Cf.

Thou hast conquered, O pale Galilean—
Swinburne, *Hymn to Proserpine.*

Viribus unitis. (With united
strength)

JOSEPH VON BERGMANN—motto
adopted by the Emperor of Austria
Francis Joseph I, Feb. 12, 1848.

INDEX OF NAMES OF PERSONS.

Abbott, Charles, Lord Tenterden : 17.
à Beckett, Thomas : 16, 25, 32.
Aberdeen, Lord : 139, 145, 233.
Adalbert : 170.
Adam, Dr. Alexander : 35.
Adams, John : 45, 69.
Adams, John Quincy : 69.
Addison, Joseph : 29, 42.
Æsop, 210, 231.
Affre, D.A. : 168.
Agatharcus : 211.
Agesilaus : 210, 212, 215, 220, 229, 231.
Agesistrata : 217.
Agis II : 220, 222.
Agis III : 214.
Agis IV : 215.
Alava, General : 47.
Albert, Prince : 27.
Alcibiades : 211, 213, 221.
Alexander, Emperor of Russia : 113.
Alexander II (of Russia) : 185.
Alexander the Great : 210, 212, 214, 215, 216, 217, 219, 221, 228, 229, 231, 247.
Alexander (the tyrant) : 210.
Alford, Dean : 78.
Alfred the Great : 11, 69.
Almaric, Arnauld : 183.
Alviano, General : 118.
Amantius : 251.
Ames, Fisher : 8, 43, 55.
Amurath (Murad) II : 210.
Amyot, Jacques : 132.
Anacharsis : 23.
Anaxagoras : 222, 231.

Andrassy, Count : 204.
André, Charles : 102.
André, Major John : 37.
Andrieux : 160, 179.
Andronicus : 228.
Angelo, Michael : 232.
Anisson, A.J.L. : 108.
Anne of Austria : 188.
Anson, Lord : 31.
Antalcidas : 215.
Antigonus : 213, 230.
Antigonus, the elder : 110, 219.
Antipater : 211, 214, 219.
Antoinette, Marie. V. Marie Antoinette.
Antisthenes : 221.
Antoninus. V. Aurelius, Marcus.
Apelles : 245.
Appleton, T.G : 19.
Aram, Eugene : 45.
Aratus : 224.
Arcesilaus : 209.
Archelaus : 223.
Archestratus : 221.
Archias : 213.
Archibald, 8th earl of Argyle : 24.
Archidamidas : 218.
Archidamus : 175.
Archimedes : 211, 214.
Arcole. V. Fournier, J.
Argyle, 8th earl of. V. Archibald.
Aristides : 220, 228.
Aristotle : 237.
Arminius : 248.
Armin-Boytzenburg : 196.
Armistead, L.A. : 18.
Arnauld, Antoine : 154.
Arnold, Dr. T. : 3.

Arnould, Sophie : 94, 97, 157.
Arria : 247.
Artemisia : 218.
Arthur III (duke of Brittany) V. Richemont, Comte de.
Augusta Charlotte, Princess : 80.
Augustus : 209, 224, 237, 248, 250, 251.
Aurelius, Marcus : 220.
Auriol : 176.
Avinain : 154.
Axel. V. Oxenstiern, Count.

Babington, Anthony : 63.
Bacon, Francis : 29, 39, 238.
Bacon, Sir Nicholas : 21, 80.
Bailly, J.S : 114, 183.
Ball, John : 75.
Ballantyne, James : 62.
Ballestrem, Count : 195.
Barbazan : 169.
Barbour. Dr : 68.
Barentin, C.L.F.de : 122.
Barère de Vieuzac, Bertrand : 111, 130, 132, 153.
Barnave, P.J.M. : 88, 142, 186.
Barra, J : 185.
Barré, Isaac : 68.
Barrot, O. : 90, 107.
Bart, J : 186.
Bassompierre, maréchal de : 180.
Battie, William : 80.
Baudin, J.B.V : 186.
Bautru, G. : 100, 156, 188.
Baxter, Richard : 28.
Bayard, chevalier : 83, 85, 110, 134, 180.
Bayle, Pierre : 180.
Beaconsfield, Earl of. V. Disraeli, Benjamin.
Beard, Dr. G.M. : 34.
Beaton, David : 22.
Beaufort, Cardinal Henry : 33.
Beaujeu, Anne de : 123.
Beaumanoir, J.de : 87.
Beaumarchais : 84, 94.
Beauvais, Abbé de : 143.
Beckerath, H.von : 203.
Bede, The Venerable : 18.
Bedford, Duke of : 123.
Bee, General B.E. : 54.

Beecher, Henry Ward: 20,44,46,75.
Bekker, I. : 200.
Benedict XI, Pope : 235.
Benserade : 152.
Benso, Camille (Conte di Cavour) : 22, 185, 194, 234.
Bentham, Jeremy : 25.
Bentinck, Lord George : 60.
Bentley, Dr. Richard : 25.
Bergmann, Joseph von : 251.
Berlier : 143.
Berrier : 167.
Berry, Captain : 58.
Bertin, Mlle. : 109.
Berwick, Duke of. V. Fitzjames, James.
Betterton, Thomas : 2
Beugnot, comte J.C. : 111, 120.
Beurnonville, General : 139.
Biancolelli, J. V. Dominique.
Bias : 211, 226, 246.
Bigod, Roger, Earl of Norfolk : 55.
Bion : 215, 225, 226.
Biron, Charles de Gontaut, duc de : 91, 120, 150.
Biron, General Armand Louis de Gontaut, duc de : 114, 151.
Bismarck, Prince : 105, 141, 190, 191, 192, 193, 194, 195, 196, 197, 198, 199, 200, 201, 202, 203, 204, 205, 206, 207, 208.
Bismarck-Schönhausen : 194.
Black Prince, The. V. Edward.
Blake, Admiral : 10, 36.
Blandan, Sergeant : 152.
Blessington, Lady : 76.
Blood, Thomas : 24.
Blossius : 225.
Blucher : 204, 207.
Bohun, Humphrey de, Earl of Hereford : 54.
Boieldieu : 150.
Boileau, N. : 90, 118, 123, 164, 166, 168, 176.
Bois-Reymond, E. du : 242.
Boleyn, Anne : 36, 81.
Bolingbroke, Viscount Henry St. John : 19, 35, 73.
Bonchamp, marquis de : 104.
Bonaparte, Joseph. V. Joseph, king of Naples.

Bonaparte, Mme. Lætitia : 170.
Boniface VIII, Pope : 235, 248, 249.
Bordeu, T.de : 120.
Borgia, Cæsar : 238.
Bosdari : 235.
Bosquet, P.J.F. : 92.
Bossuet, J. : 130, 143, 148, 149, 184.
Bougainville : 167.
Bouhours,D. : 119.
Bouillon, duc de : 181.
Boulanger, General G.E.J.M. : 87, 112, 138, 171.
Boulay de la Meurthe : 92.
Bourbon, duc de : 138.
Bourdaloue, L. : 89, 107, 115.
Bourdon : 148.
Bourmont, General : 142.
Bouvard : 96, 120.
Boves, Geoffrey de : 87.
Bowen, Lord Charles : 4, 11, 32, 39, 56, 72, 78, 80.
Boyle, Robert : 74.
Bradford, Alden : 50.
Bradford, Andrew : 48.
Bradford, John : 9.
Bradlaugh, Charles : 61.
Bradshaw, President J. : 53.
Bragg, General : 3.
Brainerd, David : 41.
Brand, von : 200.
Brantôme, P.de B. : 118.
Brass, A. : 208.
Brébeuf, G.de : 117.
Brennus : 225.
Breslaw, Meyer : 192.
Bresse, comte de. V. Savoie, duc de.
Bressolles, General : 104.
Brienne, comte de : 108.
Bright, John : 2, 5, 9, 14, 16, 51, 58, 131.
Brissot, J.P. : 164.
Brocklesby, R. : 74.
Brontë, Emily : 45.
Brontë, Rev. Patrick : 76.
Brougham, Lord : 62, 65, 66, 67, 251.
Brown, John : 43.
Brown, John : 15, 22, 32.
Browning, Elizabeth Barrett : 35.

Bruce, Robert : 30, 47.
Brueys d'Aigalliers, Admiral F.P. de : 243.
Brummell, "Beau" : 33.
Brunswick, Duke of. V. Christian.
Brutus : 209, 215, 230.
Bryant, W.C. : 77.
Buchanan, George : 37.
Buchanan, James : 48.
Buckingham, Duke of. V. Villiers, George.
Buckingham, Duke of, & Normanby V. Sheffield, John.
Buckle, H.T. : 51.
Bucknill, Dr. : 3.
Buffon, 136, 144, 148.
Bull, George : 5.
Bunyan, John : 78.
Burgon, Rev. J.W. : 72.
Buridan, J. : 130.
Burke, Edmund : 3, 5, 8, 9, 12, 13, 18, 24, 32, 33, 35, 36, 40, 43, 60, 63, 64, 67, 70, 75, 76.
Burleigh, Lord. V. Cecil, Sir Wm.
Burn, Andrew : 45.
Burney, Dr. : 55.
Burns, Robert : 48.
Burton, Sir R.F. : 48.
Bushnell, Rev Dr. : 56.
Butler, Benjamin Franklin : 29.
Butler, Bishop Joseph : 28.
Butler, Samuel : 35.
Byron, Lord : 16, 23, 31, 41, 47, 50, 59.

Cabanis : 151.
Cadogan, W.B. : 35.
Cæsar, Julius : 210, 212, 214, 215, 216, 218, 219, 230, 238, 240, 242, 243, 248, 249, 250, 251.
Calderon : 151.
Calhoun, J.C. : 52, 66.
Caligula, Caius : 251.
Calloun, S.H. : 74.
Calonne, C.A.de : 86, 172.
Cambon, J. : 105.
Cambronne, P.J.E. : 98, 127.
Camillus : 225.
Camoens, L.de : 243.
Campbell, Thomas : 45.
Canning, George : 23.

Canute, King : 70.
Capet, Hugues : 170.
Capèce-Latro : 105.
Caprivi, Chancellor G.L.von : 191, 193, 195, 201.
Carlo Alberto : 234.
Carlyle, Thomas : 8, 18, 24, 28, 66, 67, 69, 79.
Carnot, L.N.M. : 148.
Caroline, Queen : 49.
Caroline Matilda : 158.
Cary, Alice : 37.
Casanova, J. : 129.
Casaubon, Isaac : 168.
Casca : 216.
Castlereagh, Lord : 62.
Catherine de Medicis : 98.
Catherine, Electress of Brandenburg : 204.
Catherine of Arragon. V. Katharine.
Cato Major : 210, 214, 215, 225, Catiline : 237, 241.
Catinat, Marshal : 109, 110. 229, 230, 239, 244, 247.
Cauchon, P. : 188.
Caulaincourt, M.de : 182.
Caussidière, Marc : 147.
Cavour, Conte di. V. Benso, Camille.
Cecil, Sir Wm, Lord Burleigh : 13. 42, 78.
Cephalon : 224.
Chabot, F. : 135.
Chabrias : 229.
Challemel-Lacour, P.A. : 104.
Chamfort, S.R. Nicolas : 105, 121, 134, 137, 147, 169, 186.
Chamouroux, Lieut-Col. de: 177.
Champesnetz, Chevalier de : 101.
Channing, W.E. : 80.
Chanvallon, Abbé de : 124.
Chapelle, C.E.T. : 104.
Chares : 220.
Charilaus : 223.
Charlemagne : 243.
Charles I : 17, 20, 25, 26, 27, 28, 46, 51, 52, 53, 57, 64, 73, 75, 80, 241, 245.
Charles II : 7, 9, 12, 36, 43, 51, 68, 77.

Charles V : 124, 134, 178, 187.
Charles V (the Wise) : 149.
Charles VI : 128.
Charles VII : 106, 141, 160.
Charles IX : 120, 132, 168, 187.
Charles X : 106, 111, 124, 185.
Charles de Bourbon : 83.
Charles the Bold . 90, 97, 242.
Charlotte, Princess Augusta. V. Augusta Charlotte, Princess.
Charlotte (Lucien Bonaparte's daughter) : 158.
Chateaubriand, F.R.vicomte de : 92.
Châteauroux, duchesse de : 102.
Chatham, Earl of. V. Pitt, Wm., Earl of Chatham.
Chatillon, G. de : 169.
Chaulnes, duc de : 84.
Chénier, A : 165.
Chesterfield, Lord : 17, 19, 28, 56, 57, 71.
Chilo : 211, 226.
Chius, Theodotus : 217.
Christian, Duke of Brunswick : 198.
Christina, Queen of Sweden : 234.
Chudleigh, Elizabeth, Duchess of Kingston : 38.
Cicero : 212, 237, 239, 241, 247, 249.
Cinna : 225.
Cinq-Mars, marquis de : 125.
Civinini, G : 235.
Claimant, Tichborne. V. Tichborne Claimant.
Claus : 193.
Clavier, E : 100.
Clay, Henry : 5, 55.
Clémenceau, E. : 133.
Clement V, Pope : 95.
Clement VII, ,, : 245.
Clement XIII, ,, : 250.
Clement XIV, ,, : 250.
Cleobulus : 216, 227, 228.
Cleomenes : 217, 220. 226.
Cleveland, President G. : 32, 52.
Clodius : 249.
Clovis : 244.
Cocault, Arnoul : 107.
Cockburn, Sir A. : 67.
Cœur, Jacques : 82.
Coke, Sir E. : 11, 70.

Colbert : 117, 119, 173, 176.
Coleridge, Sir John : 78.
Coligny, Admiral de : 102, 187.
Collings, Jesse : 70.
Collins, Anthony : 27.
Colman, George (the younger) : 41.
Colombo, Guiseppe : 233.
Coluche, Jean : 159.
Compton, Sir Spencer : 11, 71.
Condé, Prince de : 107.
Condé, The Great : 85, 123, 143, 155, 165, 188.
Condorcet : 105.
Constans : 142.
Constantine the Great : 243.
Conti, Prince de : 128.
Cookman, Rev. Alfred : 23.
Coombe, Mr. : 75.
Cooper, Sir Anthony Ashley. V. Shaftesbury, Earl of.
Cooper, Dr. Thomas : 47.
Cornelia : 241.
Cornelius, Caius : 217.
Corbinelli : 97.
Corday, Marie-Charlotte de, d'Armont : 136.
Corneille, Pierre : 117.
Cornuel, Mme : 110, 129, 153.
Correggio : 232.
Corse, General : 21.
Cortez, F. : 124.
Corvisart-Desmarets, Baron J. N. : 118, 169.
Cowley, Lord : 134.
Cowper, William : 74.
Craik, Professor : 65.
Cranmer, Thomas : 11, 69.
Craterus : 211.
Crébillon, P.J.de : 86.
Créqui, marquise de : 122.
Crillon, L.de : 163.
Crispi, F. : 234, 236.
Crittenden, J.J. : 49.
Crœsus : 223, 231.
Crome, John : 48.
Cromwell, Oliver : 2, 6, 10, 29, 38, 43, 44, 52, 75, 79.
Crosby, Howard : 43.
Cruger, Mr. : 33.
Cullen, William : 38.
Cumberland, Bishop R. : 35.

Cummings, Bishop G.D. : 39.
Curran, J.P. : 14, 76.
Curtius : 141.
Cyrus : 169, 222.

Dahlmann, F.C. : 205.
d'Aiguillon, duchesse : 172.
d'Alembert, J. : 86, 99.
d'Alençon, marquis : 125.
d'Angoulème, comte. V. Francis I.
d'Angoulème, duc : 152.
d'Anjou, comte. V. Foulques II.
d'Anjou, duc : 174.
Danton : 84, 90, 96, 97, 101, 102, 115, 148, 149, 151, 159, 163, 166, 181, 183, 184.
d'Argenson, comte (1696-1764) : 121.
d'Argenson, M.R. : 97.
d'Argental, comte : 115, 121.
d'Argout, : 107.
Darius : 215, 221.
d'Artois, comte. V. Charles X.
Darwin, Charles : 22.
Darwin, Erasmus : 65.
d'Assas, Chevalier : 85, 180.
d' Aubigné, comte : 187.
d'Aumale, duc : 87.
d'Aumont, duc : 93.
d'Auteroches, comte : 138, 150.
Davy, Sir Humphry : 75.
Davinain. V. Avinain.
D'Azeglio, Massimo : 194, 234.
Decatur, Stephen : 49.
Delon : 106.
Delphic, Oracle : 210, 212, 213, 222.
Demades, 214, 223.
Demeas : 214.
Demetrius : 216.
Democritus : 131, 222, 226.
Demonax, 216, 237.
Demosthenes : 175, 213, 214, 223, 228.
d'Enghien, duc : 92, 179.
Denman, Lord : 2.
Dennis, John : 4, 68.
Depretis, A. : 235.
Darby, Lord : 42, 55, 63, 73.
Des Barreaux : 185.
Desfontaines, abbé : 121.

Desgenettes : 151.
Desmoulins, Camille : 88, 135, 185, 186.
d'Este, Cardinal : 235.
d'Estrées, Gabrielle : 142.
d'Harcourt, Princess : 125.
Dickens, Charles : 49.
Dillon, Wentworth (Earl of Roscommon) : 43.
Diogenes : 185, 209, 210, 212, 214, 216, 219, 221, 225, 227.
Dionysius, the tyrant : 227.
Disraeli, Benjamin : 1, 2, 3, 5, 6, 7, 8, 9, 10, 11,13,14,16,19, 20, 22, 23, 24, 27, 29, 30, 31, 33, 35, 36, 37, 38, 42, 44, 49, 50, 51, 52, 53, 54, 59, 60, 62, 63, 64, 65, 66, 67, 68, 70, 80, 143, 243, 249.
Dix, John A : 25.
Dodwell, Professor : 21.
Domergue, U. : 119.
Dominique : 238.
Domitian, Emperor : 247.
Donaldson, Thomas : 48.
Donne, Dr. John : 21, 37.
Dorat, C. J. : 119.
Dorney, Henry : 21.
Douglas, Archibald, 5th earl of Angus : 30.
Douglas, Sir James : 47.
Douvrier, L. : 244.
Drake, Sir Francis : 26, 68.
Dreux-Brezé, H. E. de : 157.
Drew, Samuel : 57.
Drouot, General : 182.
Drummond, Henry : 68.
Drummond, Thomas : 52.
du Barry, Mme. : 143.
Dubois, Sergeant : 85.
Ducis, J. F. : 125, 134.
Ducrot, General A. : 153.
Dudevant, Mme. V. Sand, George.
Dufor : 101.
Dumas, A., fils : 105.
Dundas, William : 66.
Dundee, Viscount. V. Graham, John (of Claverhouse).
Dupin, A. M. J. J. : 94, 101, 126, 140, 144.
Duplessis-Mornay : 96.

Dupuis, F. : 88.
Dupuy, C. : 149.
Duruy : 141.
Dwight, Timothy : 50.
Eckermann, J. P. : 191.
Edward I : 10, 34, 54.
Edward III : 40, 106, 116.
Edward IV : 71.
Edward VI : 42.
Edward VII : 73, 77.
Edward, Prince (son of Henry VI) : 71.
Edward the Black Prince : 27, 40, 199.
Edward the Confessor : 118.
Edwards, Jonathan : 72.
Egbert, Col. H. Clay : 19.
Eiserne, Ludwig der : 202.
Eldon, Earl of. V. Scott, John.
Elisabeth de France, Mme. : 118.
Elizabeth, Queen : 3, 6, 9, 10, 15, 16, 18, 27, 29, 30, 32, 39, 42, 44, 56, 63, 65, 78, 79, 80, 144, 237, 241.
Elizabeth, Margravine of Brandenburg : 204.
Elizabeth of Bohemia: 39.
Ellenborough, Lord : 61, 80.
Elliot, Ebenezer : 8.
Emerson, R. W. 18, 49, 57, 66, 76.
Emmet, Robert : 45.
Enfantin, Père : 145.
Epaminondas : 226.
Epicurus : 250.
Erasmus, Desiderius : 240.
Erskine, Thomas : 57, 58, 81.
Essex, Earl of: 16, 18.
Estienne, Henry : 120
Eteokles : 221.
Etty, William : 31, 78.
Eugénie, Empress : 92.
Eulenburg, Count : 196.
Euripides : 219.
Eurybiades : 222.
Fabert, A. 83, 129.
Fabius, Maximus : 209, 242.
Failly, General P. L. C. A. de : 155.
Fairfax, Lady : 20.

Fairfax, Lord : 20.
Falk : 195.
Falkland, Lord : 23.
Farini, L. C. : 233.
Faversham, Lord : 13.
Favras, Marquis : 187.
Favre, Jules : 155.
Fawkes, Guy (Guido) : 12.
Felton, John : 18.
Fénelon, F. de S. de la Mothe- :
115, 132, 146.
Ferdinand I (of Germany): 193,
240.
Ferdinand VII : 158.
Ferry, Jules : 171.
Feuillet, abbé ; 149.
Feuquières, marquis de : 138.
Fiesque, comte de : 153.
Firmont, abbé Edgeworth de : 103.
Fitzgerald, Thomas (Earl of
Kildare) : 63.
Fitzjames, James : 93, 106.
Fitzstephen, Thomas : 78.
Flaxman, John : 17, 55.
Fléchier, E. : 155.
Fleckamore, C : 244.
Fletcher, Dr. Richard 56.
Fleury, Cardinal : 148.
Floquet, C. T. : 87, 138, 185.
Florian : 151.
Foley, Sir Thomas : 33.
Fontenelle, B. le B. de : 84, 87, 89,
99, 108, 121, 164, 174, 177,
181.
Forey, Marshal E. F. : 132.
Forster, W. E. : 67, 72.
Foucault, Col. de : 100.
Fouché, J. : 92, 178, 179.
Foulon, J. F. : 128, 172.
Foulques II (Count of Anjou) : 185.
Fouquet : 119.
Fournier, J. : 178.
Fox, Charles James : 5, 22, 24, 30,
39, 62, 63, 64, 68, 91, 93.
Fox, Edward (Bishop of Hereford) :
71.
Fox, George : 44.
Foy, General : 113, 147.
Francis I : 85, 89, 104, 123, 134,
169, 174, 179, 182, 184, 216.
Francis Joseph I : 251.

Franklin, Benjamin : 2, 18, 28, 34,
35, 53, 70, 73, 88, 98.
Frederick (II) the Great : 86, 89,
113, 129, 160, 184, 198, 199,
200, 201, 205, 207, 246.
Frederick III (1415-93) : 201.
Frederick III (1831-88) : 202.
Frederick Augustus, Duke of York :
7.
Frederick Charles, Prince : 202.
Frederick-William III : 203, 204.
Frederick-William IV : 146, 190,
192, 197, 200, 205, 208.
Frere, J. Hookham : 2.
Frochot : 120.
Froude, J. A. : 79.
Fugières, Col. : 184.
Furcroi : 168.
Fuseli, J. H. : 34.

Gagern, President H. W. A. von :
194.
Gainsborough, T ; 73.
Galba : 217.
Galileo Galilei : 232.
Galvagno, G. F. : 235.
Gamba, Count : 51.
Gambetta, L. : 97, 109, 123, 128,
135, 137, 144, 155, 157, 164,
171, 185.
Gardiner, Bishop S. : 240.
Gardiner, Col. James : 79.
Garfield, President J.A. : 3, 6, 18,
40, 64.
Garibaldi, G. : 117, 155, 234, 235.
Garth, Sir Samuel : 4, 11, 22.
Gascoigne, Sir William : 20.
Gassendi, P. : 124.
Gassion, maréchal de : 121.
Gaussin, Mlle. : 88.
Gay-Lussac, J. L. : 91.
Gensonné, A. : 108.
Gentz, Friedrich von : 194.
George I : 27.
George II : 6, 23, 24, 32.
George III : 4, 9, 52, 55.
George IV : 6, 73, 80.
George V (of Hanover) : 192.
Gerard, General : 142.
Gersdorff, J. : 248.
Gibbon, Edward : 66.

Giorgini, G. B. : 233.
Giotto, G. di B. : 235.
Girardin, E. de : 184.
Givré, Desmousseaux de : 171.
Gladstone, Rt. Hon. W. E. : 5, 11, 22, 31, 35, 36, 40, 42, 53, 60, 61, 62, 63, 64, 66, 70, 223.
Glynn, Serjeant : 61.
Godwin. Mrs. V. Wollstonecraft, Mary.
Goethe, J. W. von : 191, 203.
Goldsmith, Oliver : 21, 45, 246.
Goltz, President von der : 199.
Gonzalvo, General : 104.
Gordon, Alexander (of Glenbucket) : 48.
Gordon, General : 55.
Gordon, Lord George : 46.
Goudchaux : 145.
Gournay, V. de : 128.
Grafton, Duke of : 58.
Graham, John (of Claverhouse) : 48.
Graham, Sir James : 6.
Gramont, maréchal de : 84, 152.
Grant, President U. S. : 29, 40, 73.
Grant, Sir William : 67
Granville, Lord : 90.
Grattan, Henry : 22, 33, 79.
Gray, Thomas : 42.
Greeley, Horace : 35.
Green, J. H. : 56.
Gregory I, Pope : 245.
Grenville, George : 17, 52.
Grétry, A : 180.
Grey, Lady Jane : 41.
Grey de Wilton, Lord : 42.
Grimaldi, B : 234.
Grotius, Hugo : 244.
Guiscard, R. : 177.
Guise, duc de : 91, 102, 109, 168, 170.
Guizot, F. : 101, 160, 167.
Gustavus Adolphus : 200.
Gwynn, Nell : 12.
Gyulai : 206.

Hadrian : 240.
Hale, N. : 33.
Hall, Dr. Robert : 12.
Hamilcar Barcas : 224.

Hamilton, Alexander : 21.
Hampden, John : 48.
Hancock, John : 73.
Handel, G. F. : 3, 73.
Hannibal : 209, 220, 224, 241, 242.
Hanover, Duke of : 142.
Hansemann, D. : 200.
Hardy, T. M. : 68.
Harel : 131.
Harkort, Deputy : 196.
Harlay, Achille de (1536-1616) : 91.
Harlay, Achille de (1639-1712) : 122, 172, 173.
Harley, Robert, Earl of Oxford : 16.
Harmodius : 225.
Harold, King : 10.
Harrison, President B. : 7.
Harrison, President W. H. : 38.
Hastings, Warren : 32.
Hautefort, Mlle. de : 164.
Havelock, Sir Henry : 10.
Hay, Lord Charles : 150.
Hayes, President R. B. : 21.
Hayne : 5.
Healy, T : 146.
Hecataeus : 218.
Heinrich LXXII : 190.
Helvétius : 83.
Henrietta Maria : 52.
Henrietta of England (Duchess of Orleans) : 148, 184.
Henry I : 160.
Henry II : 54.
Henry IV : 20.
Henry, Prince (Henry V) : 20.
Henry VII : 63.
Henry VIII : 5, 11, 26, 30, 42, 79, 85, 216, 239, 245.
Henry II (duc de Montmorency) : 145.
Henry III (of France) : 89, 109, 136, 153.
Henry IV (of France) : 94, 96, 100, 116, 118, 120, 124, 125, 126, 141, 142, 149, 150, 159, 160, 161, 162, 163, 170, 179, 186.
Henry IV (of Germany) : 204.
Henry of Navarre : 90.
Henry, Patrick : 17, 26.
Heraclitus : 188, 223.

Hermodotus : 219.
Herschell, Lord : 58.
Hervey, James : 51.
Herwegh : 200.
Hessen, Erbprinzen von : 171.
Hicks Beach, Sir Michael : 70.
Hill, Rev. Rowland : 77.
Hobbema, Meindert : 48.
Hobbes, Thomas : 46.
Hoche, Lazare : 84, 97, 99, 133.
Hogg, James : 36.
Holbein, Hans : 79.
Holland, Lord : 25.
Holmes, Oliver Wendell : 25.
Hood, Thomas : 13.
Hooper, Bishop John : 26.
Hope, Beresford : 8.
Hopkins, Mark : 39, 44.
Hopkins, Samuel : 43.
Horsman, Rt. Hon. E. : 8, 51.
Hough, John : 74.
Houston, Samuel : 57.
Howard, George : 67.
Howard, John : 39.
Howard, Dr. Samuel : 17.
Howard of Effingham, Lord : 68.
Howard, William, Viscount Stafford : 24.
Hull, Commodore Isaac : 34.
Hunter, John : 12.
Hunter, William : 41.
Hunter, Dr. William : 25.
Huntingdon, Selina, Countess of : 44.
Huss, John : 246.

Iddesleigh, Lord. V. Northcote, Sir Stafford.
Ingersoll, Robert G. : 48.
Iphicrates : 225.
Irving, Rev. E. : 25.
Irving, Washington : 31.
Ismenias : 221.

Jackson, General Andrew : 30, 49.
Jackson, General T. J. ("Stonewall") : 40, 54.
Jacoby, Johann : 192.
James I : 10, 12, 21, 38, 60, 65, 79.
James II : 13, 18, 21, 38.

James V of Scotland : 34.
James VI. of Scotland. V. James I.
James, Duke of York : 9.
Jars, Chevalier de : 99.
Jay, John : 42.
Jean II (the Good) : 174.
Jeannin, P : 94.
Jefferson, Thomas : 16, 33, 34, 69, 73.
Jenkins Robert : 23.
Jenner, Edward : 12.
Jewell, Bishop : 1, 69.
Joan of Arc : 106, 124, 173, 188.
John, Don : 146.
John, King (" Lackland ") : 26.
John XXII, Pope : 248.
Johnson, Richard : 26.
Johnson, Samuel : 1, 2, 4, 5, 7, 12, 18, 21, 32, 35, 46, 53, 55, 59, 70, 74, 76, 108, 246.
Jones, Paul : 28.
Jordan, C : 136.
Joseph, Père : 89, 96, 121, 122, 155.
Joseph II : 206.
Joseph, king of Naples : 144.
Josephine, Empress : 84, 153.
Josserand : 122.
Jourdan, General : 104.
Joyense, duc Anne de : 90, 136.
Jugurtha : 214, 251.
Julian (" the Apostate ") : 251.
Julius II, Pope : 233.
Julius III, Pope : 238.
Junot, A. : 87, 133.
Juxon, Bishop : 53.

Kallisthenes : 217.
Kames, Lord : 28.
Kant, I. : 198.
Kaunitz : 206.
Keats, John : 25.
Keith, Lord : 63.
Kell, J. : 196.
Ken, Bishop Thomas : 18.
Kent, Earl of : 56.
Kildare, Earl of. V. Fitzgerald, Thomas.
Kingsley, Charles : 21, 43.
Kingston, Duchess of. V. Chudleigh, Elizabeth.

Kingston, Sir William : 16, 20, 54.
Kirkpatrick, of Closeburn : 30.
Kléber, General : 104.
Kneller, Sir Godfey : 13.
Knox, John : 47.
Koller, von : 207.
Kosciusko : 241.
Kratesiclea : 217.
Kruger, President : 56.
Kuhmann : 147.

La Bedoyère, comte de ; 154, 169.
La Blache, comte de : 84.
Labouchère, Henry : 61.
La Châtre : 83.
Lacretelle, C. : 103.
Ladré : 88.
Laelius : 225.
La Fayette, General : 90, 107, 147.
La Fayette, Mme. de : 149.
Laffémas, I. de : 99.
La Fontaine, J. de : 87, 89, 100, 122, 152.
Laguerre : 142.
La Hire : 98, 160.
Lamachus : 221.
Lamartine : 131, 136.
Lambert, John : 45.
Lambruschini Cardinal L. : 235.
Lamennais, F. R. de : 156.
La Mettrie : 160.
Lamoignon, G. de : 119, 172.
Lamoral, comte d'Egmont : 82.
La Mothe, d'Orleans de : 171.
Lamourette, abbé A. : 87.
Landseer, Sir Edwin H. : 34.
Landsmath : 148.
Lanjuinais : 148.
Lannes, Marshal : 86.
Lanza, G. : 234.
La Palice (or Palisse), Jacques de : 104.
La Roche-Aymont, C. A. de : 96.
La Rochefoucault : 149, 181.
La Rochejacquelein, Count Henri de : 173.
Lassalle, F. : 202.
Latimer, Hugh : 9.
La Tour : 156.
La Tour d'Auvergne, T. Corret de : 119, 152.

La Trappe, monks of : 104.
Laubanie, Lieut.-gen. de : 176.
Laubardemont, J. M. : 99.
Laud, William : 41, 45.
Lauderdale, Earl of (1616-82) : 51.
Lauderdale, Earl of (1759-1839) : 91.
Lauenburg, Duke of : 200.
Lauraguais, comte de : 102, 169.
La Vallière, duchesse de : 90, 114.
Lawrence, Sir Henry : 40.
Lawrence, Captn. J. : 12.
Layard, Sir A. H. : 66.
Le Bœuf, Marshal : 157.
Leczinska, Marie : 113, 135, 142, 156, 171, 180, 188.
Lee, Gen. H. : 71.
Lee, R. E. : 57.
Lefebvre, J. F. J. : 121.
Leigh Hunt, J. H. : 12.
Le Kain, H. L. : 87.
Lemercier, Népomucène : 84.
Lemierre, A. M. : 133.
L'Enclos, Ninon de : 83, 117, 134, 158.
Lenet, P. : 181.
Lenthall, Speaker Wm. : 28.
Leo, Heinrich : 197, 199, 206.
Leo X, Pope : 233.
Leonidas : 231.
Leopold (Prince of Anhalt-Des sau) : 98.
Le Pelletier, L. M. : 115, 119.
Lesseps, F. de : 137.
Lewis, Sir George Cornewall : 40.
Levassor : 180.
L'Hôpital, Michel de : 126.
Liebnecht : 201, 207.
Ligarius, Caius : 230, 241.
Ligne, Prince de : 135.
Lincoln, President A. : 8, 12, 19, 23, 24, 36, 79.
Lippard, George : 34.
Lisle, Sir George : 27.
Livingstone, Dr. David : 4, 12.
Livius, Marcus : 209.
Locke, John : 48.
Lockhart, J. G. : 18.
Longfellow, H. W. : 47.
Lorraine, duc de. V. René II.
Lothair I (of Germany) : 246.

Louis IV (d'Outre-Mer) : 185.
Louis VI : 150, 160, 178.
Louis XI : 88, 98, 123, 141, 158, 167, 170, 248.
Louis XII : 88, 89, 118, 129, 136, 140, 150, 165.
Louis XIII : 125, 162, 164, 167, 175, 243.
Louis XIV : 83, 84, 89, 90, 92, 93, 96, 97, 98, 99, 105, 110, 112, 114, 115, 116, 117, 118, 124, 125, 128, 139, 141, 142, 144, 148, 152, 155, 158, 162, 165, 172, 173, 175, 176, 181, 182, 186, 188, 189, 237, 244.
Louis XV : 85, 86, 100, 102, 118, 129, 143, 148, 156, 157, 169, 176, 184.
Louis XVI : 86, 89, 100, 103, 115, 119, 129, 153, 165, 166, 174.
Louis XVIII : 36, 112, 120, 122, 145, 152, 182, 184.
Louis, duke of Burgundy : 176.
Louis, Baron J. D. : 102.
Louis de France : 169.
Louis-Philippe : 89, 90, 93, 96, 105, 117, 126, 137, 139, 155.
Louis - Philippe - Joseph (duc d'Orléans) : 112.
Lowe, Sir Robert (Lord Sherbrooke) : 20, 54, 74, 240.
Lowndes, William : 57.
Lucas, Sir Charles : 55.
Lucullus : 211, 212, 224.
Lulli, G. B. : 141, 171.
Luther, Martin : 199. .
Luxembourg, maréchal de : 114, 128.
Lycurgus : 166, 224.
Lyons, Archbishop of : 170.
Lysander : 218, 221, 227.
Lysimachus : 213, 215.
Lyttelton, Lord George : 9.
Lytton, Lord : 7, 11, 12.

Macaulay, Lord : 34, 64.
Mackenzie, Sir G. : 15.
Mackintosh, Sir James : 4, 20.
Mac Mahon, Marshal : 94, 126, 137. 168, 171.
Maecenas : 250.

Maharbal : 224.
Mahdi, The : 55.
Maintenon, Mme. de : 117, 122, 148, 158, 171, 182, 187, 189.
Maistre, Count Joseph de : 118, 181.
Malesherbes, G. G. L. de : 158.
Malet, Gen. C. F. de : 89, 181.
Malmesbury, Lord : 134.
Mancini, Marie : 189.
Mann, Sir Horace : 23, 67.
Mansfield, Lord : 58, 61, 241.
Manuel, J. A. : 100.
Manteuffel, Baron Th. von : 195, 205.
Marat, J. P. : 85, 136.
Marceau, General : 104.
Marcel : 168.
Marcellus : 220.
Marcotti, F. : 234.
Marcy, Governor W. L. : 3.
Mardonius : 222.
Maret : 161.
Margaret of Scotland : 103.
Margotti, G. : 234.
Marguerite de Valois : 118.
Marie-Thérèse : 186.
Marius, Caius : 209, 224, 225.
Marie-Antoinette : 109, 172, 175.
Marmier, X. : 129.
Marmontel : 186.
Martin : 125.
Martin IV, Pope : 170.
Martineau,: Harriet : 34.
Mary I : 2.
Mary II : 43.
Mary, Countess of Warwick : 73, 77.
Mary, Princess : 150.
Mary, Queen of Scots : 82, 243.
Mascaron, Bishop : 182.
Masham, Lady : 48.
Massieu : 133.
Massillon, J. B. : 98, 114.
Mather, Rev. Cotton : 22.
Mathews, Charles : 22.
Matthias : 206.
Maury, abbé : 84, 135, 174, 183, 189.
Maxentius : 243.
Maximilian I : 207.
Maximilian II (of Bavaria) : 200.

Maybach, Minister : 199.
Mazarin, Cardinal : 83, 101, 104, 107, 112, 145, 152, 165, 176, 181.
McKinley, President W. : 4, 6, 13, 49, 50, 58, 69.
Médicis, Cardinal de : 173.
Ménage, G. : 115, 249.
Menedemus : 223.
Mercier, L. S. : 125.
Meredith Read, Gen. J. : 72.
Merlin, comte P. A. : 105.
Metellus, Captain : 170.
Metternich, Prince : 147, 195.
Michel, General Count : 127.
Michelangelo, Duke : 233.
Michell, Mr. : 55.
Mikion : 230.
Milon. V. Amalric.
Miloradovitch, General Count : 159.
Miltiades : 215.
Milton, John : 49.
Mirabeau, comte de : 89, 107, 108, 120, 126, 128, 129, 132, 138, 143, 151, 157, 166, 172, 178, 188, 189, 241.
Molay, Jacques de : 95.
Molé, Matthieu : 84, 124, 167.
Molière, J. B. Poquelin : 106, 151, 161, 162, 168, 171, 188.
Molin, J. : 164.
Mollien, comte F. N. : 112.
Moltke, Count von : 194, 198.
Momoro, A. F. : 147.
Monmouth, Duke of. V. Scott, James.
Montagu, Lady Mary W. : 13.
Montalembert, comte de : 130.
Montauban, Princess of : 125.
Montausier, duc de : 162.
Monteagle, Lord : 69.
Montecuculli, General : 106, 186.
Montefiore, Sir Moses : 57.
Montespan, Mme. de : 114, 115.
Montesquieu : 145, 154, 161.
Montfort, duc de : 152.
Montfort, Simon de. V. Simon de Montfort.
Montjau, Madier de : 96.
Montlosier, comte de : 93.
Montmorency, duc de : 92.

Montmorency, duc de. V. Henry II.
Montpensier, Mlle. de : 165.
Montrond, Count : 96, 131, 141, 176.
Moody, D. L. : 33.
More, Hannah : 39.
More, Sir Thomas : 26, 33, 50, 54, 81.
Moreau, General J. V. : 100.
Morley, John : 61
Mornay, P. de. V. Duplessis-Mornay.
Morris, Miss : 18.
Morton, O. P. : 3.
Motley, J. L. : 22.
Munster, Count : 137.
Murat, J. : 182.

Napier, Sir Charles : 247.
Napier, Sir Robert : 20, 66.
Napoleon I : 83, 84 , 86, 87, 91, 94, 99, 100, 101, 104, 105, 108, 112, 116, 117, 121, 126, 127, 132, 134, 136, 138, 142, 143, 144, 145, 150, 151, 153, 155, 156, 158, 159, 160, 161, 162, 166, 177, 178, 179, 180, 182, 184.
Napoleon III : 135, 139, 160, 178, 181.
Nassau, Duke of : 111.
Necker : 241.
Nelson, Lord : 2, 8, 13, 30, 32, 33, 36, 57, 58, 68, 71, 74.
Nemours, Dupont de : 164.
Nero, Emperor : 241, 247, 248.
Neumayr, von : 200.
Newcastle, Duke of : 71.
Newton, John : 23.
Newton, Sir Isaac : 25, 47.
Ney, Marshal M. : 162, 177, 185.
Niccolini, G. B. : 233.
Nicholas I (of Russia) : 145, 146, 156, 184.
Nicole, P. : 108, 154.
Nicolet, J. B. : 97.
Niebuhr, B. E. : 200.
Niel, Marshal : 189.
Normanby, Marquis of : 52.
Northcote, James : 19, 36, 39, 62.

Northcote, Sir Stafford : 61.
Nottingham, Countess of : 18.

Oates, Titus : 35.
O'Connell, Daniel : 23.
O'Donnell, Mr. : 67.
Ollivier, E. : 136, 156, 160.
O'Meara, E : 126.
Onesicritus : 215.
Opie, John : 31.
Oppenheim, H. B. : 201.
Orange, Prince of : 146.
Orleans, Duke of : 89.
Orleans, Duke of. V. Louis-Philippe.
Orleans, Duke of. V. Louis-Philippe-Joseph.
Orleans, Duke of. V. Philippe.
Ormond, Duke of : 16.
Orthe, Viscount : 120.
Osten, Count P. : 195.
Oxenstiern, Axel, Count : 238.
Oxford, Earl of. V. Harley, Robert.

Paine, Thomas : 28.
Palissy, B : 89
Palmer, John : 65.
Palmerston, Lord : 12, 13, 51, 60, 80, 147, 238.
Pan, Mallet du : 112.
Panat, Chevalier de : 112, 162.
Pannier, Colas : 149.
Paré, A. : 118.
Parker, Archbp. : 6.
Parker, Theodore : 19.
Parmenio : 215, 225.
Parnell, C. S. : 67.
Parr, Catherine : 5.
Parr, Dr. Samuel : 3, 45.
Pastoret, marquis de : 87.
Patch, Samuel : 56.
Paterson : 53.
Patin, Gui : 116.
Patru, Olivier : 183.
Paul I, Emperor of Russia : 137, 184.
Paul, François de : 158.
Peel, Sir Robert : 1, 8, 38, 51, 59, 66, 80.
Pelopidas : 210, 229.

Penn, William : 36, 67, 71, 77.
Periander : 136.
Pericles : 216, 220, 225, 231.
Perowne, Miss : 74.
Perraud : 141.
Peschel, Dr. : 194.
Peter III of Aragon : 170.
Peters, Hugh : 17.
Peyrat, A. : 135.
Pharnace : 251.
Phemonoes : 211.
Phidias : 245.
Philip II (of Spain) : 145, 146, 244.
Philip V (,,) : 110.
Philip (II) Augustus (of France) : 177.
Philip of Macedon : 212, 221, 224, 225, 229, 231, 247.
Philippe (I), duc d'Orleans : 152.
Philippe (II) duc d'Orleans : 175, 184.
Philippe (III), le Bon : 123.
Philippe (IV), le Bel : 95.
Philippe VI (of France) : 162, 169.
Philipe-Égalité. V. Louis-Philippe-Joseph.
Phillips, Wendell : 4, 9, 12, 15, 32, 48, 50, 53, 75, 79, 80.
Philotas : 225.
Phocion : 211, 213, 214, 217, 219, 220, 222, 223, 228, 230.
Phocus : 222.
Pilou, Mme. : 113.
Pinckney : C.C. : 42.
Pindar, Peter. V. Wolcot, John.
Pinkney : 49.
Piron, Alexis : 91, 107, 113, 156.
Pitillan, comte de : 159.
Pitt, William, Earl of Chatham : 6, 11, 17, 22, 26, 31, 51, 58, 60, 64, 65, 69, 74, 76.
Pitt, William : 5, 16, 21, 22, 36, 44, 48, 74, 93.
Pittacus : 215, 226, 229.
Plato : 216, 230, 237.
Pliny, the elder : 246.
Plunket, Lord : 56.
Podbielski, General von : 207.
Podewil, Graf : 198.
Poe, E. A. : 41.
Polignac, Cardinal de : 83.

Polignac, Duchesse de : 175.
Polycrates : 222.
Pompadour, Mme. de : 85, 129.
Pompey : 218, 219, 222, 226, 242.
Pompignan, Lefranc de : 111.
Poniatowski, Prince J. A. : 98.
Pope, Alexander : 65, 69.
Porson, Dr. R. : 25, 76, 78.
Porus : 210, 229.
Poullé, abbé : 176.
Powell, William : 34.
Premier Grenadier de la France, le.
    V. La Tour d'Auvergne, &c.
Preston, Mr. : 55.
Ptolemy : 217, 227.
Purcell, Daniel : 5.
Pusey, Dr. E. B : 43.
Putbus, Prince : 190.
Pym, John : 73, 79.
Pyrrhus : 209, 213, 218, 222.
Pythagoras Zacynthias : 210, 223, 227, 228.
Pytheas : 213.

Quarles, Francis : 75.
Quesnay, F. : 128.
Quick, John : 34.
Quin, James : 24.
Quincey, Thomas De : 55.
Quincey, Josiah : 5.

Rabelais, F. : 124, 140, 180.
Racine, J. : 87.
Raikes, Thomas : 8.
Raleigh, Sir Walter : 10, 15, 29, 56, 67, 71, 74.
Raumer, G. W. von : 205.
Reade, Charles : 5.
Rechberg, Count von : 198.
Reed, General Joseph : 17.
Reggio, duc de : 182.
Reichenbach, von : 200.
Rémusat, Mme. de : 140.
René II (duc de Lorraine) : 97.
Reynolds, Sir Joshua : 4, 15, 29, 46, 55, 62.
Rhodes, Cecil : 15, 55.
Ricci, L. : 250.
Rice, Sir Stephen : 13.
Richard I : 26, 81.
Richard II : 38.

Richard III : 3.
Richelieu, Cardinal : 89, 96, 98, 105, 121, 122, 123, 155, 160, 166, 172, 174, 175, 182, 232, 241, 250.
Richemont, comte de : 125.
Richet, Dr. : 167.
Richter, E : 190, 207.
Ridley, Bishop Nicholas : 9.
Riquet, Paul de : 117.
Rivarol, A, comte de : 90, 162, 187.
Robert II (le Pieux) : 118.
Robertson, F. W. : 23.
Robespierre, F. J. M. de : 88, 115, 133, 135, 139, 164, 172.
Roche, Sir Boyle : 43, 54, 64, 77.
Rochester, Earl of : 43, 63.
Roe, Sir Thomas : 146.
Rogers, John : 41.
Rogers, Samuel : 1, 4, 76, 78.
Roland, Mme. : 158.
Roqueplan, Nestor : 147.
Roon, Count A. T. E. von : 190.
Roscommon, Earl of. V. Dillon, Wentworth.
Rossetti, D. G. : 35.
Rossini, G. A. : 102.
Rothschild, Baron J. de : 141.
Roucher, J. A. : 165.
Rougemont, de : 106.
Rouher, E. : 117, 132, 135, 183.
Routh, Dr. M. J. : 72.
Rowe, Nicholas : 4.
Royer-Collard, P. P. : 121, 139.
Rudini, A. S. di : 234.
Russell, Lord John : 41, 42, 67.
Russell, Lord William : 60.

Sablière, Mme. de la : 152.
Sabor : 192.
Saint-Aignan, comte de : 125.
Saint Ambrose : 248.
St. Augustine : 239, 248.
Saint-Cère : 236.
St. Cyprian : 239.
Saint Hilaire : 89.
Saint-Jean d'Angely : 183.
Saint-Just, A. : 139.
Saint-Pern : 100.
St. Remy : 244.

Saint-Simon : 164.
Salisbury, Marquis of : 3, 42, 51.
Salvandy, M. de : 155.
Sand, George : 128.
Sanderson, Robert : 43.
Sandwich, Lord : 49.
Santerre, C. : 165.
Santeul, J. : 238.
Sartine, G. de : 94.
Saunders, Lawrence : 73.
Saurin, B. J. : 171.
Savage, Richard : 71.
Savoie, duc de : 112.
Savoie, M. L. Gabrielle de : 93.
Saxe, Marshal : 108, 134, 159, 176.
Scarron, Mme. V. Maintenon, Mme. de.
Scarron, P. : 149.
Schill : 203.
Schiller : 197, 203.
Schleiermacher, F. E. D. : 200.
Schleinitz, Baron von : 196, 197.
Schomberg, Col. Tich de : 116.
Schulenberg-Kehnert, Count von : 205.
Scipio Africanus Major : 159, 242, 243, 246.
Scipio, Nasica, Publius, 225, 239,
Scott, James, Duke of Monmouth : 43.
Scott, John, 1st Earl of Eldon : 13, 37.
Scott, Sir Walter : 12, 18, 41, 59, 62, 70, 78.
Scott, General Winfield : 3, 39.
Sebastiani, General H. : 148.
Séchelles, H. de : 136, 151.
Séguier : 127.
Segur, M. de : 150.
Sella, Quintino : 232.
Selden, John : 1, 26.
Selwyn, G. A. : 25, 55.
Sémonville, de : 107.
Sénac : 134.
Sermoneta, Duke of : 233.
Serre, comte de : 127.
Sertorius : 225.
Severus, Septimus : 244.
Sévigné, Mme. de : 107.
Seward, William H. : 6, 65.
Sextilius : 209.

Seymour, Sir E. Hamilton : 145, 156.
Shaftesbury, 1st Earl of : 4.
Shaftesbury, 3rd. ,, ,, : 53.
Shakspere, William : 9.
Sheffield, John, Duke of Buckingham and Normanby : 38.
Shelburne, Earl of : 31.
Sheppard, Jack : 27.
Sherbrooke, Lord. V. Lowe, Sir Robert.
Sheridan, R. B. : 12, 17, 37, 46, 66, 71, 76.
Sherman, John : 35.
Sherman, General W. T : 21.
Siccard, abbé : 133.
Sidney, Sir Philip : 32.
Sieyès, abbé : 86, 108, 113, 116, 127, 129, 150, 169, 176, 185.
Sigismund, Emperor : 240.
Sigismund III : 249.
Sillery : 141.
Silliman, Professor : 27.
Silo, Publius : 224.
Simon de Montfort : 11.
Siward, Earl of Northumberland : 1.
Sixtus V, Pope : 173.
Smith, Joseph ; 58.
Smith, Rev. Sydney : 10, 13, 26, 32, 34, 45, 51, 56, 57, 60, 65, 68, 73, 75.
Socrates : 213, 216, 217, 220, 221, 223, 227, 230, 237.
Solon : 23, 213, 216, 223, 224, 226, 229, 231.
Somerset, Duke of : 13.
Soult, Marshal : 92.
Southcott, Joanna : 25.
Southey, Robert : 44.
Spuller, E : 143.
Staël, Mme. de : 21, 51, 94, 132, 140, 143, 150.
Stafford, Viscount. V. Howard, William.
Stahl, F. J. : 191, 193, 196.
Stair, Lord : 116.
Stanley, Arthur P. (Dean of Westminster) : 38.
Stanley, Lord. V. Derby, Lord.
Stanley, Sir H. M. : 12.

Stark, John : 73.
Steele, Anne : 29.
Stephenson, George : 12.
Stevenson, R. L. : 75.
Stilpo : 246.
Stowell, Lord : 2, 60.
Strafford, Earl of. V. Wentworth, Thomas.
Subarranus : 250.
Suffolk, Earl of : 3.
Sulla : 226.
Sully, duc de : 94, 125, 138, 159, 162, 167, 179.
Sulpicius : 225.
Swift, Dean : 3, 7, 19, 26, 59.
Sydney, Algernon : 46, 59.
Sydney, Sir Philip : 57.
Széchényi, Count : 194.

Tallard, Marshal : 171.
Talleyrand-Perigord, C. M. de : 90, 91, 92, 96, 99, 105, 106, 112, 114, 121, 131, 139, 154, 171, 181.
Tarente, Archbp. of. V. Capèce-Latro.
Taylor, Bayard : 37.
Taylor, E. T. : 77.
Taylor, Jane : 7.
Taylor, Jeremy ; 44.
Taylor, John (the Water Poet) : 21.
Taylor, John : 58.
Taylor, Rev. Dr. Rowland : 42.
Taylor, General Zachary : 3, 33. Duke of.
Teano, Prince O. C. di. V. Sermoneta, Duke of.
Tenterden, Lord. V. Abbott, Charles.
Tennyson, Alfred, Lord : 28.
Terrasson, J. : 168, 181, 188.
Thales : 211, 216, 219, 229.
Themistocles : 215, 216, 222, 228, 230.
Thénard, Baron : 152.
Theocritus : 229.
Theopompus : 216.
Thianges, Mme. de : 100.
Thiers, L. A. : 83, 108, 110, 133, 134, 139, 141, 144, 164, 171.
Thistlewood, Arthur : 34.

Thodippus : 213.
Thomas, Clement : 143.
Thoreau, H. D. 30.
Thurlow, Lord : 11, 30, 58, 76.
Tiberius : 225.
Tichborne Claimant : 56.
Tigranes II : 212.
Tilden, S. J. : 73.
Tillotson, Archbp. : 43.
Timrod, Henry : 44.
Tindal, Matthew : 48.
Titus, Emperor : 239, 245.
Tooke, J. Horne : 79.
Toplady, Rev. A. M. : 45.
Tournemine, Père : 154.
Townshend, Charles : 56, 68.
Trajan, Emperor : 250.
Tremblay, F. le Clerc du. V. Joseph, Père.
Tréville, de : 108, 175.
Trivulzi, Marshal G. J. de : 165.
Trousseau, Prof. A. : 179.
Trumbull, Jonathan : 74. 129.
Turenne, vicomte de : 89, 97, 106, 129.
Turgot, A. R. J. : 90.
Tyler, Wat : 38.
Tyndale, William : 41.

Uhland, Ludwig : 197.
Unruh, von : 204.
Urban VIII, Pope : 232.
Ussher, James : 41.

Vaillant : 150.
Valentine, Lord : 9.
Van Buren, President Martin : 30.
Vanderbilt, Cornelius : 79.
Vane, Sir Henry : 9.
Vanini, L. : 242.
Varus, Quintilius : 248.
Vauban, Marshal : 117.
Vega, Lopes de : 151.
Vendôme, General de : 185.
Verdi, G. : 236.
Vergniaud, P. : 108, 163, 166.
Vertot, abbé : 152.
Vespasian : 243, 245, 251.
Viali, Agricole : 119.
Victor Emmanuel II : 232, 235, 236.

Victoria, Queen : 48.
Viennet, J. G. : 129.
Vignoles, Étienne de. V. La Hire.
Vigny, A. de : 121.
Villars, duc de : 106, 124, 157, 165, 172.
Villemain, A. F. : 129.
Villeroi, Marshal : 152.
Villeroi, N. de N. : 94.
Villiers, George, 1st Duke of Buckingham : 18
Villieas, George, 2nd Duke of Buckingham : 27.
Villiers, R1. Hon. J. : 28.
Vinci, Leonardo da : 123.
Vincke, G. F. von : 197.
Virchow, Prof. : 202.
Vitellius, Aulus : 246.
Vitrolles, Baron de : 91.
Vivonne, duc de : 93, 100, 128, 162, 181.
Voisenon, abbé : 105.
Voltaire : 18, 63, 82, 89, 98, 99, 102, 108, 111, 115, 119, 156, 160, 161, 239.
Wagner, R. W. : 204.
Waldemar, Prince : 205.
Waller, Edmund : 21, 51.
Wallis, Count : 207.
Walpole, Horace : 21, 23, 59, 67.
Walpole, Sir Robert : 6, 7, 11, 14, 19, 28, 49, 68.
Walpole, Spencer Horatio : 14.
7—Index Sayings.
Warburton, Bishop : 49.
Warham, W. (Archbp. of Canterbury) : 57.
Warren, Commodore : 37.
Warwick, Lord : 29.
Washington, George : 30, 37, 40, 71, 74.
Watts, Dr. Isaac : 24.
Webster, Daniel : 5, 19, 21, 23, 27, 34, 40, 42, 48, 54, 57, 64, 65, 75.
Wedgwood, Josiah : 5.
Wellington, Duke of : 1, 6, 8, 9, 12, 14, 20, 28, 31, 33, 36, 41, 44, 45, 46, 47, 51, 59, 60, 61, 62, 65, 72, 74, 75, 76, 80, 145, 159, 210.

Wentworth, Thomas, Earl of Straf ford : 52, 79, 241, 245.
Wesley, Charles : 34.
Wesley, John : 59, 75.
Wesley, Sarah : 49.
West, Benjamin : 3, 7.
Westminster, Dean of. V. Stanley, A. P.
Whately, Archbp. : 24, 78, 81.
Wheaton, General : 19.
White, Joseph Blanco : 47.
Whitefield, George : 22, 75.
Whitehead, Dr. David : 30.
Whitman, Walt : 48.
Whittier, J. G. : 27.
Wilberforce, William : 20.
Wilbraham, Mr. : 61.
Wild, Jonathan : 41.
Wilhelm I : 191, 192, 196, 200, 202, 204.
Wilhelm III : 111, 194.
Wilkes, John : 16, 76.
Willard, F. W. : 21.
William I. (the Conqueror) : 115, 189.
William II : 31.
William III : 10, 16, 21, 38, 59.
William IV : 37.
William of Wykeham : 42.
William the Silent : 82, 247.
Windham, William : 48.
Windthorst, Dr. : 201.
Winthrop, R. C. : 8.
Wishart, George : 24, 25.
Wolcot, John (Peter Pindar) : 17.
Wolfe, Rev. Charles : 10.
Wolfe, Gen. James : 39, 46.
Wollstonecraft, Mary : 30.
Wolsey, Cardinal : 15, 16, 20, 240.
Woolton, John : 1.
Wordsworth, William : 21, 34, 38, 50, 67, 72.
Wolton, Sir H : 14, 33, 244.
Woulfe, Chief Baron : 52.
Wyatt, Sir Thomas (the younger) : 58.
Wycherley, William : 52.

Xenocrates : 216, 230.
Xerxes : 218.
Ximenes, Cardinal F. : 250.

York, Duke of. V. Frederick Augustus, &c.

Young, Dr. Thomas : 7.

Zamoiski, Jan : 249.

Zedlitz-Truetschler, Prince von : 192.

Zeno : 209, 211, 215.

Zeuxis : 211

Zola, E. : 245.

ERRATA.

Page 1, col. 2, ll. 1, 6. *For* "gentleman" *read* "gentlewoman."
,, 19, ,, 1, l. 2. ,, "1725" ,, "1751."
,, 19, ,, 1, ,, 9. ,, "ch. 66" ,, "ch. 6."
,, 21, ,, 2, ,, 7. ,, "Sharman" *read* "Sherman."
,, 30, ,, 1, ,, 36. *Insert* "of" *after* "name."
,, 31, ,, 2, ,, 31. *For* "July 28" *read* "July 27."
,, 52, ,, 1, ,, 10. ,, "Property" ,, "Protection."
,, 52, ,, 1, ,, 20. ,, "Protection" ,, "Property."
,, 71, ,, 1, ,, 23. ,, "Binsley" ,, "Brinsley."
,, 77, ,, 2, ,, 12. ,, "Roland" ,, "Rowland."
,, 78, ,, 1, ,, 4 *from bottom. For* "ilke" *read* "like."
,, 78, ,, 2, ,, 10. *For* "wondreful" *read* "wonderful."
,, 96, ,, 2, ,, 5 *from bottom. For* "la Roche-Aymond"
               read "La Roche-Aymon."
,, 102, ,, 2, ,, 27. *For* "1807" *read* "1837."
,, 160, ,, 1, ,, 6. ,, "Charles VI" ,, "Charles VII."
,, 169, ,, 2, ,, 24. ,, "Philip IV" ,, "Philip VI."